Real Estate Investment

Real Estate Investment: A Strategic Approach provides a unique introduction to both the theory and practice of real estate investing, and examines the international real estate investment industry as it reacts to the global financial crisis.

Andrew Baum outlines the market and the players who dominate it, the investment process, the vehicles available for investment and a suggested approach to global portfolio construction. The book contains many useful features for students including discussion questions, a full further reading list and case studies drawing on international examples from the UK, continental Europe, the USA and Asia.

Ideal for undergraduate and postgraduate students on all real estate and property courses and related business studies and finance courses, *Real Estate Investment* is designed to provide a foundation for the next generation of investment managers, advisers and analysts.

Further resources for lecturers and students are available at: www.routledge.com/cw/baum.

Andrew Baum is an internationally respected real estate professional, researcher and author. He is Chairman of Property Funds Research, a consulting business, and Visiting Professor of Management Practice at the Saïd Business School, University of Oxford. From 2009 to 2014 he was Honorary Professor of Real Estate Investment at the University of Cambridge. He is also Emeritus Professor at the University of Reading, visiting professor at the University of North Carolina and non-executive director of, or consultant to, several other property investment businesses.

This edition, like the others, is enriched by Baum's years and breadth of investment experience. The chapters are a lovely mix of theory and practical experience and the analysis is on the cutting edge of commercial real estate portfolio management today. Baum is effusive in thanking his colleagues for their assistance but I believe that only Andrew Baum could craft a book like this – a comprehensible piece of scholarship.

Raymond Torto, *Harvard Graduate School of Design, retired Global Chief Economist of CBRE, co-founder of Torto Wheaton Research, now rebranded CBRE Econometric Advisors*

As an international real estate fund manager, I found this new edition of *Real Estate Investment* not only provides technical knowledge but also practical examples and case studies which are extremely relevant and essential to the decision making process of real estate professionals with a global prospective. To me, this book is the bible of real estate investment.

Humbert Pang, *Managing Principal, Head of China, Member of the Investment Committee, Gaw Capital Partners*

Real Estate Investment

A Strategic Approach

Third edition

Andrew Baum

LONDON AND NEW YORK

First published 2002 by Estates Gazette
Published 2015 by Routledge
2 Park Square, Milton Park, Abingdon, Oxon OX14 4RN

and by Routledge
711 Third Avenue, New York, NY 10017

Routledge is an imprint of the Taylor & Francis Group, an informa business

First edition published by Estates Gazette 2002
Second edition published by Estates Gazette 2009
Third edition published by Routledge 2015

British Library Cataloguing-in-Publication Data
A catalogue record for this book is available from the British Library

Library of Congress Cataloging in Publication Data
Baum, Andrew E.
Real estate investment : a strategic approach / Andrew Baum.
pages cm
Includes bibliographical references and index.
1. Real estate investment. 2. Real estate investment–Finance. I. Title.
HD1382.5.B3783 2015
332.63'24–dc23 2014043136

ISBN: 978-0-4157-4160-6 (hbk)
ISBN: 978-0-4157-4161-3 (pbk)
ISBN: 978-1-315-76229-6 (ebk)

Typeset in Times New Roman
by Wearset Ltd, Boldon, Tyne and Wear

Printed and bound in Great Britain by
TJ International Ltd, Padstow, Cornwall

Contents

Part 2 The investment process

Part 3 Investment vehicles

Part 4 International real estate investment

Figures

Tables

Boxes

The author

Andrew Baum is Chairman of Property Funds Research, a consulting business, and Visiting Professor of Management Practice at the Saïd Business School, University of Oxford. From 2009 to 2014 he was Honorary Professor of Real Estate Investment at the University of Cambridge and (from 2011 to 2014) Fellow of St John's College, Cambridge. He is also Emeritus Professor at the University of Reading. He is non-executive director of, or consultant to, several other property investment businesses.

He has spent the majority of the last 30 years working with institutional real estate investors in developing global property investment strategies. His experience is primarily in the UK but he has also worked in the US and Asia. He holds BSc, MPhil and PhD degrees from the University of Reading, is a graduate of the London Business School investment management programme and is a chartered surveyor and a qualified member of the CFA institute (ASIP). He was elected a Fellow of the Urban Land Institute in 2002.

Hired as the first director of property research for Prudential in 1987, he founded RES (a property research company) in 1990 and (with his partners) sold the business to Henderson Global Investors in 1997. At that time he became CIO for property at Henderson and later Director of International Property.

In 2001 he founded OPC, a property research and investment company that was sold to CBRE in 2006. CBRE Investors' global multi-manager team was formed upon the acquisition of OPC, which created Europe's first dataset describing unlisted property funds, launched one of first real estate fund of funds vehicles in Europe and became one of the world's leading specialists in indirect property investment. On its merger with ING REIM in 2011 CBRE Global Investors Multi-Manager (now re-branded as CBRE Global Investment partners) had around $11.4 billion of indirect property assets under management. OPC's information business was re-acquired by its management in 2006 and re-named Property Fund Research, and he now chairs this real estate consulting and research business.

Foreword to the first edition

For investors, property has been something of a puzzle. Against its large share of national wealth, the representation of property in multi-asset portfolios is not only low, but has fallen to one-third of what it was 20 years ago. On the available evidence (its accuracy in turn a subject of debate) property's risk and return history refuses to fit neatly into the framework of modern portfolio theory through which investors view the world. Still worse, through much of the last 20 years property has failed to meet, either in absolute terms or relative to alternative investments, the simple return thresholds investors need to beat. And, in an era obsessed with the globalization and transparency of investment, property markets are still heavily divided by national differences in statute, regulation and culture; accurate international comparisons are at best expensive, at worst impossible to come by. Property has, indeed, looked in danger of becoming an afterthought in the asset allocations of major investors.

There is, fortunately, a brighter, more interesting side to the picture. A run of satisfactory rates of return through the last five years – in the UK and many other countries – has revived flagging investor interest. And, thanks to a burgeoning, perhaps even blossoming, in commercial property research since the mid-1980s, property investment is far better understood and far better managed than it was 20 years ago. Many of the problems which were associated with property investment at that time have found workable (if rarely ideal) solutions. We can now say that the measurement, benchmarking, forecasting and quantitative management techniques applied to property investments are comparable with other asset classes. If other problems are less fully resolved – the correct interpretation of valuation and price evidence, the relationship between the performance of unlisted and listed investment vehicles – advances in property research have at least put the ongoing debates on to a footing of solid evidence, and produced a clear formulation of the issues.

That position has been reached through many different strands of research – from academics, specialist commercial researchers and research-minded portfolio managers in different countries, not always easily communicated between those spheres. Much of it, indeed, remains private rather than public – confined to the top levels of major investors and their advisers. Having held senior positions in all those fields of research, Andrew Baum is singularly well qualified to draw the strands together into a coherent and accessible statement of the state of the art in applied property research. In a world swept by radical change – globalization of investment markets, financial engineering of investment vehicles, the collection and dissemination of information – we can be sure that the state of the art will be transformed again over the coming decade. Here too the book offers a clear view of the next steps in the evolution of the industry, which will be read with keen interest by all those involved in it.

Tony Key
Research Director
Investment Property Databank
London, May 2000

Preface to the first edition

This book is the result of the author's recently varied experience of applied property research, UK property fund management, inter-national property investment and academic research. The many challenges and questions prompted by this varied experience have led to a varied set of thoughts and writings, some previously published and some not. The book is therefore something of a set of sketches. Nonetheless, they share a common subject matter, which can be described broadly as institutional investment in real estate, and a common foundation, broadly an international and capital markets context viewed with the perspective of a UK property professional.

The picture painted is of a major industry which is going through a period of rapid modernization, facing more and more challenges as economies and markets become more global in character, as financial and investment markets become more and more creative and as the world is swept by a wave of technological change. Creativity is at a premium, but at the same time this is an industry requiring – and developing – discipline, processes and measurement.

The text concentrates on UK institutional real estate, mainly retail, office and industrial, although residential is growing in importance as a UK sector and is included in the portfolios of most non-UK institutional investors. It is designed for practitioners facing the challenges described above, and those who may have to design solutions to tomorrow's problems. It is hoped that it provides a more straightforward and integrated view of the key issues in UK real estate than will be found elsewhere.

The book is divided into three sections. Part 1 provides a description of the market, the industry and the vehicles available, and a performance history of UK real estate as an asset class. Part 2 discusses the property investment process and the tools required to develop excellence in executing that process. Part 3 provides material for debate about the changes likely to take place over the short and medium term.

I am very grateful for the many fortunate partnerships which have made it possible for this material to be produced. Over the past decade, colleagues at the University of Reading, Prudential Portfolio Managers and at Real Estate Strategy, later Henderson Investors, have been responsible either for the better ideas or the more accurate analysis contained in these pages. In particular, I would like to thank Professors Neil Crosby, Colin Beardsley, Colin Lizieri and Charles Ward at Reading, John Partridge at RES/Henderson, Paul McNamara at Prudential, and especially Andrew Schofield, Guy Morrell and Professor Bryan MacGregor with whom I was fortunate to work at both Prudential and RES/Henderson.

Andrew Schofield deserves particular mention. He was responsible for much of the analysis and some of the ideas in Chapters 3, 5 and 7, and our joint work at RES in the 1990s has influenced much of the book's content.

Tony Key has also allowed me to reproduce some of our joint work in Chapter 6, and Freeman Publishing has also allowed me to reproduce parts of my work with Peter Freeman for *Freeman's Guide to the Property Industry* in Chapters 1 and 2. Some of the ideas in Chapter 9 are based on the work of Charles Ward and Colin Beardsley, my colleagues in the property derivatives group. I am grateful to them all.

In addition, Tony Key of IPD and Richard Barkham of CB Hillier Parker acted as expert reviewers of the first draft of the text, and produced many suggestions for improvements. Tony Key proposed a much improved structure to the original book and Karen Baum acted as an expert copyeditor.

Any remaining errors are my own. In the text, he/his is meant to imply he or she/his or hers.

The place of real estate as an investable asset class is secure. The same cannot be said of existing vehicles, companies or managers, which and who will survive only through education, innovation and professionalism. I hope this small book makes at least a small contribution to their future success.

Andrew Baum
London
May 2000

Preface to the second edition

If the first edition of this book was a 'set of sketches' this new edition is more ambitious. This time, I hope we have produced a coherent and continuous book which successfully brings together theory and practice.

The global financial crisis of 2008 had its roots in property speculation. The ability of property investors and homeowners to take on debt secured on the value of property, coupled with the ability of lenders to securitize and sell those loans, created a wave of capital flows into the asset class and a pricing bubble. London and New York had become the main centres for creative property structuring through REITs, unlisted funds, property derivatives and mortgage-backed securities, and became the eye of the financial storm which followed.

When the first edition of this book was published in 2001, property had been somewhat unfashionable as an investment, but advances in property research had put the ongoing debates on to a footing of solid evidence, producing a clear formulation of the relevant issues. The last decade has seen a near-frenzy of product creation and leveraged speculation, together with true advances in the range of indirect products, in the face of which the advances in research of which we were so proud were not enough to avoid a crash. The approaches described in these pages are intended to provide a foundation for a new wave of creativity for use by the next generation of investment managers, advisers and analysts, and to encourage a responsible and professionally guided recovery. In the last decade the author has again been immensely fortunate to have worked with a series of high quality partners in business and academic life, as well as with many generous and thoughtful students in executive education classes, MBA electives and other postgraduate classes in many countries, all of whom have made a contribution to this text.

In particular, in Chapter 1 has used the work of Professor Neil Crosby and Dr Patrick McAllister of the University of Reading, and the input of Peter Struempell, research analyst at Property Funds Research 2004–6. Chapter 2 includes work produced by the Property Funds Research team, including Professor George Matysiak and Jane Fear, who also contributed to Chapters 4 and 7. Professor Bryan MacGregor, now of the University of Aberdeen and a former colleague and partner at Prudential, contributed material on forecasting in Chapter 4. Alex Moss, Head of Global Property Securities Analytics at Macquarie Capital Securities, helped with Chapter 6, and Gary McNamara, Associate Director at DTZ, did a similar job on Chapter 8, which leans heavily on work undertaken with Professor Colin Lizieri and Dr Gianluca Marcato, with Paul Ogden, at the University of Reading.

CBRE Investors have been very helpful, providing access to a wealth of research and data resources. In particular, the global multi-manager, global real estate securities and research teams have been unfailingly generous. Kieran Farrelly was instrumental in developing parts of Chapters 5 and 7, while my former partner Jeremy Plummer gave me most of the good ideas in Chapters 7, 9 and 10. Students at the Amsterdam School of Real Estate and on IPD executive education courses jointly contributed much of the tax material in Chapter 9.

Thanks to these partnerships, I am fortunate to feel – as the back cover suggests – well qualified to summarize the impact and likely future of global innovations in property research and fund management in the context of the third real estate crash I have observed over a long career. As we said in the preface to the first edition:

> In a world swept by radical change – globalization of investment markets, financial engineering of investment vehicles, the collection and dissemination of information – we can be sure that the state of the art will be transformed again over the coming decade. Creativity is at a premium, but at the same time this is an industry requiring – and developing – discipline, processes and measurement.

It is also thanks to these partnerships that this book offers a unique theory/practice perspective of the evolution of the international real estate investment industry at a time when the asset class has become critically important to the world economy.

Again, any remaining errors are my own, and in the text he/his is meant to imply he or she/his or hers.

This edition was completed in January 2009, in the eye of a 'perfect storm' in the global real estate market. However, analysis and data tables use different periods depending on when they were undertaken. This is deliberate, as updating them all would not have achieved the objective of illustrating market conditions and behaviour at the relevant point in time. Nonetheless, I apologize for any lack of clarity which results.

Andrew Baum
London
January 2009

Preface to the third edition

As real estate investment has begun to embrace more property types, including in particular more focus on several forms of residential property, *Commercial Real Estate Investment: A Strategic Approach (second edition)* has now become *Real Estate Investment: A Strategic Approach (third edition)*.

The book began its life as very UK oriented, including a performance history of UK real estate as an asset class. This has now gone, and the book is now aimed firmly at a global audience.

Nonetheless, I continue to use a lot of UK examples. For this I can offer my first apology: the UK is where most of my work has been based, and it is easier for me to write from first-hand experience. I can also offer a justification. The UK is officially the world's most transparent real estate market (JLL Transparency Index, 2014), and UK data is relatively long, comprehensive and well founded, making the UK market an excellent laboratory for the forming of ideas that will hopefully have a global application. Still, I would prefer to have used more examples from outside the UK, especially the Asian and emerging markets. So, in the hope that *Real Estate Investment: A Strategic Approach (fourth edition)* will be on its way in a few years, I'd like to make an open invitation to readers to contribute global examples for the next edition. Please feel free to send any ideas to me at ab@andrewbaum.com.

My second apology is less easy to temper with a justification. The book contains too many references to my own research and published work, not to mention the businesses I have worked with, and it may appear that I regard myself as the key reference source on all matters real estate. I don't, but frankly it has proved easier to cut and paste from my own work than to be the perfect scholar and look for better sources in order to misquote them; and having written the book from both an academic and practitioner perspective, I wanted to write about issues with an 'I was there' perspective. My apologies are unreserved to those whose relevant and first class work I have failed to reference, especially if I have used my own less impressive material in their place.

This re-write has involved updates to all chapters, with some more serious pruning and additions, including a re-write of Chapter 2 and a major revisions of Chapters 6, 7 and 8. My thanks remain due to those whose work is incorporated in the first and second editions, and with this particular edition in mind are again offered to Alex Moss (now of Consilia Capital), Jane Fear, Nick Colley and the PFR staff and Gary MacNamara (now of Arca Property Risk Management). This time, I would also like to thank Malcolm Frodsham, Rupert Kirby and four anonymous referees whose suggestions were extremely helpful and very largely incorporated in this edition, which has benefited greatly from their efforts. Finally, Ed Needle's persistence in getting this edition into print and David Hartzell's understanding in allowing this book to survive alongside our book *Global Property Investment*, with which a considerable amount of material has been shared, are very much appreciated.

Andrew Baum
Oxford
October 2014

Abbreviations

AFFO	Adjusted Funds from Operations
AIFMD	Alternative Investment Fund Managers Directive
AIFs	Authorized Investment Funds
APUTs	authorized property unit trusts
CAPM	capital asset pricing model
CBD	central business district
CEPR	Centre for Economic Policy Research
CFO	chief financial officer
CMBS	Commercial Mortgage-Backed Securities
CSFB	Credit Suisse First Boston
CV	coefficient of variation
DSCR	debt service coverage ratio
EMEA	Europe, Middle East and Africa
EPRA	European Public Real Estate Association
ERV	estimated rental value
ETFs	exchange traded funds
FAD	Funds Available for Distribution
FFO	Funds from Operations
FOX	London Futures and Options Exchange
FSA	Financial Services Authority
FT	*Financial Times*
FX	foreign exchange
GAV	gross asset values
GDP	gross domestic product
GFC	global financial crisis
GP	general partner
ICR	interest cover ratio
IPD	Investment Property Databank
IPF	Investment Property Forum
IRR	internal rate of return
ISDA	International Swaps and Derivatives Agreement
LIBOR	London interbank offered rate
LGP	Legal & General Property
LP	limited partnership
LTV	loan to value
MPT	modern portfolio theory

MWRR	money-weighted rate of return
NAPF	National Association of Pension Funds (UK)
NAREIT	National Association of Real Estate Investment Trusts (US)
NAV	net asset value
NCREIF	US National Council of Real Estate Investment Fiduciaries
NOI	net operating income
NPI	NCREIF Property Index
NPV	net present value
OEICs	open-ended investment companies
OTC	over the counter
PAIFs	property authorized investment funds
PFR	Property Funds Research
PICs	Property Index Certificates
PREA	Pension Real Estate Association (US)
PropCos	property companies
PUTs	Property Unit Trusts
REIM	real estate investment market
REIT	Real Estate Investment Trust
REOCs	real estate operating companies
RICS	Royal Institution of Chartered Surveyors
RMBS	residential mortgage backed securities
S&P	Standard and Poor's
SD	standard deviation
SIIC	*Sociétés d'Investissements Immobiliers Cotées*
SML	security market line
SPVs	special purpose corporate vehicles
TI	Transparency Index
TWRR	time-weighted rate of return
UPREIT	Umbrella Partnership REIT
WALT	weighted average lease term

Part 1

Introduction to real estate and the real estate market

Real estate – the asset class

1

1.1 Property – a global asset class?

This book is about real estate (or property) investment. In finance, 'investment' means putting money into an asset with the expectation of earning interest or dividends plus capital appreciation. Most or all forms of investment involve some form of risk, including investment in equities, and even fixed interest securities, which are subject to default and inflation risk (the prospect that the spending power of the income will erode).

Property is that which is capable of belonging to somebody. Depending on the nature of the property, an owner of property has the right to consume, alter, share, redefine, rent, mortgage, sell, exchange or transfer it.

Real property and personal property are the two main subunits of property in English common law. Real property, real estate, realty or immovable property are land and the improvements made to it (usually buildings). Scottish law calls real property 'heritable property'; French-based law calls it 'immobilier' (immovable). Immovable property is also the term used in Canada, the US, India, and in countries where civil law systems prevail, including most of Europe, Russia and South America.

An estate is a common law term for someone's property; hence real estate is real property. The term real estate has become globally recognized, and for our purposes means the same thing as (real) property.

Commercial real estate is a large part of the universe of potential investments available to global investing institutions. As PREA (2013) suggests, it is very difficult to measure the size of the market exactly; but a report from the US-based Prudential (2012) estimates the size of the global institutional-grade commercial real estate market as being over US$26 trillion. (Other updated estimates put this figure at $32 trillion: see Chapter 2.) For comparison, the end-of-2012 total market capitalization of publicly traded equities was US$55 trillion. If we had no view of its likely risk or return attributes, its size as an asset class suggests that commercial real estate should be seriously considered as a significant part of any investor's portfolio, say around 50 per cent of the typical equities allocation, which (in the UK, for example) has varied between 40 and 80 per cent of all assets over time (NAPF, 2013).

Yet this simple proposition raises bigger questions. Is commercial real estate (property used solely for business purposes) the correct definition of the asset class we are discussing in this book? Clearly not; many investors are interested in residential real estate (rented, rather than owner-occupied), including what is called in the US multi-family and in the UK the private rented sector; in student accommodation and senior housing; and in hotels, self-storage and an emerging sub-class of social infrastructure real estate (uses such as hospitals, prisons, schools and universities).

By some estimates (for example Ibbotson Associates, 2006) real estate represents 50 per cent by value of all global assets. So we could justify an even bigger allocation to real estate. But we can observe that most professional investors do not hold the 'neutral weight' in real estate. Between 1980 and 2000, US and UK insurance companies reduced their property holdings from allocations as high as 20 per cent to around 5 per cent today (Association of British Insurers, 2012). No doubt this can be explained partly by the introduction of new alternative asset classes, some offering the income security and diversification benefits associated with real estate, including index-linked gilts, private equity and hedge funds. But this fall in property weightings raises other issues.

What do we know about the likely risk or return attributes of real estate as an asset class? What other factors colour the attitude of large investors? We know, for example, that there are operational difficulties involved in holding property, including illiquidity, lumpiness (specific risk) and the difficulties involved in aligning the property and securities investment management processes. We also know that there is a lack of trust in property data, due to the nature of valuations, suspicions of smoothing in valuation-based indices and the lack of long runs of high-frequency return histories. The result has been a mismatch between the importance of the asset class in value terms and its weighting in institutional portfolios.

Thanks to continued investment in commercial property research and creative product development, by 2007 property investment had become better managed and packaged than it had been in 1980. Many of the problems that were associated with property investment at that time had found workable solutions. The measurement, benchmarking, forecasting and quantitative management techniques applied to other asset classes had begun to be used by property investors. Advances in property research had provided ongoing debates with a foundation of solid evidence, and produced a clear formulation of many relevant issues. The result was an unprecedented boom in commercial and residential real estate investment across the globe, accompanied by such excellent returns that by 2005 property had become the best performing major asset class in the UK over five, ten and 15 years.

However, by 2007 clear overpricing had become evident in housing and in commercial property of all types in the UK, US and elsewhere. The ability of property investors and homeowners to take on debt secured on the value of property, coupled with the ability of lenders to securitize and sell those loans, created a wave of capital flows into the asset class and a pricing bubble. Professional responsibility took a back seat to the profit motive. Academics and researchers became fund managers, boardrooms lacked the detached yet experienced voice that advances in information and research should have made available, and detached analysis gave way to greed. London and New York had become the main centres for creative property structuring through REITs, unlisted funds, property derivatives and mortgage-backed securities, and became the eye of the financial storm that followed.

The technical advances made in information and research, and the spreading of risk made possible by the development of property investment products, did not prevent a global crisis from being incubated in the world of property investing. Worse, the global financial crisis of 2008 had its very roots in property speculation, facilitated by the packaging and repackaging of equity, debt and risk. By the end of 2013 UK property was no longer the best performing asset class over five or ten years.

So what now for international property investment? Is the asset class a worthy component of a mixed asset portfolio? The purpose of this book is to demonstrate how to approach and answer this question.

1.2 What makes property different?

As with all equity-type assets, the performance of property is ultimately linked to some extent to the performance of the economy, and like all assets its performance is linked to the capital markets. The economy is the basic driver of occupier demand, and, in the long term, investment returns are produced by occupiers who pay rent. However, in the shorter term – say up to ten years – returns are much more likely to be explained by reference to changes in pricing, or capitalization rates, which are in turn driven by required returns. Required returns do not exist in a property vacuum but are instead driven by available or expected returns in other asset classes. As required returns on bonds and stocks move, so will required returns for property, followed by property capitalization rates and prices.

Nonetheless, history shows that property is a true third asset, distinctly different from equities and bonds. The direct implication of property being different is its diversification potential within a multi-asset portfolio, and hence the justification for holding it. Generally, the impact of the real economy and the capital markets on the cash flow and value of real estate is different from the impact on stocks and bonds, and is distorted by several factors. These are as follows.

- Property is a real asset, and it wears out over time, suffering from physical deterioration and obsolescence, together creating depreciation.
- The cash flow delivered by a property asset is controlled or distorted by the lease contract agreed between owner and occupier. US leases can be for three or five years, fixed or with pre-agreed annual uplifts. Leases in continental Europe may be ten years long, with the rent indexed to an inflation measure. Leases in the UK for high quality offices are commonly for ten years, with rents fixed for five-year periods after which they can only be revised upwards.
- The supply side is controlled by planning or zoning regulations, and is highly price inelastic. This means that a boom in the demand for space may be followed by a supply response, but only if permission to build can be obtained and only after a significant lag, which will be governed by the time taken to obtain a permit, prepare a site and construct or refit a property.
- The short-term returns delivered by property are likely to be heavily influenced by appraisals rather than by marginal trading prices. This leads to the concept of smoothing.
- Property is highly illiquid. It is expensive to trade, there is a large risk of abortive expenditure and the result can be a very wide bid–offer spread (a gap between what buyers will offer and sellers will accept).
- Property assets are generally large in terms of capital price. This means that property portfolios cannot easily be diversified, and suffer hugely from specific risk.
- Leverage is used in the vast majority of property transactions. This distorts the return and risk of a property investment.

- Property is a hybrid asset, with similarities to stock and bonds, but different. While real estate is not technically a good inflation hedge, property rents appear to be closely correlated with inflation in the long run, producing an income stream that looks like an indexed bond. But rents can be fixed in the short term, producing cash flows that look like those delivered by a conventional bond, and the residual value of a property investment after the lease has ended exposes the owner fully to the equity-type risk of the real economy.
- The risk of property appears low. Rent is paid before dividends, and as a real asset property will be a store of value even when it is vacant and produces no income. Its volatility of annual return also appears to be lower than that of bonds. This is distorted somewhat by appraisals, but the reported performance history of real estate suggests a medium return for a low risk, and this can appear to be a mispriced asset class.
- Unlike stocks and bonds, real estate returns appear to be controlled by cycles of eight to nine years.

These factors will now be considered in more detail.

1.3 Property depreciates

- *Property is a real asset, and it wears out over time, suffering from physical deterioration and obsolescence, together creating depreciation.*

Commodities (say coffee, or oil) are by nature different from paper assets. Commodities will normally depreciate over time; they can have a value in use that sets a floor to minimum value; and they are generally illiquid. Finally, they may have to be valued by experts rather than priced by the market. Examples include property of all types (that is, both real and personal).

Real property is, unlike equities and gilts, a physical asset. While, unlike much personal property, it is durable (and immovable), the physical nature of commercial property means that it is subject to deterioration and obsolescence, and needs regular management and maintenance. Physical deterioration and functional and aesthetic obsolescence go together to create depreciation, defined as a fall in value relative to an index of values of new buildings (see Box 1.1).

The problem of building depreciation or obsolescence of freehold buildings should not, as has usually been the case in the property world, be understated. Poorly designed office buildings located in business parks in low land value areas will suffer more deterioration in performance over time than will city-centre shops and shopping centres, and even sheds (industrial properties), located in high land value areas. A failure to identify the potential impact of depreciation is very dangerous. The office sector has generally failed to out-perform national property indexes over the long run, and depreciation is probably one of the major causes of this.

Depreciation can affect the performance and value of real estate vehicles in a number of ways. In the context of real estate, depreciation has been defined by Law (2004: 242) as follows: 'the rate of decline in rental (capital) value of an asset (or group of assets) over time relative to the asset (or group of assets) valued as new with contemporary specification'.

Box 1.1: Depreciation and its impact

The extremes of performance are illustrated by the following two office properties in the City of London.

21 Great Winchester Street, a building of 18,000 sq ft, which, in 1986, was 16 years past a major refurbishment, was valued at that time at £369 per sq ft. The ERV (estimated rental value) was £24; the capitalization rate at which a sale might be expected following a new letting was estimated at 6.5 per cent.

Token House, at 8–10 Telegraph Street, a 17,000 sq ft building having undergone a major refurbishment in 1985, was valued at that time at £674 per sq ft, with an ERV of £32 and a capitalization rate of 4.75 per cent. In terms of underlying value (in other words, ignoring the impact of lease contracts), it was worth roughly 80 per cent more than the value of 21 Great Winchester Street per unit of space.

In 1996, 26 years since refurbishment, 21 Great Winchester Street was valued at £19.50, at 7 per cent and at £279 per sq ft. This was a decline in capital value of £91 or 25 per cent. Some 72 per cent of its underlying 1986 value remained, and it had declined in value at the same rate as the market (3 per cent). Ageing had not therefore severely affected the underlying value of the building.

In 1996, 11 years old and just past its second review, Token House was worth £133 per sq ft, valued at £10 and 7.5 per cent. It was now worth less than half the value of the comparable property. It had fallen in value by £540 per sq ft, or no less than 80 per cent of its underlying 1986 value: 20 per cent of that value remained. It had suffered depreciation of 15 per cent each year, of which perhaps 3 per cent can be blamed on the market.

This definition relates to the economic depreciation of assets. This is distinct from depreciation as used in corporate accounting, which is a method of reducing the book value of assets through time (and the annual profit of a company) to reflect the consumption of capital assets that will need to be replaced. It is also a topic distinct from depreciation as a source of tax relief.

The definition above does not indicate the causes of such depreciation, which it is helpful to briefly consider. Baum (1991) sets out the following causes of depreciation in commercial property values.

- Physical deterioration: this relates to the wearing out of the building through time.
- Building obsolescence: this refers to changes in what is expected from buildings, the most obvious source of which are changes in technology that impact upon occupier requirements and may render a building's design or configuration redundant.

These factors can affect rental values and capital values, as they will influence the rent that a potential tenant would be prepared to pay, and they will have consequences for future cash flows either in the form of reduced rents and/or capital expenditure in order to combat their effects.

Several UK studies have attempted to measure the impact of depreciation on property values. Those conducted for the UK commercial real estate market include CALUS (1986), Jones Lang Wootton (1987), Baum (1991, 1997), Barras and Clark (1996) and College of Estate Management (1999). More recently the Investment Property Forum has commissioned research (IPF, 2005 and 2011).

The full cost of depreciation includes capital expenditure needed to maintain and renew the properties in a portfolio and a fall in rental values as a building ages. The 2011 IPF study suggested an average rental depreciation rate across the UK market of 0.6 per cent per annum before capital expenditure (see Table 1.1). The combined depreciation rate was higher for offices and lower for shops.

Table 1.1: Rental depreciation and capital expenditure, UK, 1993–2010 (% per year)

	Rent depreciation (%)	CapEx (% of value)
Office	0.8	0.6
Industrial	0.5	0.3
Standard shop – south-eastern	1.0	0.3
Standard shop – rest of UK	–0.7	0.5
Shopping centres	0.1	1.4
Retail warehouses	0.9	3.4
Office – City	0.5	0.3
Office – West End	1.1	0.7
Office – south-eastern	0.8	0.9
Office – rest of UK	1.8	0.6
Industrial – south-eastern	0.3	0.3
Industrial – rest of UK	1.0	0.3
All property	0.6	–

Source: IPF, 2011

It is clear, therefore, that property investment differs from investment in securities, and equities in particular, due to its physical nature and the consequent depreciation it suffers. This means that the rate of income growth that the asset class can deliver is constrained, and that the assumption of constant growth used in the analysis of property needs to be adjusted to reflect this fact.

Baum and Turner (2004) argue that the depreciation phenomenon is disguised by the market practice of making a full distribution of rental income, when the maintenance of capital value might require that a retention be made. The effect is to support income return, and in an era of low inflation this might create excessively confident expectations regarding capital and total return. Higher total returns might be achieved by re-investment rather than through a full distribution policy and a full income distribution might therefore damage returns in property markets. In some markets a full distribution policy is necessitated by common leasing convention; and this might lead to higher depreciation rates than in those markets where leasing practice allows owners to actively manage their assets (for example, the US, where multi-tenanted office buildings may be occupied on three- or five-year leases and the freeholder retains responsibility for internal repairs and maintenance).

To test this, Baum and Turner measured and compared retention rates across European office markets, and found interesting differences related to lease length and the landlord's repair and management obligations. Where leases are short and landlords retain responsibility (as in Stockholm), reported depreciation rates were lower than in London, where leases were long and leases were 'triple net', so that landlords have little responsibility for ongoing repairs and maintenance.

It appears that some re-investment of income is necessary to maximize returns, and, more importantly, re-investment relieves depreciation and thereby improve net income growth. Nonetheless, depreciation is an unavoidable and understated problem in real estate investment.

1.4 Lease contracts control cash flows

- *The cash flow delivered by a property asset is controlled or distorted by the lease contract agreed between owner and occupier. US leases can be for three or five years, fixed or with pre-agreed annual uplifts. Leases in continental Europe may be ten years long, with the rent indexed to an inflation measure. Leases in the UK for high quality offices are commonly for ten years, with rents fixed for five-year periods after which they can only be revised upwards.*

Unlike equities, property's income stream is governed by lease contracts, and, unlike bonds, the income from a freehold is perpetual. Property income is affected by 'lease events'; it may be expected to increase at rent reviews and to change at lease ends. Property's cash flow and investment character flow from the effects of the customary occupational lease, supported by statute and case law (see Baum and Sams (2007) from which the following paragraphs are paraphrased).

Any large commercial building involves a complex pattern of relationships created by the unique nature of property as an economic commodity. The market for property is not driven wholly by the desire to own land and buildings. It is instead a market for rights in the product that may have many tiers of ownership. Consequently, a single building might represent the property rights or interests of several different parties.

For a given unit of property, there is a basic dichotomy of rights. These are the right of ownership, which may be fragmented, and the right of occupation, which (allowing for the existence of time shares and joint tenancies) is usually vested in a single legal person. In fact, the 'given unit' is commonly delineated by its exclusive occupation by an organization, family or individual.

It is especially typical in the case of commercial property (all office, shop, industrial and institutional property, for the purposes of this book) that buildings are 'owned' by non-occupiers, in contrast to residential property, where the rights of ownership and occupation are more often fused within the same person. This decomposition of the ownership of commercial property produces the probability of the existence of contractual landlord/tenant relationships. A property adviser is often employed as an agent on behalf of one of the parties to negotiate an acquisition or disposal of an interest or a variation thereof. The medium for these negotiations is a contract or a lease, which defines the contractual relationship between the parties.

There are many factors contained in a lease that directly affect the value and performance of interests in land and buildings. For instance, repairing liabilities, lease length, break clauses, user and assignment restrictions and rent review patterns may all, individually or collectively, have an impact on the cash flow delivered by the property and its resulting capital or rental value. The differences between a short US lease, a UK lease governed by five-yearly, upward-only rent reviews, a French 3–6–9 lease (a nine-year lease with tenant breaks and reviews every three years) and a German 10-year indexed lease produce very different cash flow characteristics and different assets.

Baum (2005), Baum and Brown (2006) and Robinson (2012) explore the potential mispricing of leases caused by these differences.

1.5 The supply side is inelastic

- *The supply side is controlled by planning or zoning regulations, and is highly price inelastic. This means that a boom in the demand for space may be followed by a supply response, but only if permission to build can be obtained and only after a significant lag, which will be governed by the time taken to obtain a permit, prepare a site and construct or refit a property.*

The supply side of property is regulated by local and central government. The control of supply complicates the way in which an economic event (such as a positive or negative demand shock) is translated into return. A loosening of policy, such as happened in the UK and US in the mid-1980s, created the conditions for an immediate building boom, which, in the context of the following recession, led to the property crash of 1990–5. It is difficult to vary the supply of property upwards, and even more difficult to vary it downwards. This is termed price inelasticity.

The supply side can be both regulated and inelastic, and will sometimes produce different return characteristics for property from equities in the same economic environment. A good harvest will damage the price of wheat in a strong economy, just as oversupply held back office returns in the recovering mid-1990s economic environment.

More elastic supply regimes, such as those pertaining in loose planning environments in parts of Texas, or for industrial property in regeneration cities, will produce different cash flow characteristics for property investments than will highly constrained environments, such as the West End of London. The industrial investment will typically deliver less volatile rents, and will show less rental growth in times of demand expansion, than will the West End office.

1.6 Valuations influence performance

- *The short-term returns delivered by property are likely to be heavily influenced by appraisals rather than by marginal trading prices.*

In the absence of continuously traded, deep and securitized markets, commercial property valuations perform a vital function in the property market by acting as a surrogate for transaction prices. Property asset valuations are central to the process of performance measurement, but within both the professional and academic communities there is considerable scepticism about the ability of appraisals or valuations to fulfil this role in a reliable manner.

There has been a considerable amount of research into the operation of the valuation process in various parts of the world, especially in the US and the UK. Research has tended to concentrate on the methods used by valuers and the way that valuation information is processed. For example, Baum *et al.* (2003), Crosby *et al.* (2010) and Crosby and Hughes (2011) deal in particular with the following questions.

- How accurate are valuations? What is the probable margin of error and what is the impact of smoothing?
- How does the client/valuer relationship operate? Is there evidence of client influence or other external influences on valuations?
- Are valuation approaches consistent across borders?

1.6.1 Valuation accuracy

There is a consensus that individual valuations are prone to a degree of uncertainty. At the macro-level, it is clear that few analysts accept that appraisal-based indices reflect the true underlying performance of the transactional property market. It is commonly held, for example, that such indices fail to capture the extent of market volatility and tend to lag underlying performance. As a consequence, issues such as the level and nature of valuation uncertainty and the causes and extent of index smoothing have generated a substantial research literature.

Some of this research indicates that valuations both lag the market and smooth the peaks and troughs of 'real' prices. Valuations – and, if valuations affect market psychology and hence prices, real estate prices – can be 'sticky'. Sticky is a term used in the social sciences and particularly economics to describe a situation in which a variable is resistant to change. A variable that is sticky will be reluctant to drop even if conditions dictate that it should. The suggested reasons for this are as follows.

Anchoring

According to Wikipedia in 2014, anchoring is

> a cognitive bias that describes the common human tendency to rely too heavily on the first piece of information offered (the 'anchor') when making decisions. During decision making, anchoring occurs when individuals use an initial piece of information to make subsequent judgments. Once an anchor is set, other judgments are made by adjusting away from that anchor. For example, the initial price offered for a used car sets the standard for the rest of the negotiations, so that prices lower than the initial price seem more reasonable even if they are still higher than what the car is really worth.

It seems that trading prices or previous valuations of a piece of real estate can provide a very heavy anchor influencing subsequent valuations and (sometimes) prices.

In many jurisdictions, the fiduciary responsibility of the valuer towards the client is an important influence on valuer behaviour. Claims based on accusations of professional negligence are not unknown and judicial precedent is a powerful influence on the valuation process. It is not therefore surprising if a valuer, retained to produce a portfolio valuation on a three-year contract, pays attention to his/her year-end 2014 valuation when undertaking the 2015 equivalent and ensures continuity by limiting the number and size of shocks a client might suffer. This can reduce changes in valuation from one period to the next.

Temporal averaging

Stock markets rise and fall on a daily basis, sometimes significantly. Market price changes between 31 December 2014 and 31 December 2015 are fully affected by the end-of-trading price on each day, and it is perfectly possible for the year-end 2014 market to be at a temporary low and the year-end 2015 market to be at a temporary high. In property, however, year-end valuations are undertaken over a period of up to three months, and even where the valuation date is set at 31 December an averaging effect is inevitable. This is likely to result in lower price volatility from year to year.

The lagging effect of comparable evidence

Real estate valuation is founded primarily on the use of comparable sales evidence. Similarity in property characteristics is paramount, and finding relevant recent transactions may not be easy to do. Hence the evidence used to value a property as at 31 December 2015 may use evidence collected over the period July to December 2015. In a rising or falling market, this will again result in a lower variance of prices. Hence valuations will be based upon the previous valuation plus or minus a perception of change. The perceived changes, unless based on very reliable transaction evidence, will be conservative.

The resulting valuation 'smoothing' has been widely analysed. It is generally presumed to reduce the reported volatility – or risk – of real estate investment below the real level of risk suffered by investors who have to sell in a weak market or buy in a strong one.

1.6.2 Client influence

Valuers may be influenced by their clients. This is likely to be damaging, as client influence creates a conflict of interest between professional responsibility and client satisfaction, interfering with objective professional judgement.

Attention has been paid to the moral hazards or conflicts of interest present when an auditing firm provides additional non-auditing services, with the result that the Sarbanes-Oxley Act of 2002 forced the providers of auditing services to be more accountable regarding client influence. But such issues are not unique to the auditing/accountancy/consultancy profession, and there is some evidence of problems existing within the client/valuer relationship.

Issues raised by an investigation of the 'moral hazards' (conflicts of interest) involved in the principal/agent (client/valuer) relationship include the following.

- When acting for a purchaser, investment brokers who also act as valuers may have an incentive to provide a confirmatory valuation since their fee income depends upon completion of the transaction.
- Valuers will be motivated to retain the client's valuation business, and the implications of lost clients – both for individual careers and for success at firm level – may encourage valuers to keep clients happy.
- Property advisory firms often provide non-valuation services to clients, providing an incentive for that firm to respond positively to client influence.
- Fund managers have clear incentives to attempt to influence valuations since they are used in the measurement of performance.

- In a period of falling values, the minimum loan to value ratios required by lenders may be breached – or supported – as the result of a valuation, which may, as a result, be subject to client influence.

As a result, we need to be aware that (while professional valuers acting properly will resist such pressures) valuations might change in response to client pressure, especially when the valuations are important, typically at the year end. Valuation smoothing, lagging and inaccuracy may all be supported by the relationships between clients and valuers. Research (for example, Baum *et al.* 2003) suggests that valuations may be distorted by the influence of clients as well as by the procedures that form the valuation process. Valuations are used to re-negotiate prices (which, in turn, may be used by valuers to support subsequent valuations). In addition, valuations often go through a process of negotiation with clients, and this is especially evident at the year-end December valuation. This may lead to improved valuations, bolstered by enhanced information quality; but it also may lead to biased and less valid figures. If the latter is the case, valuations may be far from independent of the market. Ultimately, market credibility relies on the professionalism and integrity of valuers and other advisers.

Recommendations to limit the impact of client influence by (for example) changing valuers on a regular basis have been considered in the UK (see the RICS-sponsored Carsberg Report, 2002).

(The lack of independence between valuations and achieved sale prices means that a natural lag would appear to be built into monthly and quarterly indices in an upswing or a downswing. This became a significant problem for open-ended property funds in 2007–8: see Chapter 7.)

1.6.3 Cross-border valuation consistency

Are valuation approaches the same from country to country? Does a valuation in one market mean the same as a valuation in another market? Crosby and Hughes (2007), who focus on differences in approach in UK and Germany, suggest not. They found that German valuations have been much less volatile than UK valuations. Is this the result of differences in the markets, or a difference in approach to valuations?

To test this, we would need to set up an experiment to examine valuations of the same assets over time by valuers from different backgrounds. Crosby and Hughes come close to achieving this by their analysis of two datasets: one, a set of valuations of UK assets (largely owned by UK institutions) undertaken by UK valuers; and the second, a set of valuations of UK assets owned by German investors undertaken by German valuers.

Table 1.2 shows that the volatility of the German approach to capital value change is much lower than in the UK. This is the clearly the result of differences in the approach to valuations.

Table 1.2: UK and German valuations of UK assets, 2000–9: capital change

	Average	**Standard deviation**
German valuers	0.37%	3.67%
UK valuers	1.20%	13.54%

Hence the smoothing of values may vary from market to market, somewhat compounding the problems of valuation accuracy for an international investor.

1.7 Property is not liquid

- *Property is highly illiquid. It is expensive to trade, there is a large risk of abortive expenditure and the result can be a very wide bid–offer spread (a gap between what buyers will offer and sellers will accept).*

It costs much more to trade property than it costs to trade securities. There are both direct and indirect costs.

The direct costs include taxes paid by buyers on property transactions (stamp duty in the UK, for example, is levied at a rate of 4 per cent of the purchase price for transactions of commercial property worth more than £500,000) and fees paid to professional advisers by both buyers and sellers. In addition to taxes, buyers will incur survey fees, valuation and brokers' fees and legal fees, totalling up to (say) 1.75 per cent. The buyers' costs, including taxes, would therefore be 5.75 per cent. Sellers will incur legal fees (say 0.5 per cent) and brokers' fees (say 1 per cent), so that up to 1.5 per cent can be the total seller's cost, and (in the UK) a round trip purchase and sale can cost up to 7 per cent.

These costs, which can be even higher in other jurisdictions, define one cause of the 'bid–offer spread' which inhibits liquidity. It is natural for a seller to wish to recover his total costs, so that having bought a property for $1 million he will wish to get back $1.07 million in order not to have lost money. But in a flat or falling market buyers will not pay this price, and sellers are tempted to hang on until the selling market is stronger. Hence liquidity will be positively related to capital growth in the market.

There are also indirect costs of transacting property. Every property is unique, which means that time and effort have to be expended on researching its physical qualities, its legal title and its supportable market value. In addition, the process by which properties are marketed and sold can be very risky to both sides. In many markets, including the US and England and Wales, there is a large risk of abortive expenditure, because buyers and sellers are not committed until contracts are exchanged, and last minute overbids by another buyer, or a price reduction (or 'chip') by the buyer, are common. The role played by professional property advisers, and the integrity of all parties who may wish to do repeat business with each other, create a sensitive balance and risk control in the transaction process. This transaction risk must also be built into a bid–offer spread.

Bond and Lizieri (2004) review the definitions of liquidity provided within both finance and real estate markets and conclude that liquidity relates to sales rates or turnover, but also has cost and risk dimensions (so that a long sales period directly increases the risk of property).

Crosby and McAllister (2004) suggest that the ability to enter and exit property markets at specific times is constrained by the time transactions take, any difficulties in identifying and bringing specific properties to the market, and uncertain prices, including changes to prices over the transaction period. A preliminary analysis of 187 transactions suggested a median transaction time of 190 days, or just over six months. The vast majority of time to sale is in the marketing and due diligence periods, with the marketing period (median 88 days) slightly longer than the due diligence period (median 62 days).

Finally, the lack of a formal market clearing mechanism for property, such as is offered by the stock market for securities, means that on occasion there may be few or no transactions, reducing the flow of comparable sales information and further increasing the perceived risk of a transaction, creating a feedback loop and self-sustaining illiquidity. This appeared to be the case, for example, in the UK in 1991–3 and 2007–9. Devaney and Scofield (2014) found an increase in the time to transact for properties that sold during the post-GFC downturn alongside falling transaction volumes and an increase in aborted deals during this period. After the trough in the UK market around Q2 2009, transactions then became even slower, especially from introduction to price. Such relative changes in the time taken to complete each stage of a transaction provide important insights into buyer and seller behaviour during different market conditions.

1.8 Large lot sizes produce specific risk

- *Property assets are generally large in terms of capital price. This means that property portfolios cannot easily be diversified, and suffer hugely from specific risk.*

Property is 'lumpy'. Lumpiness – the large and uneven sizes of individual assets – means that direct property investment (buying buildings) requires considerably higher levels of capital investment when compared with securities, and, even with significant capital investment, diversification within property portfolios will prove to be more challenging than in equity and bond portfolios. As a result, typical property portfolios contain high levels of specific risk. This fact, coupled with the growing globalization of property portfolios, largely explains the boom in indirect vehicles (see Part 3).

There is also some evidence that large lot sizes have been high beta investments (more responsive to the economy and to rises and falls in the investment market). This adds a further layer of risk.

Specific risk in property, whether measured as a standard deviation or as a tracking error against a benchmark, is a key problem, especially for international investors. Unlike securities, large average property capital values, an uneven distribution of these values and the inability of investors to match competitors' portfolios creates very different real estate portfolios across investors. Property funds offer a way to limit this problem, as all three issues are minimized by investing indirectly by using diversified funds. But specific risk varies significantly between sectors, and unlisted funds (which add other risks) may be more useful in some sectors and countries than others. This is not simply a function of lot size, but also of 'diversification power' within sectors, defined as the efficiency of specific risk reduction through adding properties.

Investors who have targeted property as an asset class will most likely be seeking to replicate the benchmark performance with few surprises; after all, the decision to invest in property is often based on an analysis of historic risk and return characteristics produced from a market index or benchmark. The tracking error of a portfolio is therefore likely to be seen as an additional and unrewarded risk. As a result, managers may be charged with minimizing tracking error – but with limited sums to invest. This is a very difficult challenge: how many properties are needed to reduce tracking error to an acceptable level?

Various studies, all of which concentrate on portfolios of properties of mixed types and geographies, have suggested that the appropriate number of properties is very large. Relevant sources in general finance include the work of Markowitz (1952), Evans and

Archer (1968) and Elton and Gruber (1977). A more limited number of studies investigate risk reduction and portfolio size in the property market. They include Brown (1988), Brown and Matysiak (2000a), Morrell (1993), Schuck and Brown (1997), Baum and Struempell (2006) and Callender *et al.* (2007). It is concluded that many assets are needed to reduce risk to the systematic level when value-weighting returns, depending on the degree of skewness of property values in the portfolio.

It is also well known that the necessary level of capital required to replicate the market will be greatly dependent on the segments of property in which one wishes to invest, as different segments of the property market exhibit vastly different lot sizes. For example, it appears obvious that a very large allocation of cash may be needed to invest in a sufficient number of shopping centres to replicate the performance of that segment with a low tracking error.

In addition, there are significant differences in the performance characteristics of properties within the different segments. Properties in some segments – for example London offices – appear to experience higher variations in return than others, resulting in the probability that more properties will be needed to minimize tracking error within the segment. If London offices are also relatively expensive, the problem of assembling a market-tracking portfolio at reasonable cost is magnified. The vital question is again: how many properties are needed to reduce tracking error to an acceptable level?

Baum and Struempell (2006) and Callender *et al.* (2007) used market data to examine the extent of the problem of specific risk for domestic UK property investors. Comparing results across segments, both research projects simulated returns on portfolios of properties comprising randomly selected properties located within each market segment to examine the number of assets needed within each segment to achieve particular levels of tracking error against Investment Property Databank (IPD) Annual and Monthly benchmarks. Conclusions were drawn about segments where diversification is relatively easy and those where it is relatively hard.

To produce low tracking errors, returns on the simulated single-sector property portfolios would need to be highly correlated with returns on the same sector. This is more likely to be the case if returns on the portfolios have a similar variance to the sector variance of returns. The greater the average single property variance is in comparison to the sector variance, all other things being equal, the greater will be the tracking error. The more correlated the properties within a sector portfolio are, all other things being equal, the greater will be the tracking error. Low tracking errors will result when single property variance is low and properties within a sector are highly correlated with one another.

Also of relevance is the amount of money needed to achieve particular levels of tracking error within each segment against the benchmarks, determined by the average lot size of assets within each segment.

Clearly, shopping centres have larger average lot sizes than standard shop units. All things being equal, more money will be needed to reduce tracking error within the shopping centre segment than within the standard shop unit segment. However, the covariance issue referred to above means that all things are not equal. Meaningful results are only available when the two factors are combined. The result for shopping centres, for example, is not exactly as one would expect, wholly as a result of the covariance effect. Shopping centres appear to behave more like one another than do London offices.

In Baum and Struempell, a sample of annual direct UK property returns was assembled and grouped by each of nine standard segments (defined by property type and geographic location) in collaboration with IPD. The data used is derived from the IPD UK Universe and covers properties held continuously over the period 1990 to 2004, thus providing 15 data points for each property (with two exceptions, where data limitations required a slightly shorter analysis period). Table 1.3 lists the property type/geographic segmentation used and the respective sample size (number of properties) used in this study.

IPD provided the following data for each segment:

a the average variance of individual properties;
b the average covariance of individual properties;
c the average covariance of individual properties with the IPD market segment returns; and
d the average lot value as of June 2005 for each segment.

Table 1.3: UK market segmentation and data

Property type	Geographic location	Sample size
Standard shops	UK	381
Retail warehouses	UK	33
Shopping centres	UK	26
Other retail	UK	60
Offices	London	73
	South-east	45
	Provincial	38
Office parks	UK	26
Industrials	UK	130

Source: Baum and Struempell, 2006

Using this data, simulated portfolios of direct properties were constructed with increasing numbers of properties for each segment. The portfolio sizes range from one to 100 underlying properties. For each portfolio the expected (simulated) tracking error against the respective market segment was computed. As the number of underlying assets in a portfolio is increased, the specific risk element of the portfolio is reduced; as the portfolio size tends to the market, the portfolio's risk approaches the market (systematic or non-specific) risk level.

To achieve a 5 per cent tracking error, the results are as follows. Fewest properties are needed in the shopping centre segment, followed by office parks, retail warehouses, south-east offices, provincial offices and industrials; and most in the London office segment, followed by other retail. The full results are shown in Table 1.4.

The high covariance of returns between individual shopping centres and the segment coupled with the small number of properties present in the segment at any time mean that only three properties will reduce the tracking error to 5 per cent; only 11 are needed to achieve 2 per cent.

On the other hand, the high variance of London office returns coupled with the low correlation characteristics of properties in this segment means that, on average, ten properties are needed to achieve a 5 per cent tracking error, and no less than 81 properties are needed to reduce tracking error within the segment to 2 per cent.

These results ignore the average costs of buying properties in these segments, which are shown in Table 1.5. Clearly, while shopping centres are apparently easy to diversify,

Table 1.4: Number of properties needed to achieve tracking error targets

No. of properties segment	5% tracking error	4% tracking error	3% tracking error	2% tracking error
Standard shops	6	9	16	34
Retail warehouses	4	6	12	47
Shopping centres	3	4	6	11
Other retail	8	12	20	34
London offices	10	16	30	81
South-east offices	5	7	12	24
Provincial offices	5	8	12	23
Office parks	4	6	11	21
Industrials	5	8	14	33

Source: Baum and Struempell, 2006

they are not cheap. A £40 million average lot size compares with average values of between £4.6 million and £7.2 million in the standard shop, other retail, industrial and south-east and provincial office segments.

Table 1.5: Average lot sizes by segment

Property type	Geographic location	Average lot value (£m)
Standard shops	UK	4.6
Retail warehouse	UK	21.5
Shopping centres	UK	39.5
Other retail	UK	5.0
Offices	London	15.2
	South-east	7.2
	Provincial	7.2
Office parks	UK	10.0
Industrials	UK	6.4

Source: Baum and Struempell, 2006

Table 1.6 combines the impact of average lot sizes and the efficiency of diversification within segments. The figures show the differing levels of capital investment in the UK direct property market by segment required to achieve reducing levels of tracking errors within each segment.

Figure 1.1 illustrates how tracking error falls in one segment – London offices – as investment increases. The required capital investment depends on both the efficiency of diversification within the segment and upon the average lot size within each segment. Investors with higher levels of risk aversion require more capital investment in property segments in order to reduce the specific risk component of the portfolio to the desired level.

Both Baum and Struempell and Callender *et al.* found that to achieve a given tracking error, the least investment is needed in the standard shop, provincial office, other retail and

Table 1.6: Capital investment required for target tracking errors

Capital required (£m) segment	5% tracking error	4% tracking error	3% tracking error	2% tracking error
Standard shops	28	42	74	157
Retail warehouses	86	129	259	1,013
Shopping centres	118	158	237	434
Other retail	40	60	100	169
London offices	152	243	455	1,229
South-east offices	36	50	86	172
Provincial offices	36	58	87	166
Office parks	40	60	110	210
Industrials	32	51	90	212

Source: Baum and Struempell, 2006

Figure 1.1: Tracking error and portfolio value in London offices

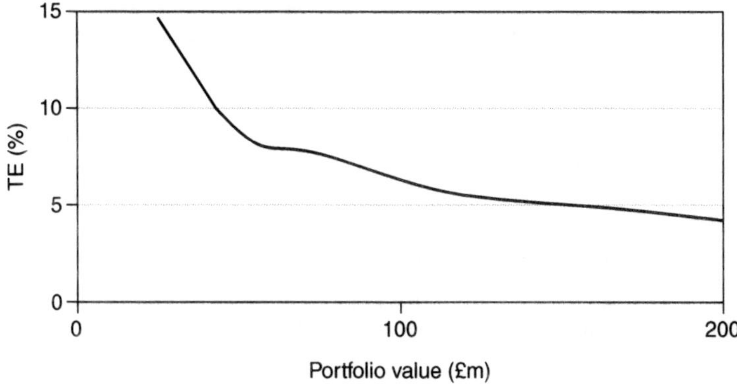

Source: Baum and Struempell, 2006

south-east office segments; most investment is needed in the London office, retail warehouse and shopping centre segments.

1.9 Leverage is commonly used in real estate investment

- *Leverage is used in the vast majority of property transactions. This distorts the return and risk of a property investment.*

Leverage is a term used to measure the level of a company's debt as a proportion of its equity capital, or of its total capital, expressed as a percentage. The term 'gearing' is also used, usually to measure debt as a percentage of equity. So a company with gearing (debt to equity) of 60 per cent (say $60 million) has levels of debt that are 60 per cent of its equity capital ($100 million). Alternatively, leverage might be expressed as the level of a company's debt compared with its gross assets (debt plus equity, $160 million). In that case, the above example would produce a leverage (debt to gross assets, or loan to value) ratio of 37.5 per cent ($60 million/$160 million). In this book we will use the term leverage and gearing interchangeably to mean debt as a percentage of gross assets, and we focus on capital structure (the use of debt and equity) in Chapter 2.

This concept is very important in the world of real estate investment. In the right market conditions, banks have been willing to lend more against the security of property than against other assets such as equities. This is a result of property's income security and the land, bricks and mortar or salvage value of a non-performing property loan. As a result, banks have been keen to lend against the collateral security offered by real estate assets, especially when the rental income more than covers the interest payments on the loan.

The use of gearing will change the financial mathematics of the real estate investment. It reduces the amount of equity that needs to be invested; it reduces the net cash flow available to the investor by the amount of interest paid and it reduces the net capital received by the investor on sale of the asset by the amount of the loan still outstanding. This issue (which is more fully discussed in Chapter 2) has some complex tax and currency effects in the international context (see Part 4) and allows more diversification of specific risk at the asset level as the investor can buy more properties for the same total outlay of equity. It also has two more direct implications, on return and risk.

If the prospective return or IRR on the investment without using leverage is higher than the interest rate charged then leverage will be enhance the expected return; and the greater the leverage, the greater will be the return on equity invested. In addition, the risk of the investment will be greater. The chance that the investor will lose his equity is greater the higher is the level of gearing, and the sensitivity or volatility of the prospective return will be greater.

This is illustrated by Table 1.7, which summarizes an example whose details are not reproduced here showing how changing capitalization rates on the sale of a property produced a wider range of returns on equity (using 70 per cent debt) than on the unleveraged investment.

Table 1.7: The impact of exit yields on the risk to equity: 0 and 70% leverage

Exit yield (%)	IRR (%)	IRR on equity (%)
7.50	12.00	18.77
8.50	10.00	15.10
10.50	6.00	3.90

Source: Baum and Crosby, 2008

The history of ungeared direct property returns, such as is produced by IPD in Europe and NCREIF in the US, disguises the returns that have been available to investors' equity over most sub-periods of the past 25 years. Just as homeowners can, in times of rising house prices and low interest rates, significantly enhance the return on the cash they invest by borrowing, property companies and private property investors use debt finance to increase returns on equity.

By using rents to pay interest and (if possible) some capital repayment (amortization), investors can enjoy a return on their equity investment in excess of the reported total return available to whole-equity investors, such as pension funds. These geared returns are rarely reported in indexes such as IPD and NCREIF (the US National Council of Real Estate Investment Fiduciaries), but explain most private capital investments in global commercial property. Leverage is also discussed in Chapters 2, 7 and 9.

1.10 Is property an inflation hedge?

- *Property is a hybrid asset, with similarities to stocks and bonds, but different. While real estate is not technically a good inflation hedge, property rents appear to be closely correlated with inflation in the long run, producing an income stream that looks like an indexed bond. But rents can be fixed in the short term, producing cash flows that look like those delivered by a conventional bond, and the residual value of a property investment after the lease has ended exposes the owner fully to the equity-type risk of the real economy.*

Property is usually described as a medium risk asset. Its returns should therefore be expected to lie between those produced by equities and those produced by bonds, and its risk profile should be similarly middling. The risk of property seems to have been lower than the risk of the equity market, and some data suggests a risk even lower than that of the bond market (but see Section 1.6.1).

The uncertainty of the nominal dividend income produced by equities over a given holding period compares with the absolute certainty of nominal income produced by a fixed interest security held to redemption (see Table 1.8). Commercial property falls somewhere

Table 1.8: Illustrative returns available on equities, bonds and property

Year	Equities	Property	Bonds
0	–100.00	–100.00	–100.00
1	3.00	6.00	6.00
2	3.23	6.00	6.00
3	3.47	6.00	6.00
4	3.73	6.00	6.00
5	4.01	6.00	6.00
6	4.31	7.30	6.00
7	4.63	7.30	6.00
8	4.98	7.30	6.00
9	5.35	7.30	6.00
10	197.48	128.19	106.00
IRR (%)	10.00	8.00	6.00

Notes

1 The equity is bought with an initial dividend yield of 3%; the initial yield on the property is 6%; the bond has a running yield of 6%.

2 Dividend growth for the equity is a constant (and demanding) 7.5%; the property's rental growth begins at 4% but slows to 2% after the first review as the building tires and depreciates.

3 The property capitalization rate or yield increases by 1% over the 10-year holding period, while the equity yield remains constant.

between the two in terms of certainty of income. In a standard UK lease with upward-only rent reviews, the initial rental income set at the start of a lease remains certain, with only the uplifts expected at each rent review being uncertain. Given long leases, the principal return to the investor is an income return; and the value of the reversion at the expiry of the lease (while largely uncertain) is of reduced importance. In a shorter US lease, the income return is less guaranteed. In a German or French lease of nine or ten years with some indexation to an inflation measure, income return is again more important. Depending on the typical lease, therefore, commercial property should be a low to medium risk asset, compared with bonds at the least risky end of the spectrum and equities at the most risky.

To explore this, we can set up a theoretical return model. Table 1.8 shows the returns that would be generated by the three asset classes under a set of plausible assumptions. (Property is assumed to be subject to five-year leases at a fixed rent.) A 6 per cent ten-year bond bought at par will produce 6 per cent if held to redemption; an equity producing an initial return of 3 per cent with dividends rising at around 7 per cent will produce 10 per cent, fairly reflecting the higher risk in equities and the lower risk in bonds. Under these conditions, which are arguably rosy for equities and neutral for bonds, it can be shown that property can be expected to generate a return midway between those of bonds and equities.

For many investors, particularly pension funds which have liabilities linked to future wage levels, the need to achieve gains in money value (in nominal terms) is of less concern than the need to achieve gains in the purchasing power of assets held (in real terms). Again, property might be viewed as a medium real risk asset. Data suggests a correlation between rents and inflation in the long run, and the cash flow might (although subject to deterioration and obsolescence) be expected to increase in line with inflation over a long period. However rents may be fixed in the short term, which means that in the short run the income produced is of a fixed interest nature and hence prone to damage by inflation. This is not true of equities, but is even more true of conventional (not indexed) bonds.

Blake *et al.* (2011) find that while UK property has delivered positive long-run real returns, it is not, in most cases, a hedge against inflation, where a 'hedge' is defined strictly as an asset moving *at the same time* as inflation, or reacting to it, rather than merely keeping pace with it over time. This may depend upon the underlying economic conditions and type of inflation. Equities tend to be a far better hedge against inflation in the formal sense.

1.11 Volatility and risk appear to be low

- *The risk of property appears low. Rent is paid before dividends, and as a real asset property will be a store of value even when it is vacant and produces no income. Its volatility of annual return also appears to be lower than that of bonds. This is distorted somewhat by appraisals, but the reported performance history of real estate suggests a medium return for a low risk, and an apparently mispriced asset class.*

Return is one side of the coin; risk is the other. Property is typically regarded as a low-risk asset: rent is a superior claim on a company's assets, and paid before dividends. Property's downside risk is limited, because as a real asset property will be a store of value even when it is vacant and produces no income. In addition, leases determine the delivery of income and produce short-term bond characteristics with longer-term equity performance.

Investment professionals, including the actuary working with a pension fund or life assurance company, use measures of risk based either on the concept of volatility or on the probability of a potential loss.

Volatility is the fluctuation of returns around an average return. For example, one property (A) might show a 10 per cent return each year for five years (see Table 1.9). Over the five-year period, it would have shown 0 per cent volatility as the actual return in each year was the same as the average return. If another property (B) had shown a positive return of 20 per cent for the first two years, followed by a negative return of 40 per cent in the third year and two further years of a positive return of 25 per cent, it would have produced the same average return of 10 per cent per annum. However, the volatility in returns would have been much greater. This is usually measured in units of standard deviation. This is (approximately) a measure of the average distance of each observation or data item from the mean of that data.

Table 1.9: Return and volatility

Year	Property A	Property B
1	10	20
2	10	20
3	10	–40
4	10	25
5	10	25
Average	10	10
Standard deviation	0.00	28.06

The total returns delivered by UK commercial property over the period 1971–2013 (see Table 1.10) have been less volatile even than the returns from gilts (UK government bonds). This data is now unsupported by US data shown in Table 1.11, using US equities (S&P 500), treasuries (Merrill Lynch AAA) and real estate (NCREIF NPI), which appears to suggest that property has a slightly higher risk than treasuries, as might be expected.

Table 1.10: UK property risk and return, 1971–2013

	Return (%)	Risk (%)
Equities	12.6	28.9
Gilts	9.7	13.4
Property	10.7	11.2

Source: IPD, time-weighted returns

The Sharpe ratio is a combined measure of risk and return. It can be defined as follows:

Sharpe ratio = (return on asset – risk free rate)/standard deviation of asset return (risk)

Table 1.11: US property risk and return, 1978–2013

	Return (%)	Risk (%)
Equities	11.8	16.7
Treasuries	7.9	7.0
Property	9.2	7.9

Source: NCREIF, Merrill Lynch, S&P, time-weighted returns

Assuming a long-term average risk free rate of (say) 4 per cent, real estate has the best Sharpe ratios in both the UK (0.9) and the US (1.2) compared to the other asset classes.

However, despite the data, any conclusion to the effect that property returns have been less volatile than the returns from gilts or treasuries is flawed. Low volatility of delivered nominal returns disguises the illiquidity (or lack of easy or regular sale) of property, which introduces a risk not reflected in the volatility of notional returns based solely on valuations from period to period. In addition, valuation-based returns are themselves believed to be biased towards lower volatility than typical underlying market conditions support. There are several reasons for this, discussed in Section 1.6 above, but the effect is serial or auto-correlation between consecutive values.

Brown and Matysiak (2000a), show that where autocorrelation is present, the current valuation (Vt) is a weighted function of the present market value (Vt^*) and the immediate past valuation ($Vt-1$), so that:

$$Vt = aVt^* + (1-a)Vt - 1$$

Using this formula, a series of valuations can be 'unsmoothed' to present a representation of the imagined (unobservable) market values. Given Vt and $Vt-1$, we need to assign weights (a and $(1-a)$) to each. If $a=0.5$, then the current valuation (say £10 million) is 50 per cent of last year's valuation (say £8 million) and 50 per cent of the present market value, which solves to £12 million. The unsmoothed series will consequently demonstrate greater volatility.

1.12 Real estate cycles control returns

- *Unlike stocks and bonds, real estate returns appear to be controlled by cycles of eight to nine years.*

It has been suggested (by, for example, Barras, 2009) that repeatable patterns, or cycles, can be seen in the history of development, occupier and investment markets. These are expressed in the form of real estate developments, rents and yields, with these in turn driving capital values and returns.

Figure 1.2 illustrates what many would describe as a cycle in UK property returns over the period 1971–2013.

The graph shows three sharp UK commercial property downturns, in 1974, 1990 and 2007. This sets up an interesting hypothesis – is there a 16- to 17-year cycle? This type of

Figure 1.2: UK property returns, 1971–2013 (%)

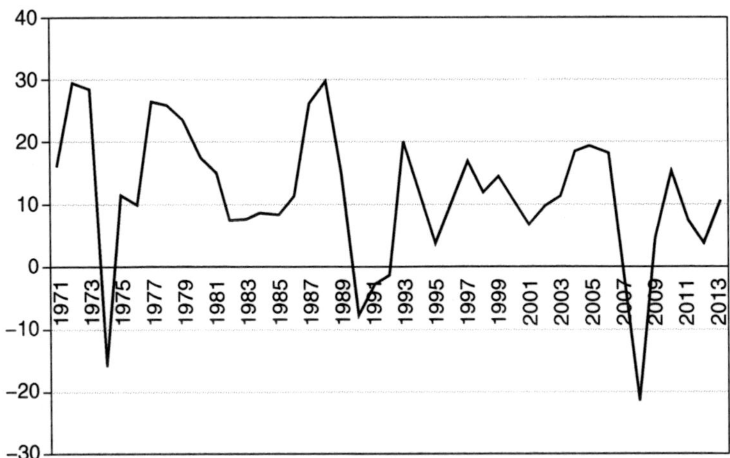

Source: IPD

'technical' analysis is intriguing, but is ultimately less valuable than a 'fundamental' view of the property cycle, which begins with property development.

1.12.1 Developments

The inelasticity of property supply in response to price changes is perhaps the most important variable that explains the existence of a cycle of supply, rents, capital values and returns. Empirically, a cycle in property development is apparent, and most obvious in the London office market. Barras identified short cycles (four to five years, the classic business cycle operating on occupier demand), long cycles (nine to ten years, a tendency for severe oversupply in one cycle to feed part of the next demand cycle), long swings (20 years, associated with major phases of urban development) and long waves (50 years, technology based). More recent data suggests long cycles of seven to eight years from peak to peak of development activity.

Development activity appears to be highly pro-cyclical with GDP growth and property values (rising and falling at the same time), but exhibits sharper rises and falls. As property values rise in a strong economy, developers gain confidence and construction activity increases. Hence, current development profits drive development activity.

There is a strong relationship between office development and changes in rents, suggesting a degree of adaptive behaviour among lenders, investors and developers with a tendency to follow the market, often in an exaggerated fashion. A period of excessive optimism is followed by a period of excessive pessimism. Adaptive behaviour can explain much of the late-1980s boom and bust development cycle. As prices rise, prices are more likely to be expected to continue to rise; development profits are a function of continued price rises; hence price rises lead to ever-increasing supply levels, which create the conditions for lower prices (disaster myopia). The time lag between the inception and completion of developments creates an inevitable supply cycle.

1.12.2 Rents

Rents have also been strongly pro-cyclical with GDP. Barras shows how periods of growth in GDP above the long-term trend rate of growth have been coincident with periods of growth in rents above long-term trend growth. The demand side is pro-cyclical with economic growth indicators, but the inelasticity of supply means that even highly regular demand cycles can generate irregular rental cycles. Hence rents will rise in response to economic growth and a static supply in the short term, and will continue to rise as construction activity gathers momentum; but the peak in construction activity may arrive after the peak in GDP growth, and an oversupply will result.

1.12.3 Yields and capital values

Some evidence of cyclicality in property yields of cap rates around a flat (mean-reverting) trend may be discernible over a long period. A negative correlation between cap rates and rental growth results in an extremely strong relationship between rental growth and capital value growth, both strongly pro-cyclical, although some extreme market movements have been strongly yield-driven (examples include the UK in 1973–4, 1993–4 and 2004–6).

1.12.4 Returns

There is some relationship between returns and the business cycle, but this is less strong than the relationship between changes in rents, capital values and economic growth simply because income returns have been reasonably stable from period to period, thereby reducing the sensitivity of total returns to economic growth variables.

Work by IPD, drawing on historic data from Scott (1996), and updated by Property Funds Research, provides the fullest picture of long-term UK performance yet available. Data assembled from various sources covering the period 1921–2013 shows several 'fairly distinct' peaks and troughs in the market. IPD identify six completed cycles, with peaks in 1925–8, 1935, 1950, 1954, 1960–4, 1973, 1979–81 and 1989, now augmented by 2007. They suggest that those cycles have ranged in length from four to 12 years, with an average of eight years; upswings have run from two to seven years, and downswings from two to nine years. The average cycle length of eight years is interesting, as after roughly two more eight-year periods beyond 1989 the next peak of 2006–7 emerged.

The latter part of Scott's long-term data (Scott, 1998), supplemented by the more recent IPD data, is shown in Figure 1.3.

Scott's eight-year estimate for the average cycle is interesting in the context of the 16-year period from trough to trough in the UK between 1974 and 2013. The 16-year cycles may contain two eight-year cycles, where the interim cycle is less severe because the memory of the last severe crash is still fresh – but, by the second time around, adaptive behaviour has encouraged complacency among market participants and a large correction is necessary. Within Figure 1.3 one might suggest an interim downturn in 1981, the lowest return year between the troughs. Projecting forward, then, we might look for a minor correction around 1998 (not apparent) and a severe crash around 2006 (very clear!).

We can conclude that the property cycle is linked to the economic cycle, but the precise nature of the relationship varies from one cycle to another. These property cycles appear to be clearer in form than equity and bond cycles and more exaggerated in effect than economic cycles. Why might this be the case?

Figure 1.3: UK property returns, 1947–2013

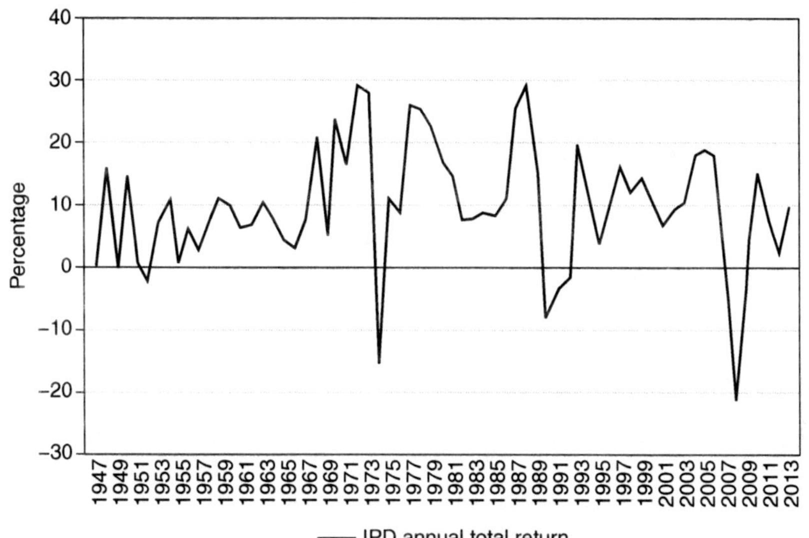

Source: IPD, Scott (1998), Property Funds Research

1.12.5 Cycles: the result of market inefficiency?

Bjorklund and Soderburg (1997) suggest that auto-correlation (previous upward movements in prices leading to increases in prices in the next period) affects real estate returns to the point that a speculative bubble can be proven to have formed. Antwi and Henneberry (1995) identified what they called habit-persistent (another term might be adaptive) behaviour by lenders and by developers. Wheaton (1999) suggests that forward-looking (rational) expectations by agents lead to stability, while myopic (adaptive) behaviour promotes oscillations – or cycles.

Grenadier (1995) examined the way owners of space will restrict supply in an upswing. Letting space at a market rent on a five-year lease involves the giving up of a five-year American option (the right to call a higher rent at any time). In an auto-correlated occupier/rental market, it is easy to see how letting at the market rent may appear to be a sub-optimal financial decision, especially when the supply side is so slow to respond to demand and price. Withholding space or delaying development in this way exaggerates the supply shortage and the cyclical upswing. It may also lead to empty space in a downswing: the well-known 1974 case of Centre Point in London, which was withheld from the market at a time of rising rents in 1973 but remained vacant for much of the remainder of the decade, is a good example.

These concepts indicate inefficiency in real estate markets. They affect the way space is developed, the way rents are agreed for space and the way prices are paid for real estate investments. They exaggerate and elongate upturns and downturns, and create the appearance of definable cycles in real estate markets. 'Sticky prices' (see Section 1.6) affect occupier, investor and developer markets, elongating and exaggerating real estate cycles.

Rates of change in rental values and vacancy rates are small, due to the actions of intermediaries or agents and the costs of moving. Occupiers have to take account of the cost of moving in bidding for new space. Intermediaries, in the form of real estate brokers, tend to smooth rental value fluctuations by relying on historic comparable evidence in assessing new market rent levels. Development cycles are slow to reverse due to the commitment created by the large amounts of sunk (human and physical) capital required to complete a project.

Rates of return are also auto-correlated, due to valuation smoothing. This goes some way to support conventional views of the low volatility of real estate returns and the poor correlation of property with the main asset markets. Cycles appear to be the inevitable result of human psychology, and real estate provides an extreme illustration of this, as the events of 2004–9 clearly demonstrated.

1.13 Diversification – the evidence

Mathematical models based on modern portfolio theory (MPT) play an important role in the investment market, especially in the advice on investment strategy and asset allocation given by actuaries and consultants to pension funds and insurance companies.

MPT reflects the desire of investors to achieve higher returns, low individual asset risk and (more importantly) a smooth return on the entire portfolio. Asset allocation advice has, since the acceptance of MPT, traditionally required a view on three values: the likely future return on an asset class; its risk (usually defined as volatility and measured in units of standard deviation of return over a given period); and its correlation with other asset classes. This last factor measures the extent to which upward and downward movements in the values of two variables are linked together.

MPT has both led to, and has been further encouraged by, the development of asset allocation models. Strong prospective returns, coupled with low standard deviation of returns and a low correlation with equities and gilts, would provide a very strong argument for holding property assets.

When assets are combined in a portfolio, the expected return of a portfolio is the weighted average of the expected returns of the component assets. However, unless the assets are perfectly correlated, the risk is not the weighted average: it is determined by the correlations of the component assets. The way in which assets co-vary is central to portfolio risk, as low covariance produces diversification opportunities.

IPD's UK annual index and NCREIF's NPI provide the longest available runs of consistent annual data describing the performance of a well-diversified portfolio of real properties. The results show the following:

- UK and US property returns have been lower than the return on equities but better than the return on gilts and treasuries (see Tables 1.10 and 1.11).
- UK property volatility has been less than the volatility of both equities and gilts (see Table 1.10) while US property volatility has been less than the volatility of equities but slightly higher than the volatility of treasuries.
- UK property has been much less well correlated with equities and gilts than equities and gilts have been correlated with each other. In other words, while equities and gilts have usually performed well or badly at the same time, property has out-performed or

under-performed at different times, thus smoothing out the overall performance of a portfolio with assets of all three classes. In the US, all assets appear poorly correlated.

This is illustrated by Tables 1.12 and 1.13. Both UK and US data suggest that property offers portfolio risk reduction to holders of bonds and equities. The UK data suggests that gilts and equities are more highly correlated, so that property is a more efficient diversifier, but this is not true in the US.

Table 1.12: UK asset class correlations, 1971–2013

	Gilts	Property
Equities	0.56	0.28
Property	0.04	1.00

Source: IPD

Table 1.13: US asset class correlations, 1978–2013

	Treasuries	Property
Equities	–0.04	0.14
Property	–0.01	1.00

Source: NCREIF, Merrill Lynch, S&P

The result of using UK return, risk and correlation data in an MPT framework is a high property allocation, as shown by Table 1.14. Using data to 2009, we constructed the optimal (lowest risk) portfolios for portfolio target returns of 11.5, 13 and 14.5 per cent respectively.

The low return/risk portfolio not surprisingly has plenty of gilts (40 per cent), but the optimizer selects 60 per cent property, as this reduces the portfolio risk even below the risk of a portfolio of 100 per cent gilts.

Table 1.14: Illustrative asset class allocations (%)

Target return	Volatility	UK property	UK stocks	UK gilts
11.5	9.2	59.7	0	40.3
13.0	14.0	61.5	31.5	7.0
14.5	22.4	34.5	65.5	0

Source: IPD, PFR

The high return/risk portfolio – not surprisingly, again – has plenty of stocks, but the optimizer selects 35 per cent property, as this again reduces the portfolio risk without excessively damaging returns.

Property comprises between 35 and 60 per cent at all target return levels.

Yet the actual allocation for UK institutional investors in 2009 was around 8 per cent, up from around 6 per cent in 2005 (see Table 1.15), but around one-sixth of the optimized level. What explains the huge difference between unconstrained theory and practice?

Table 1.15: Observed asset class allocations – institutional investors

Country	Real estate as % assets	% direct	% indirect*
Australia	11.0	45.0	55.0
Germany	12.0	58.0	42.0
Netherlands	10.0	56.0	42.0
UK	6.0	Not known	Not known
US	3.5	46.0	54.0

Source: PREA, 2005

Notes
* See Chapters 6 and 7.

Smoothing (see Sections 1.6 and 1.11) is a large problem colouring this data. In some years, property yields do not appear to change; and it is clear that this can be the result of a scarcity of transaction evidence and the behaviour of valuers rather than a steadily performing market.

The smoothing problem also affects the correlation numbers. Reported property correlations, such as volatility, may be artificially low. The greater the fixity of the property return series – the greater the amount of smoothing, or serial correlation – the greater will be the tendency of the correlation of that series with returns in efficient markets to be close to zero. (The correlation coefficient is determined by the covariance of two series divided by the product of their standard deviations. Low volatility depresses both the numerator and denominator of this equation, but the impact of the covariance is likely to be greater.)

Given that three indicators are needed for assessing the appropriate weight of property in a multi-asset portfolio, two of which present two large problems, it is not surprising that property allocations in practice do not match the MPT solution. Standard deviations of returns from year to year understate true property risk; and correlations between property and the other assets may be unreliable. For this reason, various efforts have been made by academics to improve the position, which usually imply the use of statistical techniques to adjust the data (see Section 1.11).

In addition, year-on-year correlations between the asset classes may be said to be of limited interest to pension funds and insurance funds with longer-term liabilities. They are more likely to be concerned with their ability to match liabilities (wage inflation-linked pensions or nominally fixed endowment mortgages) without increasing the contribution rate of the employer or employee, or to declare a bonus.

A more interesting measure for long-term investors might therefore be the coincidence of good or bad returns on different asset classes over longer periods. It is then possible to judge whether the poor correlation between property and equities is merely the result of valuation lags or smoothing, or alternatively whether there is something more fundamentally different about the way the assets perform. Encouragingly for property, an analysis of long-term returns suggests that the best and worst periods of performance for property have not coincided with those periods for bonds and equities, and that property offers long-term advantages for investors with long-term liabilities. While the property data used in a 75-year analysis is very thin indeed, it shows that property has performed well at wholly different times from equities and gilts, and that equities and gilts have been disturbingly closely correlated. For example, in terms of real returns the best rolling 25-year period in the last 75 years has been the same (1921–46) for equities and gilts but different (1944–69) for property. The worst rolling 25-year period in the last 75 years has been the same (1950–75) for equities and gilts but different (1969–94) for property. Should not pension funds and insurance companies value property more highly for this finding?

However, there are more limitations to this type of optimization analysis that need to be considered, especially in a global context. These are as follows.

Specific risk

The data used describes the returns available on the index universes of asset classes. For stocks and bonds, it is possible for investors to replicate these universes in an investment portfolio, as they are highly divisible assets and index-tracking products are available. For property, the universe used to compile the UK annual index at the end of 2013 comprised over 21,000 properties worth around £153 billion (including 9,000 residential assets worth £6 billion); over 7,100 properties and $382 billion comprise the US NCREIF universe, suggesting a much bigger average lot size.

Unlike stock and bond indexes, these real estate universes are not investable, because the assets which comprise the index are not all available for sale, and (even if they were) too much capital would be required for the vast majority of global investors to hold the index. The investor therefore faces an additional layer of risk, which is the sampling error created by the heterogeneity and specific risk of real estate (see Section 1.8).

Leverage

The majority of property transactions involve the use of leverage (see Section 1.9). Even where the institutional investor does not use leverage on direct property acquisitions, REITs or unlisted funds will commonly be used for specialist or international investments (see Chapters 6, 7 and 10), and these will typically be geared. Hence, ungeared returns may not be fully representative of the risk and return profile of the investment vehicles used by investors.

Illiquidity

Real estate, unlike securities, is not a liquid asset class (see Section 1.7). This is not reflected in the volatility and correlation data. Chapter 6 shows how the introduction of liquidity into a property structure can significantly change the return characteristics of real estate to the point that it ceases to be attractive. Arguably, therefore, illiquidity is a necessary evil in justifying the role of real estate, but it is an evil that clearly reduces the attraction of the asset class.

Taxes, currency and fees

Property investment may require the services of specialist fund managers (see Chapter 2), who will typically charge *ad valorem* management fees and performance fees. Taxes may be paid, even by tax exempt investors, when investing internationally, and in such cases unhedged currency risk (see Chapter 9) will colour returns.

These variables all challenge the value of UK IPD or US NCREIF index data in deciding on an allocation to global commercial property. These describe a single country, gross of tax and fees, domestic currency, unleveraged, universe of returns. Until recently, however, little else was available, and, adding the operational challenges of investing in real estate alongside faster-moving securities, it is not surprising that allocations do not reflect the outputs of an MPT optimizer. Now the IPD Global Index (and various fund indexes) promises a better solution, but this is still in its infancy.

Asymmetry

The GFC added extra spice to the debate about real estate in the mixed asset portfolio because real estate plainly failed to act as a diversifying asset when everything was going wrong – indeed, it is plausible to suggest that a real estate crisis triggered a collapse in all markets. If real estate fails to provide diversification gains when they are most needed then the defensive qualities of the asset class are called into question.

In 2013, Lizieri *et al.* produced a report for the Investment Property Forum which set out to examine the extent to which UK real estate returns have been correlated with other asset classes in poor economic environments. They noted that the standard approach to portfolio diversification relies on measures of mean return and the variance or standard deviation around that return, with the relationship between assets captured by the covariance or correlation. This assumes a particular distribution of returns – that individual returns are broadly normal and that the joint return distributions are normal. But evidence might challenge this assumption, meaning that the portfolios derived from mean-variance analysis are sub-optimal.

They found that real estate returns appear to be skewed and to have 'fat tails', so that there is a higher probability of extreme downside returns than would be expected for a normal distribution. They also found that when equity markets are performing poorly (or where real interest rates rise sharply), property exhibits strongly negative returns. There is also evidence that valuation smoothing effects are more pronounced in extreme markets so that appraisal-based performance indices may understate property market risk.

They find that the inclusion of real estate in a mixed asset portfolio is likely to improve the risk-adjusted performance of that portfolio, but real estate returns are not normal and there is a higher than expected risk of strong negative shocks in real estate, shocks that are likely to coincide with difficult capital market conditions.

Alternative approaches to asset allocation do exist. The most popular alternative is the so-called 'equilibrium approach' (Litterman, 2003), which advocates a neutral position determined by the size by value of the asset class (see Chapter 2) with positions taken against that neutral weight determined by the attractiveness of market pricing. This more closely reflects the practice of professional and institutional market participants.

1.14 Challenges

1.14.1 The limitations of direct real estate investment

The past can be used to suggest many things, both factual and false. It would clearly be incorrect to assume that history will repeat itself, following a standard pattern. Nonetheless, data can be used to show that property markets, both occupier and investor markets, clearly respond to economic cycles and economic events. Property advisers certainly need to understand these linkages and the way market inefficiencies serve to exaggerate or disguise the impact of the economy and the capital markets on commercial property performance.

The UK 'cycle' of the 1990s was sufficiently different in its shape (a gradual recovery of values and activity, interrupted by the sharp value rise driven by falls in the gilt yield in 1993–4) to prompt commentators to suggest that cycles are a thing of the past. Better, or wiser, management, better market information, better management and pricing of the debt supply were all suggested as reasons why this may be the case. An alternative view is that cycles are an inherent feature of property performance, and that (while they may appear in different forms, and may not be perfectly predictable) some evidence of property cyclicality will always emerge. The boom and bust of 2004–11 may not have been driven by a development bonanza, but a 'cycle' clearly re-emerged and the conditions of 2014 suggest the likelihood of a coming development boom – and subsequent slowdown. For the benefit of investors, efforts to anticipate economic and property market change are essential in the property investment process.

For the purposes of this book, the importance of real estate lies in the fact that it has been one of three major asset classes that insurance companies and pension funds like to invest in, either directly or through property funds or REITs and property companies, which have become accepted as a major sector of the global stock market. However, the cult of the equity has dominated western investment strategy to the extent that equities dominate many institutional portfolios, especially in the US and the UK. On the other hand, in Germany and some other continental European countries, bonds have always been the largest component of the mixed asset portfolio. In either case, property is treated as the third asset class – and often a very poor third.

UK institutions, for example, held over 20 per cent of their investments in real estate in 1980. The average fell to around 5 per cent by 2014. There are two reasons for the decline. First, the long-term returns on property relative to equities have been low, so that the allocations to equities have increased as a result of the unmatchable growth in the capital values of equity portfolios. Second, the positive performance characteristics of property, traditionally seen as reasonable return, low risk and a good diversifier, have been challenged, and for good reasons.

The experience of property investors in the early 1990s and late 2000s was enough to persuade many of them that it was time to abandon the asset class. Property companies became bankrupt; banks developed severe shortfalls in their loan books through exposure to property loans; householders found they owed more than they had borrowed by developing negative equity; and, worst of all, it became acutely apparent that the liquidity of property was not the same as the liquidity of equities and bonds.

1.14.2 Securitization and globalization

Because of the liquidity and management problems associated with direct real estate ownership, the property investment market has become mesmerized by the potential for securitization or unitization of real estate.

Over the period 1990–8, real estate investment trusts in the US and listed property trusts in Australia each saw explosive growth in markets where the legal and regulatory framework permits privately held real estate assets to be transferred into tax-efficient public vehicles. Following a boom in the creation of unlisted funds in the 1999–2006 period (see Chapter 7), the UK and Germany introduced REITs in 2007 (see Chapter 6) and other markets (India and China, for example) are poised for a similar revolution. Table 1.15 shows that as at 2006 PREA estimated that roughly half of all new real estate investment by institutional investors in the countries selected was through indirect vehicles.

Property derivatives became a realized concept in the UK in 2005 and there are now swaps, structured notes and even futures trading globally (see Chapter 8).

In addition, the search for return and diversification led to globalization, meaning a transfer of attention from domestic investors and investments to international investors and assets (see Part 4). But we must remember what makes real estate attractive to these investors, which is low volatility and the opportunity to diversify a securities portfolio.

Property is illiquid. This means that its required – and expected – return is higher than it would otherwise be. So introducing liquidity in the form of securitization may damage returns. The largest impact of improved liquidity, however, would be upon risk and diversification. Surveys have consistently shown that diversification is a powerful driver for pension funds and insurance companies to become involved with real estate as an investment. Diversification surely works only as long as the asset is truly different. Property is a diversifier away from equities because it has bond and commodity characteristics. Taking away the long lease and the physical, heterogeneous, commodity nature of real estate would take away a large part of its diversification potential. A quoted, liquid property vehicle will inevitably have performance characteristics that are shared with the equity market. In other words, 'be careful what you wish for'.

Direct real estate (dealt with in Part 2) is lumpy and illiquid. But it appears to diversify a portfolio. REITs are liquid and divisible, but they may not be good diversifiers, and unlisted funds and synthetic property (derivatives) bring their own challenges. Part 3 deals with these issues. Building the global real estate portfolio requires a compromise between the diversification offered by direct real estate and the costs of wrapping the asset into a securitized or unitized fund structure, the subject of Part 4.

As you can see, investing successfully in real estate requires quite some preparation.

2 The market – and who makes it

2.1 The global property investment universe

2.1.1 The size of the market and its regional composition

In Chapter 1 we introduced the idea that we might be able to assess the size of the global property market. We noted that US-based Prudential estimated the size of the global institutional-grade real estate market as being over US$26 trillion in 2012.

Using similar methods, Property Funds Research has re-estimated the value of property owned by institutional investors around the world as around $32 trillion at the end of 2014. This reflects a surge in investment in Asia and other emerging markets, as well as a rebound in values following the global financial crisis (GFC). This $32 trillion is the investable stock, meaning stock that is of sufficient quality to become institutional investment product.

This estimate must be taken as the broadest possible guide. There is a lack of transparency in many markets, and the generally low levels of information available in Asia and the emerging markets of the world mean that data limitations are even more stark. For example, we do not know much about the size of the investable property markets in China, India and Brazil, despite their huge populations and increasingly significant GDP.

The $32 trillion investable stock of property can be broken down to the regional level. The global market is split by GAV into 30.5 per cent Europe, 26.5 per cent North America, 30.2 per cent Asia, 2.4 per cent Australasia, 5.8 per cent Latin America, 3.5 per cent Middle East and just 1 per cent Africa (see Table 2.1).

This universe does not provide the basis of any commercial index or benchmark for investors. The best available option, the IPD Global Annual Property Index, weights real estate investment returns across 25 countries. North America and EMEA (Europe, Middle East and Africa) each comprise 42 per cent of the weighted total, with the remaining 16 per cent in Asia Pacific. IPD processes investment performance details using a dataset of over 62,000 at least annually appraised individual assets valued at US$1.4 trillion. This index should be seen as sub-set of the true global universe, limited to properties owned by investors who are keen to share information (typically, institutional investors). Given the lower

Table 2.1: The global property investment universe ($bn)

Europe	Asia	Australasia	Latin America	North America	Middle East	Africa	Total
9,637	9,545	759	1,841	8,381	1,097	379	31,639
30.5%	30.2%	2.4%	5.8%	26.5%	3.5%	1.2%	100%

Source: Property Funds Research, RREEF, EPRA, 2014

levels of transparency in Asia and other markets, North America and EMEA is clearly over-represented in the IPD Global Index.

2.1.2 Revenue models

Risk and return characteristics vary from property to property and from sector to sector. A key issue is the nature of the revenue that is produced.

Traditionally, risk-averse and dominant owners of commercial real estate in some countries have appeared to impose unreasonably one-sided lease terms on tenants, resulting in a non-volatile stream of lease rents, especially applicable to offices, shops and industrials. As we have seen, these rents might be agreed in advance for three to 15 years, or reviewed to market every three to five years, in some countries upwards only; they might be indexed, or stepped, again upwards only. The nature of real estate as an investment asset relies on these lease terms to provide a stable revenue stream and a non-volatile asset class. However, the universe of investable real estate has expanded, for a variety of reasons.

First, global markets throw up different ways of developing land into stabilized property assets. High quality traditional single unit shops, for example, are common in London and Paris but rare in the US, the Middle East and Asia where strip malls, shopping centres and big box retail are typical. The revenue model for a shopping centre is likely to be different from the revenue model for a single unit shop, allowing (for example) rents to be charged based partly on retailers' turnover (which can be influenced by the owner using advertising to attract shoppers to the centre). In addition, the leisure sector (hotels, restaurants, casinos) has been an investable asset class in some markets (for example the US), and is now being introduced into others (for example, the UK).

Second, the impact of the internet on real estate has been recognized primarily by concerns about on-line retailing, but this also has an impact on industrial and distribution units. In addition, working from home and the associated move to hot desking has had some impact on the traditional office.

Third, demographic, lifestyle and political changes (primarily expressed through the privatization of former public services) have produced a need for new formats, including rental housing, affordable housing, senior housing and student accommodation; self-storage; medical centres; data centres; and others. These emerging residential and social infrastructure sectors have become increasingly popular with investors.

The main effects of these changes on real estate investment are (i) a wider choice of asset types to invest in, and (ii) a bigger range of revenue models for investors to consider. Take the example of hotels.

Hotels had not been considered as core real estate investments up until the mid-2000s, and thus attracted relatively low capital flows. Depending on the operational model used, real estate-backed hotels might not earn stable lease rents and did not as a result have the 'fixed-income' aspect of other real estate investments. The freehold owner of a hotel might operate the asset personally, employ a manager or lease the asset to a hotel group. Similarly, a hotel group could procure its real estate in a number of ways: it could buy a freehold, it could sign a lease for the asset or it could enter into a management contract.

Where the freehold owner of a hotel operates the asset personally this is not real estate investment, and the asset is removed from our investable universe. Where the hotel operator signs a lease, this arrangement can produce a traditional, low-risk real estate investment, especially when the operator is a well-known and financially secure company. Where the operator signs a management contract, the property owner's revenue will be the revenue of the operation, determined by the room rate, the occupancy rate and any additional revenue streams, less the manager's fees and costs (which may include a share of revenues or profits). In this case the property owner's revenue will not be a stable lease rent but will be exposed to the risk of the underlying business. (The biggest private equity profit in history was made by Blackstone's real estate and private equity funds in the purchase and flotation of Hilton Hotels, 2007–14, a deal which was a classic combination of real estate dealing and operational expertise – see Phalippou and Baum, 2014.)

The same revenue model might operate in bars and pubs, restaurants, self-storage, cinemas, student accommodation, senior housing and other revenue-generating property types. Owners of offices and industrials will likely be excluded from the possibility of being exposed to the underlying operation but retail property, especially shopping centres, might be let on a lease with a rent component being determined by revenues or turnover (a 'turnover' or 'percentage' rent).

Traditional investors in 'core' real estate (see below) generally avoid anything other than low-risk lease income, but their ability to do so as new property formats enter the universe is being reduced.

Core, core-plus, value-add and opportunity

These terms have become popular descriptors for property investments with different risk profiles and different revenue models. We can also add prime/secondary/tertiary (and even super-prime) as a set of quality measures.

Core, core-plus, value-add and opportunity are terms which carry with them judgements about property risk, including leverage, and expected returns. The following definitions (Cacciapaglia, 2011) are taken from the Active Rain website and blog in the US.

> *Core*: These are fully stabilized properties with credit quality tenants on long term leases. These investments are well located in primary and secondary markets. Usually these properties are purchased by institutional investors that are looking for a safe reliable return. Core investments in commercial real estate are often purchased as a way to diversify an investment portfolio.
>
> *Core Plus*: Investors who generally want a safe return, but are looking for a little bit of upside prefer Core Plus. These properties match the physical description of Core investments, but usually have some opportunity to increase NOI [net operating income]. A common Core Plus investment would be a class A office building in a CBD in a primary market. The property would have good tenants, but might have a lot of upcoming lease roll [lease ends, or break clauses]. Core investors would see this lease roll as a threat to their reliable income, but Core Plus investors might see this as an opportunity to increase rents.

Value Add: This strategy is exactly what it sounds like. Value Add investors are looking for the opportunity to increase the value of their commercial real estate investments. Often these properties will have a high vacancy rate or some physical obsolescence. Value Add investors will buy these properties at a discount, and work to increase the occupancy or fix the physical deficiencies. Once the property has been stabilized, these properties may be sold to Core investors.
Opportunistic: There are a lot of different types of investments that fall into this category, from ground up development, to adaptive re-use, to emerging markets. The unifying principle is that the investor is willing to take entrepreneurial risk to achieve out-sized returns.

It should be added that leverage can be applied to any of these categories, further increasing risk (see Section 2.2).

2.1.3 The market sectors

To take the UK as an example, Mitchell (2013) estimated that, within the total value of all commercial property in the UK, 40 per cent is retail property, 40 per cent is office property, 11 per cent is in industrial use and the remaining 9 per cent is largely made up of health, education and public service buildings. The value of the residential market is much greater, but very little of this is investable, because a majority is owner-occupied. However, more investable residential property is being developed, and Mitchell's split is very unlikely to reflect the pattern of investment going forward. Globally, the traditional interest in commercial real estate (offices, shops and industrials) is being augmented by a new wave of non-traditional asset types.

Retail

Retail property can be split into standard (high street) shop units, shopping centres and big box retail or retail warehouses. There are over 500,000 shops in the UK and about 500 locations which attract a reasonable spread of multiple retailers, but this format is less common outside Europe. High street shop unit values are on the low side, offering the potential for effective diversification, and as single tenant investments they are straightforward to manage.

They depreciate very little, as much of the value resides in the land. Supply is restricted by the importance of the location, so owners are protected from competition in many cases. Nonetheless, smaller high streets have suffered in recent years as shoppers have sought greater shopping choice and convenience in out of town retail warehouses and shopping centres and as the impact of on-line retailing has hit the sector.

While the US market tends to suffer from over-supply, retail warehouses and parks were the best performing sector for UK investors through most of the 1990s. Single units have lost popularity at the expense of retail parks, which combine large areas with unrestricted planning consents and have as a result become more like shopping centres and command much higher rents. Good parking and highway access are of vital importance, and planning and zoning restrictions are very important in protecting investment values.

Shopping centres can be in-town centres, typically providing 20–60 retail units, or out of town and as big as one million sq ft, commanding values of up to £2 billion. Refurbishment, depreciation and service charges for common parts are big issues for shopping centre owners and their tenants. Specialist managers are necessary to manage the shopping mix and to extract full value from the centre; each centre is a major business in its own right.

Because lot sizes can be as high as £1–2 billion, diversification can be a challenge (see Chapter 1), although unlisted funds have taken a share of this market and offer some divisibility.

Offices

Traditional offices and business parks have not performed well in most markets over the long run, probably as the result of unanticipated depreciation (see Chapter 1). Depreciation and obsolescence have badly affected performance as occupiers' needs have changed and flexibility of layout and services has become the key issue. Many of the earlier buildings were incapable of providing air-conditioning and raised floors for computer cabling. Now green and sustainability issues are challenging energy-inefficient office property, as well as the opportunity for those employed in services to work from home, resulting in hot-desking and reduced space needs.

Some business parks began to command higher rents than town centre offices; a movement towards the much higher levels of out-of-town or suburban offices common in the US had begun by the turn of the millennium, but sustainability issues are now a challenge for the sector.

Industrials, distribution and storage

Generally, the perceived value of the industrial sector has increased with greater recognition of the lower risk to total returns associated with higher income returns. Many older industrial buildings have shown surprising resilience to obsolescence and are still lettable several decades after construction, but more interest is now attracted by large distribution warehouses with floorplates of 10–30,000 sq m and eaves heights of 12–25 m.

Distribution warehouses have attracted investors because they offer new highly specified buildings and tenants with good covenant strength, albeit often on shorter leases. The impact of on-line retailing on distribution has yet to be fully understood, but this trend is generally believed to require more distribution facilities. However, rents will be held down by a ready supply of land and the willingness of developers to work on narrow profit margins due partly to the abundance of pre-lets.

In addition, the self-storage sector has become an emerging global property sector, driven by urbanization, employee mobility and space shortages. Petrol filling stations and the associated retail facilities are also of interest, as are car parks and marinas.

Leisure schemes and hotels

US format leisure parks, normally anchored by a multi-screen cinema, a themed restaurant, a fast food restaurant and a mixture of bowling, discotheque and other facilities became a popular investment globally in the 1990s. Hotels, traditionally not a part of the UK commercial property sector, have become more investable, through increased investor risk appetite, multi-sector city regeneration projects and the development of unlisted funds. Pubs and standalone restaurants can also be investable. Investors may be able to access pure lease income supported by a high quality tenant covenant, but may be exposed to operational revenues (a share of profit or turnover).

Residential

Population growth and demographic change in combination with a wave of privatization of public sector assets have worked together to create a strong demand for private sector investment in income-generating residential property.

The US multi-family sector (purpose-built apartments for rental) has been a major part of the market for some time, and a strong performer. This is being exported into what is known as the private rented or rental sector in the UK and Australia. The main investment characteristics of this sector are the short nature of leases (usually one year) and the large operating expense burden which falls on the owner, meaning that the difference between the gross and net income yield often causes concern to investors. However, the impact of the depreciation of multi-family compared to (say) offices is not yet well understood, and may be a positive factor as regular maintenance is applied to these properties. In addition, voids (vacancies) have been limited.

Student accommodation has become a highly popular sector, similar to the private rental sector as it provides purpose built accommodation for multiple occupation managed by a specialist operator, with a similar revenue model (albeit considered more secure due to the implicit guarantee of rents offered by parents).

Senior housing (or care homes) is another example of a newly investable and under-supplied asset type. The revenue model is less clear, as pure rentals may be found in some assets while operational revenues are delivered in more specialist properties with medical or hospital facilities.

Social infrastructure

Privatization has become a popular method of reducing government expenditure. Student housing is an example of the private sector stepping in to provide what might otherwise be regarded as a public sector asset. Medical centres provide another example, and the list can include hospitals, graveyards, libraries, sports facilities, schools and nurseries, airports, harbours and other specialist property. As above, the key question to be asked by a potential investor is to do with the revenue model employed or proposed and whether a government or quasi-government body is responsible for the rent. If it is, the value of such a guarantee is considerable.

The private sector has also embraced out-sourcing, so that specialist operational property assets may be sold by (and leased back to) corporates. Telecoms companies, for example, might be best advised to release capital from property assets to re-invest in more profitable technology operations, providing an opportunity for a real estate investor to earn a high quality income stream from the asset. This might apply to specialist properties and infrastructure (including cabling, telephone masts and so on), but also to more traditional office and industrial property. (Note that pure infrastructure has been – and may continue to be – regarded as a specialist asset class of its own.)

Land

As the global population burgeons and exceeds seven billion, concerns have risen concerning food production. Agricultural land used for food production has not been especially remunerative historically, but has become more popular globally as food prices rise. Australia and New Zealand have become particularly popular investment targets, and Chinese investors have attracted publicity by buying land in Africa. Forestry has also been a popular investment, but the extent to which this is a real estate investment rather than a crop or commodity is debatable.

2.2 Capital structure

2.2.1 Four quadrants

In a developed market, with large pension funds and other institutional investors, we might wonder where we will find suitable assets into which we can sink our capital. We can call this area of enquiry real estate investment.

In a developing market, with lots of need and occupational demand for new real estate assets, we might wonder where the capital will come from to finance those assets. We might describe this area of enquiry as real estate finance.

The two main sources of real estate finance are equity and debt. In a developed market awash with pension fund equity, debt may be unimportant (or even disallowed). But there is little doubt that in recent times the use of debt has become a standard part of the real estate investment toolkit.

We can source equity and debt from the public markets (the global stock markets) or the private sector. Listed property companies and REITs (real estate investment trusts: see Chapter 6) can raise debt finance by issuing corporate bonds, and they can raise new equity finance through a rights issue. If as private buyers we wish to buy a large piece of real estate, we can raise (private) equity from our bank account or from co-investors, and we can raise (private) debt by taking out a bank loan.

So, if we are thinking about where finance might be sought for a new real estate development, or the deal's *capital structure*, we can construct a four quadrant classification. Public equity will be the way a listed property company raises most of its finance, by

Figure 2.1: Four quadrants

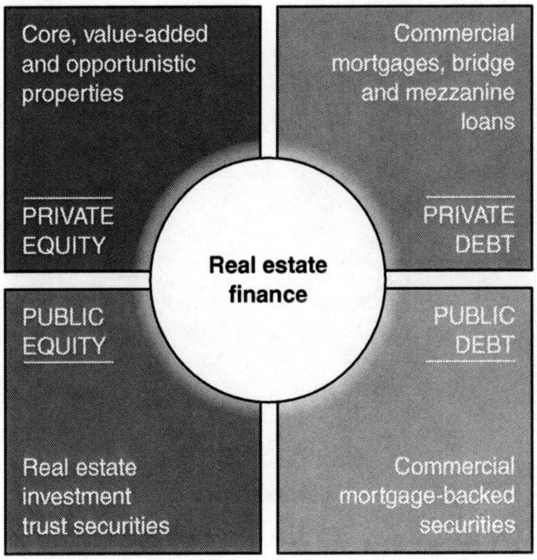

issuing shares. Private equity describes the vast majority of pension fund and insurance company investments in real estate; it also describes the initial capital resource of a universe of unlisted real estate funds (see Chapter 7). Public debt is available to listed companies that can issue debentures or corporate bonds secured against their balance sheet, while private debt is available from banks in the form of loans or overdrafts, and from debt funds in the form of senior debt or mezzanine finance. Figure 2.1 illustrates what has become known as the four quadrants of real estate finance.

Some have argued – erroneously, in our opinion – that the four quadrants can be used to drive a portfolio strategy (see, for example, Rees *et al.*, 2006), but this is merely an elegant way to categorize products and market real estate services, originated in the US and discussed, for example, by Hudson-Wilson and Guenther (1995).

2.2.2 The capital stack

The capital structure of a real estate transaction can consist wholly of equity capital, but it may, for reasons discussed below, include some debt. Where this is the case, the term 'capital stack' is used to describe the diagrammatic representation of the capital structure. The rectangle shown in Figure 2.2 is typical of this.

Senior debt is the least risky form of investment by the capital provider. In the event of things going wrong, this is the capital that has the highest repayment priority. Typically, up to 65 per cent of the property's initial capital value at the time of a transaction or capital re-structuring may be provided by senior debt. It is shown at the bottom of the rectangle, meaning it has low risk relative to the other forms of capital.

Equity debt is the most risky form of investment by the capital provider. In the event of things going wrong, this is the capital that has the lowest repayment priority, and if values fall equity is wiped out first. As little as 5 per cent of the property's initial capital

Figure 2.2: The capital stack

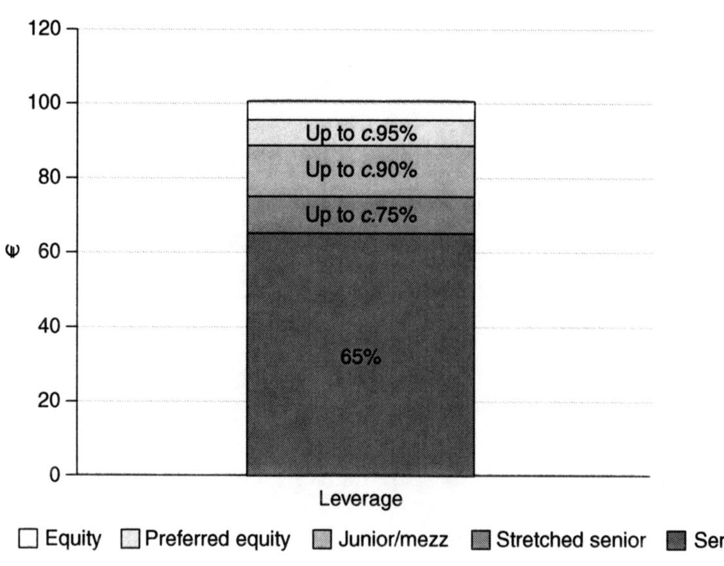

value at the time of a transaction or capital re-structuring may be provided by equity, although history shows that this can be dangerous for debt and equity providers alike.

Where the equity provider is constrained in the amount of equity available for a deal, and this can often be the case (see Chapter 1), senior debt plus equity may provide a sum which falls short of the total capital required. In such a case a variety of intermediate forms of higher risk debt and lower risks equity is available. Stretched senior debt describes riskier senior debt that may be pushed beyond normal senior debt limits (and earn a higher interest rate). Junior debt (often provided by a different capital source than the senior debt provider) will have a much higher interest rate. Mezzanine finance will also earn a much higher interest rate, and may also share in any gains to equity (earning, say, a percentage of the IRR delivered over 10 per cent). Preferred equity may also earn a 'guaranteed' coupon or interest rate, plus a priority receipt of capital when the asset is sold.

(Note that the y axis goes beyond 100 per cent: this is because subsequent fails in market value might cause the initial capital provided to exceed the capital value of the asset after the initial financing or re-financing, causing distress to at least the equity provider, and maybe others.)

2.2.3 Debt and real estate – the theory

Debt is a very important issue in the world of real estate investment. The main reason for this was discussed in Chapter 1 (Section 1.8). Real estate is a large, lumpy asset class and, on average, it costs a lot to buy real property. In order to do so, an individual may have to borrow money, and even a global institution may find it hard to fully diversify its portfolio (see Chapter 3), so using debt is a way of stretching its equity capital across more assets.

Happily for such investors, banks like to lend against real estate. Banks lending to a real estate investor earn arrangement fees and interest, and they have a double layer of security. First, the borrower will promise to pay interest and repay capital, and may provide a personal guarantee secured against any other assets they own. Second, if the borrower fails to fulfil its promise the bank will be able to take control of the property, keep the rent and sell it.

Leverage and return

If debt is used in a real estate transaction, the financial mathematics of the deal changes. Let us develop a very simple example. We can buy a property for €1 million, including all costs. We can lease it for five years at a fixed net rent of €50,000, paid at the end of every year. We expect to sell the property in five years' time for the price we paid, net of all costs. Our cash flow (in €) is shown in Table 2.2.

Table 2.2: Cash flow

	Capital	Income	Total
Year 0	−1,000,000	–	−1,000,000
Year 1	–	50,000	50,000
Year 2	–	50,000	50,000
Year 3	–	50,000	50,000
Year 4	–	50,000	50,000
Year 5	1,000,000	50,000	1,050,000

The internal rate of return (IRR) of this cash flow is 5 per cent, because 5 per cent is the discount rate which, when applied to the cash flows of years one to five, produces a total present value of €1 million (see Table 2.3).

Table 2.3: Cash flow and present values

	Capital	Income	Total	PV €1*	PV
Year 0	–1,000,000	–	–1,000,000	–	–
Year 1	–	50,000	50,000	0.9524	47,619
Year 2	–	50,000	50,000	0.9070	45,351
Year 3	–	50,000	50,000	0.8638	43,192
Year 4	–	50,000	50,000	0.8227	41,135
Year 5	1,000,000	50,000	1,050,000	0.7835	822,702
					1,000,000

Note
* This is given by $1/((1+i)^\wedge n)$, where i is the discount rate of 5% and n is the relevant number of years.

If we borrow 50 per cent of the purchase price at an interest rate of 4 per cent, with no amortization (meaning no capital is repaid until the asset is sold), then the cash flow to the investor changes. The capital outlay falls to €500,000; the net annual income received is now €50,000 less interest paid of 4 per cent of €500,000, or €20,000; and the capital received on sale is reduced by the capital to be repaid (€500,000). The net cash flow now looks like this (Table 2.4).

Table 2.4: Cash flow after debt

	Capital	Income	Interest	Total
Year 0	–500,000	–	–	–500,000
Year 1	–	50,000	–20,000	30,000
Year 2	–	50,000	–20,000	30,000
Year 3	–	50,000	–20,000	30,000
Year 4	–	50,000	–20,000	30,000
Year 5	500,000	50,000	–20,000	530,000

This now delivers an IRR of 6 per cent. This illustrates the following rule:

Return on leveraged equity > return on unleveraged equity

when

Return on unleveraged equity > interest rate on debt

In this case:

Return on leveraged equity (6%) > return on unleveraged equity (5%)

when

$$\text{Return on unleveraged equity (5\%)} > \text{interest rate on debt (4\%)}$$

The transformation is explained by the following formula:

$$ke = [ka - (kd^*LTV)]/(1 - LTV)$$

where:
ka = return on unlevered asset;
kd = cost of debt;
LTV = loan to value ratio.

In this case:

$$ke = [ka - (kd^*LTV)]/(1 - LTV) = [0.05 - (0.04^*0.5)]/(1 - 0.5) = (0.05 - 0.02)/(0.5) = 0.03/0.5 = 0.06 \text{ or } 6\%$$

(However, we should note that while a 1 per cent increase in the IRR is a good thing, this information is not enough to persuade us to use leverage because we are taking more risk – see below. We would also need to assume that we do not have €1 million or that, if we did, we would be able to use the remaining €500,000 efficiently, that is to earn a better return than 4 per cent, or to diversify the portfolio.)

The interest rate on debt may be variable over time, and we are very unlikely to know with certainty what will be the rate of return on unleveraged equity. This makes the analysis above less useful in practice.

However, it is common for borrowers to enter into an interest rate swap, taking a fixed rate in exchange for a floating rate, often with the lender's active encouragement. And borrowers may comfort themselves with the idea that much of their return will come in the form of income, so they may be interested in the relationship between the swap rate and the initial yield on the asset, as debt can enhance the net income return. (This is often believed by investors, wrongly, to be the relevant rule governing the profitability of leverage, but it does give an initial indicator of the likely appeal of borrowing.)

Figure 2.3 shows the relationship between the five-year swap rate and property capitalization rates (or so-called equivalent yields) in the UK, 1992–2013. Swap rates exceeded yields for much of the 1990s, but as interest rates fell in the period 1999–2006 property became more attractive, and the crash in prices (rise in yields) accompanied by a further fall in interest rates post-GFC made property – and leverage – appear to be more attractive than ever by 2012.

Leverage and risk

Using gearing means that returns can be enhanced if the IRR on the 100 per cent equity transaction exceeds the cost of borrowing. The cost of borrowing may be known, but the IRR on the deal is likely to be unknown, so we need to take account of the impact of leverage on risk.

What would happen, for example, if we can sell the asset for only €800,000? Our IRR falls to 1.09 per cent, but with 50 per cent leverage it becomes negative (–3.27 per cent). Leverage clearly increases risk. Table 2.5 shows the various IRRs before and after 50 per

Figure 2.3: The property/swap rate gap, UK, 1992–2013

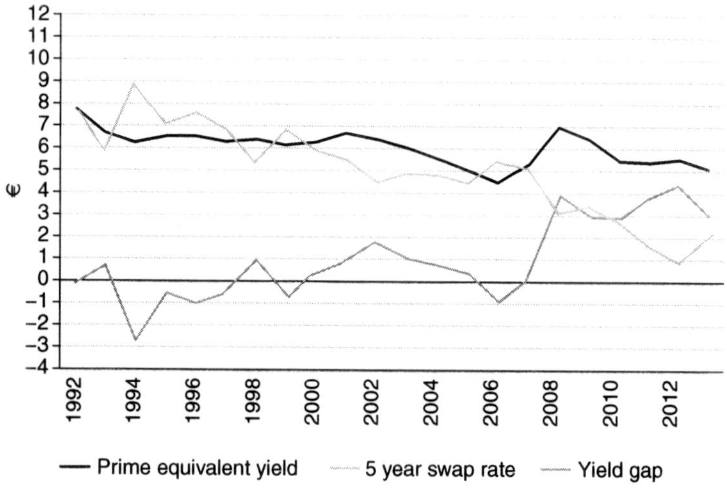

Source: Property Funds Research, IPD, Bloomberg

cent leverage assuming different resale prices, ranging from a low €500,000 to a high of €1,500,000. The results are interesting. The base case, which provides the expected value for the IRRs pre- and post-leverage, is an enhancement of the 5 per cent pre-leverage IRR to 6 per cent, as we noted above. As the resale prices rises above €1,000,000 the pre-leverage IRRs rise, but the post-leverage IRRs are all higher and rise by increasingly large amounts. As the resale prices fall below €1,000,000, the pre-leverage IRRs fall, and the

Table 2.5: IRRs with and without 50% leverage, varying resale prices

Resale price	Return, no leverage	Return, 50% leverage
1,500,000	12.75%	19.56%
1,400,000	11.38%	17.33%
1,300,000	9.92%	14.91%
1,200,000	8.38%	12.26%
1,100,000	6.75%	9.32%
1,000,000	5.00%	6.00%
900,000	3.12%	2.17%
800,000	1.09%	-2.39%
700,000	-1.14%	-8.11%
600,000	-3.60%	-16.00%
500,000	-6.35%	-30.19%
Expected value	5.00%	6.00%
Mean	4.30%	2.26%
Standard deviation	6.27%	15.38%

post-leverage IRRs are lower by increasingly large amounts. And the effect is non-symmetrical: as things get worse, the damage caused by leverage becomes more amplified than the benefit enjoyed as things get better. This is illustrated by the means – the *mean* leveraged return is actually lower than the mean return before leverage, because of this asymmetry, despite the fact that the *expected* return is higher with leverage. In addition, the standard deviation (volatility) of the leveraged return has more doubled compared to the unleveraged returns.

The impact of leverage is illustrated by Figure 2.4, which demonstrates the asymmetric impact of leverage on returns.

Figure 2.4: The impact of leverage on return

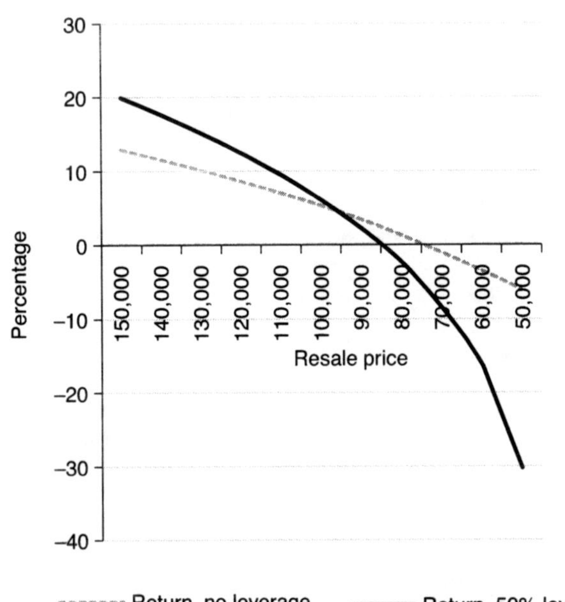

This somewhat challenges the Modigliani–Miller (1958) theorem which concerns capital structure, arguably forming the basis for modern thinking on capital structure. The basic theorem states that in the absence of taxes, bankruptcy costs and agency costs, and in an efficient market, the value of a firm is unaffected by how that firm is financed. It does not matter if the firm's capital is raised by issuing equity or raising debt. Therefore, the Modigliani–Miller theorem is also often called the capital structure irrelevance principle. The theorem effectively suggests that while leverage can increase expected return, it will also increase risk, and that produces a fair game (in other words, each outcome is as attractive as the other).

Currency and tax

There are other reasons for using debt. Using local debt as a form of currency hedging is sometimes cited by investors. This is a flawed argument – see Chapter 9 – but has some intuitive appeal. If I am from China and invest in Frankfurt, I can use €1 million in equity, meaning that I will need to exchange €1 million for its equivalent in renminbi, exposing all of this to the risk that the euro depreciates against the Chinese currency. If I can borrow €500,000 from a German bank, only half of my investment is exposed to this risk. If the euro depreciates, the value of the €1 million asset falls in renminbi, but so does the cost to the Chinese investor of the €500,000 debt. So only the equity of €500,000 is exposed to currency risk. (The flaw in this argument is that the equity is exposed to currency risk and is also now leveraged, so the risk to equity is now even greater.)

Using debt to reduce tax is a more sound reason to consider leverage. This device is used by many, including both taxpayers and investors who are tax exempt in their own jurisdiction but taxed if they invest abroad. Following the rule that the best way to reduce income tax is to reduce income, and taking advantage of the allowability of loan interest as a deduction against income for taxation in many jurisdictions, investors commonly reduce income tax as far as possible by introducing borrowing, so that the interest charge will be set against rental income to reduce annual profit and tax. (This qualification to the capital structure irrelevance theorem was noted by Modigliani and Miller in 1963.)

Table 2.6 shows the after tax cash flow before leverage. The total tax bill is €75,000 and the IRR is reduced by a proportion of 30 per cent from 5 per cent to 3 per cent.

Table 2.6: After tax cash flow and IRR, no leverage

	Capital	Income	Tax	Total
Year 0	–1,000,000	–	–	–1,000,000
Year 1	–	50,000	–15,000	35,000
Year 2	–	50,000	–15,000	35,000
Year 3	–	50,000	–15,000	35,000
Year 4	–	50,000	–15,000	35,000
Year 5	1,000,000	50,000	–15,000	1,035,000

Table 2.7 illustrates the after tax cash flow with 50 per cent leverage. The total tax bill is reduced from €60,000 to €45,000. In this case the IRR is reduced by the same proportion of 30 per cent, from 5 per cent to 3 per cent.

Table 2.7: After tax cash flow and IRR, 50% leverage

	Capital	Income	Interest	Tax	Total
Year 0	–500,000	–	–	–	–500,000
Year 1	–	50,000	–20,000	–9,000	21,000
Year 2	–	50,000	–20,000	–9,000	21,000
Year 3	–	50,000	–20,000	–9,000	21,000
Year 4	–	50,000	–20,000	–9,000	21,000
Year 5	500,000	50,000	–20,000	–9,000	521,000

However, if we re-introduce scenarios with varying capital growth, we can see that the proportion of pre-tax returns retained post-tax when leverage is used is higher than the

Table 2.8: After tax cash flow and IRRs, 50% leverage, varying resale prices

Resale	Pre-tax	Post-tax	Proportion	Pre-tax	Post-tax	Proportion
	No leverage	No leverage		50% leverage	50% leverage	
1,000,000	5.00%	3.50%	70.00%	6.00%	4.20%	70.00%
1,100,000	6.75%	5.30%	78.52%	9.32%	7.63%	81.87%
1,200,000	8.38%	6.98%	83.29%	12.26%	10.67%	87.03%
1,300,000	9.92%	8.56%	86.29%	14.91%	13.39%	89.81%
1,400,000	11.38%	10.05%	88.31%	17.33%	15.86%	91.52%
1,500,000	12.75%	11.46%	89.88%	19.56%	18.14%	92.74%

proportion of pre-tax returns retained post-tax when leverage is not used. This illustrates the 1963 Modigliani and Miller qualification to their earlier theorem of capital structure irrelevance.

2.2.4 Debt and real estate in practice

We can see from Section 2.2.3 why real estate investors might use leverage. But why do banks lend? This may seem to be a curious question – after all, banks are set up to take deposits and lend them out. But what specific motivations are there for banks to lend against real estate assets, given that we know that the global financial crisis (GFC) of 2008–11 caused such huge distress in the banking system?

It would not be a surprise if we suggest that banks are in it for the money. Lenders' returns include fees (an arrangement fee when the loan is provided, and sometimes a fee when the loan is repaid) and loan officers may be motivated through bonus payments to generate as many fees as possible. Banks also earn margins – this is the profit, or reward for risk, earned over the cost of funds. The interbank rate (such as LIBOR or Euribor) determines the interest rate at which banks lend to each other, and this, together with the rate of interest earned on deposits provided by the public, determines the bank's cost of capital. When it lends, it will earn a margin (or profit) on top of its cost of capital. It may, in some circumstances, earn a commitment fee (of say 50 per cent of the margin) for standing ready and committed to provide capital as it is required or drawn. Surprisingly, perhaps, it may also earn a fee for early repayment of a loan. If the borrower defaults, meaning that he fails to make an interest payment, or the value of the real estate asset falls below a certain value (see below), the bank may make an extra penalty charge, increase the margin or both. In extreme cases of default, the bank may gain control of the asset, although that may not be a good thing in a highly distressed marketplace.

Corporate and project finance, secured and unsecured

Loans made against real estate assets may be corporate (secured against the borrower's balance sheet or assets) or project-specific (project finance means that the debt is secured against a single asset). Debt finance may also be unsecured (meaning that the bank has no access to any specific assets in the event of default), a facility usually only made available

Table 2.9: Unsecured corporate bonds issued by UK property companies, 2012–13

Date	Sponsor	£m	Rate	Comment
Sep. 12	British Land	400	1.5%	Convertible, matures in 2017
Oct. 12	Capital Shopping Centres	300	2.5%	Convertible, matures in 2018
Jun. 13	Helical Bar	75	6.0%	Matures in 2020
Jul. 13	Derwent London	150	1.125%	Convertible, matures in 2019
Sep. 13	Great Portland	150	1.0%	Convertible, matures in 2018
Sep. 13	UNITE	90	6.125%	Matures in 2020

to high quality REITs (see Chapter 6) and other companies. Such companies might issue their own unsecured corporate bonds – see Table 2.9. These are sometimes convertible into equity (shares in the company) at maturity.

Debt is more commonly secured by a charge against assets, meaning that in the event of major default the bank will own and be able to take control of the asset. The security may be against a property or a portfolio. Lending is often to 'special purpose vehicles', or SPVs, which are companies set up specifically to own an asset or portfolio and to be 'bankruptcy remote' from a larger entity. In such cases loan covenants are transaction-related and not set at the corporate level. These arrangements are suitable for joint ventures and funds (see Chapter 7) where assets are held 'off-balance sheet' (meaning not on the balance sheet of the holding company). This type of debt is also known as non-recourse, meaning that the lender has no resource to other assets owned by the borrower in the event of a default.

Senior debt

In the diagrammatic layering of risk shown by Figure 2.2, senior debt provides the low-risk debt capital essential to many real estate transactions. The key measure used by senior lenders is the loan to value (LTV) ratio, meaning the amount of debt provided as a proportion of the value of the asset. Senior loans are usually made for a term of around five years, often by reference to the typical lease length or a period of certainly regarding the initial rent paid. After this term, a re-financing will be required – through 100 per cent equity (a sale), or a new loan.

Figure 2.5 shows that LTV ratios fell from around 80 per cent to around 65 per cent in the UK following the GFC. This means that pre-GFC values could fall 20 per cent before the banks' security was directly threatened, but post-GFC that figure rose to 35 per cent (which compares with a peak-to-trough fall in values of 40 per cent between 2007 and 2009). Margins vary with market conditions and the security offered by the borrower, but typically range from 1.5 to 3.5 per cent. Arrangement fees can be around 0.75 to 1 per cent of the loan. Margins and arrangement fees for lending against developments are higher.

Stretched senior debt

Sometimes known as whole loans, stretched senior loans are typically (in 2014) issued at up to 75 to 80 per cent of LTV. These are effectively a blend of senior debt and mezzanine, and some lenders (especially the new debt funds launched in the 2009–13 period) issue

Figure 2.5: Loan to value ratios, senior debt, UK offices, 1999–2013

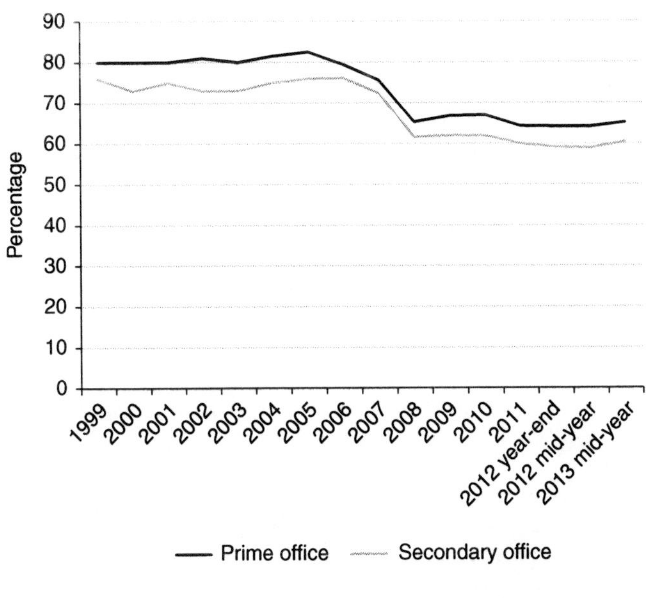

Source: Maxted, 2013

such stretched whole loans in order to sell off the senior 'piece' and retain an engineered mezzanine or junior debt position.

Margins will, as always, vary with market conditions and the security offered by the borrower, but typically range from 2.75 to 4 per cent. Given the mathematics of leverage, this can mean that the stretch component earns a much higher interest rate (see Box 2.1).

> **Box 2.1 Engineered mezzanine**
>
> The Moontree debt fund issues stretched senior debt at 80 per cent LTV against a portfolio of property assets valued at $100 million including purchase costs. It earns a total fixed rate of interest of 6 per cent over five years and an arrangement fee of 1 per cent. It immediately sells down $60 million of this debt secured by a first charge over the assets, and the buyer accepts a 5 per cent fixed rate of interest and pays a fee of 0.75 per cent. If the debt is fully repaid in five years' time, what IRR does Moontree earn?

Junior debt or mezzanine finance

Subordinated or junior debt describes loans made where the lenders' security is subject (or 'subordinated') to the prior charge of the senior lender. Issued at up to around 90 per cent of LTV on top of senior debt at up to say 65 per cent, junior debt is governed by a second charge and an inter-creditor deed. Pricing is naturally higher than for senior or stretched senior (interest rates of 8 to 12 per cent have been common relative to inter-bank rates of 1 to 3 per cent).

Mezzanine debt is a form of junior debt where there is some alignment with the equity position, usually through a share of profit of IRR (see Box 2.2).

Box 2.2 Mezzanine investment, 2011

An industrial portfolio was valued in 2011 at £148.5 million. It generated a net income of around £15.75 million, a 10.1 per cent yield on total purchase costs including fees and taxes of £156 million.

When it was acquired by a private property company, a senior loan of only 50 per cent of the total outlay was available, because banks had become risk averse in the aftermath of the global financial crisis. Interest was charged based on a fixed rate of 3.5 per cent plus a margin to the lender of 3.0 per cent, a total 6.5 per cent interest charge, plus an arrangement fee of 1 per cent.

The property company had around 50 per cent of the required equity capital available, roughly £39 million. It approached a provider of mezzanine finance, who offered to provide the equity shortfall of £39 million on the following terms: a 14 per cent coupon or interest rate; an arrangement fee of 4 per cent of the capital provided; 2.5 per cent amortization, meaning 2.5 per cent of the capital would be repaid on top of interest every year; and a profit share of 30 per cent of the delivered IRR over 14 per cent on resale or re-financing. (This is calculated by estimating the capital receipts needed to deliver a 14 per cent IRR, and then splitting the extra capital 70:30 in favour of the equity owner.)

The two directors of the property company were very keen to do this deal. Assuming 2 per cent rental growth per annum over the holding period of five years, they assumed capitalization rates would fall and values would rise.

They estimated that if they resold the asset on a 10 per cent capitalization rate they would earn a return of 10 per cent. At an 8 per cent resale capitalization rate, which was their base case or expected outcome, they would earn 27 per cent even after paying the mezzanine provider the high interest rate, the arrangement fee and the split of IRR.

The property was re-valued in 2014 at the same rental value and 7.1 per cent (a price just in excess of £220 million). It was then re-financed wholly through a new senior loan of around £130 million in 2014. The mezzanine provider was paid back plus a share of the IRR generated, making an IRR on their capital in excess of 30 per cent, while the property company more than doubled their money.

Can you validate these calculations?

Preferred equity

In a joint venture, two equity providers might choose to engineer a different risk-return position. One, typically the junior partner with energy and a keen desire to undertake a transaction, finds a deal and ask the senior partner to share the equity commitment. Either because he/she is in a powerful position, is more risk-averse or because he/she has less knowledge of the transaction, the senior partner may insist on a preferred equity position. This will normally be subject to the junior partner putting in at least 5 per cent of the purchase price as pure equity, and the senior party holding preference shares, warrants or convertibles in the vehicle used to hold the asset. Preferred equity returns rank before equity but are subordinated to all other debt, and can earn returns in excess of 15 per cent plus fixed exit fees and/or a profit share. Sometimes the preferred equity revenue will be rolled up and paid out on exit.

Debt covenants

When a bank issues debt, the loan officer will take account of the risk involved in the transaction in order to decide whether to make the loan and on what terms to lend. The asset location, specification, lease profile (specifically the weighted average lease term or WALT), tenant quality and the diversification of risk by building, tenant and lease expiry will all be relevant. An exit analysis will be undertaken. What exit yields can be expected in the context of the lease profile, the projected capital value and the value of the property as empty, and who is the likely buyer of the asset at the loan expiry? For example, would a five-year loan issued against a seven-year lease be wise if buyers will regard a property subject to a two-year lease remainder as highly risky?

Once the initial decision to lend has been provisionally made, there are two important metrics that will dominate negotiations and remain of vital importance until the debt is fully repaid. These are the loan to value ratio and the interest cover ratio.

The LTV ratio enables the lender to assess the likelihood that it will be able to recover its loan in full in the event of default. Hence the LTV on loan issue may be the subject of the initial negotiation, but the LTV over the life of the loan – say five years – is more important. In the case of a development loan, the loan to cost ratio may be more commonly used.

In the example used in Table 2.4, the LTV ratio is initially set at 50 per cent. This means that the value of the asset can fall by up to 50 per cent before the bank would suffer a loss on taking control of the asset. If the LTV were set at 60 per cent, the value of the asset can fall by up to 40 per cent before the bank would suffer a loss.

The interest cover ratio (ICR) enables the lender to assess the likelihood that the borrower will be able to pay interest on its loan out of the rental income generated by the asset. The debt service coverage ratio (DSCR) includes amortization in the calculation. A typical minimum ICR set by a lender might range from 1.25 (meaning net rental income is 125 per cent of the interest payments) to 2.5, and it is reasonable for banks to prefer borrowers to swap from a variable rate to a fixed rate simply in order to have more certainty over the ICR for the period of the loan. In the example in Table 2.4, the initial ICR is 2.5, and this remains in place for five years.

Generally, financiers are concerned with the legal documentation which controls the subordination of the more senior tranches of capital, with particular attention paid to what rights each tranche has in the event of a failure to pay interest, or receivership/liquidation.

(For more on real estate debt, see Baum and Hartzell, 2012.)

2.3 Market players

The global property investment market is driven by investors, lenders and fund managers, guided by advisory firms. Together, they dominate the market for property owned by institutional investors, for which Property Funds Research has estimated the value as around $32 trillion at the end of 2014.

This universe is held in one of three ways: it may be owned directly; it may be owned by listed property companies, including REITs; or it may be held in unlisted property funds, such as open-ended funds, unit trusts, limited partnerships and others. According to Property Funds Research (PFR), 77 per cent is held directly (although this will include joint ventures and 'clubs' – see Chapter 7), 14 per cent is owned by listed companies and 9 per cent is held in unlisted funds.

2.3.1 Investors – equity providers

The structure of ownership (or, more accurately, control) of investable property has been changing in both obvious and subtle ways over the last 35 years. First, the combined forces of privatization and globalization have had their intended and inevitable impact. The traditional owners – old established families in the US, the great private landed estates in the UK such as the Church, the Crown and the Oxbridge colleges, and central and local government organizations in most global economies – have, as a whole, lost relative influence, while international institutional owners and wealthy individuals have increased their presence.

Until the turn of the millennium the UK, the US, Australia and a limited number of European markets such as Paris were exceptional markets capable of attracting a wide range of overseas property investors. Many had been particularly attracted to the London office market, home to more international banks than anywhere else in the world, and New York. As an example, the City of London (the financial district) property stock was almost wholly domestically owned until Big Bang in the mid-1980s, after which successive waves of Japanese, American and German capital took levels of overseas ownership from under 10 per cent to over 50 per cent (Lizieri *et al.*, 2011).

In the last ten years, however, many international markets have become investable, even for risk-averse institutions, and the pace of exchange of assets among international players has been remarkable. Much of this has been facilitated by unlisted real estate funds – see Chapter 7. The category of cross-border multi-national owners includes property companies, wealthy individuals and family offices, US-based (and other) pension plans and endowment funds, international insurance companies, pension funds, German open-ended funds and now sovereign wealth funds.

The recent pace of change in investor attitudes has been rapid. Taking UK pension funds as an example, in 2000–5 balanced, unlisted property funds dominated the UK and European markets and domestic-only mandates were common. In 2005–6, pan-European pension fund mandates became typical. Global mandates started to appear in 2006–7, and in 2007 the first global listed/unlisted mandates were being agreed. Meanwhile, increasingly established derivative markets were, by 2007, allowing property hedge funds (such as ReechAiM's Iceberg fund) to create 'market neutral' absolute return funds. Given time, and after a long pause for breath following the crash of 2007–9, the standard pension fund mandate is becoming global. CBRE Global Investors' Global Alpha fund, for example, grew to more than $1 billion of private, indirect assets in 2014. We may also see the market develop further with requirements for global funds investing in listed and unlisted property funds and long/short solutions to achieve absolute returns.

Pension plans and endowment funds, insurance companies, pension funds and sovereign wealth funds make up the vast majority of real estate investors in the markets we know something about. Collectively, they can be called institutional investors, operating professionally, usually across borders, and in some scale, large enough to build diversified real estate portfolios.

Table 2.10: The largest global investors

Capital name	Domicile	Type	Total value of fund (US$m)	Invest in real estate?
Japanese Government Pension Investment Fund	Japan	Government fund	1,261,616	Yes
Norwegian Government Pension Fund Global	Norway	Government fund	736,071	Yes
Abu Dhabi Investment Authority	United Arab Emirates	Government fund	626,770	Yes
State Administration of Foreign Exchange (SAFE)	China	Government fund	589,768	Yes*
China Investment Corporation	China	Government fund	574,789	Yes
Teachers Insurance and Annuity Association – College Retirement Equities Fund	US	Pension fund	529,806	Yes
Korean National Pension Scheme	Korea	Pension fund	486,781	Yes
Saudi Arabian Monetary Agency Foreign Holdings	Saudi Arabia	Government fund	472,937	Yes
Kuwait Investment Authority	Kuwait	Government fund	385,859	Yes
Hong Kong Monetary Authority Exchange Fund	Hong Kong	Government fund	320,782	Yes

Source: Property Funds Research

Note
* Through a subsidiary

Of the top ten global investors in the Property Funds Research database, all are institutional (sovereign wealth or government funds, or pension funds). All except one (the Chinese State Administration of Foreign Exchange, or SAFE) have global investment portfolios with significant exposure to unlisted funds, or in the case of the largest of all, the Japanese Government Pension Investment Fund, have announced plans to invest in global real estate for the first time in 2014 (see Table 2.10) and in 2015 SAFE had begun to invest through a subsidiary, Gingko Tree.

2.3.2 Lenders – debt providers

Historically, banks have dominated the market for real estate debt, although insurance companies also provided mortgage lending in the 1930–60 period. Post-GFC, attractive returns have been on offer in a recovering market that was starved of bank debt but in which the opportunity cost or actual cost of low-risk capital was at a historically low point. Entrepreneurial investors observed the possibility of making higher returns on low-risk debt than they were able to envisage as equity investors. Imagine that the income return on a prime piece of real estate in Germany in 2014 is 4 per cent, that growth prospects are severely limited by very low inflation and a low growth environment, and that stretch senior debt (to 75 per cent of value) can earn a margin of 4 per cent over Euribor of 1.5 per cent. Given the lower risk of debt, plus the possibility of earning fees on top of a 5.5 per cent return, it may appear to be more interesting to some than equity investment.

While this is likely to have been a relatively short-lived anomaly, post-GFC economics appear to have encouraged a new wave of private equity capital providers into the private debt quadrant through the medium of co-mingled, closed ended, unlisted debt funds (see Section 2.3.5). The result is that senior and stretched senior debt is provided by international banks, insurance companies and debt funds, while junior debt and mezzanine lenders are more likely to be investors who would otherwise be attracted to higher-risk private equity.

Table 2.11 illustrates the range of lenders in the UK market in 2014.

Table 2.11: Senior debt providers, UK real estate, 2014

UK banks	Barclays, HSBC, RBS, Lloyds, Santander
German banks	Aareal, Helaba, Deutsche Pfandbriefbank, Deka
Other international	Royal Bank of Canada, BNP Paribas, Credit Agricole, OCBC, Sumitomo Mitsui, Bank of China, Investec
North American lenders	Wells Fargo, BAML, Morgan Stanley, JP Morgan
Insurance companies (20% of all lending in the US)	Aviva, Cornerstone, M&G, AXA, MetLife, Pricoa, L&G, Canada Life
Other non-bank lenders (including debt funds)	AEW Europe, Henderson, Topland, Pears Group, Omni Capital, Aeriance, M&G

Source: Property Funds Research

2.3.3 Fund managers

There has been a less apparent shift in management away from the insurance companies and pension funds which were so dominant in 1980, when property made up as much as 20 and 10 per cent respectively of their total assets, towards fund managers and property companies (the distinctions between which are occasionally blurred). Through the 1980s the institutional investor dominated the higher levels of the industry, controlling the larger transaction business and (in collaboration with real estate service providers and chartered surveying businesses) driving best practice and forming industry lobbies.

In the 1990s the effects of privatization and out-sourcing reached down to the institutions. There was a re-structuring of their investment and property divisions, with the result that the power base now lies within specialist fund management operations, which may themselves be owned by what used to be insurance companies and are now financial services groups. Table 2.12 shows the top 25 global managers of unlisted property funds and the value of the assets held in those funds in Europe, North America, Latin America, Australasia and Asia. The top three are North American in origin; three of the top ten are European in origin. Significantly, as yet there are no large Asian-based managers.

Around half of these fund managers are (former) institutional fund managers owned by bank or insurance businesses, but many of the risk takers are private equity groups (such as Blackstone and Starwood) or property companies (such as Brookfield). In Asia, this is likely to be where the next phase of growth will come from. Several global exemplars and models exist of property companies moving into fund management. Popular motivations may be to add high quality earnings to volatile development profits to create value through diversifying a mix of risk styles; to maintain employment for a large asset management team when the core business is challenged by low share prices; to add some new expertise motivated by a more direct interest in new business; or to disinvest from large assets while maintaining an interest in ownership, fee flow and a form of control.

2.3.4 Advisers

Developments in the investor and fund manager communities have created a more complex industry structure and a confusion of ownership and management. The traditional and now global property service providers, originally the chartered surveying practices in the UK, have been severely challenged by these changes. While there has been no serious threat to the transaction-based business of the traditional surveyor/agent/broker, often a poorly capitalized partnership, their control of investment management is another story. First, bank-backed fund managers can access large sums of capital for business development or for co-investment in large blocks of property alongside clients, which traditional partnerships cannot do. Second, regulation has imposed discipline on the securities businesses – and more recently the private investments – of financial services groups.

Even before these regulations applied to direct property, they suggested the possibility of unmanaged conflicts of interest among the traditional service providers which earn the majority of their fees from transaction business while at the same time acting as investment managers. The rise of indirect forms of ownership has brought financial regulation more clearly into play, and now the GFC has brought the gaze of the regulator round to real estate (through, for example, the 2011 Alternative Investment Fund Managers Directive or AIFMD in Europe).

Even so, many of these businesses have been successful in maintaining their own fund management operations by creating their own 'Chinese walls' (CBRE, for example, is now a top three global property fund manager by assets under management, separately branded as CBRE Global Investors). Some now have access to significant capital, but this has been at the cost of their independence. An epidemic of takeovers in the mid-1990s resulted in

Table 2.12: The PFR global manager survey, 2014 – top 30 managers – total value of global real estate equity AUM ($m)

Fund manager	Europe	North America	Latin America	Australasia	Asia	Middle East and Africa	Global	Total
Blackstone Group	23,535	79,242	606	–	4,824	–	–	108,207
Brookfield Asset Management	4,437	91,081	3,677	8,655	–	–	–	107,850
CBRE Global Investors	48,000	33,300	–	–	7,800	–	–	89,100
AXA Real Estate	65,236	123	–	158	266	–	–	65,783
UBS Global Asset Management	23,563	22,439	–	–	9,499	–	10,259	65,760
MetLife Real Estate Investors	3,406	56,605	363	2	1,923	–	–	62,299
TIAA-CREF Asset Management	3,602	25,823	–	–	–	–	32,077	61,501
Pramerica Real Estate Investors	9,120	35,384	4,009	–	7,188	–	–	55,701
Invesco Real Estate	7,297	20,457	–	–	4,867	–	23,078	55,699
JP Morgan Asset Management	7,816	44,277	–	–	997	–	–	53,090
Credit Suisse AG	48,011	1,288	1,625	521	452	–	–	51,897
AEW Global	25,709	24,136	–	–	1,481	–	–	51,325
Hines	10,879	34,906	2,826	386	1,240	–	–	50,237
Principal Real Estate Investors	507	46,940	–	235	1,052	2	–	48,799
LaSalle Investment Management	20,907	12,386	–	–	4,737	–	9,959	47,989
Deutsche Asset and Wealth Management	20,170	23,165	–	1,802	1,917	–	–	47,053
Cornerstone Real Estate Advisers LLC	2,038	40,674	–	8	41	–	–	42,761
Aviva Investors	38,168	502	–	–	1,092	–	–	39,763
Tishman Speyer	5,552	25,372	1,493	–	4,179	–	–	36,596
Starwood Capital Group	7,369	26,335	338	–	197	–	–	34,240
Morgan Stanley Real Estate Investing	7,103	17,900	100	3,670	5,264	147	–	34,184
Cohen and Steers Capital Management	2,488	26,808	31	1,003	2,052	6	–	32,388
M&G Real Estate	26,518	1,949	–	540	1,326	–	–	30,334
Clarion Partners	–	29,873	100	–	–	–	–	29,973
Heitman	5,141	22,911	–	687	399	–	–	29,138
Aberdeen Asset Management	27,584	222	–	–	860	–	–	28,666
BNP Paribas Real Estate Investment Management	24,499	–	–	–	124	–	–	24,623
Prologis	11,394	8,616	256	–	4,355	–	–	24,620
BlackRock	7,515	8,255	–	–	7,978	–	–	23,749
Bentall Kennedy	70	23,165	–	–	–	–	–	23,235

Source: Property Funds Research

the sale or merger of many of the most respected chartered surveyors to or with US-based real estate businesses. As examples, Jones Lang Wootton merged with LaSalle, Richard Ellis and St Quintin were sold to Insignia, Hillier Parker was sold to Coldwell Banker, and Healey and Baker was sold to Cushman and Wakefield. The subsequent 2003 merger of Insignia and CB created CB Richard Ellis, now CBRE, the world's largest property services business in 2014.

Other advisers or service providers have become essential to the working of the commercial real estate investment market. These include placement agents and promoters of property funds, lawyers, tax advisers, derivatives brokers, trustees and custodians, and good, old-fashioned property managers, who are most easily found within the traditional service providers, but with new competition in the form of specialist facilities management businesses.

2.3.5 Funds and vehicles

Several problems are associated with property investment. These include illiquidity, specific risk and a lack of trust in valuation-based property return indices (see Chapter 1). An apparently obvious solution for many of these problems is the use of liquid traded property vehicles in place of the direct asset.

Many legal structures exist which are capable of providing a vehicle for investment in domestic or international real estate. These include REITs and listed property companies, and a new generation of unlisted property funds, both open-ended and closed-ended. In addition, much work has been expended in the development of synthetic vehicles (derivatives) to provide this solution, with some already in place, including property swaps, structured notes and property derivatives funds.

REITs and property companies

Securitization has enabled real estate investment to be executed through an accepted industry sector of the global stock market. This includes debt (Commercial Mortgage-Backed Securities, or CMBS) and equity (Real Estate Investment Trust, or REIT) formats, both of which grew rapidly in the 1990–2007 period.

The US REIT is a tax transparent, quoted vehicle which is forced to distribute the majority of its earnings and to limit its gearing. This provides the features which many would look for in the ideal property vehicle, providing pure property performance features in a liquid form. Its growth in the 1990s to a current market capitalization of around $1.1 trillion demonstrates this. The REIT format has now been exported around the world.

However, REITs are in essence listed property companies, and, over the longest time series available, returns on investments in listed UK property companies have only just matched the returns on direct property investment, and have significantly under-performed the UK equity market. The volatility of property company shares has been much higher than that of the direct property market, and the performance of property company shares has not mirrored that of direct property, but has instead been highly correlated with the equity market in the short term (see Chapter 6). In other words, UK property company shares look a little like equities, although the result of any analysis is subject to the time period used. For example, the relationship between property company shares and the UK equity market was very strong in the 1970s while the relationship between property company shares and the direct property market has been stronger since 1980.

US REITs have a more encouraging track record, and appear to have out-performed direct property, even after adjusting for leverage and differences in the property type held (Ling and Naranjo, 2014).

Property companies have been successful at surviving two severe challenges to their very existence, in 1973–5 and in 1991–3. Another severe challenge was confronted in 2009. In all of these property recessions, many famous property companies became insolvent and disappeared. While the extremely strong performance of the stock market in the 1980s, coupled with a growing demand for liquid (easily traded) property investment vehicles, has provided some support to the albeit poorly performing share prices of the survivors, its weighting as a proportion of the global stock market has declined since 1989. Nevertheless, with 14 per cent of the current global market, the listed property company and REIT market trebled in size between 2001 and 2006, before the GFC, as the REIT format was applied in more and more countries.

Unlisted funds

The unlisted fund sector grew from very small beginnings in the 1970s, sprang into life in the late 1990s and now holds over 9 per cent of the global property market. Surveys by PFR and INREV (the European Association for Investors in Non-listed Real Estate Vehicles) suggest that there is potential for further growth. In the long run, it is reasonable to suppose that more listed and unlisted property funds will follow to convert the huge pool of government and owner-occupier held property into an investible form. It is expected that growth in the creation of funds will continue, supported by booming fund of funds and multi-manager solutions (a form of indirect investment in which a manager is appointed to select funds on behalf of an investor; see Chapter 7). Investors are taking more risk in search of maintaining attractive return levels, resulting in an increased appetite for what are called 'value-added' (higher risk) funds. There is also growing interest in emerging markets on the fringes of Europe, the Middle East and North Africa, Sub-Saharan Africa, South America and Russia.

These vehicles may have the primary objective of reducing tax, of achieving liquidity or of aligning the interests of the investors and the managers. They may exist to permit co-mingling of investors, or they may be special purpose vehicles for the use of one investor acting alone or two parties acting in a joint venture. Their use has multiplied in recent years as a result of the increase in cross-border investment activity, often more attractive in a co-mingled format, and the generally more punitive impact of tax on foreign investors. Unlisted funds are more fully described in Chapter 7 of this book: what follows is a brief summary.

Many professional investors use what are known as collective investment schemes or co-mingled funds. Typically managed by fund managers, these are pooled funds which allow smaller insurance companies and pension funds and other investors to achieve diversification without the high fixed costs and illiquidity of holding direct property. The main types of pooled fund are open-ended property unit trusts, closed-ended limited partnerships and offshore trusts. Special purpose corporate vehicles (SPVs) are also used, usually for tax efficiency or to permit the use of gearing which does not appear on the investor's balance sheet.

Special purpose corporate vehicles

The company is a popular format for the ownership of both domestic and international property. Its prime advantage is to allow complete flexibility in the size and quantity of the number of investors in the vehicle; in addition, it introduces the possibility of liquidity if the vehicle is offered in the public markets. In many countries, however, tax is paid on the profits made by these companies. In addition, tax is paid by shareholders on the dividends distributed by companies out of already-taxed profits, so the conversion of freehold ownership into a corporate structure introduces an extra layer of tax.

This is more of a problem for taxpayers, typically overseas owners or private individuals and corporates, than it is for pension funds and other tax exempt investors. However, pension funds may be caught in this net if they invest across borders. As we discussed in Section 2.2, leverage can be used to reduce tax. In addition, interest received may be taxed differently from dividends, and a second means of reducing income tax is to introduce 'equity' in the form of debt. This can be achieved by issuing investors with loan notes instead of, or alongside, share certificates.

Closed-ended unlisted core funds: limited partnerships and trusts

Specialist unlisted property funds in the form of offshore unit trusts were increasingly popular in the UK at the turn of the millennium. For example, the Hercules Unit Trust, which by 2006 held over £2 billion by value of out-of-town retail parks in the UK, is a Jersey-based property unit trust vehicle managed for the benefit of a mix of domestic and international investors. There has been a reasonably active secondary market in units in this fund, and in several other similar structures.

The limited partnership structure offers less liquidity. It is unregulated, and simpler to operate than the unit trust. It has been very successful in attracting investors, usually into specialist funds or single property investments. Limited partnerships are tax neutral or tax transparent vehicles, meaning that the vehicle itself does not attract taxation, and partners are treated exactly as if they owned the assets of the limited partnership directly. This creates an enormous advantage for the vehicle, which has become increasingly popular as the standard vehicle for co-mingled property ownership. The ownership of Bluewater Park, for example, a £2 billion shopping centre developed in the UK by LendLease, was converted to a limited partnership in 1998 and partnership shares were sold to investors. Many similar structures followed, and this is now the most popular global format of unlisted fund (see Chapter 7). The main disadvantage of the limited partnership structure may be limited liquidity, with stakes tradable only on a matched bargain basis.

The new debt funds are also examples of closed-ended unlisted funds operating at the core end of the risk spectrum.

Private equity real estate funds

In the late 1980s, the US saw the launch of a new generation of co-mingled funds looking to buy cheap, distressed property assets popularly known as 'vulture funds'. These were the first generation of closed-ended real estate funds, usually set up in a corporate or partnership format. For many reasons the format became largely discredited, but the access provided to difficult markets for foreign investors, tax efficiency and a lack of alternatives have all helped to overcome resistance to the vehicle.

A more acceptable name ('opportunity funds') was found for these funds in the 1990s; later 'private equity real estate funds' became a popular broader descriptor for higher risk, higher return, illiquid real estate funds modelled on private equity structures. They are always closed-ended, meaning there is a finite number of units in issue at any time and the manager will not issue or redeem units on demand. It follows that they almost always have a limited life in order that investors can force a sale to receive a return of equity. They are usually limited partnerships.

Fee structures in such vehicles, modelled initially on US private equity funds, typically attempt to 'align' the interests of investor and manager by rewarding the manager on a performance basis. The manager may charge a base fee calculated as a percentage of the value of the assets managed, and additionally take a proportion (say 20 per cent) of the total return over a minimum hurdle (say 12 per cent).

These structures can be employed in cross-border investing, which often involves the creation of several special purpose vehicles. The often-complex structure can be purpose-made and therefore tax effective for certain investor domiciles and types. Gearing is common, at levels up to 60–80 per cent, both for performance and tax purposes. This carries inherent risks which were revealed in full in 2008–9. The fund manager often invests capital alongside clients.

This vehicle carried much of the US-originated 1990s investment in markets such as Eastern Europe and China. While there are many flaws in this investment format – the limited life format and its lack of liquidity being two – its main advantage is that it clearly accesses the performance characteristics of private real estate rather than listed equities.

Open-ended funds

Open ended property funds are popular in the UK, Germany, Australia and the US, and have been the main vehicles used by many pension funds to gain access to diversified portfolios of real estate in a form that allows replication of direct market performance characteristics. They are unlisted, the unit prices are determined by valuations, and liquidity is limited to a small amount of secondary market trading activity and the guarantee that managers will buy and sell units, albeit (in the UK) at spreads which replicate the cost of buying and selling direct property.

Such funds (unauthorized property unit trusts and property authorized investment funds, or PAIFs, in the UK) are usually tax free for qualifying pension funds. While they have to invest in domestic property to protect this status, they can be established offshore to appeal to international investors.

The open-ended nature of these funds means that investors can deal directly with the manager rather than with each other through a secondary market. This dual liquidity mechanism can fail in rising and falling markets. Flows of capital into and out of the vehicle can create greater difficulties for the manager than rising and falling share or unit prices would create for the managers of a closed-ended listed vehicle such as an opportunity fund or a property company. In strong markets, intense performance pressure can be placed on managers by net inflows of cash. Managers are forced into a position where they wish to invest quickly, but only in attractively priced assets.

Weak markets create greater problems. Particular difficulties were evidenced in 1990–3, when net sales of units led to forced sales of property, damaging the performance of some unit trusts. This in turn led to more investors wishing to exit, forcing further sales of units and then forced sales of properties in a vicious downward spiral.

A more severe crisis erupted in 2007–8; see Chapter 7. The open-ended fund market in Germany, which managed €82 billion of assets at 2014, all but closed down and several funds were forced to liquidate all assets by 2017. The largest example of the UK property unit trust, the Schroder Exempt Property Unit Trust (now converted to a PAIF and known as the Schroder UK Property Fund), managed at May 2000 over £1.1 billion of commercial property assets for more than 600 different corporate pension fund unit holders. In December 2006 the gross assets had risen to £2.3 billion; by the end of 2008 this had fallen back to £1.3 billion, and the gross value at 2014 had not recovered.

Despite these problems, open-ended funds have survived. In general they appear to behave like direct property. Liquidity is not significantly better than for direct property, but these funds are ideal for small funds due primarily to professional management and the diversification benefits offered by a pooled vehicle, coupled with some liquidity.

Synthetic vehicles

Property index certificates, launched by Barclays in the UK in the mid-1990s, were the first European derivative property investments. Buyers are provided with synthetic returns matching the annual return on the IPD annual index. As in the gilt or bond market, the buyer pays a capital sum which is either par value or a price representing a premium or discount to par depending on demand in the market. The issuer provides a quarterly in arrear income based on (but not exactly the same as) the IPD annual income return, and following expiry the par value is repaid together with a large proportion, but not all, of the capital appreciation in the IPD index.

While performance is directly linked to the capital performance of the IPD annual universe, under normal circumstances property index certificates lock in marginal underperformance of the IPD annual index due to the management costs charged. Correlation with the direct market is nonetheless very high, and in a multi-asset or international context these instruments provide the pure diversification benefits of UK property. However, liquidity is low due to the small size of market and the lack of a true secondary market.

These are now a sub-set of a broader 'structured note' market, which developed in the UK in the period post-2004 when tax and regulatory clarification made a property swap market – and later a traded futures market – more efficient for institutional investors. Derivatives are dealt with in more detail in Chapter 8.

2.4 Conclusions

The crash of 2007–9 means that the generic case for investing in real estate will be re-examined, and it will need to be made with care. Methods of portfolio management will need to be highly professional: this is dealt with in Part 2 of this book.

After the shock caused by property's key role in the GFC, the industry will attempt to resume its growth as a proportion of global stock markets and attract more recognition, creating more unlisted funds, more property share funds and funds using derivatives. These developments are dealt with specifically in Part 3.

Finally, the cross-border real estate investment industry remains healthy, and various global markets, having paused for breath and weathered a period of retrenchment, are now moving from the emerging stage, through the development phase, to become maturing markets. International real estate investing is the subject of Part 4.

Part 2

The investment process

3 Building and managing the portfolio

3.1 Real estate portfolio management

Should investors include real estate in mixed asset portfolios? If so, how much? In Chapter 1, Section 1.13, we examined the risk, return and correlation data which is used by many to answer this question. We also noted the practical difficulties associated with using an MPT approach: valuation smoothing, specific risk and lumpiness, illiquidity, the common use of leverage, the fees and costs involved in managing real estate and asymmetry are the main problems. Nevertheless, we suggested that property can appear to be a low-risk asset class, and a good portfolio diversifier, offering long-term advantages for investors with long-term liabilities.

In this chapter we will use a similar approach, taking account of its limitations, to focus on the issues that arise when building a real estate portfolio, and then turn to real estate portfolio management.

Until the 1980s in the developed markets, property portfolios tended to be seen as simple aggregations of individual buildings. There was little reference to portfolio theory in practice or in university courses, and little was made of the linkages between the property market and the macroeconomy or the capital markets. This changed in the late 1980s and 1990s, and with it the emphasis shifted from property and asset management to portfolio and fund management until the importance of the individual asset was re-asserted, with the healthy result that both portfolio level expertise and asset level expertise are regarded as essential components of property investment expertise.

Already in this chapter we have made use of four different management terms, which we now need to define.

Fund management is the administration of a pool of capital, with the intention of investing the majority or all of the capital in a group of assets. Hence a property fund may have some cash, or utilize gearing.

Portfolio management is the administration of the property assets within the fund, not including the cash or gearing, but taking account of the structure of the portfolio as a whole. All or part of this function could be sub-contracted by a fund manager to a property specialist. Sales and purchases might be left to the discretion of the portfolio manager (a discretionary appointment) subject to net inflows or outflows of cash imposed by the fund manager or client. More commonly, however, the property fund manager will act as the portfolio manager.

Asset management is the administration of individual property assets, not taking account of the structure of the portfolio as a whole, but with the objective of maximizing the financial performance of each property asset for the client. All of this function might naturally be sub-contracted by a fund manager to a property specialist. If sales and purchases require the approval of the fund manager, the appointment might be said to be advisory rather than discretionary.

Property management is the administration of the property assets, with the objective of offering satisfaction to the end-user (the occupier or customer), not necessarily with the objective of maximizing financial performance for the client beyond the efficient and prompt collection and payment of rent and service charges. This distinction explains the rising popularity of *facilities management*, a wholly and more comprehensive user-oriented approach to property management, sometimes called corporate real estate management.

This chapter focuses on portfolio management. It starts from three basic propositions.

i Investment strategies are like business plans
Investment strategies should be driven by a clearly stated and understood objective. They should take account of the fund's strengths, weaknesses, opportunities and threats (or constraints). They should be reviewed using a form of performance appraisal.

ii There are three ways to achieve performance objectives
These are:

a managing portfolio structure;

b positive stock selection and successful negotiation of transactions; and

c active management of the properties within the portfolio.

iii The necessary technology includes three sets of models, all of which can add value
These are:

a models used to produce forecasts;

b valuation models, which operate at all levels for the market down to the individual building; and

c portfolio models, used to control risk and assist in the optimization of portfolio planning.

Developing a strategy for the management of a portfolio is rather like a producing a business plan. This includes the following processes:

A clear statement of objectives
The manager needs to know what he is trying to achieve and when. This should include a statement of required return; risk tolerance; and timescale. Return and risk are likely to be relative to a benchmark (see Section 3.2). This process is analogous to the agreement of a mission statement.

Strengths, weaknesses and constraints
A portfolio analysis is a statement of where the fund is positioned and is needed to be able to establish realistic objectives. Stock characteristics, market conditions, expected flows of cash and staffing can be regarded as constraints on the fund achieving its objectives.

The strategy statement
This is the business plan. How is the objective to be achieved, and by when?

Performance appraisal
This process forces us to ask: how well did we do? Did we achieve the objective? Are there any other standards of performance we should make reference to?

It needs to be recognized that more than one set of interests needs to be considered when adopting a mission and writing a business plan. The organization may have several, sometimes conflicting, objectives. In an investment management organization, these are all likely to relate to risk and return, a common means of measuring which are the mean and variance of annual total return. Mean-variance analysis, albeit simplistic in the context of a large and complex organization, is useful because it is a commonly accepted theoretical foundation for investment and finance and it reflects the motivations of some actors in the business, for example some fund trustees and some research economists.

However, we know mean-variance analysis has limitations, and it is not a useful way of interpreting the mission of most fund management organizations. Funds or managers will be concerned with other things. The practical issues facing most investors are to do with long-term survival. This concentrates the mind on liabilities and solvency, which requires the advice of actuaries. Will the asset income stream be sufficient to pay the annual liabilities of the insurance or pension fund?

Fund managers also focus also on profits, or market share. This means that, managers should be concerned with competitors and business risk. This leads to the pinpointing of return relative to a competitor benchmark.

3.2 Absolute and relative return objectives

Investors have return objectives that are expressed in *absolute* terms, meaning a quantified nominal or real total return over a given time period. A pension fund, for example, might express its real return objective for a real estate portfolio as follows: *to achieve a 5 per cent return in real terms, after fees and taxes, for the lowest possible risk.* A nominal return objective might be 6–8 per cent at a time when inflation is expected to run at 2–4 per cent.

This is designed to allow the pension fund to pay out future pensions at a rate which covers wage inflation and to reduce the contribution rate made by employers and employees in the longer run. If the real estate portfolio can deliver these returns as well as diversifying the risk of the multi-asset portfolio and operating as a hedge against unexpected inflation, this is an attractive proposition.

Investors may, however, provide fund managers with different, *relative*, return targets. This is because investor trustees or pension plan sponsors may need to prove that their selected manager has done a good job in order that they will be retained for a further investment period.

Fund managers are generally content with relative return targets. Financial services organizations, like other businesses, concentrate on market share as one of the ways to grow profits. Like any business, they are also concerned with the performance of their competitors and business risk. To prove that they are delivering value as fund managers, there is a requirement for measuring return relative to a competitor benchmark. The property fund manager is therefore concerned not only with absolute return, but also with return relative to a performance benchmark.

The danger to fund managers departing from standard weightings is clear. For example, in 1998–9 a well-known fund manager lost mandates to manage many billions of pounds of client money after reducing his stock market holdings in mistaken – or more accurately, premature – anticipation of a fall in share prices.

Table 3.1 shows how the fund manager views relative risk. Absolute volatility, as measured by standard deviations, shows manager B to be much worse than manager A. However, this is of less concern than the riskiness of excess returns (returns delivered relative to an index or benchmark). The standard deviation (SD) of return relative to the index is called tracking error.

Table 3.1: Excess returns and tracking error

Year	Index	A	B	A excess	B excess
1	18	10	20	–8	2
2	17	10	20	–7	3
3	–30	10	–40	40	–10
4	20	10	25	–10	5
5	21	10	25	–11	4
Average	9.2	10	10	0.8	0.8
SD	21.97	0.00	28.06	21.97	6.14

In the table, manager A has no volatility, but the index does. Hence the returns achieved by A relative to the index (A excess) are volatile. They are in addition more volatile than the excess returns, or the tracking error, on B. Manager B produced more volatile returns, but they were more in line with the market and probably introduced less business risk for manager B than manager A, who would have been uncomfortable in all years except year 3.

Good or widely accepted benchmarks are not, however, available in all property markets. Investors offering global real estate mandates cannot set a relative return target if there is no acceptable global return benchmark. Hence global real estate mandates have typically set absolute return objectives: for example, '*to invest in global real estate to achieve a 5 per cent return in domestic currency in real terms, after fees and taxes, for the lowest possible risk*'.

This reversion to an absolute return objective is understandable, but dangerous for investor and manager alike. Investors are unlikely to be satisfied with 5 per cent real returns when the market booms and delivers 20 per cent, and managers will be unhappy being charged with failure to deliver if the market turns down badly. A global benchmark remains a key requirement for a professional sector, and work continues to bring this closer.

3.3 The top-down portfolio construction process

3.3.1 The relative return target

Where good benchmarks are available, a strategic approach has become popular in property portfolio management. This involves consideration of the structure of the portfolio

Figure 3.1: The investment process

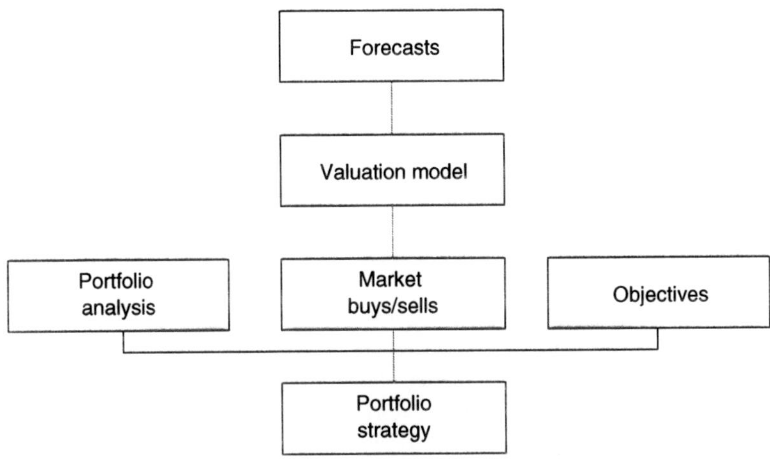

relative to a benchmark; forecasts of return and risk for the portfolio, often top-down by property type or location; and a strategy which involves buying and selling. The investment process which has become typical in the better developed property investment markets is shown in Figure 3.1.

Commonly, forecasts of rental growth and yield movement are applied at the market, sector, region, city and property level. These, fed through a discounted cash flow valuation model, will suggest market buys and sells – those sectors, cities and buildings where the returns on offer, as estimated by the investment manager, exceed the risk-adjusted required return.

A valuation model is simply a way of comparing the expected or forecast return with the required return (the risk-adjusted cost of capital) or, equivalently, the correct initial yield with the current market capitalization (cap) rate. The inputs into a valuation model are the investor's views on rental growth, depreciation and risk. These are used to establish the correct cap rate or the expected return. This is compared with the current market cap rate or the required return to establish whether the asset is correctly priced, under-priced or over-priced. This produces market buy and sell decisions. This process is described in detail in Chapter 4.

Deciding whether assets or markets look cheap is not sufficient to determine a portfolio strategy. The current portfolio structure is also significant, and a portfolio analysis will be undertaken to identify where the manager is underweight or overweight relative to a given benchmark. In addition, the manager's or trustees' objectives must be taken into account in determining what action needs to be taken. That action will be prescribed in the form of a business plan or portfolio strategy.

3.3.2 The absolute return target

Where an absolute return target is unqualified by a benchmark, the investment manager may be tempted to employ a form of MPT-based optimization process. This approach is challenged by the limitations listed in Chapter 1, and applications in practice tend to be heavily qualified and adjusted.

Alternative approaches include the equilibrium model, which when applied within a property portfolio would begin with a neutral position, determined by the size by value of the market, with positions taken against that neutral weight determined by the attractiveness of market pricing. This more closely reflects the practice of professional and institutional market participants. Figure 3.1 applies equally well to a portfolio whose investor or manager has an absolute return objective.

3.4 Setting investment objectives

We have seen that an investment portfolio may have an absolute or relative return target. Whichever of these is in place, several criteria should determine the precise framing of the performance objective. These will have an impact on the return target and risk tolerance, the benchmark adopted and the timescale over which performance is measured.

3.4.1 Criteria for investment objectives

Objectives should be achievable, yet testing. They should be marketable, in other words capable of attracting investors. They must be testable, so that performance measurement is capable of determining success or failure. This should then be capable of leading to a reward of some sort (performance fee, bonus). Finally, the objective must be specific in terms of risk control.

3.4.2 Return and risk

The absolute return objective is common in the absence of acceptable benchmarks, but it has to be said that this type of objective is sub-optimal for the investor. Investors are unlikely to be satisfied with low real returns when the market booms. Managers will also be unhappy being charged with failure when the market crashes, but they may prefer absolute return targets if they have engineered a bonus payment for good absolute performance. This is accepted by, or even popular with, some investors, but this can be short-sighted.

Typically, so-called carried interest or performance fees might give the manager extra remuneration (say 20 per cent of the excess return over a 10 per cent IRR target). Let us assume that a property acquired in 2014 is to be held for five years. It will deliver a 5 per cent income return. In order to deliver a 10 per cent IRR it needs to be sold in 2019 for $15 million. If it is sold for $20 million, the manager 'earns' 20 per cent of the extra cash, which is $1 million. There are two problems with this. First, it is more likely that the market, and not manager skill, will drive the value beyond $15 million. Second, there *are* ways in which the manager can boost returns, but these probably mean increasing risk. Risk can be taken at the property level, by buying a volatile asset, or financial risk can be introduced, by using more leverage. If things go wrong, the investor suffers; if things go well, the manager gets a large bonus. This is a bad idea for investors.

The better return objective will be expressed relative to the benchmark. This could be to achieve average performance, to achieve above median performance, to achieve a return of 2 per cent (or any other number) above average, to achieve upper quartile performance or a combination of these. Best practice carried interest structures in the modern marketplace can combine an absolute benchmark and performance fee with a relative performance objective. An example would be '*to be paid 20 per cent of IRR returns in excess of 10 per cent as long as the return is in excess of the benchmark by at least 1 per cent on an unleveraged basis*'.

The return objective should be realistic when considered against the current structure of the portfolio, possible restructuring and transaction costs, staff levels and other constraints.

Any investment carries risk and there is a trade-off between return and risk. Thus the higher is the required return, the higher is the risk to be taken. If the manager seeks to achieve top quartile performance, he must take a higher risk of achieving lower quartile performance than if the objective is median performance. Because of this, the investor's risk tolerance should be made explicit.

Because information is relatively scarce, properties are heterogeneous and there is no central marketplace, property is traded in a relatively inefficient market. As a result, and because specific risk is such a significant problem (see Chapter 1) it is arguably easier to out-perform (or under-perform) the index by sector structure and by stock selection (see Chapter 5) than it is in the securities markets. Considerable data exists to enable this potential to be measured.

The opportunity to add value is illustrated by Table 3.2, which shows the range of returns that managers of various asset classes achieved in a typical single year. It illustrates the enormous range associated with property.

Table 3.2: WM percentile rankings, 1994 total returns (%)

	95th	Median	5th	Range
Property	3.0	13.0	20.8	17.8
UK equities	–8.4	–5.8	–2.3	6.1
Gilts	–12.4	–9.6	–5.1	7.3
Overseas equities	–9.9	–5.4	–2.3	7.6

Source: The WM Company

3.4.3 Benchmarks

The universe used to compile the IPD UK annual index at the end of 2013 comprised over 21,000 properties worth around £153 billion; over 7,100 properties and $382 billion make up the US NCREIF universe. Table 3.3 shows the breakdown of the UK universe by sector.

The neutral or equilibrium UK portfolio comprised 46.8 per cent retail property, 26.5 per cent offices, 15.4 per cent industrial, 3.8 per cent residential and 7.5 per cent 'other'. (Note that this has shifted significantly over the last few years: 'other' property and residential had a combined weight of only 3.7 per cent in 2007.) This can be suggested as a reasonable portfolio shape to begin with. As noted in Chapter 1, the tracking error between a real estate portfolio and a benchmark can be very high, but a portfolio constructed with this shape is likely to perform more closely in line with the return delivered by the universe in 2013 than a portfolio with different constituent weights.

Typically, pension plan sponsors and trustees will expect to earn the benchmark average return: that is the most widely accepted measure of the market. This has the

Table 3.3: The IPD UK universe, end 2013

Sector	No of properties	Value	Proportion
IPD UK Retail	4,156	£71,463	46.8%
IPD UK Offices	2,663	£40,446	26.5%
IPD UK Industrial	2,850	£23,525	15.4%
IPD UK Other	2,379	£11,461	7.5%
IPD Residential	9,127	£5,755	3.8%
IPD UK All Property	21,175	£152,652	100%

Source: IPD

advantage of convenience, but can cause problems for some fund managers if the size of fund they manage differs greatly from the average. Performance differentials between large and small funds are inevitable for a number of reasons.

- Larger funds can gain access to large lot size markets such as London or New York offices, or large size assets such as shopping centres.
- The impact of stock-specific characteristics may be smaller in a large fund because of greater opportunities to diversify.
- Larger funds can undertake developments, which can produce high returns but are typically riskier.

For example, large life funds out-performed the UK IPD average by 0.9 per cent on average each year during the 1980s. Occupational pension funds under-performed the IPD average by 1.3 per cent on average each year during the same period. In simple terms, London offices and developments and active asset management were positive performers over that period, and pension schemes had less access to these sectors and activities.

Cash and leverage will also be an issue. There are significant differences in this respect between a property benchmark such as NCREIF or IPD, which ignore the impact of cash and gearing, and property fund measures which measure fund performance as affected by cash, gearing levels and fees. Examples include the Open-ended Diversified Core Equity (ODCE) and NCREIF Townsend Real Estate Fund Indices in the US, the Association of Real Estate Funds (AREF) in the UK, the Association of Investors in Non-Listed Real Estate Vehicles (INREV) in Europe, and the IPD Fund Indices, which include several country-specific indexes as well as the IPD Global Quarterly Property Fund Index, the IPD Pan-Europe Quarterly Property Fund Index and the IPD Nordic Quarterly Property Fund Index. (These benchmarks are referred to again in Chapter 7.)

3.4.4 Time horizons

It is unrealistic to expect core fund managers or investment portfolios to deliver returns of 2 per cent above average every year. This target level is highly testing, and consistency is nearly impossible. A level of 1 to 1.5 per cent above the median return has typically been sufficient to produce upper-quartile performance. In addition, property's specific risk means that it is more realistic to set a target in terms of three- or five-year averages; the effects of valuation timing, illiquidity and specific risk are then reduced.

3.5 Strengths, weaknesses, constraints: portfolio analysis

There are three broad parts to the portfolio analysis. These are an analysis of recent performance, a statement of current portfolio structure and an assessment of the strengths, weaknesses and constraints affecting the organization.

3.5.1 Recent performance

Fund manager appointments in property are most commonly made subject to a three- or five-year review. The performance objective may be framed in these terms. Whether or not this is the case, the manager's strategy will be influenced by his recent performance. There will be times when greater risks are encouraged to recover lost ground; there will other times when the appropriate strategy will be designed to lock in the fruits of good past performance by eliminating tracking error from the portfolio.

3.5.2 Current portfolio structure

It is necessary to examine the structure of the portfolio relative to the chosen benchmark. The region is a highly dubious unit of analysis (see Table 3.4 below), but some portfolio analysis focuses on the sector/region because benchmarks use this level of market disaggregation. These sector/region combinations are the asset classes: they are groups of properties which are thought to be affected by the same broad economic factors.

If the portfolio structure is identical to the benchmark, the only risk remaining relative to the benchmark is specific to individual buildings rather than systematic. This could be diversified away by having a large number of buildings, although in practice this is rarely possible because of costs and lot size (see Chapter 1).

The analysis of structure identifies those sector/regions in which the fund has an above- or below-average representation relative to the benchmark. This analysis is combined with forecasts of the sector/regions. If the fund has less than the benchmark in a sector/region that does well, the fund will perform below average. If the fund has more than the benchmark in a sector/region which does poorly, the fund will also perform below average.

When taken together with market forecasts and the fund objectives, an analysis of the structure of the fund relative to the benchmark will suggest sector/region combinations to buy or sell.

3.5.3 Strengths, weaknesses, constraints

It is not wise to determine the fund's ideal objective without considering how easy it is to achieve. Implementation may be helped or hindered by a number of factors, a number of which have already been covered. Others include the following.

- The scope for changing the shape of a fund will depend on whether new money is coming in or money is being withdrawn. Cash inflows can create opportunities to change the fund shape, or to apply capital to active management. Cash outflows can create enormous pressures on performance, especially in an illiquid market.

- It is also necessary to consider practicalities: whether it will be possible to undertake the proposed level of sales and purchases in a sensible time. This is a particular concern in inactive or small markets and for large funds.
- Particularly for small funds, there may be stock-specific factors (such as lease renewals) which mean that the required sales cannot or should not be made.
- The cost of sales and purchases should be included in the analysis.
- The impact of taxation needs to be considered in some cases.
- For small funds, it may not be possible to gain exposure to large value markets with large lot sizes. Using unlisted funds may be an option, but this brings other challenges (see Chapter 7).
- The fund may not have the necessary expertise in-house and may require external advice.
- The timing of any change in strategy and changes in tactics is important: it is necessary to anticipate market movements and to buy and sell at the most advantageous moments. In property, as is the case with many investments, it is rarely time to buy or sell when the consensus agrees with you.

3.6 Structure and stock selection

The most commonly accepted way of summarizing the skills available to a property fund manager is to separate the performance impact of portfolio structure from the performance produced by stock selection. This is covered in more detail in Chapter 5.

3.6.1 Structure

In considering a plan for altering the structure of a portfolio, relevant issues include the appropriateness or otherwise of sector/region classifications, the accuracy and value of forecasts, and portfolio size as it impinges upon the manager's freedom to balance the portfolio across three, five, ten or 50 sector/regions. This will also be affected by research staff size and expertise and by the culture of the organization, which may or may not apply similar processes to those used for other asset classes.

It is natural for managers to attempt to reduce risk by matching the sector/region composition of an index. At the same time, managers may believe in their ability to spot underpricing in property types – for example, secondary or high yield property. In equity fund management, this is called style management. This risk control with a style bias can also be called tilting the portfolio. This involves creating a bias within an asset class. Thus, a fund could hold the benchmark proportion for the asset class but select particular types within the class. Examples in equities would include concentrating on the shares of small electronics companies within the electronics sector; a property example would be to concentrate on shopping centres within the retail sector; or, as above, concentrating on secondary or value-add investments.

Table 3.4: Target portfolio weights (%)

	ABC	Benchmark (ex. ABC)	Current ABC tilt	Target tilt	Position relative to target tilt
Standard shop units	11.8	17.2	–5.4	–7.5	2.1
Shopping centres	12.7	10.3	2.4	1.5	0.9
Retail warehouses	27.1	21.5	5.6	7.5	–1.9
All retail	**51.6**	**49.0**	**2.6**	**1.5**	**1.1**
City	10.9	5.1	5.8	2.0	3.8
West End/mid-town	7.0	5.3	1.7	5.0	–3.3
South-east offices	10.6	7.8	2.7	0.0	2.7
Rest of UK offices	0.5	6.8	–6.3	–4.5	–1.8
All office	**28.9**	**24.9**	**4.0**	**2.5**	**1.5**
South-east industrials	10.0	11.3	–1.3	1.5	–2.8
Rest of UK industrials	5.1	11.8	–6.7	–5.0	–1.7
All industrial	**15.1**	**23.1**	**–8.0**	**–3.5**	**–4.5**
Residential property	**3.8**	**0.0**	**3.8**	**2.5**	**1.3**
Other property	**0.7**	**3.0**	**–2.3**	**–3.0**	**0.7**
Total	100.0	100.0	0.0	0.0	0.0

Source: IPD/Manager

Note
Weightings are calculated on a GAV basis.

Table 3.4 illustrates a typical analysis of a current portfolio (the ABC fund) and a desired set of 'tilts' against the benchmark. The final column indicates a strategy for trading (meaning a need to buy and sell assets, so that, for example, some standard shop units need to be sold).

3.6.2 Stock selection

Forecasts (see Chapter 4) help to identify the sector/regions to buy. This provides a basis for stock selection (the buying and selling of individual properties) and focuses the work of those who have to identify actual buildings to buy or sell. The traditional approach to property investment has been to look for 'good' buildings, regardless of the impact on structure and consequent return and risk. However, an investment that appears 'good' in its own right need not be good in a portfolio context.

Forecasts may also be available at the city level and these forecasts might direct sales and purchases. Deeper analyses may suggest sub-sectors to buy or sell. But there is no doubt that individual property forecasts are most useful.

For small portfolios, it is essential to look at the individual buildings in the portfolio when considering strategy, and specific risk is an issue that will affect all direct property investors. Research by Morrell (1993) suggested that the impact of uneven lot sizes has a major impact on the risk of many portfolios. This is because the direct property market is characterized by assets which are both heterogeneous and indivisible. The ability of many portfolios to diversify away specific risk by holding many assets is often limited because a relatively small number of properties often accounts for a large proportion of the fund by value. (The impact of specific risk is also explored in Baum and Struempell (2006) and by Callender *et al.*, (2007).)

In addition, there may be some particular feature of a property which means it should be sold or not sold despite the sector/region weighting. Examples include potential marriage value, development potential, refurbishment potential, and leases which need to be re-negotiated before sale.

3.6.3 Passive and active strategies

Examining the capabilities of the investment or fund management organisation with particular respect to portfolio structure and stock selection enables a view to be formed regarding an appropriate strategy. This is summarized by Figure 3.2.

Figure 3.2: Passive and active strategies

	Market forecasting ability	
Stock selection skills	**Good**	**Poor**
Good	Concentrate on underpriced properties	Concentrate on underpriced properties
	Shift sector weights based on forecasts	Hold market weights
Poor	Diversify: hold many properties	Diversify: hold many properties
	Shift sector weights based on forecasts	Hold market weights

A large property investment fund or organization with a belief in its central research and forecasting capabilities might reasonably expect to add to its returns by taking active positions against a benchmark. This is the expected behaviour of a large balanced fund such as an open-ended fun run by a well-resourced fund manager.

An organization with a highly skilled and motivated acquisitions team which enjoys the benefit of asset-specific performance fees or carried interests (see above and Chapter 7) might reasonably be expected to focus on a small number of deals which it expects to add to performance rather than to buy a large number of properties whose performance will tend towards the mean return for the sector or market. This is the expected behaviour of a private equity real estate fund or opportunity fund.

True excellence might imply that the investment manager can both take sector positions and focus on good deals. Alternatively, realism, modesty, very thin resources or compensation packages that do not provide a performance fee or bonus might suggest holding benchmark sector weights and diversifying at the asset level in order to limit the tracking error of the fund relative to the benchmark.

Investors who employ fund managers should focus on their investment objectives and on the fee structures of their managers in order that behaviour appropriate to the investor's requirements is encouraged. Performance fees and carried interest have a particularly powerful effect: see Chapter 7.

3.6.4 Asset quality

Forecasts of the outlook for commercial real estate usually focus on the relative prospects for different segments of the market that are defined by sector and region, for example the expected returns from City of London offices relative to those for shopping centres. These indices mask within them a wide variation in performance, with individual assets delivering very different returns from the average recorded for the segment as a whole. However, investors should also pay attention to the structure of the portfolio, or the characterization of assets, by reference to investment quality (prime, secondary and tertiary, or core, value-added and opportunistic).

The rental trends for high quality assets, for example, are frequently perceived as being different from those of poor quality assets. The different income security of properties of varying investment quality is also perceived as crucial to asset pricing, regardless of property type or the location of the asset, reflecting the risk attached to the cash flow. Hence, according to Real Estate Strategies (2014), investment quality is a function of asset quality and income security. If asset quality and income security are shown to be major drivers of returns, then forecasts that differentiate between assets of different levels of quality and income security would provide investors with a better way of building a portfolio.

Figure 3.3: An investment quality taxonomy

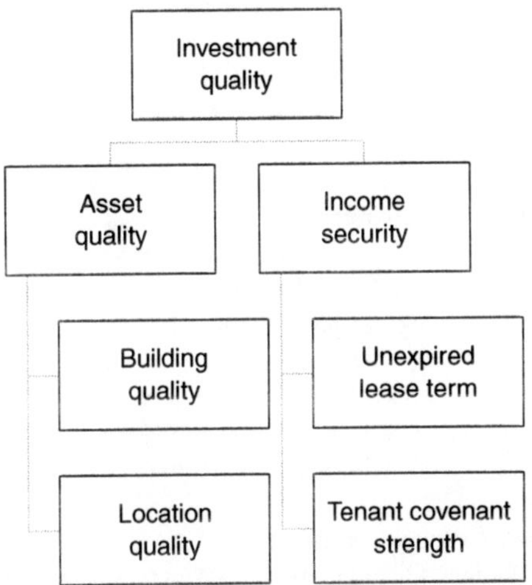

Source: Real Estate Strategies

Within any market, assets will have contrasting degrees of income security and strong asset quality will perform relatively well in weak markets, while poorer quality assets will out-perform in very strong markets. Another insight is that asset returns will vary over time, which reduces building quality through depreciation and erodes income security as leases shorten.

So, in addition to the property type and location, any asset can be considered to have two important investment characteristics that explain returns: these are asset quality and current income security. There is an interaction between income security and asset quality in determining asset returns, and this taxonomy allows further enhancements to asset allocation and portfolio risk management. If returns can be measured by type and region, asset quality and income security, then these risk/return characteristics can be used in portfolio structure. If these returns can be forecasted, then portfolio structure can be tilted to benefit.

3.7 Asset management

The slope of the 'yield curve' from low income security to high income security for an asset of the same quality can be used to quantify the opportunity for active lease management, such as extending a lease. A lease 're-gear' enhances the security of income, which is rewarded by a reduction of the appropriate cap rate and therefore a higher value. Similarly, the slope of the 'yield curve' from poor quality to high quality for an asset of the same degree of income security can be used to quantify the opportunity for refurbishment. This was further discussed by Goshawk/IPD in 2014's Asset Management Report, from which the following extract is taken.

> **Refurbishment**
> Expenditure on refurbishments is a fundamental and significant form of active asset management. Investors target expenditure to ensure a building remains fit for use and avoids functional, aesthetic and technological obsolescence. However, any expenditure by an investor will be a short term drag on return performance. The boost to relative performance will come if the cost of refurbishment expenditure is outweighed by future rental (and income) growth. In 2013, the relative contribution to total returns was +0.0 per cent, meaning expenditure was cancelled out by rental/income growth following refurbishment.
>
> **Re-gear**
> The re-gearing of leases is all about mitigating the risk of an investor's cash flow from a property. A longer lease, with fewer break clauses, means a more secure income and thus a more secure investment over a longer period of time, which will be valued more highly than a riskier property. This also means the investor will not have to re-let the property as soon as expected under the previous lease terms, meaning less risk of vacancy, and less exposure to the potential risk, cost and uncertainty of an earlier void period. Therefore, there is a strong incentive for investors to engage with lessees to renegotiate lease terms. In 2013, the re-gearing of leases provided a modest positive relative performance for investors, with a relative return of +0.07 per cent.
>
> **Break removal**
> A break clause in a lease means that a tenant could opt to break the lease on a certain date. Like lease expiries, this is another potential risk to an investor's cash flow, and the presence of a break clause often has negative impact on valuation. Therefore, there is an incentive for investors to negotiate terms with lessees to remove these clauses. Those who actively engaged with tenants in 2013 and mutually agreed to remove break options, often in return for a rental abatement, saw relative returns of +0.02 per cent. This would most likely result in a short-term fall-off in income, and the corresponding increase in value may not be realised until future yield compression kicks in.
>
> **Vacancy**
> Vacant properties proved a drag on performance, with a relative return of –0.09 per cent. Void properties are unrealised potential income. Any portfolio with a vacancy rate, or properties falling vacant during the period of analysis, are not realising their full income potential. Vacancies are also a cost burden for investors as maintenance, upkeep and rates must still be paid while a property is vacant.

Lettings

As would be expected, new lettings provided a boost to overall returns, with a relative return of +0.18 per cent. This was the largest contribution to asset management relative return in 2013. New lettings mean new income for an investor, improved security of cash flow and typically an enhanced capital value through a more favourable yield which recognises the elimination of the investor's void risk. Ensuring a property is producing a consistent income stream and vacancies are kept to a minimum is one of the most fundamental of active asset management activities.

3.8 Using forecasts and valuation models

3.8.1 Forecasts

At the national level it is possible to build econometric models linking rental growth in each sector to the main macroeconomic variables which influence rents, and to changes in supply. It is possible but a little more difficult to do this at the regional level; it is also necessary to have a view at the city level, but this is the most difficult to construct by using purely econometric methods.

Rental growth forecasts are the basic inputs into the valuation model (see Chapter 4). However, if all investors expected high rental growth, cap rates should fall to reflect this and total return would be reduced for buyers. On the other hand, low rental growth need not indicate poor performance. The important analysis is of price against value. The valuation model inputs are rental growth forecasts, assessments of depreciation and risk and the required return (see Chapter 4).

The valuation model inputs can be used to forecast returns for each sector/region. They can be regarded as forecasts of return (IRR) or as buy/sell rules (NPV). These forecasts are then used as inputs into portfolio analysis models.

We may suggest that forecasts are necessary and valuable. But there are suggestions from time to time that forecasts are of no value because even government economists make errors. Against this, it can be argued that the process which is created by forecasts is valuable in itself; but there is no denying that bad forecasts can damage performance. What is our experience?

In the 1990s Henderson Global Investors measured the accuracy of its forecasts by measuring the performance of a notional portfolio which is re-balanced annually by sector and region using one-, three- and five-year forecasts. The results are shown in Table 3.5.

Table 3.5: Forecasts and notional fund performance (%)

Target	0.5	1.0	2.0
National sectors	0.4	0.9	1.8
Retail regions	0.1	0.2	0.2
Office regions	0.2	0.4	0.9
Industrial regions	–0.2	–0.2	0.2
Regional total	0.1	0.2	0.5
Total	0.5	1.1	2.3
Tracking error	0.3	0.6	1.3

Source: Henderson Global Investors (now TIAA Henderson Real Estate)

For the optimized fund, we set a target of half of the total out-performance to be achieved through sector/national structure and a half through sector/region structure. The portfolio optimizer model was then run to create an appropriate fund structure. This structure is combined with achieved returns to calculate an out-performance figure. This out-performance figure relative to the specified target is a good indicator of the effectiveness of the return forecasts.

The first line posits the required level of out-performance against the index. The second line of the table represents the fund out-performance relative to the benchmark produced by the bets at the sector/national level. The next four lines represent the out-performance at the sector/region level as if each sector/region were a separate fund plus the total figure, which is the sum of the regional out-performance figures. The total out-performance, reported in the penultimate line, should be compared with the target. On average over the three years from 1991 to 1993, the optimized fund would have achieved or exceeded its objective.

Naturally, as the target performance increases, so does risk or tracking error. In addition, transaction costs which are the product of sector switches that are not necessary for stock selection or active management purposes will reduce the out-performance estimates by up to a half. This suggests that managers using forecasts in this simplistic way need to double the bets taken against the benchmark to achieve their structure-based return objective.

3.8.2 Valuation models

Many professionals believe that property markets are not efficient. As a result, it may be possible to identify cheap or expensive markets. Inefficient local markets can at certain times produce forecastable excess returns for investors using rational decision models, even without rent forecasts.

For example, consider office markets across Europe. In very simple terms, given economic and market fundamentals, the following factors, among others, are likely to hold for a set of non-domestic markets.

- Rents look low against other global markets.
- Capitalization rates look high against other property markets.
- Capitalization rates look high against other asset classes in the same domicile.
- Capitalization rates look high against other asset classes in the home market.

For example, in between 2009 and 2014 rents in Central London offices rebounded to all-time highs; yet rents in other major UK cities (for example, Birmingham) remained depressed. Given that capitalization rate differentials had remained broadly the same over the period and taking account of given reasonably similar demand and supply fundamentals (vacancy rates, economic growth forecasts and so on), an allocation choice between London or a set of non-London UK markets was clear. London was expensive relative to these markets.

The concept of rent pressure – a means of identifying markets where rents are higher or lower than spatial, demographic or economic fundamentals suggest – has been successfully applied by a small number of investors across UK cities for several years, with powerful performance implications.

In Chapter 4 we examine forecasting and pricing models in more detail.

3.9 The role of leverage

Large lot size assets can cause problems for real estate portfolio managers. It may be possible to use leverage secured against (say) a large London office building to reduce the equity capital allocated to that asset or sector and to enable the portfolio to be better diversified. Unfortunately, this does not work, because the sensitivity of the portfolio return to the asset return is driven by gross asset value, not net asset value.

For example, assume we have two equally valued investments, each worth £50 million. The portfolio value is £100 million. Assume one asset (A) is financed 100 per cent by equity, while the other (B) is financed by 50 per cent equity and 50 per cent debt, so that its gross asset value is £100 million.

If A doubles in value, the portfolio value rises by £50 million to £150 million, so that a 100 per cent increase in value in A is tempered to a 50 per cent rise in portfolio value through the effect of diversification across two assets, as we should expect.

If B doubles in value, the asset is now worth £200 million. Deducting the debt, we now have an investment worth £150 million and the portfolio value rises by £100 million to £200 million. Hence, the effect of portfolio diversification is cancelled out by the effect of leverage, and using different levels of debt secured against a range of assets can distort the portfolio.

Tyrell and Bostwick (2005) examined the role of leverage in real estate investments and developed an optimization approach. From a theoretical perspective, they argued, leverage should be preferred so long as the marginal increase in expected return per unit of extra risk from leverage exceeds that obtained from buying riskier assets. Since there are diminishing returns to leverage – primarily because costs rise as borrowing levels rise relative to value – this trade-off will become less attractive as leverage rises, leading to an equilibrium optimal level of leverage.

Farrelly (2012) developed a simulation framework to provide a practical framework for assessing the risk arising from financial leverage and providing a quantitative portfolio risk estimate. Simulating portfolio returns using historic return data and varying leverage levels, he found that portfolios with loan to value ratios exceeding 40 per cent do not provide attractive long-term risk adjusted returns (see Chapter 2). Leverage substantially increased downside risk, and its asymmetric impact on return requires risk measures (beyond standard deviation, which assumes normal distributions) that account for this.

3.10 Modelling the portfolio risk and return

The expected return on each asset in a portfolio should be modelled using a discounted cash flow procedure. The most attractive property will be the one for which the expected return exceeds the required return by the greatest amount (see Chapter 4). In most circumstances, this process may be optimal. However, in other circumstances it may not.

First, this ignores the impact of tax and gearing, which is dealt with in Chapter 9. Second, it ignores the impact of the purchase on the shape of the portfolio as a whole. Third, it ignores the different outlays involved. Is an excess return of 1 per cent on a £5 million outlay superior to an excess return of 0.5 per cent on an outlay of £10 million?

These latter two problems can be dealt with very simply in a portfolio model. The objective of a portfolio model is to forecast cash flows and values, year by year, on all buildings held within the portfolio, in such a form as to enable the manager to model the impact of altered expectations on portfolio performance. The model allows scenarios concerning purchases, leverage, major expenditure and sales to be explored. Hence, in the above example the impact on portfolio return – and, with the necessary inputs, risk – of the two alternative purchases may be appraised. This deals quite easily with the difference in outlays, as the optimal decision will be the one which (subject to risk) has the greatest positive impact on portfolio return. The impact on the shape of the portfolio and its risk profile is also easily dealt with in the model.

Table 3.6 shows how, assuming rising rental values and varying market capitalization rates, a single property moving through its five-year review pattern and valued using an annually in arrear equivalent yield approach will vary in capital value. There are three years until the rent review, and market capitalization rates fall and then rise over the period. The property enjoys a sharp fall in capitalization rate as it passes through its rent review, reducing the risk to the investor. The property's capital value is sensitive to four variables:

a the income, or rent passing;

b the estimated rental value;

c the period to the rent review; and

d the capitalization rate.

Table 3.6: Portfolio modelling (1)

Data	Year 0	Year 1	Year 2	Year 3	Year 4	Year 5
Income	£1,500,000	£1,500,000	£1,500,000	£2,050,000	£2,050,000	£2,050,000
ERV	£2,000,000	£2,000,000	£2,050,000	£2,100,000	£2,200,000	£2,220,000
Review term	3	2	1	5	4	3
Yield	7.50%	7.40%	7.00%	6.50%	7.25%	8.00%
Capital value	£25,366,404	£26,201,550	£28,771,696	£32,099,908	£29,733,893	£26,901,093

In Table 3.6 the impact of the changing value and rental income on the total return delivered by the property is shown, based on the following simple return definitions.

Income return is the net rent received over the measurement period divided by the value at beginning of period.

$$IR = Y_{0-1}/CV_0$$

Capital return is the change in value over the measurement period divided by the value at beginning of the period.

$$CR = [CV_1 - CV_0]/CV_0$$

Total return is the sum of income return and capital return.

$$TR = [Y_{0-1} + CV_1 - CV_0]/CV_0$$

Table 3.7: Portfolio modelling (2)

	Year 0	Year 1	Year 2	Year 3	Year 4	Year 5
Capital value	£25,366,404	£26,201,550	£28,771,696	£32,099,908	£29,733,893	£26,901,093
Income	–	£1,500,000	£1,500,000	£1,500,000	£2,050,000	£2,050,000
Income return	–	5.91%	5.72%	5.21%	6.89%	7.62%
Capital return	–	3.29%	9.81%	11.57%	–7.37%	–9.53%
Total return	–	9.21%	15.53%	16.78%	–0.48%	–1.91%

Table 3.7 shows the results. As the capital value rises and falls, the capital return is strongly positive, then negative. The income return is less volatile. The total return rises and falls in line with changes in capital value.

Combining this data for one property into an aggregate table describing all properties in the portfolio allows the portfolio return going forward to be modelled. Most importantly, different scenarios can be modelled, not only for out-turns of rental growth and capitalization rate movements, but also for sales from the portfolio, additions of new buildings and so on. In addition, a full risk model can be developed, using simulation to model all possible portfolio cash flows and measure the resulting spread of returns, or risk.

For advanced applications, financing and taxation impacts need to be dealt with, and the portfolio model can be adapted to facilitate linkages to portfolio and facilities management systems and client reporting.

The portfolio model can also be developed further into an arbitrage pricing system, designed to explore the sensitivity of portfolio return to various economic and capital market factors, such as changes in rates of interest, changes in expected inflation rates, changes in the value of sterling and other relevant factors.

Portfolio performance measurement is more fully addressed in Chapter 5.

Box 3.1 Portfolio distress, 2007–9

The following facts are based on a real case, but facts have been altered and names are fictitious.

In 2005, pension fund A appointed manager B to act as A's professional investment manager and property adviser. Fund A's desired risk profile in respect of its property portfolio was 'medium'. In 2006, manager B proposed that fund A should diversify its portfolio and invest 8 per cent of its total property allocation in a high quality, prime, office building in London. Due to the high lot size of this asset, manager A recommended that fund B should purchase the property through an SPV funded by both equity (8 per cent of the allocation) and debt. The debt element was 75 per cent of the purchase price of the asset. There was no debt elsewhere in the portfolio.

Post-acquisition, the value of the property fell and the lending bank took over the asset and sold it to recover its loan. A small amount of equity was released, but fund A lost most of its equity.

Did manager B act prudently? Was the investment a medium-risk investment or a high-risk investment? Given that the debt finance provided was subject to an 80 per cent LTV value covenant which would be breached if the property's value fell by as little as 5 per cent, was a 5 per cent decline in value a foreseeable likelihood?

Table 3.8 proves data describing the volatility of the UK sectors.

Table 3.8: Standard deviation of returns, IPD PAS segments, 1981–2006/11

Segment	to 2006	to 2011
PAS standard retail south-east	8.1	9.3
PAS standard retail rest UK	6.8	8.8
PAS shopping centre	6.3	9.2
PAS retail warehouse	8.5	11.3
PAS office City	12.2	13.0
PAS office West End and mid-town	13.9	14.1
PAS office rest south-east	9.2	10.1
PAS office rest UK	8.2	9.8
PAS industrial south-eastern	9.4	10.8
PAS industrial rest UK	8.8	10.4

Source: IPD

How sensitive was the return on the portfolio to the return on the leveraged asset? Should we be concerned by exposure to its gross asset value or net asset value? Consequently, was the portfolio well diversified?

15 per cent would be a typical limit for exposure to a single asset. The NAV of the office represented 7.9 per cent of the investor's real estate capital to a single asset. However, the investor's exposure to this asset measured by its gross asset value was over 25 per cent of the portfolio.

To judge whether the portfolio was reasonably well diversified can be judged by reference to its constitution relative to the IPD benchmark in two respects: (i) by portfolio structure and (ii) by asset concentration. Each of these needs to be judged relative to the portfolio size, which was not large and limited the ability of the manager to achieve a spread of risk both by number of assets and by creating a structure which is a close match to the benchmark. The reported portfolio shape (by net asset value) relative to the IPD benchmark (reported second) was as follows:

all retails, 27 per cent v. 45 per cent (shopping centres, 0 per cent v. 17 per cent);

all offices, 49 per cent v. 36 per cent (Central London, 12 per cent v. 15 per cent);

all industrials, 16 per cent v. 15 per cent;

other commercial, 0 per cent v. 4 per cent;

unattributed indirects, 8 per cent v. 0 per cent.

(The SPV is accounted for as the 'unattributed indirect'.)

What do you think?

4 Pricing real estate: the purchase and sale process

4.1 Introduction

In this chapter, we set out a simple process which investors and fund managers can use to identify attractive markets and properties, and to decide which markets and assets should be sold. This pricing model can be applied at all levels: asset classes, countries, market sectors and possibly for individual assets. However, it is a simplified approach used primarily in developing a strategy, and is not a substitute for the type of detailed cash flow analysis which is necessary to set out accurately the prospective returns available from a property asset taking account of the lease contract, leverage, tax and costs. (For more on this, see Baum and Hartzell, 2012.)

In this chapter we also discuss the purchase and sale process in the context of the investment strategy decision. Buying and selling properties involves a series of processes (see Chapter 3). First, the ideal portfolio structure needs to be determined. Once this target structure is in place, the manager needs to identify which market sub-segments are attractively priced and should be targeted. Next, stock needs to be sourced from the market. Appraisals of the available properties need to be undertaken. In addition, the impact of proposed purchases on portfolio risk and return needs to be modelled.

In the acquisition process, negotiation skills need to be employed; and 'due diligence' needs to be carried out. Due diligence describes the legal, physical and planning enquiries and explorations prior to exchange of contracts and completion that are necessitated by the unique nature of the asset type.

It is also necessary to think about the demands placed on the investor when selling property. In the sales process, the issues to be considered again include appraisal and assessing the impact on portfolio risk and return, but also require specific reference to the tax and cash/gearing impacts of a sale, as well as the process of broker appointment, sales and marketing.

In this book we make only passing reference to the separate skills and disciplines involved in marketing, negotiation and sales and in diligence processes. Instead we concentrate on the research and high level (strategic, or top-down) appraisal process used in property acquisitions and sales. When should investors decide that a market, a sector or a property is attractively or unattractively priced, and once this decision has been taken how does an acquisition proceed? We begin with the latter before dealing with the appraisal process in detail in Section 4.4 onwards.

4.2 Sourcing stock

Many property fund managers pride themselves on their access to stock, due either to a large scale of operation leading to a high number of transactions being offered, or on their carefully nurtured relationships with brokers and vendors in the market. Buying 'off-market' has become a watchword for doing good deals, and consultants who advise on manager selection are often very concerned with a fund manager's access to market information and buying opportunities.

The property acquisition process has not yet been transformed by the opportunities offered by the internet. Ideally, all vendors of property investments would access a common website, post details of the properties they wish to sell as well as the types of properties they are interested in buying and execute a transaction on line. However, the subtleties of this process make its complete substitution by a successful internet-based trading market unlikely for larger and more complex commercial property, certainly for some time. This type of facility has been more useful for the registration of introductions, information transfer and monitoring of marketing programmes.

While internet-based property investment sites have been useful in automating the marketing and registration process, brokers and principals (owners) have remained in control of the purchase and sale process. The investment property market remains de-centralized and somewhat inefficient, and is dependent upon the interpersonal skills of buyers, sellers and brokers operating in the complex market web of telephone, e-mail and socializing. In addition, the potential buyer will need to be able to command loyalty from brokers if he or she wishes to access the appropriate quantity and quality of deals. This will often depend upon his perceived trustworthiness in following through on offers.

Brokers can act as very effective agents for vendors if they are able to establish a relationship with their client, as well as improving the efficiency of the market by matching buyers and sellers and recommending buyers who are most likely to proceed with the deal at the required price. Typically, fund managers will use a property registration system to record the invitations to treat which are delivered in the form of posted or e-mailed particulars and determine the broker's right to charge a commission on completion of the sale. This process is under strain, however, as investors begin to source more deals directly and value specialist advice, challenging the concept of a commission for a mere introduction.

Brokers may be retained by vendors, which means they will not seek commissions from purchasers. Alternatively, they may act on an unretained basis, seeking a commission from the purchaser and expecting to undertake advisory analysis work to help the client to make an informed decision. The quality of this advice will increase the chances of repeat commissions, just as the reliability of the purchaser will increase the quality of offers from retained and especially unretained agents, who will lose the opportunity to act for another purchaser if they spend too much time advising their first choice.

Vendors will use their brokers to help decide on the appropriate course of action when offers are made. A contract may be offered to a purchaser at a certain price, but whether this happens will depend not only upon the price offered but also upon the buyer's trustworthiness and creditworthiness and the quality of other offers. Often, a second buyer will be kept in the wings in case the due diligence process throws up a reason – or excuse – for the purchaser to re-negotiate or 'chip' the price.

The nature this sale process contributes to the illiquidity of the asset class (see Chapter 1, Crosby and McAllister, 2004, and Devaney and Scofield, 2014), and there are regular attempts to improve efficiency by encouraging vendors to keep adequate information so that properties are put, and remain, in a state of 'readiness for sale'.

4.3 Due diligence: the building purchase process

In brief, this crucial aspect of the property purchase decision involves the employment of specialist property skills, in-house or out-house, to ensure that the asset being appraised is all that it appears to be. The introducing agent may be expected to produce an external valuation report, including comparable evidence and opinions concerning the strength of the local market. Whether this can be regarded as impartial professional advice will depend upon the broker and the buyer's relationship with him. Where debt is involved, a truly independent valuation may be commissioned.

Often a purchase will be subject to board approval. This will be a true corporate board in the case of property or special purpose companies, or an internal committee in the case of most institutions. Surveys dealing with building structure and in some cases with land contamination, are likely to be required. Finally, legal advice will be used to check ownership and the quality of the lease contract and the purchase contract.

4.4 A property appraisal model

4.4.1 Introduction: the excess return

A key part of the due diligence process is the appraisal. According to Baum and Crosby (2008), it is important to distinguish between three concepts.

- Value is the investment worth of an asset, or the true equilibrium price of an asset traded in a market where full information is available.
- Price is the market's estimate of value.
- A valuation of property is usually an estimate of the most likely selling price.

This section establishes a basic framework for the estimation of the value or investment worth of an asset and how it can be compared to price for buy and sell decisions, or (in other words) whether a property will deliver its required or target return. The investor will typically buy in or undertake research aimed at enabling a view to be formed of rental growth and movements in cap rates (commonly but misleadingly called yields), usually derived from a view of the economy and other capital markets, determine a target rate of return for an asset and use a discounted cash flow approach to judge whether a property is likely to achieve that target. Appraisal models will usually be fed with projected rents and cap rates. The investor's view of the value of the asset will typically be arrived at by using discounted cash flow, with internal rate of return the typical buying rule despite a clear view among academics that net present value produces a superior decision. It is not surprising that a total return or IRR measure is used in appraisals when the manager's objective is framed in terms of a total return, but the IRR rule may produce sub-optimal decisions. (However, NPV can also be criticized by those familiar with option pricing techniques.)

The value of an investment is the present value of its expected income stream discounted at a rate which reflects its risk. However, any estimate of value depends on the views of the investor making the estimates, and is subjective (for more about this, see Baum and Crosby, 2008). Price may therefore differ from value in a variety of circumstances, for example if the vendor has to make a forced sale for any reason, or if the investor has different views or better information, or is better able to use the available information.

(Investors may be more interested in the return on equity after tax and fees: see Chapters 2 and 9.)

4.4.2 The initial yield – a simple price indicator

The property types and segments described in Chapter 2 have differing qualities which are translated into the price paid for a standard unit. It is sometimes useful to describe property prices in terms of a single unit price per acre, hectare, square metre or square foot; more often, prices are described in terms of initial or equivalent yield.

In theory the standard multiple applied to the unit of rent could more usefully be used as a unit of comparison. For example, a retail property leased for £100,000 a year which sells for £2 million shows a multiplier of 20. This property would be regarded as superior to one whose multiplier was 12.5. This measure is commonly used in some markets, most notably Germany.

However, the reciprocal of the multiplier (100 per cent divided by the multiplier), known as the cap rate, or the initial yield, or the all-risks yield, is the common measure used. Hence a retail property leased for £100,000 rent a year which sells for £2 million shows a multiplier of 20 and more importantly a yield of 5 per cent; an industrial property leased for £100,000 a year which sells for £1.25 million shows a lower multiplier of 12.5 and conversely a higher yield of 8 per cent.

Why would a purchaser of typical industrial property require a higher initial income per £100 invested (and therefore pay a lower multiplier) than he would from a prime retail property or, in other words, what makes an industrial property less attractive to a purchaser? One way of attacking this problem is to use a constant growth model, which suggests (assuming that yields do not change) that the initial yield is a function of the total required return less the net growth in income which is expected.

$$\text{Initial yield} = \text{required return} - \text{net income growth}$$

The required return is itself a function of the *risk free rate* and a *risk premium*; and the net income growth is a function of the rate of *rental growth* expected for new buildings in the market and the rate of *depreciation* suffered by a property as it ages. In full:

$$\text{Initial yield} = \text{risk free rate} + \text{risk premium} - \text{market rental growth} + \text{depreciation}$$

The closest available proxy for the *risk free rate* is the yield to redemption on fixed interest bonds. The cash flow for the bond, especially a government bond, is certain; the investment is liquid; and it is cheap to manage.

The *risk premium* covers factors such as:

a uncertainty regarding the expected cash flow, both income and capital;

b illiquidity; and

c management costs.

Rental growth is the rate at which the rental value of a new building at some date in the future is expected to be higher than the current rental value of a new building. It can be separated into two components: growth in line with inflation and 'real' growth, that is growth in excess of general inflation. So market rental growth can be expanded as follows:

$$\text{Market rental growth} = \text{inflation} + \text{real growth}$$

Depreciation is the rate at which the rental value of a property falls away from the rental value of an otherwise similar new property as a function of physical deterioration and of functional or aesthetic obsolescence (see Chapter 1). Hence:

$$\text{Initial yield} = \text{risk free rate} + \text{risk premium} - \text{inflation} - \text{real growth} + \text{depreciation}$$

Another way of arranging this formula allows us to compare the required return with the expected return:

$$\text{Risk free rate} + \text{risk premium} = \text{inflation} + \text{real growth} - \text{depreciation} + \text{initial yield}$$

Table 4.1 shows how typical yields for good quality properties in the major segments may be explained by different values for these variables. In each case the risk free rate plus the risk premium comprise the required total return from the investment, or hurdle rate; from this rate is deducted the expectation of net rental growth (inflationary growth plus real growth less depreciation) to produce the appropriate initial or all-risks yield. If future changes in yields are ignored, note that the total return expected for the investment is the initial yield plus net rental growth. So, for example, the required return on standard shops is (5.5%+2%=) 7.5 per cent; the expected return is (5%+2%+1%−0.5%=) 7.5 per cent.

In the following section, we explain how this process can be developed.

4.4.3 The Fisher equation

The Fisher equation (Fisher, 1930) considers the components of total return delivered by an investment. It states that:

$$R = l + i + RP$$

where:
R is the total required return;
l is a reward for liquidity preference (deferred consumption);
i is expected inflation;
RP is the risk premium;
'l' is given by the required return on index-linked government bonds (let us assume 2 per cent). '$l+i$' is the required return on conventional government bonds or gilts (for simplicity, ignoring an inflation risk premium: let us assume 4.5 per cent). These may be regarded, respectively, as the real and nominal risk free rates (RF_R and RF_N). Note that if we assume that there is no inflation risk premium in the pricing of the bond $RF_N = RF_R + i$, and $RF_N - RF_R = i$, so i appears to be 4.5%−2%=2.5%.

Table 4.1: Indicative sector/region yields (%)

Sector	RFR*	+	Risk premium	–	Inflation	–	Real growth	+	Depreciation	=	Initial yield
Standard shops	5.5		2		2		1		0.5		5
Shopping centres	5.5		3		2		1		1.5		7
Retail warehouses	5.5		2.5		2		1		0.5		5.5
Central London offices	5.5		2		2		0		1		6.5
Secondary offices	5.5		4		2		0		2		9.5
Industrials	5.5		4		2		–1		1.5		10.0

Note
* Risk free rate.

While RF_N can be measured by examining the redemption yield offered by bonds, the required risk premium on any asset is expectations-based and is therefore harder to estimate. For equities a reasonable estimate might currently be 2.5 per cent (for an approach to measurement, see below, from Aswath Damodoran's blog).

There are three ways of estimating an equity risk premium. One is to look at the difference between the average historical return you would have earned investing in stocks and the return on a risk free investment. This historical premium for the 1928–2013 time period would have stood at about 4.2 per cent, if computed as the difference in compounded returns on US stocks and on the ten-year US treasury bond. (I know. I know. We can have a debate about whether the US treasury is truly risk free, but that is a discussion for a different forum.) The second is to survey portfolio managers, CFOs or investors about what they think stocks will generate as returns in future periods and back out the equity risk premium from these survey numbers. In early 2013, that survey premium would have yielded between 3.8 per cent (from the CFO survey) to 4.8 per cent (portfolio managers) to 5 per cent (analysts). Finally, you can back out a forward looking premium, based upon current stock prices and expected cash flows, akin to estimating the yield to maturity on a bond. That is the process that I use at the start of every month to compute the ERP for US stocks...

The link between real and nominal risk free rates is given by Fisher (1930). The return available on index-linked gilts selling at par is the coupon plus realized inflation. The real return therefore equates closely with the coupon.

This rate is defined by Fisher as the reward for time preference. Investors, according to Fisher, also require a reward for expected inflation, otherwise investment in real assets would be preferable and paper-based investments such as conventional gilts would sell at lower prices. Hence if 4.5 per cent were available on 15-year gilts, this might include 2 per cent for inflation and 2.5 per cent for liquidity preference.

However, for an investor interested in real returns (say an immature pension fund) conventional gilts are less attractive than index-linked gilts. There is a risk of inflation expectations not being realized, so that higher than expected inflation will lead to lower than expected returns; and, second, there is a general discounting of investments where investments are risky. In a market dominated by investors with real liabilities, risky (in real terms) conventional gilts would be discounted, meaning the required return would be higher. If required returns equal the available return in an efficient market, then the 4.5 per cent available on the conventional gilt must include a risk premium. Following Fisher again, the full explanation of a required return is

$$R = l + i + RP$$

If an inflation risk premium of 0.5 per cent in the pricing of the conventional gilt is assumed, the rate of expected inflation implied by a comparison of index-linked and conventional bond yields is 2 per cent.

Let us assume that RP is 3 per cent. The Fisher equation can then be rewritten as:

$$R = RF_N + RP$$

R is 4.5%+3%=7.5% in this case.

4.4.4 A simple cash flow model

Consider a simple nominal cash flow:

I is the constant income, received annually in arrears

R is the discount rate (the required return, consisting of a risk free rate (*RFN*) and a risk premium (*RP*))

Then investment value (*V*) is found as follows:

$$V = I/(1+R) + I/(1+R)^2 + \ldots (I/(1+R)^n + \ldots$$

The discounted cash flow is a geometric progression which simplifies to:

$$V = I/R$$

or

$$I/V = R \text{ (the } \textit{correct} \text{ yield)}$$

It is then possible to compare *R* with *I/P* (the *current market* yield) to determine if the asset is mispriced. This is a simple valuation model which ignores the possibility of income growth. In equilibrium, the current market yield would be 7.5 per cent in our example.

4.4.5 Gordon's growth model (constant income growth)

Expected income growth became embedded in the behaviour of equity and property investors by the late 1950s in the UK. It became necessary to extend the simple cash flow model by introducing a constant rate of growth in nominal income (G_N). Following Gordon (1962), let us assume 3 per cent constant growth in rents, which is received annually in arrear but agreed annually in advance.

$$V = I/(1+R) + [I(1+G_N)/(1+R)^2] + [I(1+G_N)^2/(1+R)^3] + \ldots [I(1+G_N)^{n-1}/(1+R)^n]$$

Again, this is a geometric progression which simplifies to:

$$V = I/(R - G_N)$$

or:

$$I/V = R - G_N \text{ (the } \textit{correct} \text{ yield)}$$

Where *P* is price, it is then possible to compare ($R-G_N$) (7.5%−3%=4.5%) (the correct yield) with *I/P* (the current market yield). If the correct yield exceeds the current market yield the asset should be sold, or not bought; if the current market yield exceeds the correct yield the asset should be bought, or held.

4.4.6 A property valuation model including depreciation

The analysis can now be extended by introducing a constant rate of depreciation (D). This produces (approximately):

$$I/V = R - G_N + D \text{ (the correct yield)}$$

Let us assume a constant depreciation rate of 2 per cent. It is then possible to compare $R-G_N+D$: 7.5%−3%+2%=6.5%) with I/P (the current market yield).

Alternatively, it is possible to compare the required return:

$$R = RF_N + RP$$

with the expected return:

$$(I/P) + G_N - D$$

The comparison of required return with expected return is equivalent to comparing correct yield with current yield. The correct yield is 'value' and the current is 'price'.

In more simple terms, let us call the initial yield K. Then, in equilibrium, and assuming annual growth in rent,

$$K = R - G_N + D$$

and

$$\underbrace{RF_N + RP}_{\textit{required return}} = \underbrace{K + G_N - D}_{\textit{expected return}}$$

When markets cannot be assumed to be in equilibrium:

if $K > R - G_N + D$, buy;
if $K < R - G_N + D$, sell;
if $RF_N + RP > R - G_N + D$, sell; and
if $RF_N + RP < R - G_N + D$, buy.

In our example, let us assume a current market yield of 4.5 per cent. In this case:

$4.5\% < (7.5\% - 3\% + 2\%)$, and
$(4.5\% + 3\%) > (4.5\% + 3\% - 2\%)$

so the market is a sell.

This is a simple framework, assuming that property behaves as a pure equity investment with annually reviewed rents and (in addition) perpetually flat yields. The real word is somewhat more complicated. Rents may be fixed for periods of time, or indexed, or stepped. As a useful progression from this simple world, therefore, property cash flows need to be explicitly modelled; and the cash flow will reveal that the asset may have the characteristics of an equity, or a bond, or both.

This complexity needs to be reflected in the two component parts of an appraisal. These are the cash flow forecast and the discount rate.

4.5 The model components

The fundamental equivalent yield relationship is given by:

$$K = R - G_N + D$$

Given that both the risk free rate and growth have both real and inflation components, this can be expanded as follows:

$$K = RFR_R + i + Rp - (G_R + i - D)$$

where:
K = the property initial yield;
RFR_R = the real risk free rate;
Rp = the risk premium;
G_R = expected long-term real rental growth;
i = expected inflation;
D = depreciation.

This process requires estimates of K, RFR_R, Rp, I, G_R and D for the market or sector. These are dealt with in turn below, using as an example the UK market in 2014.

4.5.1 The risk free rate

This is defined as the expected redemption yield on the benchmark ten-year government bond at the exit date. This was (at October 2014) around 3 per cent.

4.5.2 The risk premium

We estimated a value for the expected long-term risk premium for the property market as 3 per cent, the mean of a historic range. Our evidence for 3 per cent comes from an analysis of *ex post* delivered returns on the property market minus returns on risk free assets (treasury bills) adjusted for changes in the expected attractiveness of the asset class. Figure 4.1 profiles the historic risk premium over the period 1920–2004.

It can be seen from Figure 4.1 that the delivered risk premium has shown considerable variation over the period, varying between extreme values of almost plus/minus 30 per cent. We have used the historic profile to help inform our view on what the expected average risk premium is likely to be in the long term.

Table 4.2 summarizes some of the basic statistics on a sub-period basis. The sub-periods are chosen to reflect the different sources of data making up the long-term historic profile. The delivered risk premium is a flawed measure of the estimated future risk premium, which should be expectations-based. However, plausible forward estimates are produced by an adjusted historic analysis. The mean long-term delivered risk premium has been close to 3 per cent, but has fallen over the analysis period.

Figure 4.1: Annual delivered risk premia, 1921–2013

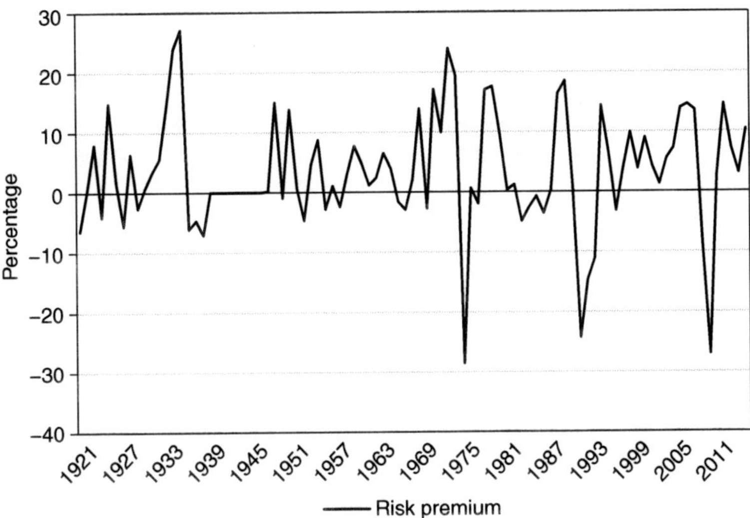

Source: PFR, IPD

Table 4.2: Annual average risk premia: supporting statistics (%)

Period	1921–38 (18 years)	1947–70 (24 years)	1971–2013 (43 years)	1981–2013 (33 years)	1921–2013 (85 years)
Risk premium	3.84	3.69	3.5	2.5	3.6
Min.	-7.11	-4.69	-28.5	-27.0	-28.5
Max.	27.15	17.15	24.0	18.5	27.2
SD	10.34	6.22	11.9	10.8	10.2
Jarque-Bera	2.80	2.59	7.19	6.15	9.74

Source: PFR

The message that emerges is that the average risk premium over different periods has varied within a narrow range. Indeed, it is statistically difficult to distinguish between risk premium figures ranging from 1.4 to 3.8 per cent. A rounded mean value of 3 per cent with a tolerance of 1 per cent either way is supportable.

4.5.3 Inflation

Long-term inflation expectations can be set at the government's target inflation rate of 2 per cent, in line with market consensus expectations.

4.5.4 Real rental growth

Table 4.3 shows the historic values of nominal and real rental growth at the segment level. Negative real rental growth of 0.5 per cent is the average for all property.

Table 4.3: Segment rental growth, 1981–2013 (%)

Segment	Nominal rental growth	Inflation	Real rental growth
Standard shop	3.57	4.00	–0.4
Shopping centre	4.05	4.00	0.1
Retail warehouse	4.45	4.00	0.5
City office	1.83	4.00	–2.2
Mid-town office	2.77	4.00	–1.2
West End office	3.40	4.00	–0.6
Rest of south-east office	1.30	4.00	–2.7
Rest of UK office	2.73	4.00	–1.3
Business park	2.06	4.00	–1.9
South-east industrial	2.25	4.00	–1.8
Rest of UK industrial	2.13	4.00	–1.9
Distribution warehouse	2.02	4.00	–2.0
All property	2.93	4.00	–1.1

Source: PFR, IPD

4.5.5 Depreciation

Table 4.4 shows depreciation expectations at the segment level based on research undertaken over a period of years by various researchers, the latest of which is Investment Property Forum (2011). Mean deprecation of 0.75 per cent is the all property average.

Table 4.4: Rental depreciation

Office	0.8
Industrial	0.5
Standard shop – south-eastern	1.0
Standard shop – rest of UK	0.0 (adjusted)
Shopping centres	0.1
Retail warehouses	0.9
Office – City	0.5
Office – West End	1.1
Office – south-eastern	0.8
Office – rest of UK	1.8
Industrial – south-eastern	0.3
Industrial – rest of UK	1.0
All property	0.75 (adjusted)

Source: IPF, 2011

4.5.6 'Correct' yields

Using the relationship $K = RFR_N + Rp - (G_R - i + D)$, the correct yield level emerging from the reported components is shown in Table 4.5.

Table 4.5: 'Correct' yields (1)

	RFR_N	$+Rp$	$-G_R$	$-i$	$+D$	$=K$
Mean	3.0	3.0	–1.0	2.0	0.75	5.75

Source: PFR

Table 4.5 suggests a correct fundamental yield level of 5.75 per cent as at the end of 2014, compared with the same value of 6.25 per cent in 2005 reported in the second edition of this book. At that time, we commented that any continued yield falls would push the market into over-pricing – see Box 4.1. (Yields continued to fall for two more years, followed by a 45 per cent fall in values over the 2008–9 period. In 2014, many prime London properties were selling at cap rates of below 4 per cent.)

4.6 A real analysis

Section 4.5 suggests that the equivalent yield is driven by fundamentals: gilt yields, risk premium and growth expectations. However, there is a very strong long-run correlation (37 per cent on an annual basis) between inflation and rental growth. If property is alternatively seen as an inflation hedge, the risk free benchmark is the index-linked gilt and not the conventional gilt yield.

The fundamental equivalent yield relationship is given by:

$$K = RFR_N + Rp - G_R - i + D \text{ or}$$

$$K = RFR_N + Rp - (G_r + i - D)$$

This presumes that the risk free benchmark for investors is the conventional (fixed interest) gilt, which is regarded as defining the nominal risk free rate.

If the index linked gilt yield (RFR_R) is used and the equation is expressed in real terms, this becomes:

$$K = RFR_R + Rp - (G_R - D)$$

Current values for these variables at late 2014 in the UK are shown in Table 4.6.

Table 4.6: 'Correct' yields (2)

	RFR_R	$+Rp$	$-G_R$	$+D$	$=K$
Mean	1.0	3.0	–1.0	0.75	5.75

Source: PFR

As the market increased in price during 2006, yields fell considerably below this 'correct' level. By January 2009, yields had risen back above the 'correct' level, suggesting a rise in the risk premium, a fall in expected growth, both of these or a cheap market. In late 2014, yields were back below the 'correct' level.

Box 4.1 'Correct' asset class yields

Table 4.7 shows the initial yields available on a group of asset classes. Each asset class has a required return, determined by the real risk free rate (liquidity preference), expected inflation and a risk premium. For each asset class it is possible to estimate an expected return, determined by the income return (initial yield, or capitalization rate), plus the expected growth in income, less depreciation.

Table 4.7: Asset pricing analysis (1)

	RFR_R	$+i$	$+RP$	=	K	$+G_N$	$-D$
Indexed bonds	–	–	–		1.5	–	–
Government bonds	–	–	–		4.0	–	–
Equities	–	–	–		2.5	–	–
Property	–	–	–		6.5	–	–
Japanese bonds	–	–	–		2.0	–	–
Cash	–	–	–		3.5	–	–

The initial yield on an indexed bond defines the real risk free rate. The difference between the yield on fixed interest government bonds and the yield on indexed bonds is explained by expected inflation plus a small risk premium to deal with the possibility of the inflation expectation failing to be delivered. If we take an inflation risk premium of 0.5 per cent, deductive reasoning suggests that 2 per cent is the expected inflation rate. The indexed bond will deliver 2 per cent growth in income through indexation. In equilibrium, the indexed bond is set to deliver a total return of 3.5 per cent, the required return. The fixed interest bond will deliver a total return of 4 per cent, out-performing the indexed bond to compensate for the inflation risk.

Table 4.8: Asset pricing analysis (2)

	RFR_R	$+i$	$+RP$	=	K	$+G_N$	$-D$
Indexed bonds	1.5	2.0	0.0	=	1.5	2.0	0.0
Government bonds	1.5	2.0	0.5	=	4.0	0.0	0.0
Equities	1.5	–	–		2.5	–	–
Property	1.5	–	–		6.5	–	–
Japanese bonds	1.5	–	–		2.0	–	–
Cash	1.5	–	–		3.5	–	–

The real risk free rate is common to all asset classes. Equities and property are risky assets, riskier than bonds, and an investor will require a risk premium to compensate for this. Equities are more volatile than property, but property returns are smoothed and property is very illiquid, so a higher risk premium (4 per cent compared to 3.5 per cent for equities) might be justified.

In order that the market analysis is in equilibrium, income growth for equities will have to be 4.5 per cent, assuming that depreciation is not an issue because it is dealt with by depreciation allowances in the profit and loss account. If inflation of 2 per cent is expected, real growth in earnings of 2.5 per cent – roughly the long-term rate of UK economic growth – is needed. For property, assuming average depreciation of 1 per cent across all sectors in line with the research studies described in Chapter 1, rents need to grow at the rate of inflation.

Equities are then set to deliver their required return of 7 per cent, and property will deliver 7.5 per cent.

Table 4.9: Asset pricing analysis (3)

	RFR_R	$+i$	$+RP$	=	K	$+G_N$	$-D$
Indexed bonds	1.5	2.0	0.0	=	1.5	2.0	0.0
Government bonds	1.5	2.0	0.5	=	4.0	0.0	0.0
Equities	1.5	2.0	3.5	=	2.5	4.5	0.0
Property	1.5	2.0	4.0	=	6.5	2.0	1.0
Japanese bonds	1.5	–	–		2.0	–	–
Cash	1.5	–	–		3.5	–	–

What is the required return for a UK investor buying Japanese bonds? As a UK investor, say a pension fund, the investor's liabilities will be denominated in sterling. It is UK inflation that is important, and the required return is not affected by inflation prospects in Japan. There is, however, a risk above and beyond that involved in the purchase of UK government bonds. The income and capital return delivered by a Japanese bond is paid in yen, and the yen/sterling exchange rate will change over time, so that the income in sterling is uncertain and may be volatile. A risk premium of 2 per cent is assumed. The required return is then 5.5 per cent, and to deliver this income growth of 3.5 per cent is needed.

However, as we shall see in Chapter 9, the market's expectation of yen appreciation is defined as the difference in interest rates – in this case represented by bond yields – in the two economies, only 2 per cent in this case. Hence Japanese bonds are not attractive to UK buyers. This does not mean that the market is not priced in equilibrium: simply that the likely buyer, whose natural habitat this investment represents, is not based in the UK.

Cash – say six month deposits – is risk free and offers neither income growth (interest rates would have to rise to deliver this) nor depreciation. As in all other asset classes except Japanese bonds, the market offers the return which is required.

Table 4.10: Asset pricing analysis (4)

	RFR_R	$+i$	$+RP$	=	K	$+G_N$	$-D$
Indexed bonds	1.5	2.0	0.0	=	1.5	2.0	0.0
Government bonds	1.5	2.0	0.5	=	4.0	0.0	0.0
Equities	1.5	2.0	3.5	=	2.5	4.5	0.0
Property	1.5	2.0	4.0	=	6.5	2.0	1.0
Japanese bonds	1.5	2.0	2.0	No	2.0	2.0	0.0
Cash	1.5	2.0	0.0	=	3.5	0.0	0.0

The complications introduced by cross-border investing are dealt with in detail in Chapter 9.

4.7 The required return: additional analysis

4.7.1 The risk free rate and the yield curve

Simplistically, the risk free rate is the redemption yield on government bonds for the matched life. To be accurate, the yield curve should be taken into account, meaning that the appropriate discount rate will be different for incomes of different maturity or tenor.

4.7.2 The risk free rate: bond and equity components

For property, the required risk premium can be thought about as having two components based on the two-sided nature of real estate as a bond/equity hybrid. Property let at a fixed rent on a long lease is like a bond; a property whose rent is regularly re-set to the market is more like an equity. The bond component of the risk premium should be determined by the liquidity of the investment and by the sensitivity of the cash flow to shocks created by tenant default or other unforeseeable events. For the equity component, the cash flow comprises the exit value and/or any expected uplift at a rent review or lease renewal, and the sensitivity of the cash flow to economic shocks will be very important indeed. For those investors interested in the real cash flow, shocks to inflation may be important.

For the bond component, assuming no default risk, the sensitivity of the nominal cash flow to economic shocks is nil. Default risk is, however, highly relevant, and will be the most important factor in the risk premium. Shocks to inflation will affect bonds more than equities, because the cash flow is fixed in nominal terms and therefore has no inflation proofing quality.

In addition, all property is subject to the extra illiquidity which affects all property much more than listed bonds and equities, and which will lead to an increase in the risk premium.

4.7.3 The sub-sector and property risk premium

Certain research systems include the provision of a series of risk premiums for sub-sectors of the property market, defined by use sector and sub-sector, by region and by city. Where a sale or purchase is being assessed and the present value or net present value over purchase or sale price needs to be estimated, these systems establish a broad guide for estimating the risk premium which might be used in the discount rate. However, where an individual interest in property is being appraised, a further set of considerations needs to be taken into account.

This section summarizes one such system which measures the issues relevant to the assessment of the individual or specific risk premium. Three main categories of premium drive the specific risk premium in this particular system. These are the sector or sub-sector premium, the city premium and the property premium.

The sector premium

The system described herein assesses the risk premium based on a checklist of issues and using a variety of quantitative and qualitative measures. The starting point is the estimation of a premium for the whole equity-type property sector based on a presumption about the equity risk premium and the relative position of property. Hence the sector premium is based on the equity premium and the differential property premium.

Beyond this, the sector premiums are assessed by taking into account three factors. These are: the sensitivity of the cash flow to economic shocks, with particular reference to rental growth and depreciation; illiquidity; and other factors, including the impact on portfolio risk and the lease pattern.

The city premium

The assessment of the city risk premium is based on an assessment of the riskiness of the economic structure of a city and its catchment area, together with a consideration of competing locations. The range expands from a minimum city premium for diversified and liquid cities with healthy industries to maximum premiums for illiquid cities whose economies are concentrated in weak sectors.

Low liquidity scores are assigned to cities and sectors where it is considered relatively difficult to raise cash from a sale at short notice.

The property premium

This section deals with the components of the property premium. The first two components are related to income security; the second two to asset quality. The four factors are:

a the tenant risk class;

b the lease risk class;

c the building risk class; and

d the location risk class.

Some of these factors will be specific to sectors of the market (in-city retail, for example). The relative weighting of the factors can be assessed by multiple regression analysis, whereby (given a large sample of individual property investments) the current importance of these variables in explaining yield or risk premiums can be assessed and their future importance hypothesized.

The simple process is best illustrated by an example.

4.7.4 Example

We are considering the purchase of either of two London office buildings. Our estimate of the risk premium for a prime London office is 3.25 per cent over the risk free rate, currently 3.5 per cent.

Tenant

The tenant of property A is a FTSE 350 corporate; the tenant of property B is a partnership of solicitors. Additional premium: 0.5 per cent for building B.

Tenure

A is leasehold, for 63 years, with low gearing (the ground rent payable to the freeholder is a small percentage of the occupational rent paid to the lessor); B is a leasehold for 116 years with no gearing. Additional premia: 1.5 per cent for building A; 0.5 per cent for building B.

Leases

The sub-lease for A has 18 years to run, with no breaks and upward-only rent reviews; B has six years to run, with no breaks and upward-only rent reviews. Additional premium: 1 per cent for building B.

Building

B is an inflexible building. Extra premium: 0.5 per cent.

Location

B has a location heavily dependent on neighbouring tenants remaining in place. Extra premium: 0.25 per cent.

In Chapter 3, we discussed a way of thinking about investment quality which derives from this approach. RES (2014) suggests that within any market assets will have contrasting degrees of income security and varying degrees of asset quality. Asset quality is a function of location quality and building quality; income security is a combination of lease length and covenant strength. Returns will vary across assets of different quality, and over time, as building quality is reduced through depreciation and income security erodes as leases shorten.

Table 4.11 summarizes the cumulative effect of these individual adjustments.

Table 4.11: Building specific risk premia: an example

Factor	Building A	Building B
Risk free rate	3.50	3.50
Base premium	3.25	3.25
Income security	1.50	1.50
Lease	*1.50*	*0.50*
Covenant	*0.00*	*1.00*
Asset quality	0.00	0.75
Location	*0.00*	*0.25*
Building	*0.00*	*0.50*
Premium	4.75	6.00
Discount rate	8.25	9.50

4.8 Forecasting rents and yields

Rents can be forecast using conventional forecasting procedures but cap rates or yields pose more of a problem. Together, rents and cap rates are the key into total return forecasts. These can be used at a number of levels.

- The total return expected for property can be used in asset allocation for a multi-asset portfolio.
- Sector and region returns can be used to construct a strategy for a property portfolio.
- Sector and region and local returns can be used to identify target areas for stock selection (buying and selling); and for active asset management.

4.8.1 The origin and uses of property forecasts

Forecasting property rents, yields, prices and returns requires an understanding of fundamental analysis. Fundamental analysis is the examination of the underlying forces that affect and connect the behaviour of the economy, asset classes, industrial sectors and companies. The goal of fundamental analysis is to derive a forecast for the future behaviour of a market or asset from these underlying forces, either using current data or using forecasts of these variables. The rent for office space, for example, can be forecast by using current vacancy rates or by using forecasts of the future demand for and supply of space, which are in turn driven by fundamental economic variables. The usual approach is to use an econometric technique called regression analysis.

Modelling property yields using this type of approach is, however, known to be challenging. Regression-based yield models typically suffer from poor explanatory power or poor diagnostics (a term used to describe an analysis of the equation) or require the forecasting of independent variables such as interest rates or equity market returns which are more difficult to forecast than the dependent variable.

Origins

Formal studies of the relationships between the economy and property prices were few until the collection and publication of property return data in the 1980s. Since then it has been established that the links between property and the economy are complex but strong.

It is now clear that there are persistent relationships which link the property market to the economy. These relationships can be found in rents, development activity and cap rates. This section focuses on the links between the economy and property rents and how these can be used to forecast the income from property investment based on forecasts of key economic variables. Much more on this subject can be found in Brooks and Tsolacos (2010).

The uses of forecasts

The formal forecasting of the property market using econometric models is now relatively commonplace. To assist with investment decisions, forecasts can be produced for each sector at the national, regional, local and individual building level. As the spatial scale becomes smaller, the task of forecasting becomes progressively more difficult. Rents could be forecast for the property market as a whole, but each sector is influenced by different factors, and it is better to consider the market as the sum of the individual sectors.

Forecasts of expected market returns are used by investors to formulate portfolio allocation strategies and asset-specific decisions. They are used at different spatial levels, for different sectors and sub-sectors, and at the asset level. In addition, forecasts can be developed for different investment quality segments, driven by asset quality and income security.

Future market returns depend on the interaction of the occupier and investment markets, which determine the path of future rental values and cap rates respectively. These rental value and cap rate movements will drive future market returns, but their impact on performance will be tempered by the mechanics of income generation (the lease) and by valuations, which will drive the capital component of return until the asset is sold.

Simulating real estate market performance requires three distinct processes: an estimation of the future path of rental values and yields, simulation of the income and capital values that will result from these forecasts, and the calculation of market returns.

Figure 4.2: The return forecasting process

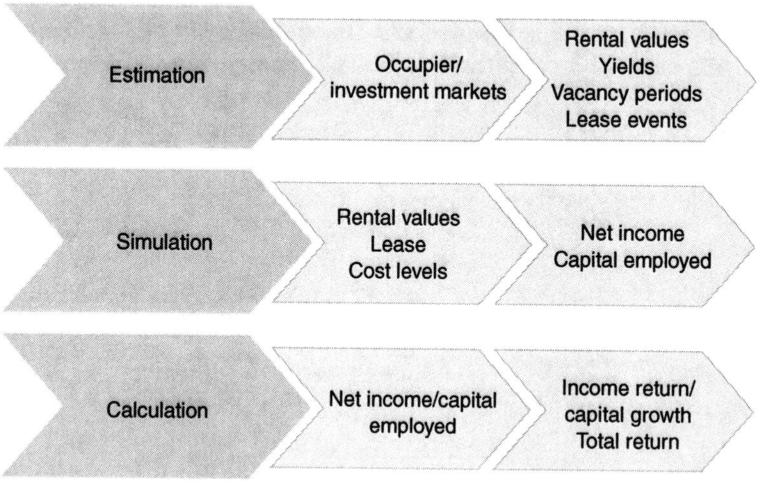

Estimation
Occupier/ investment markets
Rental values
Yields
Vacancy periods
Lease events

Simulation
Rental values
Lease
Cost levels
Net income
Capital employed

Calculation
Net income/capital employed
Income return/ capital growth
Total return

Source: Real Estate Strategies

The outlook for rental values and yields depends upon the occupier and investment markets. The occupier markets determine not just the strength of rental growth but also the behaviour of tenants at break and lease expiry ('lease events'), the length of vacancy periods and the length of new leases.

The impact of these rental value changes, lease events and vacancy periods on net income can be modelled using simulation. The lease event probabilities and the distribution of vacancy periods creates a number of potential pathways for future cash flows.

4.8.2 Forecasting rental growth: data preparation

A forecast of rental values (and net operating income) is the start of the process. Combined with the lease terms, this gives the expected cashflow (or distribution of cash flows – see Baum and Crosby, 2008) and enables us to calculate whether, given current price, the investment will deliver the required return. A large expected increase in rents need not mean a high expected return if the market has already incorporated this information into price. Such an analysis can be applied to the whole of the property market or an individual building or any level of aggregation in between.

Rental values depend upon the balance of demand and supply in the occupier markets, which are affected by the business and building cycles. Forecasts of changes in rental value levels can be made using the past relationship between exogenous economic variables and the coincident demand and supply factors, a technique known as econometrics.

For example, there is a relationship between the demand for office space and financial and business service employment. If occupier demand for office space is strong and supply is restricted, then rental values will rise. A forecast of future rental values can therefore be made from projections of financial and business service employment and the future supply of office stock (projections for which can in turn be estimated from their relationships with other economic variables).

A model links the variable being forecast (the dependent variable) with those which are used in the forecast (the independent variables). There are two types of model. The first involves establishing patterns or trends and assuming that these will continue into the future. We call this technical analysis. Examples include a linear trend (a constant increase over time) and cyclical trends. In effect, these use time as the explanatory or independent variable. All that is required is the year for which the forecast is to be made, from which it is possible to determine the value of the dependent variable.

The problem with this type of model is that external factors do not change the forecast. No matter what happens, it is assumed that the pattern will persist. Thus, in property, no matter what happens to the economy, the forecast for rents will be unchanged.

The second type of model is more plausible: it is one built from theory, that is, from a view on what causes changes in the dependent variable. This can be termed a causal or fundamental model, and everything that follows will concentrate on causal models.

A good causal model has to be logical and plausible: that is, it should be based on theory. It should also be practical: the explanatory variables must be forecastable, otherwise the model is an interesting historical model, but is of no value for forecasting.

Rent is the price paid by an occupier for the right to use the space for business activities. Basic economics points to the factors which affect price: demand and supply. This is the basis of a plausible model. However, price, demand and supply are all theoretical economic concepts. In order to use these concepts in practice, an empirical measure of each is required. This can be illustrated by using retail rents as an example.

Price (rent)

Price or rent has to be measured. At the national level, rent has no practical meaning unless it is measured as an index, that is, a weighted average of rents in different locations. This is similar to using the retail price index to measure price inflation.

In practice, issues such as the length of the time series, the robustness of the index construction and the degree of sectoral and geographical disaggregation are most important in selecting an index to model. It is also possible to combine different sources, using better quality data for the most recent period and the available, but poorer quality, data for earlier periods.

Demand

Rents are paid by occupiers, so plausible economics suggests that to understand rental levels it is necessary to understand what is happening to occupiers. It is not easy to measure demand directly, so a proxy variable is required. The demand by retailers for property and their ability to pay a price (the rent) depends on their profitability, which in turn depends on the demand for their goods from households. Other things being equal, increased demand should lead to higher profits and so to an ability to pay higher rents. Clearly, the ability of a retailer to pay rent will depend on factors other than the volume of sales, but this is likely to be the most important factor over time. Volume of sales can be measured by either retail sales or consumer expenditure.

Supply

As the supply of retail space increases, other things being equal, price will fall. Supply is a relatively straightforward concept to measure, although there are problems to do with data limitations.

Poor quality supply data is a standard problem in property research. Fortunately, this is less of a problem at the national level as supply increases relatively steadily, and national supply or stock series are usually much less volatile than rents or the demand proxies, and is less influential in the forecast.

Given adequate data describing demand and supply, the next stage is to try to build a model. Building a forecasting model involves an examination of the historical data and the determination of the relationship between the dependent variable (rent) and the appropriate independent variables. In this case, this is the relationship between retail rents, consumer expenditure and the supply of retail property.

This requires the use of econometric techniques (regression analysis). The basic model as outlined above is:

$$R = f(D, S)$$

In words, this means that rent is a function of demand and supply. A linear model would be:

$$R = aD + bS + c$$

The historical data describing R, D and S is available and is used to estimate the parameters a, b and c (where a and b are parameters and c is a constant) which constitute the model, which can be used to forecast rent using forecasts of the explanatory or independent variables. A good forecasting model is not the same as a good historical model: a model is useless for forecasting if the independent variables cannot be forecasted.

Further, in using the estimated model for forecasting, it is essential to understand that it is assumed that the coefficients a, b and c will remain constant in the future, in other words that the historical relationship will hold in the future. This is a basic assumption of any econometric model. It is possible to test statistically whether the model has been stable historically.

In practice the regression is a best fit rather than a perfect fit:

$$R = aD + bS + c + e$$

The first part of this equation is the deterministic part, in other words the model. The second part, *e*, is the probabilistic part and defines the part of the resulting forecast which is unexplained by the model: *e* is known as the error term or the residual.

The line of best fit is calculated so that the sum of the squares of the residuals is minimized. It is important to test if the model fits the data well, that is, whether the part left unexplained (the residuals) is small. If the residuals are large, then the actual values are not very near the values predicted in the model (the expected values), and the model is of limited value.There are further tests which a good econometric model must pass.

In practice, a number of adjustments are made to the basic model.

First, inflation is removed by deflating the series. If this is not done it is possible to obtain a good 'fit' purely because there is inflation on both sides of the equation.

Second, the data is transformed into logs. There are three reasons for this.

- To use regression techniques, the data has to be normally distributed and a log transformation has the effect of normalizing the data.
- With a log transformation the coefficients can be interpreted as elasticities (sensitivities), which accords well with economic theory.
- The difference in logs approximates to the growth rate which makes the model easier to interpret.

Third, as two trending variables will always have a high correlation, it is often appropriate to consider a model in differences, so that the change (rather than the level) in the independent variable leads to a change in the dependent variable.

Fourth, there may be a lagging effect. It may take some time for the change in the economy to work through to the property market. The model can be developed to include lagged effects, that is, the values of the variables in the previous period, as follows.

$$R = aR(-1) + bD + dD(-1) + fS(-1) + c + e$$

4.8.3 Forecasting rental growth: building a model

Having prepared the data, there are two approaches to building a model. The first is to start with the broadest specification, that is, to include all the possible explanatory variables and a number of lags for each, then eliminate those which are not significant in explaining the statistical relationship in the model. The second is to start with one explanatory variable and to build up a model by introducing new variables or lags.

To follow the first approach, a long time series is needed, perhaps 40 years of quarterly data giving 160 observations. In property, the longest available rent series are around 40–50 years long and include only annual observations. Thus, even the broadest specification of a property model will struggle to include a large number of explanatory variables.

Fortunately, there is a school of thought in econometrics which believes that the best model is one which contains a small number of variables. This is because adding new variables always improves the statistical fit of the model but may stretch the limits of a plausible theory and is more difficult to build and use.

When building the model, it may become clear that one (or several) of the observations of the dependent variable does not fit the model, while the others fit well. It may be that there is a measurement problem in the dataset or that in one particular year a variable not included in the model is important. In such a case, it may be appropriate to estimate the model without the observation. This is done by introducing a dummy variable. This has the effect of removing the outlying point and so preventing it being used in the estimation of the model. The use of a dummy variable requires a clear justification: it should not be used to improve a fundamentally poor model but it can often be used to deal with a shock of some sort or a data deficiency.

Broad specification models which include all the possible explanatory variables and lags may be better in explaining the past behaviour of a variable. This type of approach is flawed for forecasting, however, as it is difficult to estimate or forecast the value of a large number of independent variables.

An historical model

The following is an example of an historical model (taken from University of Aberdeen and IPD, 1994). It uses the IPD rent index as the dependent variable and had very good explanatory power (fitting the data well). Other forms of model can be produced using the same data, and choosing the best is a matter both of formal statistical tests and judgement based on an understanding of the operation of the property market.

$$\begin{aligned} \text{Rent} = {} & 0.88 \times \text{Rent}(-1) \\ & -0.28 \times \text{Rent}(-2) \\ & +1.48 \times \text{Consumer expenditure} \\ & -2.36 \times \text{Floorspace}(-2) \\ & -0.09 \times \text{Construction starts}(-2) \\ & -0.10 \times \text{Interest rate}(-1) \\ & -4.88 \end{aligned}$$

Note: the model is specified in log form and real terms.

The limitation of the historical model in forecasting is that there are several independent variables driving the dependent variable, and each of these will need to be forecast in order to arrive at a rent forecast. A model built for the purpose of forecasting will be somewhat different.

A forecasting model

The following is a model of rents in the UK retail market designed for forecasting. It explains or forecasts rent as the dependent variable, using consumer expenditure as the demand proxy and an extrapolated supply series based on government floorspace statistics. These are the main independent variables. The model also includes the rent level (Rent (–1)) in the previous year: it is clearly more parsimonious (economical) than the historical model.

Rent = 0.5 × Rent(–1)
+2.7 × Consumer expenditure
–3.0 × Floorspace
–17.0
Note: the model is specified in log form and real terms.

This model passed a wide range of statistical tests, and at the time it was developed it had an excellent forecasting ability. Its limitation is that the input forecasts may not be accurate. Accordingly, it is appropriate to develop a range of forecasts under different economic scenarios.

4.8.4 Forecasting at the local level

Local market forecasts are important for two related reasons. First, the sector/city is more useful as a segment for analysis than the sector/region, because the city is a more easily defined economic unit than the region. Second, regardless of the preferred portfolio categories, the management of real portfolios requires the selection of buildings to buy, sell, refurbish or redevelop and these require forecasts at the micro level.

The production of reliable procedures to forecast local market areas is, therefore, one of the main challenges facing the property investment market. It requires a substantial amount of work: a major investor might want views on 450 cities with populations of over 100,000 across Europe.

Formal modelling at the local level is therefore difficult. Two types of problems arise: conceptual and modelling, and data.

Conceptual and modelling problems

- The definition of the appropriate local market area for which to produce a forecast is a problem. The local market area appropriate to one sector (say retail) is unlikely to be that appropriate for another (say offices). The issue has been extensively considered in retail market modelling but has received much less attention in relation to other sectors with the exception of the London and New York office markets.
- Linked to the issue of defining local market areas is the problem that market areas for proximate centres will overlap, as the centres are in competition.
- In a local market where rental evidence has been based on rent reviews rather than on open market transactions, or is smoothed for some other reason, rental pressure may arise. This can be positive or negative; it refers to the difference between the provable rent and the open market rent. When an open market letting takes place, it is possible for the provable rent to change substantially without a change in the balance of supply and demand. There is a need, therefore, to distinguish between changes needed to reach the 'correct' rent and changes in the correct rent.
- At the local level, many factors could potentially have an important effect on rent but cannot be formally modelled. These 'soft' variables include factors such as local business confidence, changes to planning policy on city centre car parking and infrastructure developments.

Data problems

- Data for the demand variables used at the national and regional levels is generally not available at the city level. City level retail sales or consumer expenditure data or output data are usually unavailable. It is possible, however, to use population and employment as the basis for constructing explanatory variables. Population is linked to retail sales and employment is linked to output and so to rents in the office and industrial sectors.
- Whereas supply is relatively stable at the national and regional levels and so is of lesser importance in modelling, it is crucially important at the local level. A new development can dramatically change the amount of shopping space and can have a dramatic impact on rents, so supply at the local level must be closely monitored. Reliable data describing the supply pipeline is difficult to obtain and translate into a meaningful forecast of supply, but research and information services provided at the building and tenancy level by companies such as CoStar promise a solution to this problem.
- Rent data is not available for such a wide range of centres with a sufficiently long time series and of sufficient quality to give much confidence in the result of any formal modelling.

The result is that it is probably impossible to build a meaningful econometric model from local data. One possible approach is to use the coefficients calculated at the national level to forecast the local market as, in the absence of contrary evidence, it is reasonable to conclude that the same basic relationships should hold. It is, in any case, essential that a local forecast should be constrained by a framework of national forecasts. This 'top-down' approach to local forecasting can produce sensible figures.

Vacancy periods, lease events and incentive periods

Net operating income (rent less expenses and vacancy) will be adversely affected by vacancy periods, which will occur in the future if the tenant defaults, exercises a break clause in the lease or vacates at the end of the current lease term. The probability of tenant default can be estimated from the financial strength of the occupier, but individual tenant decisions to exercise a break, or not to renew the lease, will be driven by specific tenant circumstances. For example, the tenant may require larger accommodation due to business expansion or require less space due to business reorganization.

Projecting net operating income

Changes in future net operating income will be determined by rental growth, lease characteristics and lease events, and the irrecoverable revenue expenditure associated with delivering the income stream, such as rent review fees, new lease fees and irrecoverable costs.

As the determinants of income depend upon the path of lettings and these lettings are subject to the outcomes of lease events, there are multiple possible income paths for each lease. The market average net income receivable projection is an average of all of these paths. The dispersion around the average income projection for each lease can be quantified, and this provides a measure of the specific risk of an asset that can be attributed to the leasing process.

4.8.5 Forecasting cap rates

A forecast of cap rates will be determined by expected changes in yields across the financial markets and the expected outlook for growth in rental value in the real estate market. A yield projection can be modelled econometrically using these variables, but this is not straightforward, and it is well established that cap rates are more difficult to forecast than rents. However, based on the material presented earlier in this chapter we can suggest that they are driven by yields on bonds, or the risk free rate; by expectations of future net rental growth; and by the required risk premium.

The first problem is producing a good historical model. The yield series does not exhibit much volatility: property yields tend to move slowly upwards or downwards for a long period, and may simply be mean-reverting. In contrast, the many possible explanatory variables are much more volatile. This creates modelling difficulties.

The best historical model for the all property yield calculated in the University of Aberdeen/IPD report used the following explanatory variables: the property yield in the previous year, the yield on long dated gilts, net property investment, the interest rate, office and retail construction starts one year ago, property returns one year in the future and the inflation rate.

This may produce a good historic model but it is of little value for forecasting. Forecasts of the explanatory variables would be at least as difficult to produce as forecasts of the property yield. With some idea of the likely trends in these variables, it may be possible to deduce likely yield movements, but not to predict values with much accuracy.

Forecasting yields using econometric-type models is probably a waste of time, and an alternative approach using a cashflow analysis is required. There are a number of approaches that can be taken towards modelling yields. Yields may be linked to fundamentals, as above. A model which employs a fit between rental growth, swap rates and yields is described below. Event-specific factors can impact on yields: these can include the weight of money, sentiment towards property and recent rental growth experience, or simply yield movements in other assets. However, it is dangerous to use a simple lagged relationship between yields on one asset class to predict the yield on another.

Figure 4.3 illustrates the yield gap between UK government bond yields (gilts) and property. Where the gap is positive, as it was before 1993, gilt yields are higher than property yields. After 1996, property yields have been higher than gilt yields. This is not a simple lead-lag relationship, but it may be meaningful if it is set in the context of the fundamental relationship:

$$K = RFR_R + i + Rp - (G_r + i - D)$$

This tells us to expect a positive relationship between gilt yields and property yields, but one which is complicated by the risk premium and real growth expectations.

The switch to a positive yield difference post-1996 raises the question as to why this may have happened. Possible explanations are that the risk premium for property has risen, anticipated growth has fallen (meaning real growth expectations plus the ability of rents to respond to inflation) or there has been a combination of both. Alternatively, property was looking cheap before 1996. The narrowing yield difference of 2003–5 suggested that the risk premium for property fell, anticipated growth increased, there had been a combination of both. Alternatively, property had become over-priced.

Figure 4.3: The UK gilt-property yield gap, 1976–2013

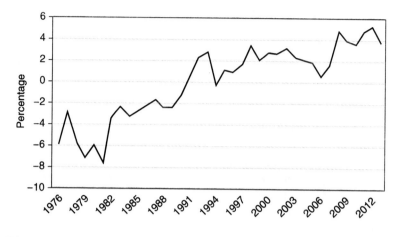

Source: IPD, Datastream

This is not a simple relationship. The yield gap between conventional bonds and real estate is affected by a large number of factors, and to some extent we are comparing an apple (a fixed interest or bond-type investment) with a pear (an equity-type investment, or at least a bond-equity hybrid).

Figure 4.4 illustrates the yield gap between UK government indexed bond yields (indexed gilts) and property ($K - RFR_R$). The gap is always positive, because property is riskier, and inflation-related income growth is common to both yield series (and cancels out).

Figure 4.4: The UK indexed gilt-property yield gap, 1976–2013

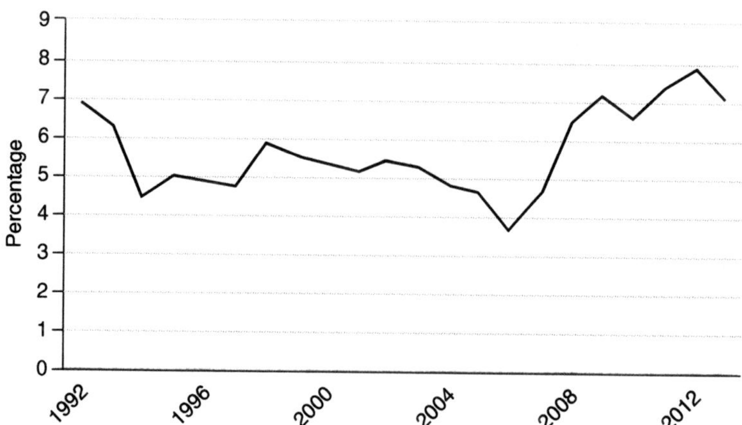

Source: IPD, Datastream

$$K = RFR_R + Rp - G_r + D \text{ and}$$

$$K - RFR_R = Rp - G_r + D$$

This appears to be a more stable series, and might appear to tend towards mean reversion. This makes sense as long as property is regarded as a good inflation hedge. If that is the case, then the yield gap will respond only to fundamentals in the occupier markets ($G_r + D$) and changes in the risk premium for real estate. The yield gap reached a low just before the crash of 2007–9, and reached a peak in 2009, indicating an excellent buying opportunity, as turned out to be the case.

The problem with relying on this relationship, of course, is that real estate can be a bond-equity hybrid, so we may again be comparing an apple (a true inflation hedge) with a pear (a asset which has some similarities to a bond-type investment)!

Figure 4.5 shows the historic relationship between rental growth and property yields. There is an obvious negative correlation, measured as –30 per cent. When rents are growing, yields are falling (in anticipation of further auto-correlated rental growth?).

Figure 4.5: UK rental growth and property yields, 1976–2013

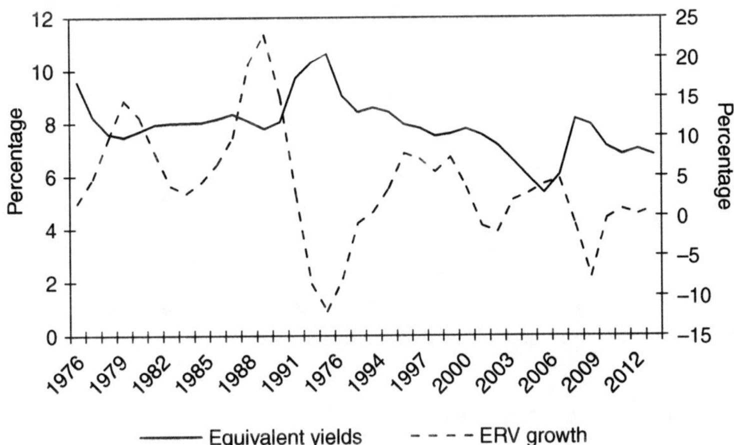

Source: IPD, PFR

An even stronger relationship can be found by combining swap rates – a measure of the cost of borrowing used to finance property acquisition (see Chapter 2) – and rental growth, a short-term measure of market strength. When swap rates are low and current rental growth is high, yields will fall.

We regressed end-year equivalent yields on rental growth over the year and 18 month lagged five-year swap rates. This resulted in a very strong and stable relationship, with some 95 per cent of the variability in equivalent yields being explained by these variables.

In 2005, we used this estimated relationship to forecast equivalent yields, assuming rental growth in line with IPF consensus surveys of 2.4 per cent for 2006 and 2.7 per cent for 2007 and the appropriate lagged values of swap rates. The equivalent yields for the end of 2006 and 2007 are both forecast to be around 7.1 per cent, which implies an increase in equivalent yields at the end of 2006. In the event, despite higher swap rates and disappointing rental growth, yields fell further to well below 6 per cent, before the inevitable, rapid and sharp correction of 2007–9. In 2009 they had risen to 8 per cent. (See Box 4.2, ending this chapter.)

Table 4.12: Annual fundamental model output

Model	2005	2006	2007
Annual	6.73	7.11	7.09

Source: PFR

4.8.6 Forecasting property cash flows

When the rental income is fixed between rent reviews, property investments have bond components to the cash flow. The expected cash flow from the typical property investment is therefore a combination of bond and equity. Even a heavily over-rented office has an equity component at the lease end; and property with rents fixed between reviews have a bond component. Property is a hybrid, and the investment strategy must reflect this by anticipating the impact of economic and capital market forces on the value of both components of the cash flow.

The cash flow should also reflect the following factors.

- Property income is subject to the lease, which determines the payment of rent. For example, the reversionary nature of some property investments will create an income uplift at the next review. Our focus should always be on the net operating income, which is rent less vacancy and expenses (see Baum and Hartzell, 2012).
- Property, more than any other mainstream investment, is a tangible asset which depreciates through physical deterioration and obsolescence.

The over-rented component of the cash flow will be subject to greater risk than the portion secured by the estimated rental value (ERV); separation of the cash flow into these two component parts would therefore be wise.

Forecasting the cash flow from a property ideally, therefore, comprises the following stages:

i an econometric model driving rental values, taking full account of depreciation;
ii a fundamental model explaining the future path of cap rates; and
iii a simulation model which overlays expected rental growth on top of the lease, so that the net operating income and resale price driven by lease events and market rental values can be estimated, plus a risk measure computed.

This process will tell us whether the investment will deliver the required return, and will also help us to calibrate the risk of the investment and whether the required return has been reasonably estimated.

The holding period used in cash flow projections should normally coincide with a lease end or review. However, this may not always be the case. In any event it should be determined with care for several reasons. These are as follows.

- The net present value (NPV) or internal rate of return (IRR) (see Baum and Crosby, 2008) will not be invariant with regard to the holding period.
- The shorter the holding period, the greater the influence of the exit value, which will be a more risky input.
- The manager or investor may have an expected holding period, which may or may not equate with lease ends or reviews.

We close this chapter by illustrating an approach to forecasting a market at what turned out to be a particularly interesting time.

Box 4.2 A bubble in UK property prices?

(taken from an unpublished client 2005 report by Property Funds Research

With equivalent yields, as recorded by the IPD UK Monthly Index, at a historic low at October 2005, the question of whether continued yield compression is possible is becoming increasingly significant. By looking at yields both in terms of their fundamental drivers and in comparison with yields in other asset markets, this report examines whether the current state of the UK property market is something of an anomaly in the context of historic patterns. In addition, the report summarises the results of a survey exploring whether the weight of money invested in UK property in recent years is likely to remain a factor.

Taken together, these research pieces allow us to explore the outlook for UK property market yields (cap rates) over the next five years.

In order to explore whether real estate yields can fall further, we undertook a technical analysis which will present alternative ways of examining yield patterns for UK property using simple relative indicators such as swap rates, long and short gilt yields, equity dividend and earnings yields, and property company dividend and earnings yields and share price performance. Whether current pricing levels for property appear to be out of line compared to other indicators will be considered here.

Technical analysis is the examination of past price movements to forecast future price movements. We address the question of whether yields can call further from a technical perspective. In order to do this, a number of approaches are employed. By looking at yields from these alternative perspectives an 'on the balance of evidence' view of the likely direction of future yield movements will be taken.

IPD equivalent yields are used as the appropriate property yield variable because they are not affected by the reversionary potential in the market, and as a result they are better (more stand-alone) measures of property pricing than the initial yield.

We have used two technical approaches to look at yields. These are as follows.

- Technical analyses of historic property yield data in isolation (univariate analysis), including mean reversion and moving averages. Do current yield levels look wrong in the light of previous levels? Can the future outlook be indicated by these measures?

- A technical analysis that looks at property yields relative to gilt yields, equity dividend yields and property share yields. Do current property yield levels look wrong in the light of previous values for these relationships?

The IPD monthly yield series are highly 'auto-correlated', the correlation coefficient between adjacent months being 0.98. The correlation between annual yields falls off to 0.67, which remains a high figure. Hence, the history of the variable is important in determining its value today. Yields exhibit underlying patterns that may be useful in making forecasts. That is, there is enough memory, or momentum, in the underlying pattern so that its correlation with previous periods contributes towards making useful forecasts. Yields are unlikely to change quickly or by large amounts.

In summary, 2004/05 clearly shows an irregularity both in terms of the size of the yield fall and in the absolute level of yields. This in turn produced an abnormally high total return.

Moving average (ARIMA) models

A well-known technical approach is to look at the time-series behaviour of yields and to try to discern if there are any systematic patterns or tendencies in the data which permit a forecast of future movements. There are many methods that can be employed in looking to determine such patterns of time series data. The approach adopted here is to estimate basic time series models. Due to their flexibility so-called 'ARIMA' (auto-regressive integrated moving average) models have been estimated.

ARIMA models are of particular use in modelling many types of economic and financial variables. They are simple to estimate, can produce reasonable short-term forecasts, and most importantly they require no knowledge of any fundamental variables that may explain what causes a variable to change.

Only the past values of a series are used to model, and to forecast, the series. No other information is used, which means that the series is explained as a purely mechanical/automated process that depends only on previous values. As indicated above, the equivalent yield series exhibits strong persistence where previous values influence current values, particularly in the monthly series. The implication is that there may be an underlying relationship between successive values. The ARIMA model identifies this dependence.

Two types of model were estimated: namely, one model using IPD monthly data and another model using IPD annual data. The annual data is more important as the impact of economic factors such as the business cycle (reflected in GDP figures) may only be detectable at annual intervals.

Table 4.13 provides the forecasts based on the ARIMA annual equation. In this equation we have estimated the value of the end year 2005 equivalent yield on the IPD annual series from movements in the monthly series to October 2005. This value has been used in the forecast.

Table 4.13: Annual ARIMA model outputs

Model	2005	2006	2007
Annual	6.73	7.17	7.11

Source: PFR

Based on the estimated annual equations yields are likely to increase. The forecasts for the monthly equations are shown in Table 4.14.

Table 4.14: Monthly ARIMA model outputs

Model	November 2005	December 2005
Monthly	6.18	6.13

Source: PFR

This says that in the very short term cap rates will fall. This contrasts with the annual figures. To reconcile these results, annual figures are picking up the implied longer-term trends which the monthly figures do not. A short term fall followed by a longer term rise is a story which makes some sense of these numbers.

Mean reversion

Robert Schiller, the renowned financial economist, has observed the following behavioural trait in prices: 'Thus there is a sort of regression to the mean (or to longer-run past values) for stock prices: what goes up a lot tends to come back down, and what goes down a lot tends to come back up.'

Figure 4.6 shows UK property equivalent yields since 1976. It is easy to conclude that there is a mean property yield of 8% or so and that yields have recently fallen below that mean. Mean reversion suggest that they will inevitably rise back to 8%. It may be argued that Figure 4.6 shows a downward trend in yields since 1992, but downward trends in yields are fundamentally unsustainable unless the real risk free rates changes significantly and for a sustained period of time.

Comparing property yields with other asset yields

We also examined movements in relationships between bond, equity and property yields in order to assess the relative attraction of each. (Note: any references made in this section to gilt yields refer to the yield on consolidated stock or consols, government bonds with no maturity date.)

Asset markets are integrated and the yield differentials between markets are likely to have an impact and trigger movement of funds between markets, exploiting any significant differences. Hence there is expected to be some link between property capitalization rates and

Figure 4.6: Ten-year gilt yield versus property equivalent yield, 1976–2005

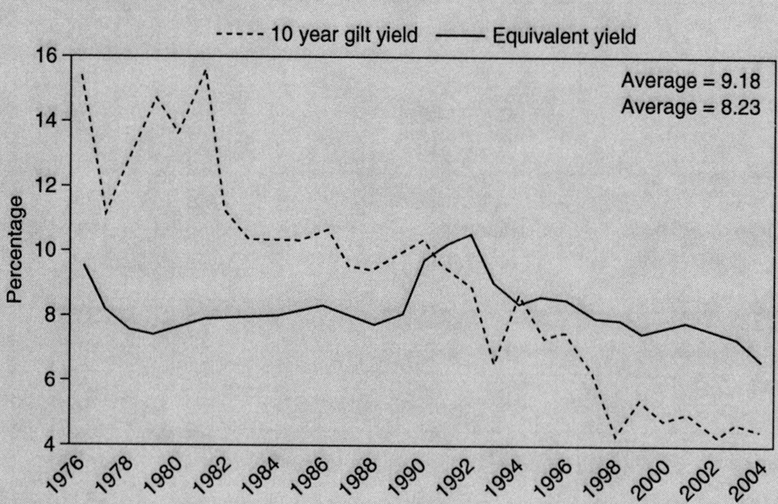

Source: IPD, Datastream

capitalization rates in other financial markets, such as the government bond and equity markets, with the risk free rate being a common component across all markets. The movement in asset yields is likely to provide an indication as to how cheap or expensive assets are relative to one another. This provides the motivation for looking at the relationships between yields across markets.

The question being addressed is as follows: do yield differences across markets contain information that is useful in determining the likely direction of future yield movements? In looking at this issue we examine yield gaps.

Property and conventional gilts

The property–gilt analysis undertaken for this report is based on 10-year gilts, the yardstick commonly used in gilt-property comparisons. Unless otherwise noted, the property yield used is the IPD annual universe equivalent yield. Inspection of the yield figures for 10-year gilts and equivalent yields for property, shown in Figure 4.6, indicates the presence of marked trends. Gilt yields (average 9.18%) have been declining since the beginning of the 1990s and property yields (average 8.23%) since the fourth quarter of 1993.

However, while the dramatic decline in gilt yields came to an end in 1998, property yields have continued to fall, now below the levels seen at any time in the IPD period of coverage (1976–2005). A key feature evident in Figure 4.6 is the switch from a positive yield gap between gilts and property evident in the early 1990s to a persistent negative yield gap from the end of 1991. This is shown in Figure 4.7. There has been a recent reduction in the gap, but it is still well below any longer term average.

Figure 4.7: Gilt-property yield gap, 1976–2005

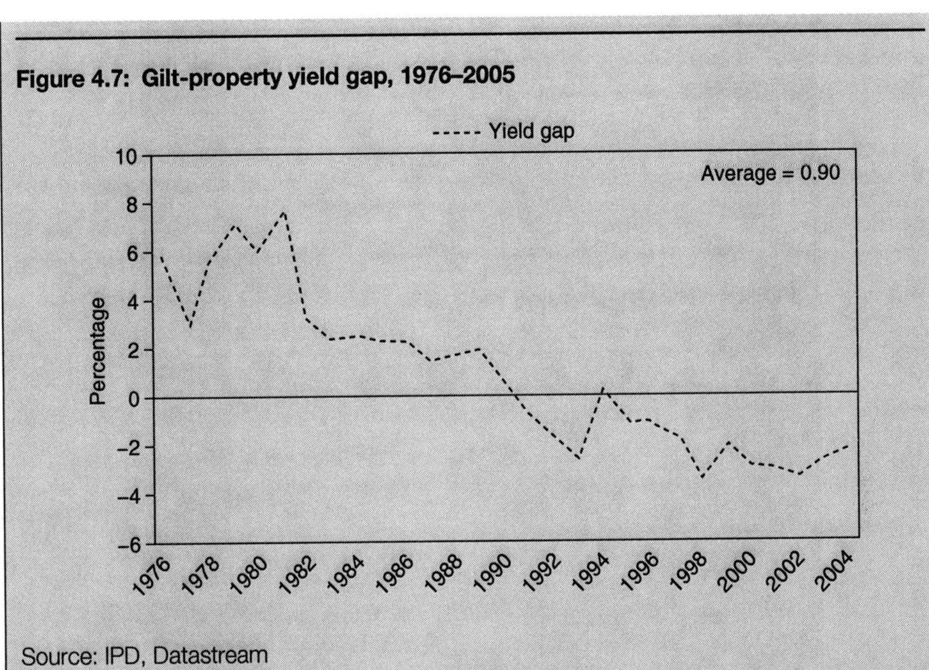

Source: IPD, Datastream

Property and index-linked gilts

In these analyses, the gilt data used is the average redemption yield on the FTA over 5-year index-linked gilt series. Figure 4.8 shows how real equivalent yields have moved in relation

Figure 4.8: Index-linked bond and property yields, 1976–2005

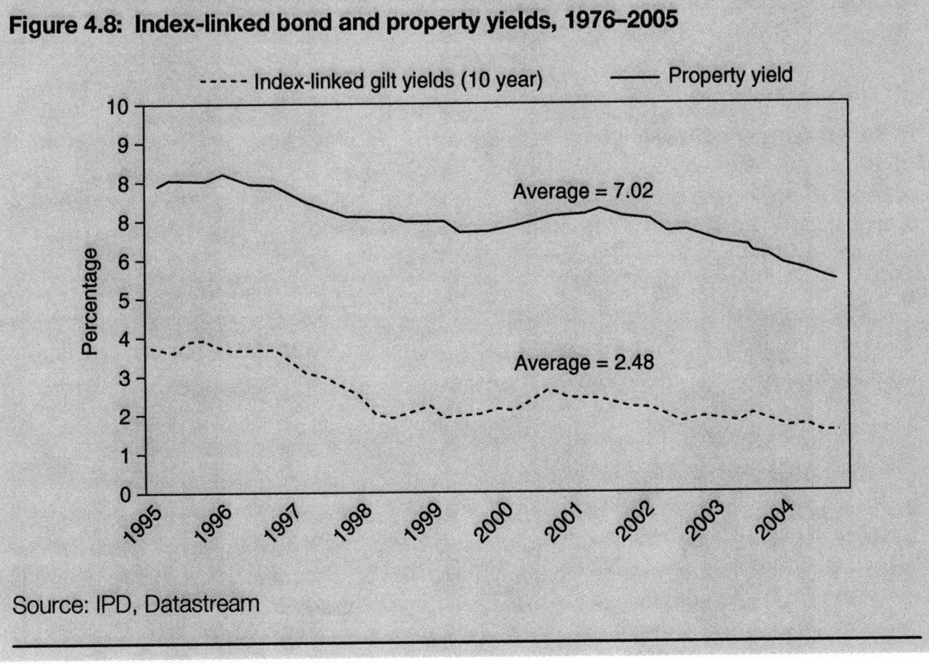

Source: IPD, Datastream

to index-linked yields since 1995. Over this period the average index-linked yield was 2.48%, compared to a property yield of 7.02%. It can be seen that real equivalent yields have tracked index-linked yields down.

Figure 4.9 shows the difference between real equivalent yields and index-linked yields over this period. This has recently closed somewhat from a mean of 4.5% to a new level of less than 4%. This suggests property yields may be on the low side.

Figure 4.9: Index-linked and property yield gap, 1995–2005

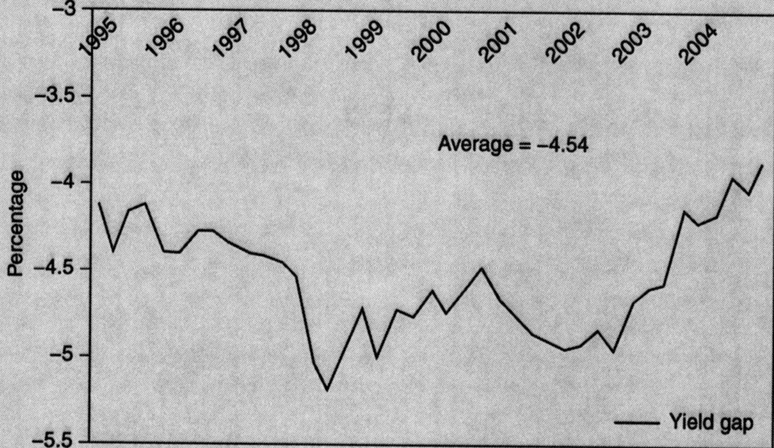

Source: IPD, Datastream

Property and equities

In the following comparison we have used the FTA All Share average dividend yield. Both might appear to have moved downwards over the period 1978–2005. However, there appears to have been a correction in the relationship over the period 2000–2005 and the reducing yield gap appears to be a sign of property over-heating. This is shown in Figures 4.10 and 4.11.

The indication is that property values relative to equities are at their highest levels since 1987. It may also suggested that property looked cheap – yields were too high – throughout the 1990s.

Property and property shares

We examined an indicator of the pricing of listed property companies, namely dividend yields measured by the FTA Real Estate Index. Again, as shown in Figure 2.9, a familiar picture emerges. Property yields have fallen over recent years and the yield gap shown in Figure 4.11 has narrowed. Property looks expensive compared to property shares.

Figure 4.10: Equity and property yields, 1976–2005

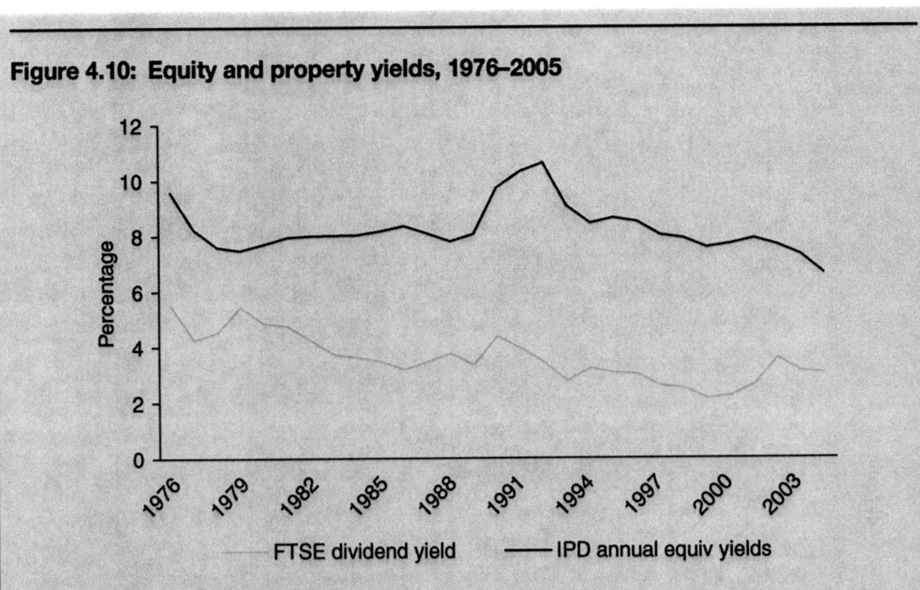

Source: IPD, Datastream

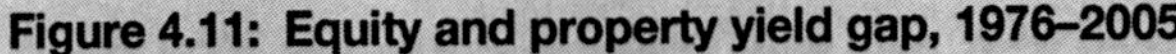

Figure 4.11: Equity and property yield gap, 1976–2005

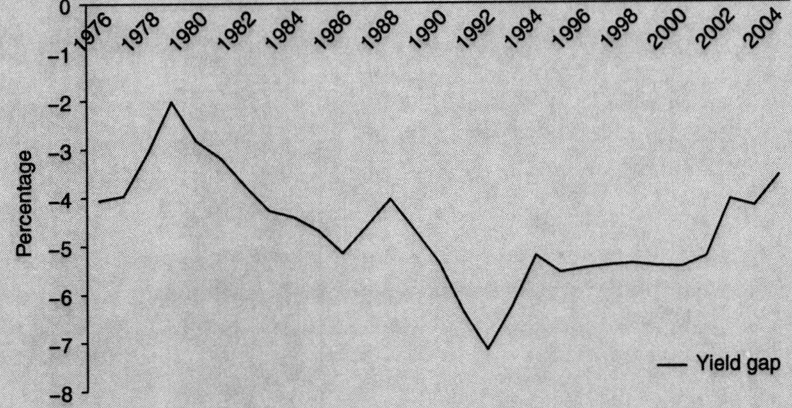

Source: IPD, Datastream

Swap rates and property yields

Finally, we compare interest rates with property yields. Debt-financed investors in property can be expected to be influenced in their bids by the effective interest rates paid on debt. This is typically the 5-year swap rate. A simple technical analysis of this relationship may reveal whether property yields look high or low relative to interest rates.

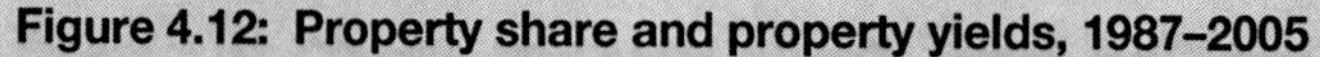

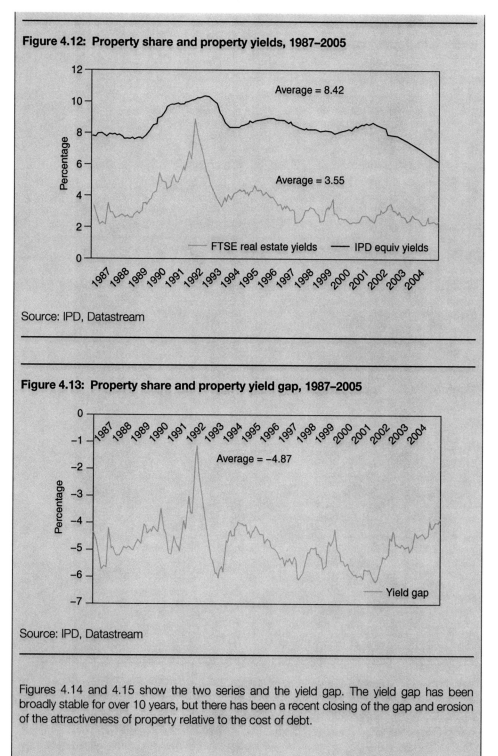

Figure 4.12: Property share and property yields, 1987–2005

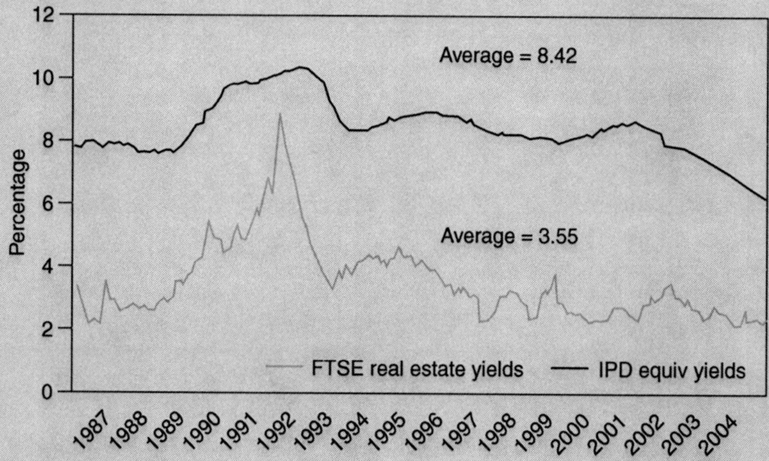

Source: IPD, Datastream

Figure 4.13: Property share and property yield gap, 1987–2005

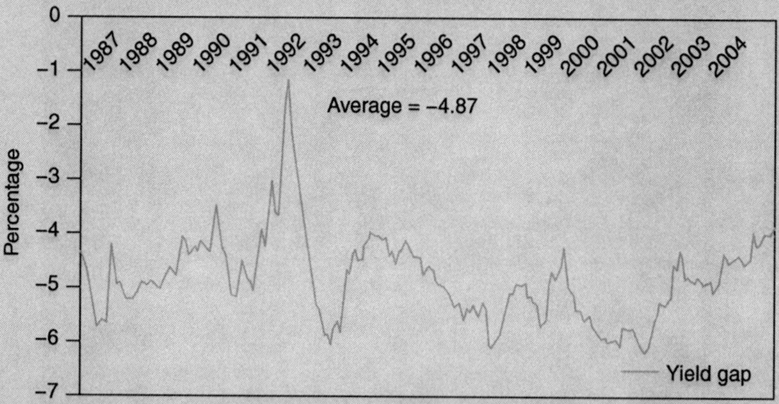

Source: IPD, Datastream

Figures 4.14 and 4.15 show the two series and the yield gap. The yield gap has been broadly stable for over 10 years, but there has been a recent closing of the gap and erosion of the attractiveness of property relative to the cost of debt.

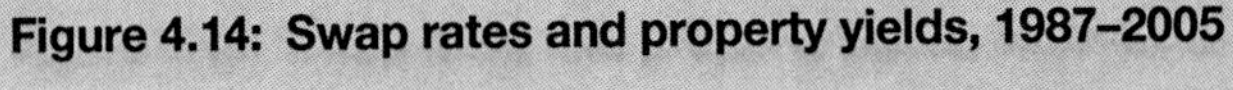

Figure 4.14: Swap rates and property yields, 1987–2005

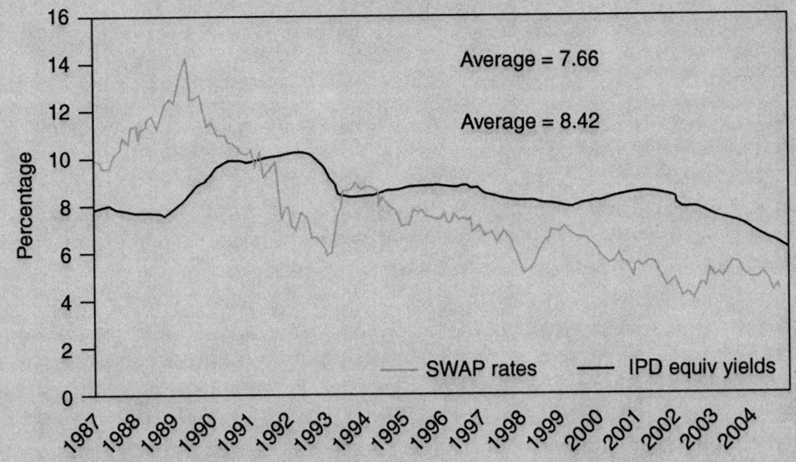

Source: IPD, Datastream

Figure 4.15: Swap rate and property yield gap, 1987–2005

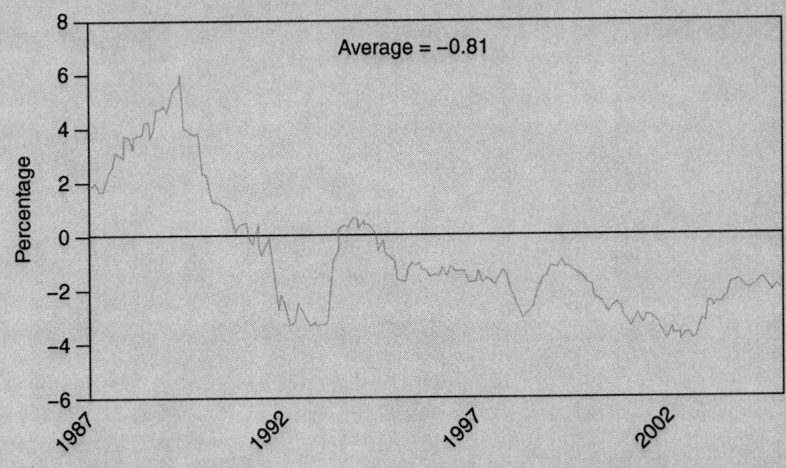

Source: IPD, Datastream

Conclusions

We used two technical approaches to look at yields. First, we examined univariate analyses of historic property yield data in isolation, including mean reversion and moving averages. Then we examined relationships between other asset prices, interest rates and property yields.

The history of the variable is important in determining its value today. Yields exhibit an underlying pattern that may be useful in making forecasts. There is enough momentum in the underlying pattern that we can say property yields are 'auto-correlated'. A basic autoregressive pattern exists, with two lags for both monthly and annual series. A short-term fall followed by a medium-term rise in yields appears to be indicated. If mean reversion holds, a sharp rise in yields back to 8% is indicated after 12–18 months.

We also used technical analysis that looks at property yields relative to gilt yields, index-linked gilt yields, equity dividend yields and property share yields. We also examined swap rates and property yields. In all comparisons, property yields appear to have fallen relative to yields on other assets. All assets have shown falling yields, but the property yield, which has been higher than the yields on all other asset classes, appears to have fallen by more. A fall in property prices appears to be likely from this evidence.

Given the out-turn, which of the forecasting approaches used by PFR appears to have made most sense?

5 Performance measurement and attribution

5.1 Return measures: an introduction

There are many confusions concerning return measurement in property. This is largely due to the unique terminology (often country-specific) which has been developed in the property world; it is also due to the unique nature of property, especially rent review patterns and the resulting reversionary or over-rented nature of interests.

There is also some misunderstanding of the difference between return measures which are used to cover different points or periods in time. Return measures may describe the future, they may describe the present or they may describe the past.

Measures describing the future are always expectations. They will cover certain periods of time and may, if that period begins immediately, be called *ex ante* measures. An example is the expected internal rate of return (IRR) from a property development project beginning shortly; another example is the required return on that project.

Measures describing the present do not cover a period, but describe relationships existing at a single point in time (usually, now). An example is the initial yield on a property investment; while this may imply something about the income return likely to be produced by an investment in future, it is simply the current relationship between the rental income and the capital value or price at that single point in time.

Finally, measures of return describing the past, or *ex post* measures, are measures of (historic) performance. An example is the delivered return on a project, or the IRR that has been produced by a property portfolio.

Performance measurement is a science which deals only with the past. It must therefore be distinguished from portfolio analysis, which is relevant to the present, and to portfolio strategy, which is relevant to the future. It deals wholly with delivered returns, and not expected or required returns (see Chapter 4).

5.2 Definitions

5.2.1 The future

The following definitions describe the future.

IRR

This is the expected total return delivered by the expected cash flows over a period of time relative to the price paid. There are similarities in other investment markets: these include the gross redemption yield in the bond market.

NPV

This is the present value of all future cash flows discounted at the required return or target rate less the initial cost or outlay. Where the NPV is zero, the discount rate is the IRR.

Required return

This is the return that needs to be produced by the investment to compensate the investor for the risks involved in holding the investment. It is also called the target rate or the hurdle rate of return.

5.2.2 The present

The following definitions describe the present.

Initial yield

This is defined as the net rental income (or net operating income, NOI) divided by the current value or purchase price, or the total outlay including costs. (Conventions vary from market to market.) There are similarities in other investment markets: these include interest-only yield, running yield, income yield, flat yield, dividend yield.

Yield on reversion

This is defined as the current net rental value or NOI divided by the current value, purchase price or total outlay. There is no equivalent in other markets.

Equivalent yield

This is the weighted average of the initial yield and the yield on reversion. It has been defined as the IRR that would be delivered assuming no change in rental value. As in the case of all IRRs, the solution is found by trial and error. There is no equivalent in other asset markets, and the term is largely confined to the UK due to the nature of the typical lease for prime property in that market.

Reversionary potential

This is the net rental income or NOI divided by the current net rental value or market rent (or sometimes vice versa). There is no equivalent in other markets.

5.2.3 The past

The following definitions are performance measures. They describe the past.

Income return

This is the net rent or NOI received over the measurement period divided by the value at beginning of period.

$$IR = Y_{0-1}/CV_0$$

Capital return

This is the change in value over the measurement period divided by the value at beginning of the period.

$$CR = [CV_1 - CV_0]/CV_0$$

Total return

This is the sum of income return and capital return.

$$TR = [Y_{0-1} + CV_1 - CV_0]/CV_0$$

Time-weighted return

This is the single rate of compound interest which will produce the same accumulated value over more than one period as would be produced by the component single period interest rates. This is related to the geometric mean rate of return.

The TWRR ignores the timing of cash injections and extraction as it is simply a type of average of individual year returns. It is appropriate for quoted unitized and other co-mingled funds. It is an inappropriate measure where the manager has discretion over the timing of an investment in assets.

Internal rate of return

This is the most accurate and complete description of historic return. It is appropriate for managers who have discretion over the cashflow and takes into account the cash invested in each period. It is not, therefore, a mean of annual returns.

Money-weighted return

This is effectively the same measure as the IRR. Its use was legitimized by investment professionals seeking an approximation prior to the development of cheap and efficient computing facilities. Given that IRR calculations are now straightforward, there is little justification for continued use of the term.

MWRR/IRR is appropriate for funds where the manager has control over cash flows. It takes account of the amount invested in each period – hence the name.

Equity multiple

When investments are leveraged, the investor's equity is put at risk. A very rough measure of success in such a case is the size of the equity that is returned after the bank has been repaid as a multiple of the equity invested. This ignores the time value of money, and is a very poor measure of return over longer periods, but its increasing use in recent times has been a response to increasing leverage and suspicions about the manager's ability to manipulate IRRs.

5.3 Example: IRR, TWRR, total return or MWRR?

By way of illustration, let us assume that the return on two funds, life fund A and pension fund B, were measured over the period 2012–14. The following performance information is available about these funds.

At the year end, the fund managers decide whether or not to buy new buildings and all expenditure takes place at that time.

Expenditure is not taken into account in the year-end valuation completed immediately before each expenditure. It is assumed instead that expenditure adds to the portfolio value at the beginning of the following year.

Table 5.1: Life fund (fund A) (£m)

	Initial value	Value at year end	Net income	New expenditure
2012	123.45	94.51	9.34	17.86
2013	–	165.50	10.12	1.45
2014	–	177.09	10.32	–

Table 5.2: Pension fund (fund B) (£m)

	Initial value	Value at year end	Net income	New expenditure
2012	12.35	9.53	0.93	0.00
2013	–	14.00	1.01	1.45
2014	–	16.50	1.03	–

The results are as shown in Table 5.3.

The life fund achieved a higher IRR over three years than the pension fund. However, the pension fund achieved a higher TWRR.

In 2012, the IRRs achieved by both funds were less than the total returns achieved. In 2014, they were both higher.

Which of these measures is appropriate?

Table 5.3: Life and pension fund performance

Year	Life fund	Pension fund
2012 total return	−15.88%	−15.30%
2012 IRR	−16.68%	−16.03%
2014 total return	12.25%	13.46%
2014 IRR	12.74%	14.04%
2012–14 TWRR	13.85%	14.82%
2012–14 IRR	14.67%	13.87%

IRR or TWRR?

The life fund appears to have out-performed on an IRR basis because the IRR (which is money-weighted) reflects the additional investment made by the fund at the start of the strong year of 2013. The extra cash outlay at the end of 2012 led to a much higher value at the end of 2013 and a stronger return over the period 2013–14.

However, the pension fund achieved a higher TWRR (which is not money-weighted), in other words a higher average annual return.

The responsibility for investing the cash determines the correct measure. Who decided to put more money in at the end of 2012? If the decision were the responsibility of the fund managers in each case, then the IRR is correct and the life fund out-performed. If the decision were the responsibility of a higher authority, then the TWRR is correct and the pension fund out-performed.

In addition, it should be noted that the IRR exceeds the TWRR only for the life fund because more money was invested in correct anticipation of the better years by the life fund, but not by the pension fund.

IRR or total return?

In 2012, the IRRs achieved by both funds were less than the total returns achieved. In 2014, they were both higher. The differences in each case are simply the result of the timing of rental income, assumed to be quarterly in advance.

Normally, that is when returns are positive, the quarterly payment of rent is an advantage and produces a higher IRR than total return. The total return effectively assumes a single end of year rent payment. In this case the IRR calculation implicitly assumes that the (quarterly) intermediate cashflows are re-invested at the IRR. Hence the 2014 returns are higher on an IRR basis than on a total return basis. On the other hand, negative returns in 2012 mean that the re-investment of quarterly income led to negative interest, a damaged IRR and a relatively higher total return.

It is often more practical to measure total return than to measure IRR, but the latter is generally a better – more comprehensive – measure. Because total returns are approximations to IRRs, direct comparisons of IRRs with total returns can be misleading. Professional performance measurement agencies, such as IPD, adjust for the timing effect in their total return calculations, and for IPD annual total returns are the average single-year TWRR of compounded monthly returns.

IRR or MWRR?

The IRR is a perfect mechanism for the measurement of fund return. The MWRR is an approximation to the IRR which was developed because it allowed manual solution by simple algebra or calculator. It is now redundant.

5.4 Capital expenditure

Performance measurement organizations in the UK and US typically use total return measures for single period performance measurement for all assets. The simple formula is as follows.

$$TR = [Y_{0-1} + CV_1 - CV_0]/CV_0$$

Property causes particular problems rooted in its unique nature as a physical asset class. Capital expenditures will be necessary from time to time to repair, refurbish, extend and improve property. How should this be dealt with? There are two alternatives. Expenditure can either be dealt with as if it causes a reduction in income, or as if it requires an increase in capital invested.

5.4.1 Reduction in income

Strict comparability with equities would suggest that minor capital improvements (CI) should be financed out of cash flow, just as a company would use cash flow to maintain its capital assets. The appropriate treatment is then quite simple. The income return is reduced by the expenditure while the capital return may be increased if the expenditure adds value to CV_1.

$$TR = [(Y_{0-1} - CI) + (CV_1 - CV_0)]/CV_0$$

5.4.2 Increase in capital invested

However, capital improvements are not always minor, and major improvements – say, extending a building – are similar to purchasing new assets. The appropriate treatment would then be to say that the amount of capital expended adds to CV_0 (and to CV_1 as long as the expenditure adds value) but does not affect the income return.

$$TR = [(Y_{0-1}) + (CV_1 - CV_0 + CI)]/[CV_0 + CI]$$

5.4.3 Timing of expenditure

These examples effectively assume that the expenditure takes place at the beginning of the year. This may not be true; for example, it may take place in stages during the year. The formula can then be adjusted to take account of timing.

For example, using the capital invested approach, expenditure at the half year stage can be dealt with by suggesting that half of the expenditure is invested for the year.

$$TR = [(Y_{0-1}) + (CV_1 - CV_0 + 0.5 * CI)]/[CV_0 + 0.5 * CI]$$

Both IPD in the UK and NCREIF in the US have used variations of this formula. However, there is a lobby in favour of the first measure (reduction in income). The effect can be significant: while the total return is unlikely to be much affected, the income return can go down (and the capital return can go up) by as much as 2 per cent over typical periods. This raises an interesting question about the income return delivered by depreciating property assets. Conventional approaches may disguise depreciation and overstate income returns: see Chapter 1. In practice the use of the month as the relevant time period for measurement greatly simplifies the treatment of the timing of expenditure.

5.5 Absolute or relative returns?

No asset can guarantee the delivery of a return fixed in nominal or real terms apart from conventional bonds or indexed bonds held to redemption and assets for which an efficient hedge can be put in place. Yet many property funds have been launched with absolute target returns (say 10 per cent nominal, or 6 per cent real) rather than relative returns (1 per cent above the IPD benchmark). This is probably a function of two drivers:

- i the desire by managers to replicate the leveraged IRR-based performance fee structures of hedge funds and to earn carried interest (see Chapter 3); and
- ii the absence of appropriate or acceptable benchmarks for international property.

The latter point requires consideration. There are now IPD Global and European Indexes, and other multi-country return measures, yet some consultants are sceptical about the objectivity and value of benchmarks that can be based upon these. However, it is now possible to specify and champion appropriate benchmarks for international relative return property funds, and if this work is put in place relative returns will be computed more often.

The relative return model is more obviously appropriate for core, low leverage funds. Opportunity funds will no doubt wish to protect absolute return targets, but even for these dual absolute and relative objectives will hopefully emerge (see Chapter 3).

5.6 Risk-adjusted measures of performance

A measure of the ten-year returns to UK property companies over the period 1981 to 1992 carried out at Reading University (Ackrill *et al.*, 1992) showed two property companies, Rosehaugh and Mountleigh, to be in the top quartile. Unfortunately, both called in receivers shortly after the end of the measurement period. While we know that past performance is no guide to the future, was past performance really no indicator of this prospect?

Happily, it was. Although the average return on these companies was very high, the high returns were concentrated in the early years of the measurement period; and the volatility of the returns from year to year was very high indeed.

A simple means of adjusting the return measure by the volatility of returns based on the Sharpe ratio (see Chapter 1) was used in the Reading study. The result was that both Rosehaugh and Mountleigh fell into the bottom quartile on a risk-adjusted basis, alongside Speyhawk, Greycoat and other casualties of the early 1990s crash. The risk-adjusted performance measure turned out to be an excellent predictor of failure.

However, just as returns can be calculated in different ways, risk adjustments can be made in different ways and often with different results.

In the following example two fund performances over five years will be compared with that of the UK property market, represented by the IPD annual index. Fund A out-performs by 1 per cent every year. Fund B has the same average out-performance, but behaves more erratically (see Table 5.4). Its volatility of return is higher.

Table 5.4: Fund A or fund B? (1)

Year	IPD	Fund A	Fund B
1	8	9	14
2	15	16	11
3	25	26	28
4	28	28	26
5	4	5	6
Average	16	17	17
SD	9.32	9.32	8.58

The most commonly used measure of volatility is the standard deviation. One simple route to risk adjustment, then, would be to divide the average return by the standard deviation of that return. This is the reciprocal of what is commonly called the coefficient of variation (CV) and ranks fund B as superior to A, which in turn is superior to the IPD benchmark (see Table 5.5).

Table 5.5: Fund A or fund B? (2)

	IPD	Fund A	Fund B
Average return	16	17	17
Standard deviation	9.32	9.32	8.58
1/CV	1.72	1.82	1.98

Note
CV = coefficient of variation (standard deviation/average return).

However, the fund manager may not be concerned about absolute volatility of performance. If he is measured relative to IPD, he may be concerned about relative performance. Dividing average out-performance by the standard deviation of return produces the same ranking (see Table 5.6).

Table 5.6: Fund A or fund B? (3)

	IPD	Fund A	Fund B
Average excess return	0	1	1
Standard deviation	9.32	9.32	8.58
1/CV	0	0.11	0.12

However, this is now comparing apples with pears; the relevant risk measure is now the standard deviation of relative performance – or tracking error. Dividing out-performance by the tracking error (a measure known as the information ratio) gives a more useful measure (see Table 5.7).

Table 5.7: Fund A or fund B? (4)

	IPD	Fund A	Fund B
Average excess return	0	1	1
Tracking error	0	0	3.58
1/CV	0	Infinite	0.28

We now have the most appropriate ranking of performance for two managers each trying to beat an index. Fund A has achieved consistent out-performance with no tracking error – infinitely good risk-adjusted performance. Fund B is less successful.

This is not, unfortunately, the end of the story. Had fund B achieved very slightly higher returns, which would have been best? How much tracking error compensates for an extra unit of out-performance?

This depends on the investor, whose tolerance for risk will vary from case to case. Nevertheless, if we believe that the past is any guide to the future, as it was with Rosehaugh and Mountleigh, we are unwise to throw these measures out, and risk measures are very important.

5.7 Attribution analysis: sources of property returns

5.7.1 Introduction

Attribution analysis separates the contribution of different variables to total return. At the single property level, the most simple attribution system separates income and capital return. Capital return can be more deeply analysed. In demonstrating this, it is useful to re-examine required and expected returns, concepts we introduced in Chapter 4.

If investors have perfect foresight, the return delivered on an asset in an efficient market will always be the return they require to make them invest. Delivered returns are not always the same as required returns, in which case single property attribution analysis becomes interesting.

5.7.2 What is a required return?

Any investment should deliver a return which exceeds the risk free rate by a premium, which in turn compensates for the disadvantages of the asset class. These are best summarized as risk, illiquidity and other factors (see Chapters 1 and 4).

The easiest starting point for considering opportunity cost is to look at a risk free asset. In nominal terms, this is represented very well by a UK conventional government bond. In real terms, it is represented in the UK by an index-linked government bond.

Whichever is used, the required return is therefore given by:

$$(1+RF_N)\times(1+RP)$$

or, as an approximation:

$$RF_N+RP$$

where RF_N is the redemption yield offered by the appropriate gilt and RP is the extra return – the risk premium – required to compensate for the disadvantages of the asset.

The full explanation of a required return is

$$R=l+i+RP$$

For conventional gilts offering a 3% yield when index-linked gilts offer 0.5%, it is possible that

$$3.5\%=0.5\%+2\%+0.5\%$$

when inflation is expected to run at 2 per cent and the extra return required to compensate investors for the risk that it does not is 0.5 per cent.

5.7.3 What is the delivered return?

Returns are delivered in two ways: through income (income return) and through capital (capital return). These combine to create total return.

$$TR=IR+CR$$

where
TR=total return;
IR=income return;
CR=capital return.

Income return over any period is the relationship of income delivered over the period and the capital value of the asset at the start of the period.

$$IR=Y_{0-1}/CV_0$$

where
Y_{0-1}=income over the period;
CV_0=capital value at the start of the period;

and

$$CR=(CV_1-CV_0)/CV_0$$

where
CV_1=capital value at the end of the period.

Capital values can be explained in terms of the relationship of the initial income on an asset and its multiplier.

$$Y^{*}1/K$$

where
Y=current income;
K=initial yield on the asset.

Hence capital values can change where incomes change or where initial yields change. Why do yields change? Following Gordon (Gordon, 1962):

$$K = R - G_N$$

where
G_N=expected income growth.

To develop this, let us use an example.

Assume that a stock has a current yield of 5 per cent. The required return is 10 per cent, incorporating a 2 per cent risk premium over local bonds yielding 8 per cent. It is priced at £20 with an expected initial dividend of £l. The expected growth in income is given as follows:

$$K = R - G_N$$

$$5\% = 10\% - G_N$$

$$G_N = 5\%$$

If expectations are correct, what total return will be delivered? Remember the required return is 10 per cent.

$$TR = IR + CR$$

$$IR = Y_{0-1}/CV_0$$

$$£1/£20 = 5\%$$

$$CR = (CV_1 - CV_0)/CV_0$$

What will CV_1 be? In one year, if expectations are correct, the income will have grown to £1.05. If initial yields do not change – and because nothing else is assumed to have changed, then initial yields will *not* change – then the value is given by

$$CV_1 = Y/K = £1.05/5\% = £21$$

$$CR = (£21 - £20)/£20 = 5\%$$

$$TR = IR + CR = 5\% + 5\% = 10\%$$

The delivered return is equal to the required return, because expectations turned out to be correct.

5.7.4 Why are delivered returns different from required returns?

It should be clear from the above that there are only two reasons why delivered returns can differ from required returns. First, expectations of income growth can turn out to have been incorrect. Second, initial yields might change.

Incorrect expectations of income growth

Let us assume that the income grows annually not at 5 per cent but at 10 per cent. What will happen? Capital value in year one will be given by:

$$£1.05/4\% = £22$$

$$TR = 5\% + (£22 - £20)/£20 = 5\% + 10\% = 15\%$$

Changes in cap rates

Let us assume now that the income grows as expected at 5 per cent but that cap rates fall from 5 to 4 per cent. Capital value in year one will be given by:

$$£1.05/4\% = £26.25$$

$$TR = 5\% + (£26.25 - £20)/£20 = 5\% + 31.25\% = 36.25\%$$

Why do changes in cap rates happen? Given, following Gordon, that

$$K = R - G_N$$

and following Fisher, that

$$R = l + i + RP$$

which simplifies to

$$R = RF_N + RP$$

then

$$K = RF_N + RP - G_N$$

and there are three reasons why initial yields would change. The risk free rate might change, the risk premium might change or expectations of income growth might change.

Changes in the risk free rate

Post-GFC, government policy has been to suppress interest rates despite continued inflation, with a resulting and targeted fall in the real risk free rate. For the sake of the following example, however, we will assume no fall in the risk free rate.

Changes in the premium

If the risk premium changes, the initial yield will change by an equal amount. Hence initial yields will fall to 4 per cent if the 2 per cent premium falls by 1 per cent to 1 per cent.

$$K = RF_N + RP - G_N$$

$$4\% = 8\% + 1\% - 5\%$$

Changes in expected income growth

If expected income growth changes, the initial yield will change by an equal and opposite amount. Hence initial yields will fall to 4 per cent if expected income growth rises by 1 per cent to 6 per cent.

$$K = RF_N + RP - G_N$$

$$4\% = 8\% + 2\% - 6\%$$

To conclude, delivered returns will differ from required returns if:

a the risk free rate falls;
b expectations of income growth are incorrect at time t;
c expectations of income growth change at time $t+1$; or
d the risk premium changes at time $t+1$.

Box 5.1 What drives returns?

Assume the required return on office property is currently driven by a risk premium of 3 per cent and that this has been a constant over the past decade. The required return on offices in 1992 would have been around 12 per cent (conventional bonds were yielding around 9 per cent). Why, then, were office returns in 1992 as low as –10 per cent?

1 Were expectations of office rental growth incorrect?

The out-turn was a fall in rental values of around –20 per cent. This was almost certainly much worse than expected.

2 Did the risk free rate change?

Bond yields were volatile at the time, but we cannot be sure that the risk free rate changed.

3 Were expectations revised?

It is a natural tendency for market participants to revise expectations based on immediate past experience. This is sometimes described as adaptive behaviour or adaptive expectations. The crash in rents in 1992 may have led to gloomier short-term expectations for 1993, no matter how irrational this might be. It would be more rational for expectations to improve as levels fall.

4 Did the risk premium change?

It is highly probable that there was an upward revision to the risk premium on offices in 1992. Canary Wharf went into liquidation, Rosehaugh and many other office-based property companies called in the receiver and the sentiment towards offices weakened significantly as rents crashed by more than expected. While such emotions may not be rational, it is often the case that the realization of a worst fear creates a new, even worse fear, rather than a feeling of relief. Such may have been the case for UK offices in 1992.

In quantitative terms, let us assume the following. Average income growth of 3 per cent was expected, the required return was 3 per cent over the 9 per cent gilt rate and initial yields were 9 per cent.

$$K=RF_N+RP-G_N$$

$$9\%=9\%+3\%-3\%$$

Let us add in the out-turn for rents (–20 per cent growth), an increase in the risk premium of 0.5 per cent and an upward revision to growth expectations to 3.5 per cent.

$$CR=(CV_1-CV_0)/CV_0$$

$$CV_1=Y_1/K_1$$

For a building previously earning £1 in rent and valued at £11.11, the new value would be (£0.80/K).

K would be given as follows:

$$K=9\%+3.5\%-3.5\%$$

$$=9\%$$

$$CV_1=£0.80/9\%=£8.88$$

$$CR=(£8.88-£11.11)/£11.11=-20.07\%$$

$$TR=9\%-20.07\%$$

$=-11.07\%$, *close to the **1992** delivered return of* –10%.

5.8 Attribution analysis for the portfolio: an introduction

Property investors increasingly used performance measurement and benchmarking services after the 1990s correction. Investors were forced to focus on risk, and needed to know that managers were professional as what had formerly been strong market returns had reversed, and the market was no longer able to disguise weaknesses in investment processes. These exist, first and foremost, to show whether a portfolio has achieved a rate of return better or worse than the 'market' average, or has met investment objectives specified in a more sophisticated fashion. Benchmarking has answered the question: *by how much* did we out- (under-) perform the benchmark? For managers, there follows an inevitable demand for portfolio attribution analysis which addresses the question: *why* did we out- (under-) perform the benchmark?

An ideal system of portfolio analysis would identify the contribution of all aspects of portfolio strategy and management to relative returns. It would separate, for example, profits earned on investments from returns on held properties. Those profits arise from two distinctly separate activities with different return and risk characteristics, and reflect different features of management 'skill'. Among held properties, relative return may be influenced by anything and everything from the broadest allocation of investment between sectors to skill in selecting tenants, negotiating rent reviews and controlling operating expenses (see Chapter 3).

In practice, the heterogeneity of individual properties and complexity of property management mean that the contributions of different functions and skills to portfolio performance are hard to disentangle. This chapter is concerned with the one tool – 'attribution analysis' – which is found in all performance measurement systems in a precisely quantified form.

Attribution analysis seeks to separate (at least) two components of a portfolio's relative return. The first is the relative return which is due to 'structure' – the allocation of investment to 'segments' of the market with different average rates of return. The second is 'stock selection' – the choice of individual assets within each market segment that have returns above or below the averages for that market segment.

Table 5.8 shows the performance of an unnamed fund in the late 1980s.

Table 5.8: Components of performance (%)

	Fund total	Sector component	Property component	IPD total
1987	13.3	–5.1	–6.0	24.3
1988	23.8	–2.4	–2.9	29.2
1989	8.3	–2.2	–3.6	14.1

Source: IPD

In 1989, for example, the fund showed a return of 8.3 per cent, which was nearly 6 per cent below the average return for the universe of properties measured by IPD. It was in the 94th percentile in that year. Over the 1980s the fund achieved an annualized total return of 11 per cent against the IPD average of 15 per cent. Returns appeared quite high, but poor relative performance meant that the management was replaced in 1990.

The poor sector mix (sector component) explained roughly half of the under-performance. The fund was overweight in retail, the under-performing sector over the period; it was particularly overweight in Scottish retail, again a poor relative performer. The remaining under-performance is explained by poor stock selection (the property component). The reason for this is that one very large asset performed very poorly. However, it is misleading to suggest that these are separable factors, because the large asset was a Scottish shopping centre. So all is not straightforward. While attribution analysis is important in property fund management – not just in terms of analysis, but also in the specification of investment objectives, the selection of managers and setting performance-related rewards – the above example shows that property is likely to present a series of challenges.

The academic and professional literature which deals with attribution of relative returns in property fund management is very thin. The literature on portfolio analysis for equities – the original source of the attribution technique – is not only surprisingly scant, but sets out several apparently different methods of defining and calculating attribution components. Following that literature, suppliers of property performance measurement services also adopted conflicting conventions.

In this section we set out a recommended approach to the application of attribution analysis to real estate portfolios. Our primary objectives are as follows.

- To give a clear statement of the purposes of attribution analysis, and its meaning for real-world property managers.
- To show, using real portfolio data from IPD's performance measurement services, the practical implications of applying different attribution methods.

The standard approach to the analysis of equity portfolios (see, for example, Hamilton and Heinkel, 1995) starts from three primary contributors to portfolio return: policy, structure and stock. (Unfortunately, the terminology for the last two contributors varies between sources. 'Structure' may alternatively be described as 'timing' or 'asset allocation'; 'stock' as 'selection' or 'property score'.)

We concentrate on structure and stock selection. By structure is meant the allocation of portfolio weights to 'segments' of the market – typically but not necessarily defined by a mixture of property types and geographical locations. By stock is meant the selection of individual investments within each segment which deliver returns above or below the average for that segment.

5.9 The choice of segmentation

An initial choice in any attribution system is critical to all that follows: what segments of the investible universe should be used to define 'structure'? Burnie *et al.* (1998) state:

> To be useful as a tool for evaluating portfolio management, performance attribution analysis should be carried out within a framework that mirrors the investment policy and the decision-making process particular to the fund under examination. A comprehensive attribution methodology will account explicitly for each key component of the portfolio management process.

In that view, the segment structure should reflect the way in which the managers of each individual portfolio choose to regard the 'structure' of their investible universe – how that

Table 5.9: IPD returns, 1998

Percentile/segment	1	5	10	25	50	75	90	99	Mean	SD	Number
Standard shops	−15.5	−5.0	−1.2	4.1	8.3	13.5	21.1	46.7	9.5	11.5	4,221
Shopping centres	−5.0	0.1	2.9	6.9	11.1	16.3	20.8	27.6	11.4	7.3	259
Retail warehouses	−10.3	−2.9	1.4	5.5	9.9	15.0	21.5	42.4	10.8	9.9	738
Stores/supermarkets	−7.4	0.2	3.7	7.6	11.5	17.7	25.2	50.7	26.5	27.3	420
Other retail	−27.7	−4.4	−0.2	5.3	9.3	13.8	24.7	105.8	11.7	18.9	271
Standard offices	−17.6	−3.1	1.3	6.9	11.2	18.2	26.9	64.6	13.3	14.3	2,693
Office parks	−11.2	−1.7	2.8	6.8	10.8	15.8	25.4	46.5	12.4	10.4	242
Standard industrials	−4.5	4.0	7.3	10.2	13.3	18.2	22.0	62.1	14.3	8.8	62
Industrial parks	−6.8	0.0	4.2	8.2	12.4	15.8	21.2	39.9	12.6	8.3	294
Distribution	−8.7	−1.5	1.7	5.5	9.7	13.5	19.9	34.2	10.0	7.7	223
Other property	−39.2	−10.5	−6.3	1.0	10.5	16.3	31.2	212.5	15.6	35.5	394
All property	*−14.9*	*−3.7*	*0.3*	*5.7*	*10.2*	*16.1*	*24.2*	*55.0*	*12.3*	*54.7*	*11,142*

Source: IPD

universe is broken down for the purposes of analysis, forecasting and setting target weights. But in practice it would then be extremely difficult for performance measurement services to operate, as it would not be possible to compare allocation and selection skills across portfolios.

For practical purposes, there has to be a standardized segmentation applied to the attribution analysis of all investors, at least as a first step. One standard IPD system is shown in Table 5.9.

Several considerations bear upon the choice of segmentation: statistical, practical and convention.

Statistically each segment should contain a sufficient number of properties for the average return to be reasonably robust: that is, each segment should ideally only reflect systematic risk. Following on from the previous point, the optimum segmentation of the market is that which statistically explains the most variance in individual property returns. Practically, segments most usefully cover property categories or areas for which property market information, with supporting information on (say) demographic and economic factors, is readily available to support analysis and forecasting. And, by convention, segments will be most acceptable to investors where they follow the generally accepted ways of dividing and analysing the market: it would be difficult to offer a detailed analysis service in the UK, for example, which did not show City of London offices as a 'segment'.

In real-world performance analysis services, the search for an appropriate segmentation will tend to resolve quite rapidly to a mixture of the dominant property types (shops, shopping centres, offices, industrials) and the geographical areas (either cities or regions) linked either to well-recognized property 'markets', or the city/regional boundaries used in the production of official statistics.

5.10 Style

Property fund managers may adopt asset allocation positions which are different from the segment weighting of the benchmark for a variety of reasons. This may be the result of forecasts driving tactical asset allocation, so that views of likely market returns influence a manager to adopt an underweight or overweight position relative to the benchmark in an attempt to produce out-performance. It may be the result of strategic asset allocation or policy, where issues other than pricing – for example, liability matching – influence the asset allocation mix. It may also be the conscious or unconscious result of the style of the fund manager.

The term is used here in an attempt to reflect more commonly used judgements of investment style in fund management. Is the manager style top-down (driven by a view of sectors) or bottom-up (driven by his choice of properties)? Is the manager a value manager or a growth manager? Such style judgements are very applicable in property fund management, and yet are rarely used. Instead, more reference is currently made to core, value-add and opportunistic as styles – see Chapter 2.

This definition of style implies a persistent bias in the property portfolio structure which is the result of preference or of habit. It may lead to long-term out-performance, or it may not. In equities fund management, value managers produced very poor returns in the dotcom boom (the period leading to 1999). Yet it was not to be expected that value managers would cease to be value managers. In UK property fund management, large prime stock out-performed secondary stock in some years, yet it was not to be expected that smaller active managers (many property companies, for example) would change their style.

Style may be associated with investment houses, or with funds. The recent focus on core, value-add and opportunistic labels is an example of style emerging as a key performance driver, and we provide evidence of this in Chapter 7.

5.11 Themes

As noted above, segment structure will typically be defined by reference to property use type and broad geographical region. Property fund managers invest in forecasting systems which enable managers to take a tactical view on prospective returns in the market 'segments' which are determined by this classification. It can be seen, then, that definitions of fund structure are of necessity rather stable. This is rational: data shows that use types in the UK have shown persistent cycles of under- and out-performance over a long period, a strong example being the continued out-performance of retail in the early 1980s and the early 1990s.

However, sector (type)/region segments are not necessarily optimal in permitting out-performance by asset allocation.

Table 5.10: Mean average deviations, IPD Irish Funds, 1986–95

Segment	Mean average deviation
Sector	2.70
Locations within retail	4.40
Locations within offices	1.80
Sub-sectors within retail	4.60
Age within retail	4.30
Age within offices	1.30
Age within industrials	5.70
Size within retail	2.40
Size within offices	1.20
Size within industrials	2.40

Source: IPD

Table 5.10 shows the mean average deviation between the mean return on the IPD index for Ireland and the returns across different segment classifications for the Irish market over the period 1986–95. The table suggests that the mean difference between the return on the individual sectors and the market as a whole in each individual year ('the window of opportunity') is less than the mean difference between the return on different age groups within the industrial market. There is more dispersion of returns across age bands *within* the industrial and retail sectors alone than there is across the three market sectors; and it would seem that concentrating on age bands across the market would have introduced the potential for greater returns that concentrating on sector choice would have done.

While sector allocations may not, in Ireland over the period 1986–95, present the maximum potential for out-performance, there is no reason why this might not be the case over some future period. An excellent manager may be expected to anticipate when this might be. Equally, he would be expected to anticipate at what point size or age becomes important. This is what we mean by themes.

The asset allocation process ideally takes accounts of themes as well as of standard segmentation. These may be new themes – sensitivity to changes in internet shopping, for example – or they may be standard, such as high yield/low yield. Themes differ from styles, because themes imply no necessary persistence in the manager's preference for segments; and themes differ from structure, because themes may not be reflected in segment classification or external performance measurement standards. Hence, a focus on short lease assets may be appropriate in some economic environments, but not in others.

5.12 City selection

An attribution system will preferably be stable and holistic. One major attraction of a regional classification in the UK, for example, is its completeness of coverage of UK property. However, this does not mean that fund managers will more effectively control risk and seek out-performance by categorizing their holdings in this way.

A regional forecasting system may or may not be effective in identifying regional markets that will out-perform a national benchmark. Even if it is, this may not be of much use to the fund manager, because he/she may not recognize the region as a useful way to think about the market. A more technical challenge to the usefulness of the region is the possibility that there may be greater windows of opportunity within a region than between regions.

The north-west of England, for example, suffered net out-migration and forecasts for population growth were negative throughout the 1990s. Within the region are two major cities, Manchester and Liverpool, one of which strengthened its position in the national hierarchy and one of which suffered extreme decline. A fund manager is likely to have considerably different views of Liverpool and Manchester; a property forecast for the north-west region is of very limited value to him.

For US and UK cities the windows of opportunity (mean average deviations from the mean) have been considerably greater at the city level than at the regional level. In addition, it appears that greater forecasting success has been associated with town or city level work than with regional forecasts. City selection is a vital input into fund management strategy.

However, portfolio structure is difficult to categorize by city. This is not a holistic system, because even if every city and town in any country were covered by the benchmark's databank there would still be outliers that fall outside defined city boundaries. This presents an attribution problem.

5.13 Calculating attribution scores

IPD records for a large number of real portfolios over a long run of years can give a fuller picture of the results for real portfolios produced by different attribution methods. The contribution of structure to variation in returns depends on the scale of differences in return across market segments. It reached a maximum in the boom and slump of the late 1980s and early 1990s, when there were spreads of up to 30 percentage points between the strongest and weakest markets. Structure accounted for 18 per cent of the variance in relative returns annualized over 17 years to 1999, but explained 42 per cent of the variance in returns over the nine years when the influence of the boom and slump was at its greatest.

The relative importance of structure and stock is as much a matter of philosophy as of statistical evidence. When calculating the attribution scores, there is even disagreement over the appropriate number of attribution components, and how they should be interpreted.

5.13.1 Two or three terms?

Brinson *et al.* (1986) identify three attribution components: timing (which is analogous to structure in our terminology), stock selection and an 'other' or 'cross-product' term.

The cross-product term is effectively a residual component that, mathematically, reflects an additional combined contribution of timing and selection. The authors' interpretation of what are termed timing and selection components broadly coincides with structure and stock selection components as defined in this chapter, but they do not offer an explanation of how the 'other' term relates to the objectives or management of the portfolio.

Subsequent authors, and suppliers of performance measurement services, divide into two camps. Experts either follow a decomposition method which calculates structure and selection scores separately from the cross-product component, or prefer to incorporate the cross-product term in either the structure or selection component, arguing that it has no useful meaning or is mathematically troubling.

According to Burnie *et al.* (1998) the cross-product term:

> represents the interaction of two other attribution effects but ... is not itself directly attributable to any one source of active management. It is therefore usually reallocated to another attribution effect or, if it remains isolated, is an ambiguous term whose value may exceed the measured effects of active management, thus rendering analysis results inconclusive.

Liang *et al.* (1999) state that the use of a two-component method is recommended 'on the basis of simplicity and ease of interpretation. Little is lost in terms of usable information, and much "noise" is avoided in efforts to explain the results to persons unfamiliar with the nuances of the calculation'. Hamilton and Heinkel (1995) and the Property Council of Australia, however, follow the three-component route, and go beyond Brinson *et al.* in suggesting how the cross-product term may be related to management decisions. As put by Hamilton and Hienkel 'the cross-product credits a manager for overweighting an asset class in which he or she out-performs the properties in that asset class in the RCPI (Russell Canadian Property Index)'.

The preferred argument is that the cross-product may reward style, when an overweighting in a segment is a persistent bias justified by consistent good stock selection in that segment; it is also an increasingly important measure of manager/fund selection in a fund of funds or multi-manager context (see Chapter 7).

5.13.2 The formulae

The dominant method of performance measurement expresses the performance of the portfolio against a benchmark as a relative return, based on the ratio of the two rates rather than the simple difference:

$$\text{Relative return} = ((1 + \text{Portfolio return})/(1 + \text{Benchmark return})) - 1$$

So a portfolio return of 10 per cent against a benchmark return of 5 per cent gives a relative return of 4.8 per cent:

$$\text{Relative return} = (1.10/1.05) - 1 = 4.8\%$$

This formula ensures that components of return and returns annualized over a run of years maintain consistent relative results, which is not possible if simple differences are used to compare returns.

Attribution scores are built up from comparisons of weights and returns in each segment of the market. Separate structure and selection scores in each segment are summed across the portfolio, to produce the portfolio level structure and selection scores which account for relative return.

The two- and three-component methods of attribution calculate structure scores in exactly the same way. In each segment:

$$\text{Segment structure score} = (\text{Portfolio weight} - \text{Benchmark weight}) \times \text{Benchmark return}$$

The alternative ways of calculating stock selection scores are:

i two-component attribution method segment selection score (the IPD method):

$$= \text{Portfolio weight} \times ((1 + \text{Portfolio segment return})/(1 + \text{Benchmark segment return})) - 1$$

ii three-component attribution method segment selection score:

$$= \text{Benchmark weight} \times ((1 + \text{Portfolio segment return})/(1 + \text{Benchmark segment return})) - 1$$

The difference lies in a single term. The three-component method multiplies segment relative returns by the benchmark weight, while the IPD method multiplies by the portfolio weight. When calculated using the IPD method, the structure score and IPD selection score in each segment add up to the weighted contribution to relative return. Summed across segments, the structure score and IPD selection score add up to the portfolio's relative return.

In the three term method, the structure and selection scores do not add up in this way, leaving a 'residual' term, the cross-product, which is the product of the segment relative returns multiplied by the difference between benchmark weight and the portfolio weight (sometimes known as the 'bet'). This is calculated as:

$$\text{Cross-product} = \text{Relative return} - ((1 + \text{Structure score}) \times (1 + \text{Selection score}) - 1) \times 100$$

Hamilton and Hienkel (1995) relate the cross-product term to management decisions. They suggest that a positive cross-product term reflects a manager's decision to focus on a segment where they have 'stock' skills or specialization. Keeris and Lanbroek (2005) highlight the potential importance of the cross-product term and show that when portfolios are structured in increasingly different ways from the benchmark, its relative importance grows.

Here is an example. The performance of a European property share vehicle which was managed by a UK fund manager was as follows, net of the effect of cash:

$$\text{Out-performance } (-2.9) = \text{structure } (-0.1) + \text{stock } (-2.0) + \text{cross-product } (-0.8)$$

The fund was overweight in countries where stock selection was poor and underweight in countries where stock selection was good, especially the UK. It would not be a surprise to the UK manager to learn that the stock selection score was better in the UK, but it may be distressing for him to realize that the stock selection under-performance was exaggerated by nearly a full point because of fund structure under-weighting the UK market. Why did he fail to take account of expected superior UK stock selection in his asset allocation?

The cross-product is also of clear relevance to multi-manager or fund of funds portfolios, indicating the portfolio manager's success in allocating money to the best fund managers or stock selectors, particularly at the higher risk (value-added or opportunity fund) end of the market.

Box 5.2 Attribution

A fund achieved the following result in 2014. Using simplified arithmetic for demonstration purposes and using the three-component attribution method:

Out-performance (1.0) = structure (0.1) + stock (–0.4) + cross-product (1.3)

What do these results signify concerning the relative importance of structure and stock?

If the cross-product is treated as part of stock selection, as in the most common two component system used by IPD and others:

Out-performance (1.0) = structure (0.1) + stock (0.9)

Stock selection contributes 90 per cent of out-performance.

If the cross-product is allocated to structure, as proposed by Burnie *et al.* for a portfolio constructed by bottom-up selection of individual assets with passive structure:

Out-performance (1.0) = structure (1.4) + stock (–0.4)

Stock selection damages performance.

The choice of method is clearly non-trivial in this example. Which is most appropriate? What else would you need to know about the manager's investment process in order to be able to answer this question?

5.14 Attribution and portfolio management

It is not clear from the mathematical construction of different attribution methods, or (pending further tests) from the real-world portfolio results they produce, that one attribution method is superior to another. Instead, they may each be valid, and particularly valid for particular styles of management.

5.14.1 Top-down portfolio building

The two-component method embodies the classic top-down model of portfolio construction. Policy dictates a benchmark against which the portfolio is to be measured, specified in terms of a portfolio weighting by segment. An 'allocator', working with market analysis and forecasts, decides which segments are likely to out-perform or under-perform the overall benchmark return, and (perhaps taking into account relative risks) determines a target weighting for the portfolio. Other things being equal, segments expected to out-perform will be over-weighted, the fund taking 'bets' against the market. The scale of the bet will depend on confidence in forecasts, on the deviations from the benchmark specifically permitted or on the manager's willingness to accept a tracking error against the benchmark.

Once the target weights have been set, the management task passes to a 'selector'. The selector chooses the specific assets to be held in each segment, with the target of choosing assets that are expected to out-perform the benchmark average for that segment. In equities, the assets will (most likely) be shares in individual companies. In property, they will (most likely) be individual buildings.

5.14.2 Backing selection skills

A portfolio constructed by backing selection skills offers a more interesting, and probably more common, case. Here managers choose to hold high weights in segments where selection skills are believed to be strong (perhaps on the evidence of track record). Here the task of the allocator is redefined to take account *both* of the overall performance of market segments and of the skills of the selector when setting portfolio weights. In this case, the three-component method of attribution offers a useful distinction between the relative inputs to portfolio performance. As before, the structure score measures the allocator's forecasting ability. The stock selection score measures the selector's skills in the purest form. The cross-product measures how far pre-judgements of selection skills have proved to be correct.

5.14.3 Specialist portfolios

A specialist portfolio could be taken as an extreme case of backing selection skills. Here the portfolio is narrowly structured on segments where selection skills are believed to be exceptionally strong, possibly in the belief that such a concentration will in itself improve selection skills. Attribution analysis as it has been defined above may no longer apply to these portfolios, because portfolio structure is defined by style rather than manager discretion. Under these conditions, an attribution analysis using a standard segmentation would show the benefits or otherwise of the overall policy choice. The performance of the manager is most appropriately measured against a benchmark limited to the segments predetermined by policy. Within those segments, special attribution analysis by sub-segment could provide information on the skills applied within that specialist area.

In the ideal world, attribution analysis should be 'carried out within a framework that mirrors the investment policy and decision making process particular to the fund under examination' (Burnie *et al.*, 1998).

5.15 Alpha and beta: a new attribution approach

In a more challenging, mature and increasingly transparent market, attribution analysis is now likely to see some development, particularly when more investment activity is undertaken through REITs and unlisted funds (see Part 3). It is increasingly possible to assemble performance records, and following this there has been more detailed analysis of those records. Potential analytical performance systems include traditional attribution methods but will also cover performance concepts widely used in other asset classes which have also seen the development of fund formats. The asset classes that are most relevant are private equity funds and hedge funds, and the most interesting attribution development in these markets is the concept of alpha and beta separation.

What creates beta, and what drives alpha in real estate investment? How can these concepts be measured and isolated? How do they relate to traditional attribution systems? Can performance records and performance fees adequately distinguish between these drivers? Baum and Farrelly (2008) illustrated these issues by reference to a case study addressing the complete performance record of a single unlisted fund, and the remainder of this chapter is derived from that paper, which is also used as the basis of the latter part of Chapter 7.

There are many references to alpha and beta as sources of risk-adjusted performance in alternative asset classes, with most work focused on hedge funds (see, for example, Litterman, 2008). The concept of alpha and beta is drawn directly from Sharpe's capital asset pricing model (CAPM): see Sharpe (1964). Anson (2002) describes CAPM as a regression model which can be used to determine the amount of variation in the dependent variable (the fund return) that is determined or explained by variation in the independent variable (the appropriate market return):

$$\text{Investment return} = \alpha + \beta * \text{Benchmark return} + \varepsilon$$

The important measure of manager performance is the intercept term α, which represents the excess return earned by the fund over and above that of the benchmark. However, it is important that this is measured as a risk-adjusted return, in other words that the effect of pure risk is taken out of the intercept.

The security market line (SML) posits that higher-risk assets and portfolios should earn higher returns. A higher-risk portfolio should out-perform a lower-risk portfolio on a risk-unadjusted basis. This does not mean that the manager has shown any skill. However, out-performance of the SML implies that skill has been demonstrated and this is measured by the intercept term, or alpha, as illustrated in Figure 5.1.

It is possible to measure alpha and beta for a property fund, provided that we have a series of fund returns and a series of appropriate benchmark returns over the same period. This is achieved by regressing the fund returns on the benchmark returns and observing the measured values of alpha (α) and beta (β). A value for β in excess of unity implies that fund returns are highly sensitive (or geared) to the market return, suggesting high-risk assets, a high-risk portfolio or a high-risk strategy. A high value for α suggests that an excess return has been earned by the fund over the risk-adjusted benchmark return.

Figure 5.1: Alpha and beta

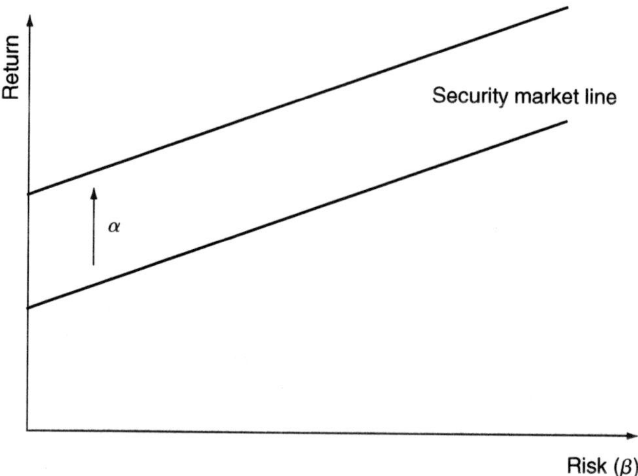

Source: Baum and Farrelly, after Sharpe, 1964

5.15.1 Sources of alpha and beta

Alpha

Positive alpha represents out-performance of the SML and implies that the manager has demonstrated skill. In property fund management managers can exercise skill when structuring their portfolios from a top-down perspective (allocating to markets and sectors) and at the stock level (sourcing and managing their assets). Out-performance at the portfolio structure level is delivered by managers who, *ceteris paribus*, allocate relatively more to out-performing sectors or geographies. This implies that the manager has a forecasting capability, which is a source of out-performance.

As noted by Geltner (2003), out-performance at the stock level is very different from that of traditional securities fund management, and this is largely due to the 'private equity' characteristics of property. Properties are selected by investor/owners and require ongoing asset management which encompasses a number of activities. These are all potential sources of alpha.

Alpha in property management can arise from operational cost control, tenant relationship management, asset maintenance, leasing strategy, marketing and capital expenditure applied to asset enhancement/refurbishment. Alpha can also be generated when assets are bought and sold. For example managers who are able to purchase assets at discounts, recognize latent value that is not reflected in valuations, or negotiate attractive prices and execute more complex deals and thus face less competitive pricing, will, *ceteris paribus*, out-perform their benchmarks.

Beta

Property investment risk (beta), like alpha, can be broadly separated into both structure and stock beta. Within the constraints of a domestic benchmark 'structure' beta arises from allocations to more volatile sectors such as CBD office markets. When mandates allow for global investment, exposures to more risky geographies such as emerging markets are then a source of additional risk. Defining structure risk in a purely quantitative manner is difficult in some situations because certain aspects are difficult to quantify. For example, differences in transparency and property rights may not be reflected in the relative performance of market data.

Stock level beta is an area of potential confusion. For example, development can often be referred to as a source of alpha in a given portfolio. This is incorrect, as development in itself is simply a more risky property strategy and should be reflected by a higher beta. Development alpha is obtained by out-performing other development managers. There is a continuum of asset level risk ranging from ground rent investments, to assets with leasing risk and high vacancy, to speculative developments, all of which should have a hierarchical range of betas.

5.15.2 Previous studies

The received wisdom is that it is easier to find alpha, those returns that are due to manager skill, in an inefficient market. It is also generally accepted that commercial property is traded in an inefficient market; however, empirical studies do not find strong evidence of delivered alpha in property fund management. Lee (2003) examines the UK pooled funds market using both the traditional CAPM equation and also the Henriksson and Merton (HM) extended CAPM model which measures the timing and selection ability of managers. Timing in this respect relates to the ability of managers to increase beta in rising markets. Using both methods Lee's study finds little evidence of manager alpha. Lee and Stevenson (2002) examine this issue using meta analysis. Again there is evidence that managers are unable to out-perform through timing, but there is evidence that they improve their risk-adjusted performance through stock selection.

In research undertaken for the UK Investment Property Forum (IPF) using data from the Investment Property Databank (IPD), Mitchell and Bond (2008) discovered little evidence of systematic out-performance for most property fund managers. Lee's (2003) study of the UK pooled funds universe again found little evidence of either short- or long-term performance persistence. However, both studies found that a small number of funds in the top decile showed persistent risk-adjusted out-performance, although most managers were unlikely to offer consistently above or below average returns.

Mitchell and Bond suggest that manufacturing beta exposure (mimicking the returns of the market) is also difficult because property is a heterogeneous asset class. In addition, the operational cost of managing passive property exposure is not significantly lower than active property management. Their research found that although the IPD property score was the strongest driver of performance and alpha in the period measured, it was of no use in predicting either in the following period. (It is also biased, as it includes the cross-product.)

This lack of alpha persistence leads to an increase in the importance of beta as a driver of performance. The study also surveyed a number of investors and consultants who saw property as a beta asset class (one for which sustained alpha is not expected), so that one could conclude that the lack of observed alpha need not be an issue for institutional investors.

Empirical work indicates that a large number of properties are required in order to get down to systematic risk levels and, on average, some 10 per cent of an individual property's return is accounted for by a broad market factor (Brown and Matysiak, 2000a). Baum and Struempell (2006) showed that specific risk is a function of lot size and diversification efficiency. Sectors in which the performance of individual assets is similar and where lot sizes are high are difficult to diversify. So we are left with evidence that a focus on beta may be a waste of time, as specific risk means that it is very difficult for managers to deliver low tracking error returns, while sustained alpha delivery is also elusive. Once again, successful property investment appears challenging!

Geltner (2003) adopts a different and original approach to performance attribution. He is concerned to dig deeper into the stock selection effect, and adds a second level of performance attribution, splitting stock effects into the following four sub-activities.

- property selection;
- acquisition transaction execution;
- operational management;
- disposition transaction execution.

If appropriate benchmark return data is available – IRRs, not time-weighted returns, he recommends, because the timing of expenditure is under the manager's control – then the manager's relative skill might be measurable. He attempts to measure the impact of these activities by reference to single property attribution using three variables: initial yield, cash flow change and yield change. Geltner makes no attempt to relate these activities to alpha and beta.

5.15.3 An attribution model

We can perhaps attempt to relate these stock selection activities to alpha and beta in the context of the higher level attribution approach. In doing so, we suggest that each of the activities shown in Figure 5.2 can be alpha-generating. The key issue, it appears, is whether

Figure 5.2: Attribution of property returns

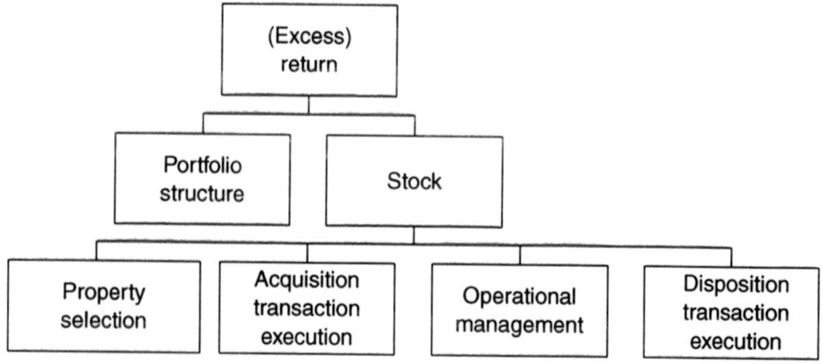

Source: Baum and Farrelly, 2008

the activities deliver extra returns through skill or through risk. If all portfolio segments are of similar risk, then positive excess returns generated by the portfolio structure relative to a benchmark will produce alpha. If they result from taking overweight positions in high-risk markets, then they generate beta.

The same distinction can be applied to some of Geltner's second tier. Property selection can deliver higher initial returns through skill or through risk. It can deliver positive cash flow change through skill (executing excellent active asset management or development) or through risk (undertaking 'average-skill' development; buying empty buildings).

The same is true of operational management. Excellence in transaction execution appears to be a pure alpha activity. All other variables may be either beta or alpha generators.

When we consider these factors in the context of unlisted funds, alpha and beta separation is somewhat easier.This is dealt with in Part 3.

Part 3

Investment vehicles

Listed real estate

6.1 What is listed real estate?

In Chapter 2 we introduced the idea of the four quadrants of real estate investing, shown here as Figure 6.1.

For investors seeking exposure to the global real estate investment universe, it is possible to invest in public (listed) securities, specifically REITs (a listed real estate company regulated by national legislation which provides tax breaks in return) or listed property companies (PropCos, or in US parlance, real estate operating companies or REOCs), or in

Figure 6.1: Four quadrants

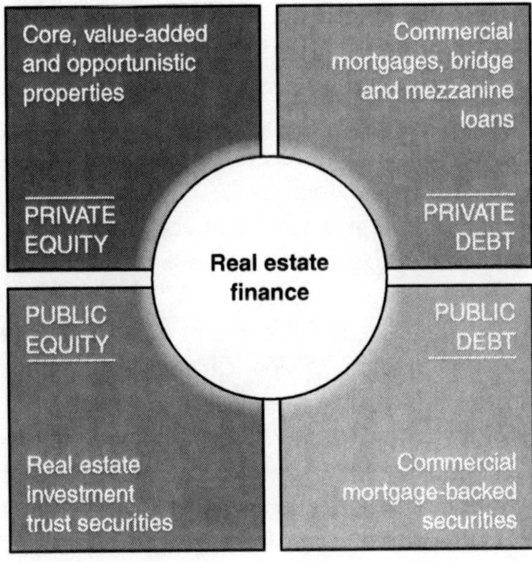

unlisted property funds such as opportunity funds. As implied by Figure 6.1, these funds primarily offer an equity-style exposure.

Banks making senior loans or providing mortgages secured on real estate are investors in private debt. Since the late 1980s, creative real estate banking professionals have developed publicly listed debt instruments, examples of which are CMBS and residential mortgage backed securities (RMBS). We deal with CMBS in Section 6.10. We should add mortgage REITs as another form of public debt; and since the GFC, unlisted debt funds have become popular. This is a new form of private debt (see Chapter 7).

For the remainder of this chapter we focus on public real estate vehicles, both equity and debt.

6.2 Public equity real estate – the background

The production and ownership of high quality real estate needs to be financed through large-scale equity and debt capital. This requires the presence of an active international banking system, which will supply most of the debt capital, but also of entrepreneurs using equity capital. Pension funds, insurance companies, endowment funds, sovereign wealth funds and family offices, the major suppliers of equity capital (see Chapter 2), have all shown a desire to access global property markets. Property companies, representing entrepreneurial equity, have offered an attractive conduit.

In Chapter 1 we identified several key problems for property investors. The main issues are (i) illiquidity and (ii) lot size and the specific risk this creates. Institutional investors often suggest that the greatest deterrent to real estate investment is illiquidity, and many believe that the best remedy for illiquidity must be a public market quotation. Baum and Struempell (2006), and Callender *et al.* (2007), on the other hand, identify lumpiness – the large and uneven sizes of individual assets – as the key inhibitor of global property investment. Direct property investment (buying buildings) requires considerably higher levels of capital investment when compared to securities, and diversification within property portfolios may prove to be more challenging than in equity and bond portfolios.

To illustrate, let us assume that there are four core global regions which investors need to access: Europe, Asia, North America and the Emerging Markets (Latin America, Africa, others). Assume that in each region there are ten markets to be accessed. (In Europe, for example, we may choose the UK, Germany, France, Spain, Italy, Poland, Netherlands, Sweden, Denmark, Ireland.) Assume there are four property types within each market: office, retail, industrial/logistics, residential.

To assemble a sample that is representative of each market (see Brown and Matysiak, 2000b; Baum and Struempell, 2006) let us assume we need ten buildings. If each costs an average of $50 million, how much capital will we need? The answer is a staggering $80 billion. If a global investor puts a typical 8 per cent of his investment into real estate, he will need assets of £1,000 billion, or $1 trillion. Chapter 2 shows that the largest real estate investment manager in the world manages assets of just over $100 billion, and there are very, very few global investors known to have $1 trillion or so in assets.

This analysis has limitations – it is highly approximate, it ignores the use of leverage and it understates the impact of diversification across markets – but it illustrates an obvious truth. The vast majority of investors do not have enough capital to build diversified portfolios of global real estate.

Listed real estate equity vehicles therefore have obvious advantages, providing access to liquidity and enabling the diversification of specific risk.

Publicly listed real estate equity securities can be split into REITs and REOCs, and the definition can be expanded to include mutual funds (Section 6.4) and exchange traded funds (ETFs, Section 6.5). Under normal market conditions, these listed markets have fewer problems with liquidity, and trades can be made quickly and easily on a daily basis, albeit sometimes with a pricing penalty for transactions of scale. Listed securities also allow immediate exposure to the market, while some unlisted funds will take capital only as it is required to buy assets. The case for these instruments is therefore strong.

6.3 Property companies and REITs

6.3.1 Property companies

In the first edition of this book, we suggested that growth in global securitized property investment seemed to be inhibited by a lack of supply, largely created by taxation and regulatory conservatism in markets outside the US, Australia and a few others. The potential for development of the European market in particular seemed great. Germany, France, Italy and Spain had less securitized real estate product per unit of GDP than any other country, while the relatively mature securitized markets of the US, Australia, UK and Hong Kong had most. One explanation for low growth in Europe had been the relatively poor performance of the listed sector, plus tax inefficiency.

A property company is a taxable entity, like any company. Profits are taxed within the firm, and management has unlimited discretion to distribute dividends to shareholders from post-tax income. Tax-paying shareholders are then taxed on the dividend income they receive, so double taxation arises in their hands. Tax leakage puts all investors in property company shares at a disadvantage to investors in direct property, who are taxed once.

In addition, in some markets, the UK being a prime example, long-term returns from property company shares had been no better than returns from direct property, while risk had been much higher (see Section 6.6). Performance had been strongly linked to equities in the short term – so property companies had not offered diversification against equity portfolios.

REITs, however, have been more popular, and both a tax advantage and improved performance characteristics appear to have been significant.

6.3.2 REITs

The global universe of real estate companies has expanded over the past decade due to the relatively strong performance of the sector, ongoing equity issuance and (most importantly) a gradual proliferation of REIT vehicles across the globe enabled by legislative changes in several countries keen to emulate the generally good experience of the early major REIT markets such as the US (1961), Australia and Canada. In the US, the REIT market has grown from tiny market capitalizations to more than $670 billion in 30 years, much of it held by overseas investors. In Australia, rapid growth in the listed property trust market over the same 30-year period created more than 70 A-REITs listed on the ASX with a 2014 market capitalization in excess of A$100 billion.

Japan, Singapore and Hong Kong followed in the 1990s. The Japanese REIT led to enacted or currently planned REIT legislation in other Asian countries including Malaysia,

Korea and India and China, while in Europe the example provided by the 2003 launch of French REITs (*Sociétés d'Investissements Immobiliers Cotées*, or SIICs) led to the UK and Germany REIT market launches in 2007 and 2008 respectively.

Now a global brand, although the regime controlling them is not formally consolidated in any way, REITs are generally distinguished from property companies or REOCs by two factors: tax treatment and regulation. The key advantage of REITs is that they generally do not pay taxes at the company level provided they conform to a number of restrictions which typically include the following:

a they discharge a majority of taxable income as a dividend;
b leverage is limited; and
c the portion of income derived from development is limited.

The key advantages created by this tax treatment of the REIT is that double taxation of income is avoided and the capital gains tax that would be charged on the disposal of assets – arguably a key reason for PropCos trading at discounts to net asset value (see Section 6.9) – is extinguished.

REITs have become more popular in some markets than others. REITs are the predominant form of public listed property equity instruments in the US, Australia, UK and France. In Japan, REITs co-exist with traditional property companies. In Hong Kong, Malaysia, Germany and several other markets REITs are a small percentage of the listed market. Time will tell how large the new European REIT markets will become, but the number of UK REITs doubled in the period 2008–14 while, despite the large size of the German direct market in 2014, there were only four German REITs in 2014.

Growth in the new REIT formats in Europe (especially the UK and Germany) appears to have been limited by bad timing, coming as these launches did at the beginning of the financial market collapse of 2007–8. Table 6.1 shows that in 2008 the total return performance of the global universe of real estate stocks, including both REITs and REOCs, was worse than –53.5 per cent. Every region was affected, with the Americas least far down at 40 per cent, and the UK most down, by a massive –61 per cent. Despite this, average returns over the nine years to 2013 have been quite acceptable, as Table 6.1 shows.

Table 6.1: Total returns, global listed real estate, 2005–13

	Asia	Eurozone	North America	UK
2005	23.37	11.52	13.21	6.72
2006	36.49	67.72	36.26	68.69
2007	14.80	−15.98	−14.92	–35.18
2008	–52.48	–45.63	–40.63	–61.09
2009	43.43	47.67	32.22	29.09
2010	17.21	7.16	28.65	1.75
2011	−19.61	−17.08	8.19	–8.62
2012	45.52	31.25	18.14	35.86
2013	4.37	11.36	1.27	26.17
Average	12.56	10.88	9.15	7.04

Source: Consilia Capital

6.4 Listed funds and mutual funds

The distinction between a company and what is commonly thought of as a fund is not based on the legal structure – funds may also be corporate structures, as explained in Chapter 7 – but on the way the two are managed. The typical listed property company is internally managed, meaning that there is no legal separation of assets and management team, while a fund (like an investment trust) has external management and a contract is put in place between the fund manager and the assets, which are held in a separate corporate structure.

Listed funds popular in the UK market include a group of Jersey and Guernsey listed investment companies created in the period before UK REIT legislation became live, seeking tax efficiency, with external management. These are usually closed-ended but may be open-ended, such as open-ended investment companies (OEICs). For more about this distinction, see Chapter 7.

A mutual fund – a US term not widely used in the UK – is a listed fund which invests in other listed companies, known in the UK as an investment trust. This is similar in effect to a fund of funds (see Chapter 7), but a mutual fund invests in companies rather than funds. Hence there are listed (mutual) funds investing in UK, European and global REITs providing a diversified exposure to the sector. Outside the US, these are more commonly known as property securities funds.

6.5 Exchange traded funds (ETFs)

Traded like normal shares, but behaving more like mutual funds in their investment performance characteristics, ETFs allow investors to spread investments even more by tracking the performance of an entire index. Investors get exposure to the ETF by buying a share in a single asset which represents that index.

The range of ETFs includes the EPRA universe of European REITs and real estate stocks, and the global listed real estate sector can be accessed through the EPRA/NAREIT Global Property Yield Fund. ETFs provide exposure to global property companies and REITs without the manager selection risk – or benefit – of a mutual fund.

Also available are short and ultra-short ETFs which provide returns which are perfectly negatively correlated with the underlying index returns. This is a useful tool for a hedge fund – see Chapter 8.

6.6 Does listed real estate offer the ideal property vehicle?

What characteristics would the ideal property vehicle have? It would deliver returns which were representative of property as an asset class, offering diversification against equities and bonds. It would have risk and return characteristics that reflected the nature of property as an asset class – moderate returns for low apparent volatility or risk. It would be divisible into small lot sizes, so that global diversification were possible for all investors. It would be liquid. It would use leverage where this was beneficial, and it would be tax efficient.

At first glance investing in listed real estate looks promising. The instruments are certainly reasonably liquid, and very divisible. But the performance characteristics offered need to be carefully examined. The ideal vehicle will offer both short-term and long-term performance characteristics in line with the asset class. Will public equity real estate do this?

6.6.1 Tactical asset allocation

When comparing returns contemporaneously, the risk-return characteristics of REITs appear to have more in common with the returns of the stock market than with direct real estate returns. For example, REITs have typically experienced significantly higher levels of volatility (as measured by standard deviation) than is exhibited by the returns of the direct market (see Table 6.1, and Myer and Webb, 1993) and higher positive correlation with stock markets (Westerheide, 2006), and in particular small cap stocks (Liu and Mei, 1992), than with direct market appraisal based indices (Lee *et al.*, 2000).

Clayton and Mackinnon (2003) present evidence of the volatility in US REIT returns in the sample period between 1978 and 1998. Volatility was correlated primarily with US large cap stocks, although it must be noted that the authors found that the level of impact had diminished over the sample period, with volatility becoming increasingly driven by small cap, bond and real estate markets. The relative short-term relationship between listed and direct markets could also be partly explained by the differences between valuation methods and trading practices adopted in the relative markets, with the appraisals used in direct market indices being subject to a smoothing effect and high levels of autocorrelation (Geltner, 1991; Brown and Matysiak, 2000b), compared to the more immediate pricing adjustments possible in daily traded secondary markets of the listed sector.

The tactical asset allocation process is designed to generate performance from short-term expectations of returns at the asset level. This means that when property is thought to be cheap, public real estate equity securities should be about to out-perform. The tactical asset allocation process, running month by month, will require this to be so, or otherwise it will be risky or illogical to go overweight, and a neutral weight or an underweight position will be maintained.

However, by examining historical monthly returns, volatilities and correlations between property, property companies and equities, it can be seen that property companies have been a hybrid between property and equities in terms of short-term performance (Hoesli and Oikarinen, 2012). Using UK data, we can see that they delivered a return between 1990 and 2013 of less than that delivered by direct property and equities, while being far more volatile than both direct property and equities. And, while correlations will always be time-variant and subject to shocks, on a monthly and quarterly basis over the longest available time period the return on property shares was much more similar to returns delivered by the equity market than to returns delivered by the direct property market.

Comparing the short-term total return of direct property (IPD), property companies (the FTSE property company sector, which include REITs from 2007 onwards) and equities (the FTSE all share index) – see Tables 6.1 to 6.6 – shows that property companies and the equity market have been very volatile compared with direct property. This is a bad thing: low reported volatility is what investors want, even if direct property returns are known to be smoothed by valuations. In it inarguable that valuations fail to report the real volatility of direct real estate, but valuation-based returns are universally accepted by pension funds and other institutional investors. And this issue is not only about volatility; it is also about correlation.

Tables 6.2 to 6.7 analyse UK data over a long time series of 1990 to 2013. Tables 6.2 and 6.3 show the short-term – monthly – performance characteristics of UK property

Table 6.2: Risk and return, monthly, UK asset classes, 1990–2013 (monthly data)

	Return	Risk
Direct property	0.71%	1.09%
Equities	0.76%	4.52%
Property companies	0.41%	5.83%

Source: IPD, Property Funds Research

Table 6.3: Correlation, monthly, UK asset classes, 1990–2013 (monthly data)

	Direct property	Equities
Direct property	1	–
Equities	0.14	1
Property companies	0.25	0.62

Source: IPD, Property Funds Research

company shares relative to property (the IPD monthly index) and equities. Table 6.2 shows the risk and return data, while Table 6.3 presents a correlation matrix.

Table 6.2 shows that property company returns (0.41 per cent per month, or around 5 per cent per annum) were less than direct property returns, despite the higher financial risk (through leverage) of property companies. This is reflected in the volatility of property company shares, over five times greater than the volatility of the direct market and greater than the equity market as a whole. In addition, property companies are highly correlated with equities. Property volatility is artificial, due to valuation smoothing (see Chapter 1), and any industry sector might have higher volatility than the equity market as a whole due simply to the smaller sample taken from a bigger market. Nonetheless, the plain reported facts remain, and UK property shares look highly inefficient over this period.

In a monthly tactical asset allocation process, it is difficult, if not impossible, to change allocations to direct property while at the same time making changes to equity and bond allocations, as it will typically take much longer than one month to complete the purchase or sale of any directly held property assets.

When equities appear expensive or unattractive and property appears cheap or attractive, then what is to be done? An increased allocation to property may fail to achieve any required result. Should the equities be sold immediately or as direct property assets are found? Selling immediately may mean investing in cash for at least one tactical asset allocation round. What happens if equities fall in price over that period and become attractive again? Should prospective property acquisitions be aborted? Clearly, this is problematic.

Alternatively, can we use property shares? Will property shares act effectively as a proxy for direct real estate in short-term asset allocation? They can be acquired with the same speed with which equities can be sold. So when equities appear expensive or unattractive and property appears cheap or attractive why not buy property shares?

Table 6.3 provides a clear answer to this. Because property company shares were correlated 62 per cent with equities, and only 25 per cent with direct property, the performance of property shares in the short term was likely to be much more like equities than property. What happens to property shares if equities fall in price over that period? Property shares were very likely to have fallen as well, while direct property is only slightly (14 per cent) correlated with equities.

Moving to a quarterly analysis, we see much the same results, shown in Tables 6.4 and 6.5.

An annual analysis, shown in Tables 6.6 and 6.7, presents a slightly different picture, especially in terms of the correlation results, which show returns on property company shares becoming more correlated with property, and more so than with equities.

This sets up the hypothesis that property shares might be good proxies for the direct real estate market over longer period, and might play a role in strategic asset allocation.

Table 6.4: Risk and return, quarterly, UK asset classes, 1990–2013 (quarterly data)

	Return	Risk
Direct property	1.75%	3.16%
Equities	2.06%	7.87%
Property companies	1.20%	11.45%

Source: IPD, Property Funds Research

Table 6.5: Correlation, quarterly, UK asset classes, 1990–2013 (quarterly data)

	Direct property	Equities
Direct property	1	–
Equities	0.23	1
Property companies	0.40	0.62

Source: IPD, Property Funds Research

Table 6.6: Risk and return, annual, UK asset classes, 1990–2013 (annual data)

	Return	Risk
Direct property	7.18%	9.98%
Equities	8.40%	16.58%
Property companies	4.90%	27.87%

Source: IPD, Property Funds Research

Table 6.7: Correlation, annual, UK asset classes, 1990–2013 (annual data)

	Direct property	Equities
Direct property	1	–
Equities	0.49	1
Property companies	0.72	0.55

Source: IPD, Property Funds Research

6.6.2 Strategic asset allocation

The strategic asset allocation process is designed to produce a set of assets that are most appropriate taking into account the liabilities of a pension scheme. The allocation to property is determined using asset-liability models and inputs that reflect the nature of the assets in terms of return, risk and correlation.

It is therefore important to examine the characteristics of indirect property vehicles compared to direct property to assess whether the use of indirect property vehicles within the property portfolio damages the integrity of the strategic asset allocation.

Comparing the longer-term annual total returns of direct property, property companies and equities shows that property companies are a hybrid between property and equities. They have delivered a return since 1971 of less than that on property while being far more volatile than direct property, indeed being more akin to equities. This is broadly true whichever time horizon is examined. However, this is not true in the US, where REITs have delivered strong performance relative to the direct market, and the pattern of delivery of the historical return on property companies has been more similar to the return on the direct property market than the return on the equity market. On an annual basis, the correlation between UK property companies and the property market was 72 per cent, while that between the property company sector and the equity market was around 55 per cent. So, over longer periods there is evidence that property companies begin to behave more like direct property.

Building from this realization that relationships change over longer time periods, Hoesli and Oikarinen (2012) set out to examine whether securitized real estate returns reflect direct real estate returns or general stock market returns using international data for the US, UK and Australia. Their work suggests that long-run REIT market performance is much more closely related to the direct real estate market than to the general stock market. This confirms the findings of studies by Pagliari *et al.* (2005) and by Ling and Naranjo (2014) in which returns were adjusted for the impact of appraisal smoothing, leverage and differences in sector composition, and no notable difference was found between the return means and variances of the NCREIF and NAREIT indices between 1993 and 2001. Consequently, REITs and direct real estate should be relatively good substitutes in a long-horizon investment portfolio.

Property shares might therefore be an appropriate way to access longer term property exposure and returns. And REITs may have advantages over REOCs. We have inadequate performance history in Europe to examine this empirically, and for evidence we must turn to the US.

6.6.3 Do REITs lead the direct market?

Given that direct market valuations are typically 'sticky' in contrast to listed real estate, pricing in an efficient market should be able to incorporate new information into pricing more quickly. It would therefore be logical for the listed real estate market to provide leading indicators for pricing in the direct market.

Several studies have provided evidence of such a link between the two markets, with direct real estate performance found to lag that of the listed sector. Listed real estate can thus be incorporated in models to predict future direct market returns (Ling and Naranjo, 2012; Gyourko and Keim, 1992). Barkham and Geltner (1995) also found evidence of a lag between markets, with pricing information from the securitized markets in both the UK and US taking up to a year before being reflected in the direct markets. Interestingly, a study by Li *et al.* (2009) presented evidence of a causality effect between the NAREIT and NCREIF indices, suggesting the presence of some form of information flow from the listed sector into valuations in the direct real estate index.

However, Baum and Hartzell (2012) warn that this lead–lag relationship between public and private market indicators may not make arbitrage gains possible. The public index, assessed in real time, is different from an appraisal-based private real estate index, which may itself lag sentiment and marginal trading prices in the private market. So the private real estate index might be tracking market prices that were set some time ago.

6.7 The US REIT experience

REITs were created in the US in the 1960s to allow smaller investors to participate in property markets. They are tax neutral, or tax transparent, vehicles provided that they meet the qualification rules. In the US, these rules include the following.

- There must be a minimum of 100 shareholders, with limited insider dominance.
- At least 75 per cent of total assets must be held in real estate assets, cash or government securities.
- At least 75 per cent of gross income must be generated from rents of real property, interest on mortgages, gains on sales of property and dividends from other REITs.

US REITs can be public or private vehicles; in this chapter we focus on the listed (public) variety. There are equity REITs, mortgage REITs and hybrid REITs. In this chapter we focus on the equity variety.

The major growth period for US REITs began in 1991, as the vehicle proved ideal for re-capitalizing a distressed real estate market. The creation of the Umbrella Partnership REIT or UPREIT in 1992 allowed a boom in securitization, as it permitted owners of assets to contribute them to a REIT in return for shares without having to pay capital tax on the transfer.

US REITs are now one of the longest-standing – and certainly the most researched – property vehicles in existence. A very large number of articles in the academic literature relate to US REITs, focused on the extent to which they perform like real estate or stocks (see reviews of the literature in Worzala and Sirmans, 2003 and Hoesli and Oikarinen, 2012). This is a key question, and there is a strong lobby arguing that REITs will be more like pure real estate equity than will REOCs. A possible reason for US REITs performing more like direct real estate are the regulations which have the effect of maintaining income distributions (see Section 6.7.1, which is derived from Baum and Devaney, 2008).

6.7.1 Distributions

When REITs were introduced in the US in 1960, a high compulsory income distribution level of 90 per cent was set. This was designed to ensure that the risk to investors was reduced (after all, 'a bird in the hand is worth two in the bush').

The distribution level was later increased to 95 per cent. These distributions were to be made from net income after the deduction of expenses, interest and (as is common in accounting for any company) a depreciation allowance, recognizing the following:

- Real estate vehicles need the ability to retain some earnings through which reinvestment and renewal of the stock can be made.
- In a particular year, a real estate owner can be faced with significant costs to repair and maintain buildings for existing or prospective occupiers.

More recently, in the REIT Modernization Act 1999, the compulsory distribution level was reduced back to 90 per cent of net income. The change did not appear to have a big impact on US REIT values. The reason for this limited impact was that REIT dividends are only partially constrained by the minimum distribution requirement. The average payout by US REITs is often over 100 per cent of accounting earnings. This is confirmed by studies by Wang *et al.* (1993) and Bradley *et al.* (1998), with the former reporting an average payout ratio of 1.65, where payout ratio is the ratio of dividends to reported net income. This was compared to an expected 0.95 if regulation were the only driver.

(In 2009, extreme circumstances forced many REITs to cut or suspend dividends. This encouraged the US Internal Revenue Service to provide REITs with the option of paying up to 90 per cent of the dividend in stock.)

The reason for these high payout proportions is that there is a big difference between reported net income and the net cash flow that an equity (property-owning) REIT has available to distribute. This difference is created by large provisions for depreciation and amortization, associated with the cost-based treatment of commercial real estate assets in accounts.

In the US REIT industry, it is recognized that the accounting measure of net income is not a useful measure of equity REIT profitability (Yungmann and Taube, 2001). Therefore, other measures have been developed, such as Funds from Operations (FFO), Adjusted Funds from Operations (AFFO) and Funds Available for Distribution (FAD). FFO adds back the depreciation allowance necessitated by cost accounting to estimate the cash flow that can be capitalized to assess value per share; AFFO makes a deduction from this cash to reflect the fact that property depreciates and that without it an over-distribution might lead to over-valuation, ignoring the cost of property refurbishment.

While these different metrics offer alternative ways of assessing REIT earnings, there is a lack of consistency in how they are calculated between firms. Nonetheless, the maintenance of higher distributions than can be relied upon from a REOC is likely to stabilize returns and create a more real estate-like asset. Does the data support this hypothesis?

6.7.2 Performance

Table 6.8 shows the annual returns on direct property (the NCREIF Property Index, or NPI), US REITs (the NAREIT Index) and US Equities (the S&P 500). Unlike UK property companies, REITs have out-performed direct property, and the increase in risk has not been disproportionate.

The correlation data shown in Table 6.9 is a little less positive for REITs. US REITs have been more highly correlated with equities on an annual basis than with direct property, although the correlation of 44 per cent is less than the UK REOC equivalent of 55 per cent.

Table 6.8: Risk and return, annual, US asset classes, 1978–2013

	Return	Risk
NPI	9.15%	7.90%
NAREIT	10.84%	18.10%
Equity	11.76%	16.17%

Source: NCREIF, NAREIT

Table 6.9: Correlation, annual, US asset classes, 1978–2013

	NCREIF	NAREIT
NAREIT	0.08	1
Equity	0.13	0.44

Source: NCREIF, NAREIT

6.8 The UK REIT

The UK REIT market began trading on 2 January 2007. A small number (eight) converted from listed property companies to REIT status at the price of a one-off tax charge, but this number included all of the largest by value of traditional property companies. The converting companies included Land Securities, Hammerson, British Land and Brixton.

The rules under which UK REITs must operate include requirements broadly to:

a carry on a 'property rental business', with at least 75 per cent of profit arising from that business and at least 75 per cent of assets dedicated to it (Corporation Tax Act 2010, s. 531). However, as long as these tests are satisfied, a UK REIT may carry out taxable ancillary activities, which can include property (re-)development; and

b distribute at least 90 per cent of the profits of the property rental business (Corporation Tax Act 2010, s. 530). This does not include capital gains from selling property, though, which can either be distributed or re-invested in the portfolio (Corporation Tax Act 2010, s. 530).

The qualifications to each requirement are important, as they appear to give UK REITs flexibility to renew their portfolios. Distributions are to be made from income profits (NOI) rather than gross income. These steps have, on the face of it, reduced the level of dividends to investors. However, because UK and European property companies adopt accounting standards that do not permit the deduction of depreciation, those profits (and therefore the distributions) are higher than would be the case in the US. If distributions were to be made from gross income, UK REITs could have been left with insufficient cash to maintain properties and thus forced to defer expenditure, sell assets or make regular capital calls, with potentially serious impacts on vehicle performance and success.

Because UK REITs are required to carry properties at market value in their accounts and no allowance for depreciation is made to offset taxable income, values change with market conditions rather than being written down each year. This key difference from the US treatment means that the distributable profit of a UK REIT will be much closer to its cash flow.

Other differences exist between the accounting practices and REIT regimes in the US and UK (and elsewhere) that may influence distribution and retention decisions. In particular, a key difference lies in the nature of the leases granted in each country. The terms and conditions of leases granted will determine whether the REIT or the tenant is responsible for repairs and maintenance. This, in turn, not only influences the pattern of income and expenditure, but potentially also the extent and amount of depreciation suffered in the portfolio (Baum and Turner, 2004). Although UK leases have become shorter and opportunities to break have increased, traditional repairing and rent review provisions still predominate (Crosby *et al.*, 2005). In the US, leases are shorter on average and more of the repairing obligations are borne by the landlord. This means that there are more opportunities for the US owner to actively manage its buildings and more incentive to do so owing to the need to achieve re-lettings more often.

In contrast, UK leases have encouraged more passive management of the stock. Responsibility for regular maintenance to combat physical deterioration is passed to the tenant, especially in single-let buildings, but there is no guarantee that the tenant will perform these obligations in the same way and, often, they are discharged through payment of a dilapidations charge at the end of the lease. While, in theory, this compensates the landlord for lost value, the impact of not performing work when it is necessary may mean greater depreciation overall.

Both accounting and property market differences mean that the experiences of the US and other jurisdictions are of limited value when assessing the likely returns from the UK and other new REIT markets around the world. In 2014, differences in the sizes of REITs and non-REITs, plus the impact of the GFC, makes it difficult as yet to compare the performance of UK REITs and UK non-REIT PropCos post-2007.

6.9 REIT pricing: introduction

6.9.1 Earnings or asset values?

The valuation of a REIT involves different approaches in different regimes. In the US, REIT valuations are typically made by reference to earnings (defined in different ways – see Section 6.7.1) and a price/earnings ratio, or a variant of this model.

In the UK, valuations of assets are available and pricing by reference to net asset value is common. It has also become common to analyse REIT prices by reference to implied yields. For example, a City of London office building yielding 6.5 per cent may appear unattractive if the 'correct yield' (see Chapter 4) is assessed as 7.5 per cent. A listed property company owning City of London offices and trading at a 30 per cent discount to NAV would have a higher implied yield, say 8 per cent, which may be attractive.

Although the pricing of listed securities is linked to that of the real estate portfolio, there is also a significant degree of variability around the underlying net asset value. This is because both REITs and property company shares are influenced by price movements in the equities markets in general. Consequently, there can be price anomalies compared with the underlying real estate market which can be exploited tactically. (It is also commonly suggested by REIT analysts that property equities, unconstrained by valuations and comparable evidence, forecast the direct market by up to 12 months ahead – see, for example, Hoesli and Oikarinen (2012) and above.) However, this issue can also increase the risk of REITs under-performing the underlying property market, and REITs are unlikely to provide access to the same level of pure real estate performance in the short term as the unlisted market.

6.9.2 Market capitalization and net asset value

EPRA and NAREIT maintain REIT and listed property vehicle data of the type one would expect to find in listed securities markets. The market capitalizations of the global REIT markets are therefore readily available. To suggest how much of the world's real estate is held by listed vehicles, as we did in Chapter 2, we estimated the gross asset value or GAV held by listed real estate vehicles. What is the connection between market capitalization and GAV?

Simplifying, GAV = net asset value (NAV) plus debt, so the vehicle's debt or gearing will give us the NAV. However, the NAV of a REIT or PropCos not exactly the same as its market capitalization because shares can trade at a premium or discount to NAV. Market capitalization is therefore equal to NAV +/– the discount or premium to NAV.

Share price * Number of shares = Market capitalization +/– Discount/premium to net asset value (NAV) = Net asset value – Debt = Gross asset value

Data produced by Green Street Advisers suggests that over the period 1990–2007 US REITs traded at an average premium to NAV (this is estimated NAV – US REITs are not required to value their assets) of 4.8 per cent. At the end of 2008, however, the estimated discount to NAV was around 40 per cent, rivalling the record discount seen in 1991, while in 1997–8 the estimated premium to NAV touched 30 per cent and in 2014 premiums were back, at an average of around 5 per cent. What explains the premium – or discount?

Figure 6.2 shows the premium and discount to NAV which coloured the performance of the UK PropCo/REIT sector over the period 1990 to 2014. It shows that there is some short-term volatility, and that significant discounts to NAV can affect pricing for periods as long as five years.

Arguments about the source of this variation can become heated. This is because the well-known valuation smoothing issue which affects direct real estate prices is seen by some – REIT proponents included – as wholly destructive of the value of valuations and, by extension, NAV estimates. Compared to 'real' pricing in the stock markets, valuations are regarded as mere opinion, and systematically flawed opinion at that. To proponents of direct property, valuations can and should be professional estimates of the most likely

Figure 6.2: UK REIT pricing relative to NAV, 1990–2014

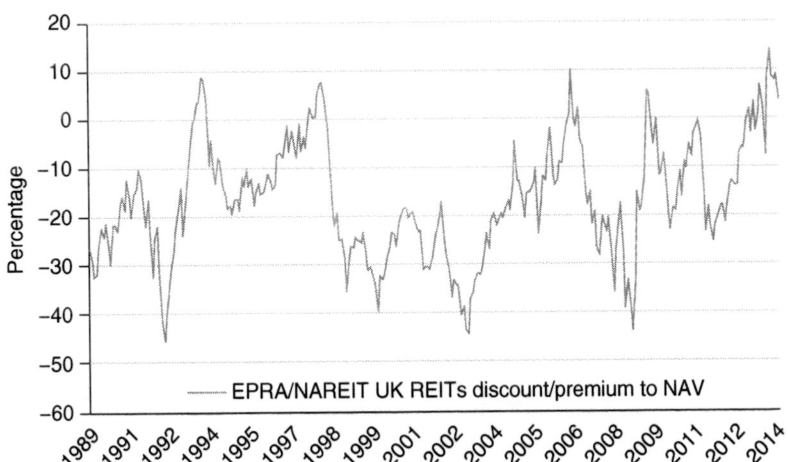

Source: Property Funds Research, EPRA

selling price of a property in the absence of a distressed market, while stock market prices are volatile, unreliable reflections of short-term sentiment in the absence of a more objective logic. The debate is philosophical and unresolvable.

Assuming that both NAV estimates and REIT trading prices contain useful information, why might the price of a REIT share be higher (or lower) than its NAV per share? Several commentators (for example, Clayton and MacKinnon, 2000) have considered this issue. In Section 6.10 we consider the more convincing propositions.

Box 6.1 Why are REITs volatile?

In December 2013, a REIT with ten million shares in issue has gross assets of €1,350 million. It has debt of €450 million. It trades at a discount to NAV of 10 per cent. By December 2014, values have risen by 10 per cent, and as sentiment improves the 10 per cent discount moves to a premium of 10 per cent.

The share price in December 2013 and December 2014 is given by:

(gross asset value–debt)/number of shares in issue+/–premium/discount to NAV)

What happens to the NAV? What happens to the share price? How many times greater is the growth in share price than the growth in NAV?

6.10 Explaining the premium/discount to NAV

6.10.1 Instant exposure

In Chapter 7, we will examine the so-called J-curve effect. This describes the phenomenon which affects any investor in direct real estate or in a blind (unpopulated by assets) real estate fund. A sum of $100 million invested in either of these formats is converted, all things held equal, into around $95 million of assets, because legal fees, other due diligence costs and property taxes (stamp duty, for example) will likely add up to around 5 per cent of the acquired property's value.

Investors in REITs and REOCs do not suffer this problem. The investor usually gains instant exposure to a fully invested real estate portfolio in the assembly of which these costs have already been incurred. All things held equal, this should drive REIT prices to a natural premium of around 5 per cent, close to the observed average premium in the US.

6.10.2 Liquidity/divisibility

What creates liquidity? Listing a security provides a shop window, advertising the product and encouraging buyers and sellers to transact. But a quotation is not sufficient to attract the attention of a market maker. Many quoted assets – including many small property companies – will not be taken on to the market maker's book. He will require matched bargains and/or require a large spread from buy to sell price.

Market makers are essential to ensure that a market can operate at volume and are important in the delivery of liquidity. In order to make a market in a stock, they ideally require:

a a spread between buying and selling prices;
b high market capitalization; and
c derivatives to offset risk.

Speculators or arbitrageurs also need to be attracted to add to market capacity. They also help to provide volume, but they require volatility to encourage them to transact. This will mean that average holding periods become shorter. They also require perfectly standard vehicles that they can understand and arbitrage between. We can now add the following requirements:

d daily quotation of prices; and
e standard vehicles.

In summary, volume is crucial: and it will be created by large market capitalization of the combined sector of standard vehicles plus short average holding periods. Short holding periods and volatility go together, hand in glove, and require the participation of market makers, investors and speculators. They in turn will be attracted by large spreads, a large volume of similar vehicles and quotation, plus the opportunity to offset risk through derivatives. Given that these conditions exist for the bigger REITs, they can surely offer a solution to the twin problems direct property investors face – illiquidity and lot size. The best remedy for illiquidity is a public market quotation, and the problem of lumpiness is solved by the securitization of real estate and the consequent divisibility of the REIT instrument.

Given a REIT's potential liquidity, these advantages should drive REIT prices to a premium to NAV. When REITs trade at premiums, the sector can be expected to grow, as REITs can buy property for less than the increase in share price which results. This is accretive to earnings. In these circumstances, rights issues by existing companies, and new REIT launches, become attractive to investors.

6.10.3 Asset values are higher than the reported NAV

If asset values are perceived to be higher than the reported NAV, then efficient REIT pricing will drive share prices above NAV. Because valuation smoothing is expected to depress valuations below trading prices in a rising market, this is a likely phenomenon in a strong market for property investing. (Observed or estimated US REIT premiums have generally been positive in strong markets and negative in weak markets.)

If asset values are perceived to be lower than the reported NAV, then REIT prices can be expected to be below NAV. This is a likely phenomenon in a falling or weak market for property investing.

6.10.4 Projected asset values are expected to exceed the reported NAV

If asset values are expected to rise, REIT prices might act as a coincident indicator of these expectations and a leading indicator of property prices. Because property prices are somewhat auto-correlated, this is a likely phenomenon in a strong market for property investing, and will work in the same direction as the perceived difference between current and reported NAVs. Note, however, that these are different, albeit related, factors.

If asset values are expected to fall, then (all other things equal) REIT prices will be expected to be below NAV.

6.10.5 Other issues

Other factors often considered in connection with the REIT premium/discount include the following.

Management skills

If management skills and efficiency are perceived to be of high quality relative to the overheads of running the business, it is argued that this would drive REIT share prices to a premium against NAV.

Tax

If there is an embedded tax liability (usually a capital gains tax liability which is contingent on the sale of assets) this is likely to drive prices to a discount to the gross of tax NAV. As with many factors, it is difficult to estimate how large this effect will be. If a property company is sold with such an embedded contingent liability, there is usually a negotiation about how much of that tax risk is deducted from the price, as it is not possible to be certain how large the tax will be or, indeed, if any tax will arise, until the assets are sold.

Debt

REOCs and REITs will have agreed debt facilities and loans in place. Interest rates will likely be fixed, or varying rate agreements may have been swapped into fixed price debt (see Chapter 2). The average interest rate on this debt may be above or below current market rates, or the average for the sector. In either case, the cost of this debt may be 'marked to market', so that expensive debt will reduce the REIT share price below NAV, while cheap debt will have the opposite effect.

The noise trader argument

Investors in REITs and REOCs may be professional and institutional investors seeking real estate exposure. as we have assumed so far in this chapter. This is not always the case, however, as larger property companies which form a part of an equity securities benchmark such as the S&P 2000 or the FTSE 250 might attract 'index' investors whose sentiments and investing behaviour may not have much to do with real estate or discounts and premiums to NAV. This issue is explored in Barkham and Ward (1999), which concludes that the behaviour of so-called 'noise traders' might affect prices in addition to the actions of rational investors, driving prices to a premium or discount.

6.11 How do global real estate investors use REITs and REOCs in practice?

Europe as a region holds a smaller percentage of its investable real estate through listed companies than is the case in either North America or developed Asia. An under-representation of listed real estate in Europe may be the result of performance (risk and return characteristics relative to equities, bonds and other assets), it may be to do with regulatory differences or it may be to do with historic organizational (or 'institutional') issues. Research promoted by EPRA (Baum and Moss, 2012) was designed to identify potential organizational issues limiting the exposure of European institutions to listed forms of real estate.

The survey found some evidence that pension funds and consultants regard (or would like to regard) listed real estate as part of the real estate allocation. However, for some European investors and managers, listed real estate is clearly part of the equity allocation. Within the sub-set of those for whom listed real estate forms part of the real estate allocation, some have an integrated approach to public and private real estate; but (unfortunately) more do not, sub-contracting public real estate to a dedicated team, the equity desk or even to an external manager, to some extent defeating the object of a combined mandate.

There is equal evidence in the survey to suggest that asset managers (with their greater experience of execution as well as a propensity for business unit separation) may not have developed a satisfactory integrated investment process. As asset managers adjust and develop their product ranges to meet what might be a gently rising demand, they also need to solve the investment process problems of integrating listed and private real estate within one business and one portfolio, a facility which currently seems either elusive or absent. They also need to be able to show that the listed portfolio is being managed with an eye on the strategic objectives of the real estate allocation, and not on a standard solution that suits the objectives of the listed real estate team.

6.11.1 Listed real estate strategies

A large number (over 670) funds of listed real estate securities have been created to facilitate a variety of potential strategies. Table 6.10 summarizes the main global fund universe, while Figure 6.3 describes the different strategies employed.

Table 6.10: Real estate securities funds by mandate, 2013

	AUM($bn)	Number of funds
Global real estate	61.2	251
US real estate	123.4	148
Asian real estate	14.2	112
European real estate	13.1	85
Global REIT	34.1	78

Source: Consilia Capital

Figure 6.3: Real estate securities funds – strategies and styles

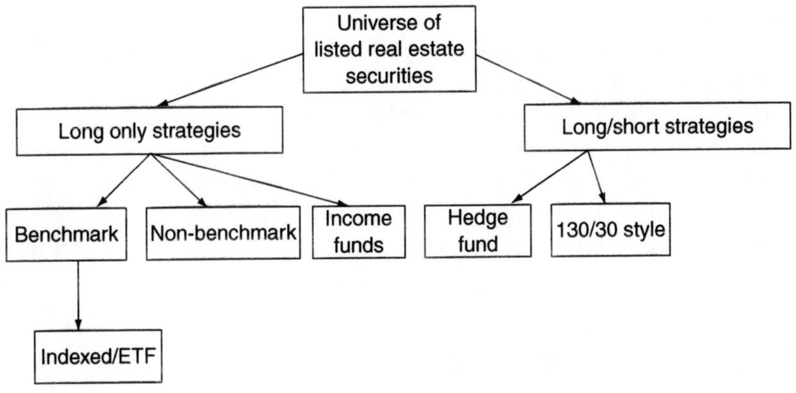

Source: Consilia Capital

'Long-only strategies' preclude a manager from running short positions (owing rather than owning stocks, meaning that money is made if values go down). If a benchmark (such as EPRA) is used, investors are likely to have a clear view of the desired risk/return profile and investment objectives of the fund, specifically to perform in line with an index of real estate stocks. Indexed funds and exchange-traded funds seek to track an index at low cost, albeit with various levels of tracking error.

Non-benchmark constrained funds seek to provide what is typically described as 'a mixture of income and capital growth'. Income funds focus on portfolios of higher-yielding REITs or write call options on the underlying portfolio (giving up some capital growth) and take a premium for this, distributing it as a dividend to unit holders.

Long/short strategies focus on absolute returns, and allow managers to hold short positions. While hedge funds are unconstrained, 130/30 funds allow a fund manager to run a maximum 130 per cent long exposure which would be offset by a maximum 30 per cent short position. If, for example, a fund had assets of £100 million and the manager was positive on the UK but negative on Europe, then instead of a £100 million UK exposure they would be allowed £130 million, enhancing returns assuming the position proved to be profitable, offset by a short position of £30 million on European stocks, leaving a net £100 million exposure.

Figure 6.4: Applications of listed real estate

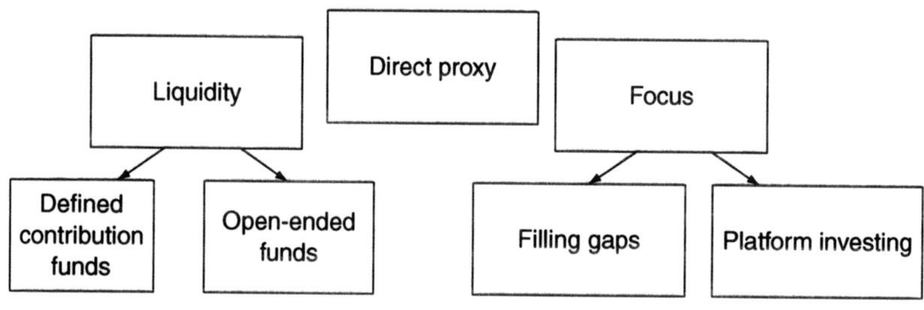

Source: Baum and Moss, 2013

Figure 6.4 shows the main applications of listed real estate in asset allocation. Securities can be used as a proxy for direct or private real estate, to add liquidity to a private real estate fund or portfolio (for defined contribution funds that require daily trading prices, or open-ended funds that need some liquidity), or when the best or only available asset manager happens to be a listed fund or company. The concept of platform investing (allocating money to specialist asset managers, or sub-contracting) is well known to real estate private equity managers, and called a multi-manager approach, but it is increasingly being used in the listed sector.

6.11.2 Combining listed real estate with other forms of real estate

Sometimes listed real estate equities will be used in isolation, and sometimes they will be combined with other real estate formats. Against a background of new risk/return requirements (such as those called for by defined contribution pension funds) the liquid listed real estate sector is increasingly used in portfolio construction with other real estate-related assets. We can think of this strategy as a palette of available real estate options with subtly different risk and return characteristics compared to a benchmarked listed real estate exposure.

Combining listed real estate equities with direct real estate is a well-established approach, illustrated in the UK by several examples.

- The HSBC Open Global Property Fund combines a geographic allocation strategy with the ability to invest in funds that are exposed to both listed and unlisted property markets.
- The listed TR Property Investment Trust mixes direct and listed real estate. Its holdings in 2014 were UK direct property 10 per cent, UK quoted shares 38 per cent and Continental European shares 52 per cent.
- In 2011, Legal & General Property (LGP) launched the Hybrid Property Fund, which invests in LGP's UK unlisted balanced fund (the Managed Property Fund) and Legal & General Investment Management's Global REITS Index Tracker Fund with a default position split of 70:30.

Combining listed real estate and derivatives is an intriguing strategy that has proved hard to deliver, although it was employed with some short-term success by the Iceberg funds managed by CBRE ReechAIM.

We can confidently expect more creativity in this space as managers continue to explore the potential uses of a combination of listed property vehicles and private real estate.

6.12 Public debt and mortgage-backed securities (CMBS)

In Chapter 2, we discussed the importance and popularity of debt in the global real estate markets. The property-backed debt market in the US, for example, has seen huge growth, and this is partly explained by the public commercial mortgage-backed securities (CMBS) market. American players and others also encouraged the securitization of property-backed debt in some volume in Europe, and as a result the European property market entered a new phase. The introduction of public debt securities provided opportunities for corporates and developers to raise finance by selling property-backed debt instruments, either quoted securities or private mortgage-type paper. It produced interesting implications for the valuation, performance and tradeability of residual property interests.

CMBS are securities which provide the right to receive interest and capital payments from a (hopefully) diversified package of borrowers. They may be listed to provide liquidity and a broader buyer universe, dominated by institutional investors seeking higher yields than government bonds provide, yet secured against low-risk real estate assets. They are debt securities collateralized by a pool of senior commercial real estate mortgage loans, themselves secured against a diverse portfolio of commercial real properties.

CMBS are credit-rated by independent agencies. The credit rating attached to CMBS securities is dependent upon several factors, including in particular the position or seniority of the securities' claim on the cash flow from the underlying portfolio of loan cash flows, which may be supporting a 'capital stack' using more than one source of debt, as shown in Figure 6.5.

The 'senior loan' will have first call on any cash flows from the asset, while the subordinated loans will have the next call. At the time the loans are made, interest cover (interest as a proportion of net rents) limits will mean that the 'stabilized' (expected) cash flow produced by the asset will be more than enough to pay all interest charges on all loans with

Figure 6.5: A typical capital structure for securitised estate

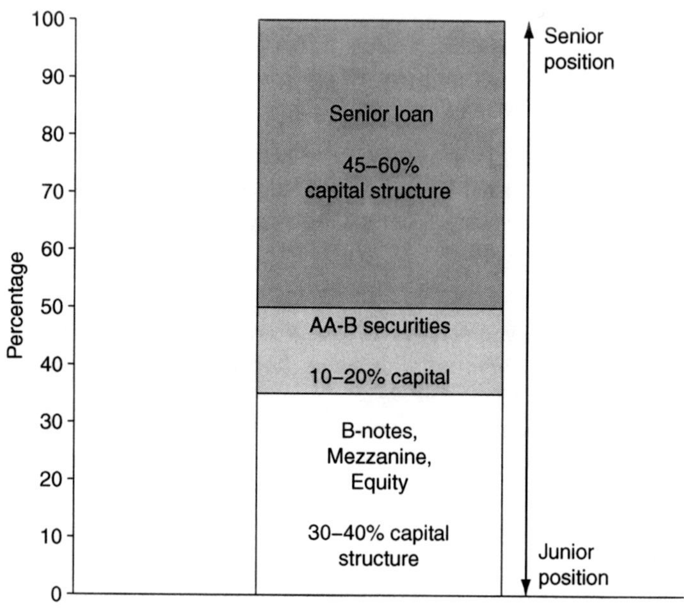

Source: CBRE Global Investors

something significant left over for the equity owners. However, things can change: variable rate interest charges can rise, and vacancies and defaults can arise in tenancies.

If and when the cash flow declines relative to its expected level, the equity owner will have to lose all of his income before the subordinated debt provider loses some of his. Only if the net income falls a long way, and both the equity owner and the subordinated debt provider lose all of their income, will the senior debt provider be at risk. Hence the senior debt will be more highly rated than the subordinated debt. This applies to CMBS issues, which will typically be split into 'tranches' of debt to maximize their value. Through this mechanism, loans could be re-engineered to have a higher aggregate market value.

A CMBS issuance comprises a pool of first or senior mortgages secured by income-producing commercial real estate (office, retail, industrial, multi-family and hotels). The mortgages are in turn bundled together into a pool or portfolio, tranched according to their priority entitlement to the underlying mortgage loan repayments, assigned a credit rating and sold to third-party investors who buy the bonds based upon their risk/return objectives.

The highest rated bonds are AAA and the lowest rated are non-investment grade. Accordingly those with the highest ratings (AAA) achieve the highest pricing and therefore the narrowest spread to the risk free rate or treasuries, while the lowest-ranking securities have higher spreads.

The probability of defaults and the expected returns for each class of a securitization vary with its rating. AAA-rated tranches offer the lowest probability of default and the lowest returns, whereas below-investment grade and unrated tranches offer higher returns as well as higher risks of default. Because the default probability is highest for below-investment grade and unrated classes, investors in these classes have traditionally been real estate private equity-focused organizations with in-depth knowledge of the underlying assets and their respective markets and with property asset management skills on hand.

As the ratings within a specific CMBS issuance decline, the interest rate spread or margin over base rate and relative to more senior and protected tranches increases. As the debt investment becomes more junior in the capital structure, the performance (return) becomes less predictable and interest rate sensitive, and more reliant on changes in the net cash flow of the collateral commercial real property.

Senior tranches (AAA through BBB), also known as 'rated' tranches, should earn their return from the coupon (interest payment) on the tranche and should be viewed as a fixed income investment in 'normal' market conditions. Moving from BB, the first level of 'unrated tranches', up the risk scale in any CMBS issuance to B and Z tranches, investors get less and less protection and more risk of loss.

The US residential sub-prime mortgage shock that emerged in mid-2007 triggered a wave of global risk re-pricing. Due to a sharp increase in risk aversion and liquidity preference, credit spreads widened dramatically on both residential and commercial real estate debt securities, as shown in Table 6.11.

Table 6.11: Indicative debt investment spreads over Treasuries, US, 2007–8

Yield range	Q1 2007	Q2/Q3 2008
CMBS – AA and A	T+5–6%	T+7–20%
CMBS – BBB	T+6–7%	T+10–25%
CMBS – sub-investment grade	T+8–20%	T+20–50%
B-notes	T+6–12%	T+7–15%
Mezzanine loans	T+7–13%	T+8–20%

Source: Markit, ING Clarion Capital

Note
T means the yield on treasuries.

As a result of the pricing change, CMBS issuance dried up completely for a period. For example, 2007 issuance was $230 billion, but only $12 billion was issued in 2008. This led to a boom and bust in CMBS issuance in the US – see Figure 6.6.

Despite the fall in new issuance, the CMBS market experienced an imbalance of supply and demand. Investors retreated in the face of aggressive underwriting standards and a lack of available capital. This imbalance placed substantial pressure on CMBS spreads to widen further and opportunities arose to negotiate investments in the secondary market on very favourable terms (high coupons or running yields).

After the credit crunch, it became clear that financial market investors failed to adequately assess real estate fundamentals and credit risk. This lack of focus on the true underlying real estate fundamentals meant that loan pools were overpriced in the period before mid-2007. In the aftermath, the spreads seen on commercial real estate debt securities, notably AAA CMBS securities, clearly exaggerated the losses that might be anticipated even in a severe recessionary phase, presenting a unique buying opportunity and momentarily replacing equity investment for some investors. This opportunity would be brief, and the normal capital return relationship began to re-assert itself, with equity expected to earn

Figure 6.6: CMBS issuance, US, 2000–13

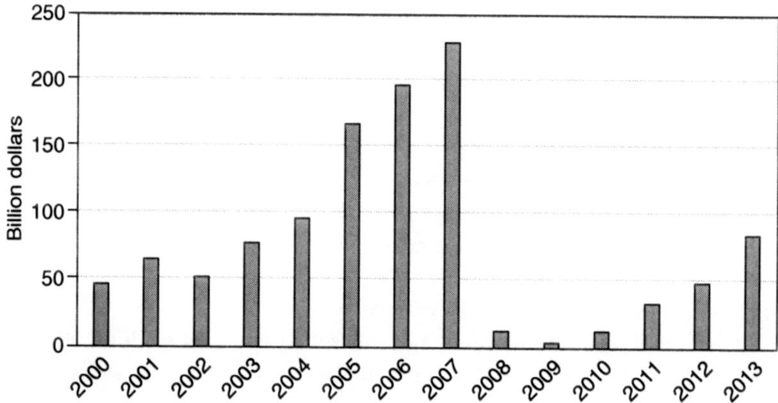

Source: Commercial Mortgage Alert

considerably more than debt as the CMBS markets began to recover in 2013–14. During the same recovery period, unlisted debt funds became very popular, and it is to the unlisted fund sector that we now turn our attention.

7 Unlisted real estate funds

7.1 Unlisted real estate funds: an introduction

Over the period 1998–2007, a change in the investment strategy of pension funds and other professional investors generated an increased investor appetite for global real estate investment. The world's top investors went global, and real estate investment managers facilitated this through the creation of innovative indirect real estate investment solutions. The most popular of these indirect solutions can be called real estate funds. While the REIT market had seen steady growth in the US and in European and Asian markets as the necessary legislation had been passed, it is the universe of *unlisted* real estate vehicles that grew more dramatically in the lead-up to the GFC.

Things came crashing down in 2008, and by 2014 it had not yet become clear whether they would ever be quite the same again. We will turn to this question later in the chapter.

The global real estate fund market can be categorized in several ways. There are listed funds and unlisted funds, although a more useful distinction is between those actively traded on major stock exchanges and those which are not; there are open-ended and closed-ended funds, both listed and unlisted; there are low-risk core funds and high-risk private equity or opportunity funds; and there are funds for private investors and funds for institutional investors. There are also different legal forms of fund: the most common forms of unlisted fund structures include limited partnerships and (in the UK and related markets) property unit trusts.

7.1.1 The appeal of the unlisted fund

The pension fund and the insurance company typically invest in property to achieve diversification and liability matching. Because some of the diversification advantages of real estate would be lost by using liquid securities, which may be highly correlated with the equity market in the short run, private real estate, including unquoted vehicles holding property assets, offer advantages. And a co-mingled fund (one through which several investors pool their capital) can offer some diversification at the asset level, thereby reducing specific risk.

Private real estate is illiquid, of course. This problem also affects unlisted funds, although some liquidity can be achieved. The manager might arrange matched bargains between buyers and sellers; the manager might deal directly with the market through an open-ended structure; and investors might be able to transact through a healthy secondary market for units in both open- and closed-ended funds (see Section 7.6.1). Liquidity will be promoted by widening the net of potential buyers, and some funds are established offshore largely to improve liquidity by attracting tax exempt international investors. Increasing harmonization of rules and taxes is expected to allow European pension funds to invest cross-border without penalty, and liquidity will improve as a result. Nonetheless, as in direct real estate, liquidity is limited.

In the 1970s and 1980s property unit trusts, unit-linked pension or insurance products and other open-ended fund formats have been regarded as perfectly adequate vehicles for providing pension funds or insurance funds with a means of diversifying into domestic property in the UK, US, France, Germany and elsewhere. These structures have now been supplemented by specialist closed-ended funds. As an example, annual growth in the gross asset value held in UK unlisted funds has averaged around 10 per cent since 2000. This data, compiled by UK research firm Property Funds Research (PFR), is illustrated in Figure 7.1.

Figure 7.1: Growth in UK unlisted real estate funds

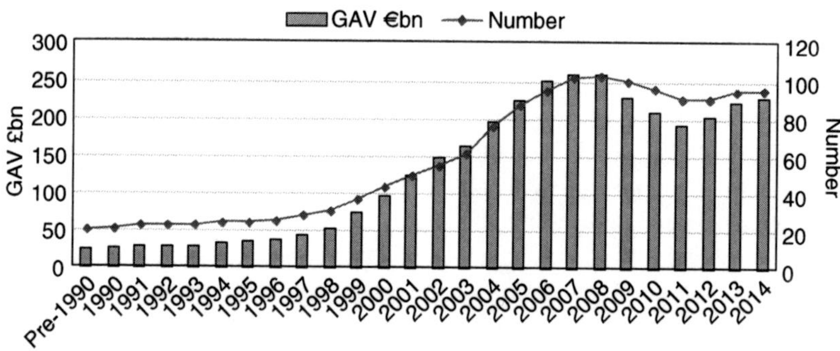

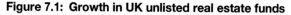

Source: Property Funds Research

In continental Europe, the number of funds in the PFR Universe grew on average by over 20 per cent per annum between 1998 and 2007 (see Figure 7.2). Over the same period, GAV grew by 14 per cent annually in the European market while explosive, albeit more recent, growth had become evident in Asia and the emerging markets. This had become a truly global phenomenon which greatly facilitated executable global real estate investment strategies and expanded the investable opportunity set for the benefit of many.

However, as we can see from Figures 7.1 and 7.2, 2008 and the following GFC period saw a downturn in activity, and the number of live funds and the gross property value held by these structures fell every year to 2011 before the market appeared to begin some sort of recovery.

Figure 7.2: Growth of the European (inc. UK) unlisted indirect market

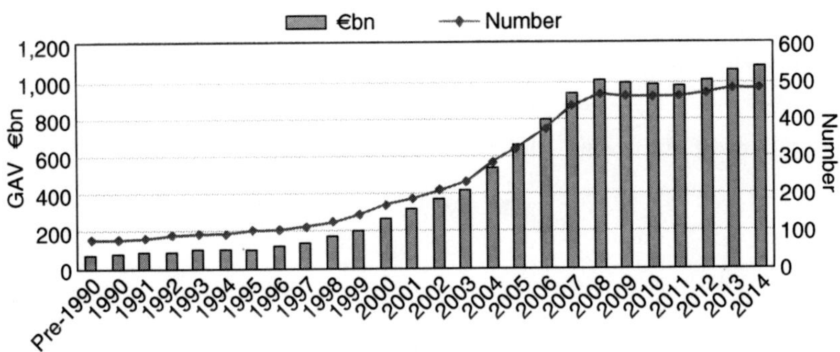

Source: Property Funds Research

7.1.2 The global unlisted property market universe

PFR's estimate of the size of this market is around $2.8 trillion (€2.0 trillion), of which data is held on funds with over $1.9 trillion or €1.5 trillion in gross assets at the end of the first half of 2014. This accounts for around 9 per cent of all global investable property (see Chapter 2 and Section 7.3). As in the UK, the global universe of unlisted property vehicles grew dramatically between 2003 and 2008. This explosive growth is demonstrated in Figure 7.3.

Figure 7.3: Growth in the PFR database of unlisted indirect vehicles, GAV (€bn)

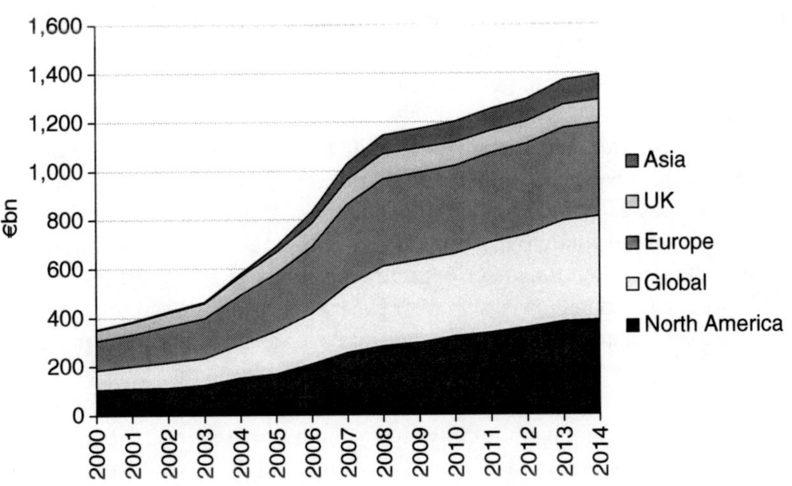

Source: Property Funds Research

The largest markets in PFR's vehicle universe are those of continental Europe, the UK and North America. As Figure 7.3 shows, growth in the European market, including the UK, was rapid until 2007 but began to tail off in 2008, as focus turned to the emerging markets of Asia, the Middle East, Africa and Latin America. From 2004 onwards, Asia in particular experienced a boom, as shown in Figure 7.4.

Figure 7.4: Growth of the Asian unlisted indirect market

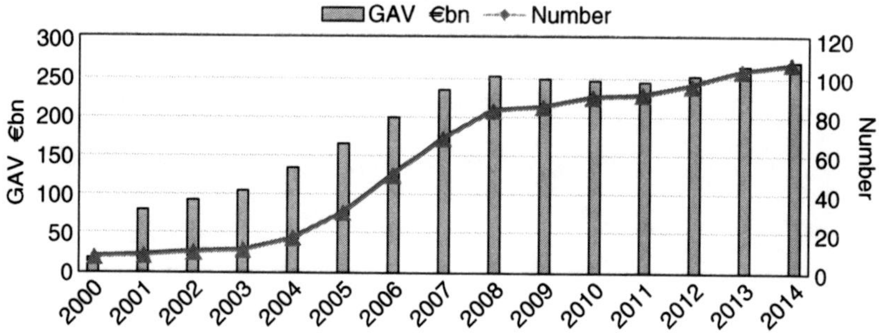

Source: Property Funds Research

By the beginning of 2009 there had been a marked global slowdown in fund launches, especially in the UK and Europe, but global growth re-started in 2011.

7.2 What is a real estate fund?

One of the primary drawbacks of investing in direct real estate is the lumpy, illiquid nature of the asset class (see Chapter 1) and a move to indirect investment is an appealing alternative. As this chapter will illustrate, real estate funds do not solve the liquidity problem, but some formats can be more liquid than direct real estate holdings. Private real estate equity funds (sometimes referred to as unlisted, or non-listed funds) are usually sub-divided into low risk core funds (often open-ended) and closed-ended private equity real estate (or opportunity) funds.

The recent pace of change in investor attitudes has been rapid. Taking UK pension funds as an example, balanced, unlisted real estate funds began to dominate institutional investment strategies early in the new millennium, and domestic multi-manager mandates which focused on these funds rather than direct real estate became common. In 2005–6, pan-European pension fund mandates became typical and global multi-manager mandates and global listed/unlisted mandates started to appear.

Since 2006, the standard pension fund mandate has begun to become more global, and will continue to require the development of more global listed and unlisted funds. This is generally a good thing: high quality real estate is a fundamental necessity for a developed global economy, and continued improvements in transparency are both essential and inevitable in the drive to attract institutional investment in the global markets that are most in need of capital investment.

These markets will also offer both diversification and the highest rewards, and unlisted real estate funds clearly have the potential to play a significant part in this process.

Funds, clubs, joint ventures and separate accounts

Professional investors often use what are known as collective investment schemes or co-mingled funds. These pooled funds allow smaller insurance companies and pension funds and other investors to achieve diversification without the high fixed costs and illiquidity of holding direct property. Typically, a third party fund manager is appointed to run the fund, or, more likely, establishes a fund and goes in search of investors.

The manager/investor relationship can be difficult when returns have been disappointing. After the GFC, when some funds delivered negative returns, tensions arose between managers and investors and also between investors with different objectives and views (some wanting their money back, some wanting to stay in hoping for a market recovery, for example).

The result has been the desire by the larger investors to take back some control. This can be done by avoiding funds altogether, and appointing a manager on a 'separate account' basis, meaning the investor loses all of the benefits of co-mingling his capital and achieving more diversification, but (if the account is advisory rather than discretionary) retains control over major decisions (to buy and sell assets). This is plainly not a fund.

Sometimes, the investor might wish to increase the extent to which his/her interests are aligned with the manager by asking the manager to co-invest capital. This is a joint venture, with the investor retaining some controls, but is likely to be set up in a format (a limited partnership) which could be expanded into a fund. If as a first step the investor invites a very small number of other investors to join the venture, this has become known as a 'club' investment, with the mandate being advisory, and the manager may or may not co-invest. A discretionary club is effectively the same thing as a fund, but a fund will have a minimum of (say) five investors.

7.3 How much global real estate is in unlisted funds?

The value of global commercial real estate owned by institutional investors was estimated to be around €23 trillion ($31.6 trillion) at the end of 2013 (see Chapter 2). This is the investable stock, meaning stock that is of sufficient quality to become an institutional investment product, and which therefore represents the potential for growth in securitized products in both listed and unlisted formats.

Using a variety of sources, PFR has made estimates of the gross asset values (GAVs) of stock held in both listed REITs and property companies and unlisted funds. The €23 trillion investable stock of real estate can be broken down to the regional level and further disaggregated by ownership structure (see Table 7.1).

Publicly available REIT and property company market capitalization data has been used and grossed up as shown to reflect the use of debt in the capital structure of the typical listed company. This represents around €3.3 trillion, or 14.4 per cent of the global market gross asset value.

PFR estimates that the much less mature unlisted real estate fund market has a value of €2.1 trillion, around 9.5 per cent of the investable stock, and that Europe (excluding the UK) represents the biggest component of this market, holding around 40 per cent of the global unlisted fund market (by number of funds). Unlisted fund GAVs have been estimated by PFR using a combination of individual fund data from the PFR fund universe and extrapolation.

Table 7.1: The global real estate investment universe (€bn)

Region	Investible stock (€bn)	Listed (€bn)	Unlisted universe ($bn)	Direct (€bn)
Africa	275	53	9	214
Asia	6,929	1,652	264	5,014
Australasia	551	200	145	206
Europe	5,960	417	556	4,986
UK	1,035	125	138	773
Latin America	1,336	92	40	1,204
Middle East	796	40	5	751
North America	6,084	617	924	4,543
World	22,966	3,195	2,081	17,691
% of investable universe	-	13.9%	9.1%	77.0%

Source: Property Funds Research, Pramerica, EPRA, NAREIT, IMF

According to PFR estimates, therefore, the €23 trillion investable market splits as follows: €5.2 trillion or just over 23 per cent of the total stock is held by listed and unlisted real estate vehicles, with 14 per cent held in listed vehicles and 9 per cent in unlisted funds. PFR's estimate of the size of the unlisted fund market is a minimum of around €2 trillion, of which data is held on over €1.5 trillion. The remaining €17.7 trillion or 77 per cent of the global universe splits into directly held investment stock and owner-occupied real estate.

The PFR fund universe comprises over 2,684 funds worth €1.5 trillion, which is therefore estimated to be a 66 per cent sample of the global market of unlisted real estate funds. This is shown in Table 7.2.

The PFR global market is split by GAV into 32 per cent Europe, 26 per cent North America, 11 per cent Australasia, 2 per cent emerging markets and 29 per cent pan-region or global in focus. Within this split, Europe is relatively fully supplied with unlisted product while Asia is under-supplied. Asia, on the other hand, has been well served by the listed sector, and (with emerging markets) has the fastest growing unlisted fund market.

Table 7.2: PFR's unlisted fund vehicle universe (€bn)

	GAV (€bn)	Number of funds
Africa	5	29
Asia	106	285
Australasia	59	114
Europe	389	909
Global	437	396
Latin America	23	91
Middle East	3	14
North America	406	744
UK	106	274
Total	1,534	2,856

Source: Property Funds Research

7.4 Unlisted fund structures

Being unlisted means there is no requirement to be public, so unlisted fund data is hard to find. Data sources include INREV (European Association for Investors in Non-Listed Real Estate Vehicles), ANREV (Asian Association for Investors in Non-Listed Real Estate Vehicles) in Asia, PFR and other sources, such as Preqin and Private Equity International, which are aimed primarily at the higher risk opportunity fund sector.

PFR suggests that there are four popular legal structures in use globally. These are (i) companies, (ii) partnerships and (iii) trusts, all backed by the general body of law relevant to each, and (iv) contractual agreements, backed by special laws, especially common in Germany, France and Luxembourg.

In the UK, core (lower-risk) real estate funds are typically open-ended property unit trusts, while private equity real estate funds are all closed-ended limited-life structures. Liquidity is the key issue which defines the relevant structure. A REIT or listed fund can usually be traded quickly on a major stock exchange, but an unlisted fund cannot. Investors in unlisted funds need to know how they can get their money back, and how much they will receive.

In the absence of an active secondary market for units in unlisted funds, which has been steadily building in the UK and is nascent in Europe but is not yet available in the US, the open-ended fund appears to guarantee 'redemption' of capital by the manager at something close to net asset value; in the absence of this, closed ended funds have to have a termination date at which point all assets can be sold and capital returned.

7.4.1 Limited partnerships

Conceived in the UK by the Limited Partnership Act of 1907, this vehicle became popular in the UK real estate market in the 1990s and limited partnership structures domiciled in many different markets are now in use throughout the globe. The limited partnership (LP) enables a pool of investors to invest together in one or more assets. The number of partners is usually unlimited in number, one of which, the general partner (GP), must have unlimited liability while the other partners have limited liability. The investment vehicle is tax transparent, because the partnership is not a legal person for tax purposes.

It is common practice that limited partnerships have a predetermined lifespan, usually of between six and ten years, in order to provide investing GPs with some reassurance that their capital will be returned. When the partnerships are established, it may be agreed that at the end of the period the partnership will be wound up and the assets disposed of, although this need not be the case if the partners vote to extend the vehicle life. Increasingly, so-called 'evergreen' or perpetual life funds are being set up, with liquidity (exit opportunities) provided at regular intervals.

LPs can be complex in their management structures, but a GP will usually be created by the originator of the concept and/or will act as lead investor. The GP may be a special purpose company owned by more than one lead investor, and will have unlimited liability in respect of the partnership. The GP will usually appoint an operator which will be responsible to the relevant regulator for a defined set of administrative functions.

In establishing the pool of capital required, the GP may appoint a promoter to raise capital from limited partners; in some cases, the promoter may be the originator of the concept and seek a GP to act as lead investor. Limited partners will contribute capital and may form an advisory board, but cannot be seen to be making decisions without losing their limited liability status. Limited partners may contribute non-executives to the GP.

The GP will also appoint an investment manager or an asset manager; in turn, the investment or asset manager may appoint a property manager. The relationships of promoter, operator, GP and asset manager can be subtly or obviously connected: in some cases, the same financial services group will provide all of these functions.

7.4.2 UK Property Unit Trusts (PUTs)

In practice, UK PUTs fall into four categories: exempt, non-exempt unauthorized UK trusts, authorized PUTs and offshore trusts. PUTs can either be authorized or unauthorized.

Unauthorized PUTs

The relatively common unauthorized PUTs are unregulated unit trust schemes which may only be offered to institutional investors. There is an exemption from capital gains tax where all issued units are held by investors who are themselves wholly exempt from capital gains tax or corporation tax (primarily pension funds and charities). The requirement is that units are held only by

> pension funds, charity or other investors which are exempt approved or treated as approved under chapter 1, part XIV of the Incomes and Corporation Taxes Act 1988 or otherwise permitted by the Inland Revenue to hold units without prejudicing the exemption of the trust from tax on capital gains under Section 100(2) of the Taxation of Chargeable Gains Act 1992.

Investors in unauthorized PUTs tend to be professional investors. While the operator/manager of the fund will be regulated in the UK by the Financial Services Authority (FSA), the fund itself will not be subject to the regulations set down by the FSA. Accordingly, the fund may be run with more flexible investment objectives and restrictions to meet the investment needs of more sophisticated investors. These objectives and restrictions will in some cases be the responsibility of a supervisory board representing the interests of investors.

Authorized PUTs

Authorized PUTs are designed primarily for retail investors. The Financial Services (Regulated Schemes) Regulations 1991 led to the authorization of unit trusts as real estate funds. These authorized property unit trusts (APUTs) were designed primarily for retail investors, giving them a medium whereby they could invest in units of a collective real estate fund offering exemption from capital gains tax on disposals of investments in the fund, with income taxable in the fund at 20 per cent. On distributions from the fund there is no further tax liability for corporate or exempt investors, but no credit of the tax paid in the fund is available.

This structure is therefore less attractive to exempt funds as there is an absolute tax cost, which can be avoided by investing through an unauthorized unit trust. Given this, and the restrictions placed on investment and liquidity, the structure has had very limited impact.

Offshore PUTs offer greater flexibility, as they are tax effective for a greater range of UK and international investors. The vehicle can be more efficient for both tax exempt and taxable institutions. Non-resident PUTs which are structured to give unit holders immediate entitlement to any income are tax transparent for income – thereby giving a cash flow advantage and preventing possible tax leakages – and are also exempt from capital gains tax at the level of the PUT by virtue of non-residence. In addition, these vehicles are less heavily regulated.

PUT structures can be complex. A supervisory board may be appointed to represent what is usually a large pool of investors. The supervisory board will appoint a trustee to operate the fund, and an investment manager to buy and sell assets and act as issuer and redeemer of units. The promoter or originator of a PUT will usually be the investment manager, who will then appoint the supervisory board and effectively appoint the trustee; but there have been examples of supervisory boards terminating their investment manager's contract and appointing a new manager. This is different from the LP model, in which the GP cannot usually be removed and also appoints the asset manager, which is often a connected company. The largest UK PUT is (at 2014) the Blackrock UK Property Fund (£2.4 billion of gross assets).

7.4.3 Property Authorized Investment Funds (PAIFs)

UK REITs (Real Estate Investment Trusts) were launched on 1 January 2007. Given that REITs were tax transparent but APUTs were not, the UK government considered the tax position of Authorized Investment Funds (AIFs) investing in real estate in order to try to produce a level playing field between listed and unlisted funds. As a result, the point of taxation was moved in the 2007 budget from the AIF to the investor, with the result that investors face broadly the same tax treatment as if they had owned real estate or REIT shares.

Access to the AIF tax regime is available only to AIFs whose investment portfolio comprises predominantly real estate or shares in UK REITs. However, unlike REITs, FSA regulations require property AIFs to value their fund each day. Property AIFs can be constituted either as APUTs or as Open-ended Investment Companies (OEICs). APUTs can convert to AIFs, but any new property AIF regime will be available only to those established as OEICs.

There are other categories of funds which could consider joining the Property AIFs regime: in addition to the existing UK-based retail APUTs these include offshore unit trusts (constituted as qualified investor schemes) and new funds constituted as retail funds or qualified investor schemes in the form of an OIEC.

At one time the largest UK PUT, the Schroder Exempt Property Unit Trust, established in 1971, converted to a PAIF in 2012. As at 2014, the M&G Property Portfolio is the biggest PAIF (£2.6 billion of gross assets).

7.4.4 UK managed funds

Managed funds (life managed property pension funds) are the insurance companies' equivalent of the pension funds' property unit trust. They are usually managed by insurance-based fund managers. Managed funds are unit-linked funds. Some are sold to retail clients; some are sold only to institutional investors.

The same fund may have both investor types, and charge different fees based on the source of capital. In return for an investment in a managed fund, a life policy is issued by the life company to the pension fund.

7.4.5 Funds of funds

There are four ways to invest in unlisted funds. Investors may:

a select a single diversified fund;
b use advisers or an in-house team to select a group of funds;

c appoint a discretionary manager to select a group of specialist funds (a multi-manager mandate); or

d invest in a fund of funds.

The multi-manager and fund of funds models are highly appropriate for pension funds of significant size without expert in-house teams.

A fund of funds is a wrapper placed around other wrappers (the underlying real estate funds). As in a multi-manager mandate, two sets of fees are charged: one by the fund of funds manager, and a second layer by the managers of the underlying funds. The fund of funds manager needs to justify the additional layer of fees either by the additional diversification and risk reduction produced by the strategy, by its skill in identifying and sourcing excellent underlying funds, or by negotiating fee reductions from the underlying managers.

The first large real estate fund of funds was launched in 2005, but this market has grown rapidly, and as at September 2014 PFR held data on over 120 real estate fund of funds products. The vast majority of UK funds of funds are open-ended, investing in a mix of open-ended and closed-ended specialist funds. The majority of continental European funds of funds are closed-ended.

7.5 Characteristics of real estate funds

PFR held detailed information on over 270 live UK unlisted real estate funds as at September 2014 with a total gross asset value of around £106 billion. (A live fund is one which has held its first close, or raised its initial capital, and has not yet been wound up or returned all capital to investors.) This UK dataset is primarily used as an example of the global market to illustrate the characteristics of unlisted funds in the following descriptive statistics.

7.5.1 Style

Funds are differentiated by risk types. While we earlier suggested splitting the universe into low risk/high risk or core/opportunity categories, some industry participants have distinguished funds by using the four styles we discussed in Chapter 2 – core, core-plus, value-added and opportunity. The vehicles included in PFR's universe are classified as being one of three styles (core, core-plus/value-added and opportunity) while the trade body, INREV, similarly recommends three styles: core, value-added and opportunistic. This classification system has become the industry standard.

Figure 7.5 illustrates the typical criteria used to distinguish global unlisted fund styles. Core funds are low-risk funds with no or low gearing, often open-ended, and should aim to closely replicate returns on the relevant index of direct real estate. The fund assets provide stable income returns which are a key element of the total return, currently in the range 5–8 per cent, and its relative target (post-tax and -fees) return is less than 1 per cent above a specified property or peer group benchmark. Permitted leverage is likely to be below 30 per cent of gross asset value.

Value-added funds have some potential for value enhancement through re-letting empty space, refurbishment work or other active asset management activity. Returns are driven by a combination of income and capital return, and target returns are currently in the range 8–11 per cent, or (in relative terms) 1–3 per cent above a specified property or peer group benchmark. Permitted leverage is likely to be between 30 and 60 per cent of gross asset value.

Figure 7.5: Unlisted fund risk styles

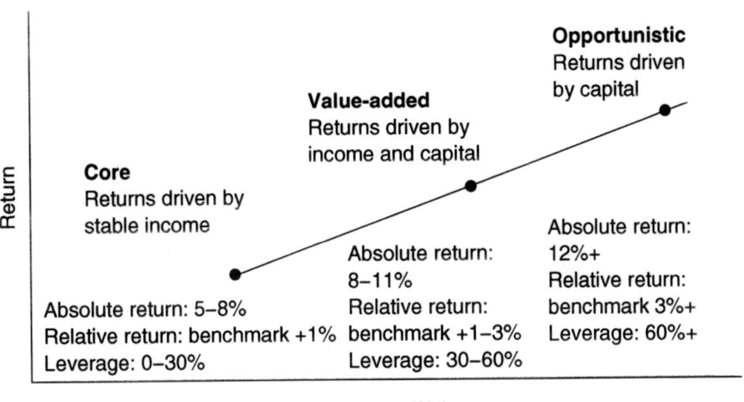

Source: Property Funds Research

Opportunity funds are higher risk, higher target return funds with high levels of gearing. Returns are driven primarily through capital return; the current target (post-tax and -fees) return is in excess of 12 per cent per annum, or its target return (post-tax and -fees) is greater than 3 per cent above a specified property or peer group benchmark; and permitted leverage is in excess of 60 per cent of gross asset value.

PFR data as at September 2014 shows the split of core, core-plus/value-added and opportunity funds, with the largest group being opportunity funds at 44 per cent, followed by value-added at 32 per cent and core at 25 per cent. Yet until the end of the 1990s European value-added and opportunity funds were barely in existence and at the beginning of the 1990s core funds accounted for 97 per cent of the market by GAV and just over 60 per cent at January 2008. Opportunity funds experienced rapid growth between 2000 and 2003 but value-added funds then emerged as the style of choice. The majority of funds launched between 2005 and 2008 were value-added, while opportunity funds made a comeback after the GFC in the 2008–14 period.

Figure 7.6 shows that core funds are more likely to be the style of choice for the more developed markets of Europe and Australasia, while opportunistic funds are the most significant fund type in most developing markets.

Vehicles in PFR's universe have a variety of investment restrictions aimed at limiting the risk of a particular portfolio of investments. Diversified funds may be permitted to invest between 30 and 50 per cent of GAV in a particular sector. Pan-European funds may have prescribed limits regarding the countries in which they can invest, which may be anywhere between 30 and 50 per cent of GAV in each country. Development is limited to anywhere between 10 and 30 per cent of GAV. There is likely to be some kind of investment restriction based on the amount invested in any single asset, typically in the region of 15 per cent of GAV. Similarly, income restrictions are likely to be placed on a fund. Income derived from a single tenant/company is typically limited to around 15 per cent of GAV.

Figure 7.6: Vehicle style by regional focus

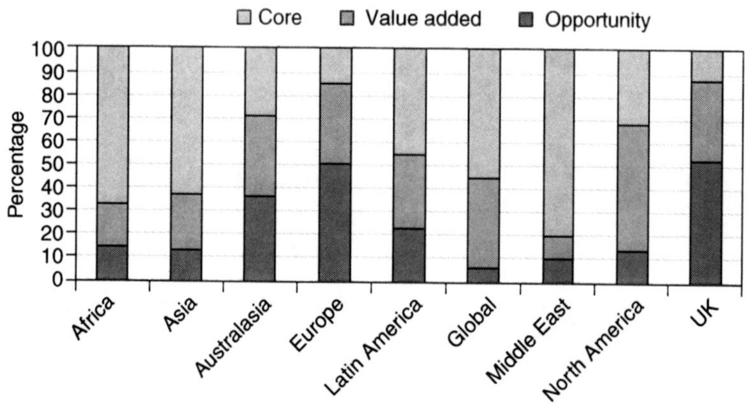

Source: Property Funds Research

7.5.2 Domicile and structure

Limited partnerships make up roughly 33 per cent and unit trusts make up around 32 per cent of the UK universe by number of funds, but PUTs are bigger in terms of current gross asset values (£37 billion for PUTs against £21 billion for LPs). The UK is the most popular domicile, as would be expected given that UK limited partnerships appear to be the vehicle of choice. Channel Islands funds (usually PUTs) define 34 per cent of the sector.

7.5.3 Sector focus

As at September 2014, 56 per cent of UK unlisted funds by number in the PFR database were diversified. Many more funds than is represented in the IPD direct real estate index were targeting residential and other real estate, including healthcare, student housing and infrastructure, illustrating the pioneering nature of many unlisted funds. Office was the most popular 'traditional' sector with 7.3 per cent of funds by number, then retail, with 6.6 per cent.

Post-GFC, the banking sector contracted and there was a shortage of debt, which meant that higher than normal returns were on offer to lenders. The result was that a large number of debt funds were launched in the 2009–13 period, issuing senior debt, stretched senior (whole loans) and mezzanine.

7.5.4 Open or closed?

More funds by number are closed-ended rather than open-ended (56 per cent against 39 per cent) but open-ended funds are larger by value (53 per cent against 42 per cent by value). Over 40 per cent of funds by value are closed to new investment, mostly closed-ended funds that had completed capital raising but including a small number of open-ended funds that had closed their doors to new investment.

7.5.5 Target equity and permitted gearing

PFR records permitted gearing based on the level of debt in all global vehicles as a percentage of GAV. Funds have had permitted gearing levels ranging up to 85 per cent, although typical gearing levels are far more conservative than this. Figure 7.7 illustrates that (as at September 2014) all vehicle styles carry a lower level of debt than is permitted, as the average is affected by funds which are not fully invested. Actual gearing levels average less than 25 per cent for core funds, just over 30 per cent for value-added funds and just under 50 per cent for opportunity funds. Permitted gearing levels are around 40, 55 and 65 per cent respectively.

Figure 7.7: Current and permitted gearing by fund style

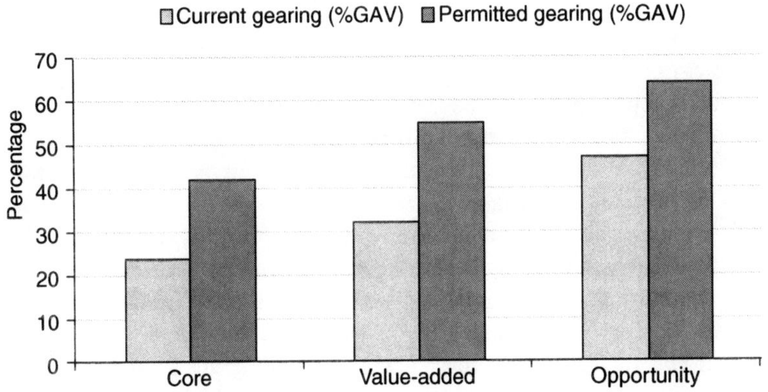

Source: Property Funds Research

In the UK sample, the average target equity level per unlisted fund is approaching £161 million. Defined as a percentage of gross target assets, permitted gearing levels vary from 0 to 90 per cent, with most funds limited to between 50 and 70 per cent. Core funds' permitted gearing levels averaged 40 per cent, core-plus/value-added 43 per cent and opportunity 70 per cent. Permitted gearing levels are shown in more detail in Table 7.3.

Table 7.3: Permitted gearing levels

Levels of permitted gearing (% of GAV)	Number	%
0–9	30	21
10–19	12	8
20–29	12	8
30–39	5	4
40–49	2	1
50–59	23	16
60–69	41	29
70–79	12	8
80	6	4

Source: Property Funds Research

7.6 Liquidity and valuation issues

7.6.1 Liquidity

The lumpy, illiquid nature of real estate as an asset class means that indirect investment may be an appealing alternative. However, liquidity in unlisted funds is generally limited. Different fund types offer different degrees of liquidity. Open-ended funds offer monthly, quarterly or annual redemptions, although sometimes with an initial 'lock-up' period of three or four years. Following the example provided by the relatively mature UK market, there is an increasingly active secondary market in European closed-ended funds and this may develop in international markets. Nonetheless, closed-ended funds generally offer little liquidity.

Given that unlisted funds are not stock market traded, an alternative mechanism is needed to provide this liquidity. The key issue is whether the fund is open-ended, semi-open-ended or closed-ended.

Open-ended fund units can be redeemed on demand, and new investors will normally be allowed and encouraged to buy new units on demand. In the UK, the manager will issue units at NAV plus an allowance for the costs of buying new properties with the new cash (the offer price), and will undertake to return capital to the investor at the latest NAV estimate less a deduction for trading costs (the bid price). (Technically, the NAV is adjusted to offer price by adding real estate acquisition costs and offer is reduced to bid by deducting the round trip costs of buying and selling real estate.) In the US, there is no bid-offer spread, and liquidity requirements are managed by a queuing system.

Semi-open-ended funds will have a 'lock-up' period, typically up to five years, during which investors are not allowed to redeem units and after which limited redemptions will be permitted.

Open-ended and semi-open-ended funds can have infinite lives, and this is an obvious attraction for managers. Closed-ended funds, on the other hand, have a limited number of units in issue at any time (hence the term) and do not have a redemption facility, so that investors are reliant upon secondary market trading, which with some notable exceptions may be thin or non-existent. The manager of a closed-ended fund is therefore usually forced to offer a termination date at which investors can force assets to be sold and capital returned. This is typically six to ten years from launch. Recently, the limitations of closed-ended funds have been recognized by the increasing popularity of evergreen funds, which have a perpetual life and regular 'liquidity events' during which windows of time the manager will offer to match those requiring an exit with those wishing to invest new capital.

Despite the obvious appeal of the open-ended structure, there are severe limitations. Investors will not redeem units from the manager if they can sell units in the secondary market for a higher price, and new investors will not subscribe for new units if they can buy units for less in the secondary market. Where there is a balance of buyers and sellers, buyers and sellers will deal directly with each other at something close to mid price (half way between bid and offer), and the bid–offer spread imposed by the manager is not justified because there is no need to undertake any direct real estate trading to grow or reduce the real estate portfolio. The manager may then wish to orchestrate a secondary market, either in search of broking fees or to offer a service to investors and to maximize the market appeal of the fund.

The open-ended structure can be fatally flawed in 'one-way' markets where there is a large preponderance of buyers or – much worse – sellers. A rush of buyers can flood the manager with cash, thereby diluting the real estate return delivered by the fund and damaging the manager's performance. A rush of sellers can be much more damaging. Unfortunately, there may be a double problem in such circumstances.

If a majority of investors feels that the time is right to sell real estate units, this may be for either or both of two reasons. First, investors may feel that the units are fairly priced but that the future market return will be relatively unattractive. Second, investors may feel that the units are over-priced and will wish to exploit a pricing anomaly by selling. On several occasions, with late 2007 being the latest example, these two factors combined to create the equivalent of a 'run on the bank'.

In 1990, Rodamco, then an open-ended Netherlands fund, was forced to close its doors to prevent investors from exiting. In 2005, German open-ended funds suffered a large exodus of investors, forcing an immediate revaluation and audit of one large fund and the risk of its closure though mass withdrawals. Following this, the pricing of German open-ended funds was publicly debated, fraud was discovered in two cases and questions about investor protection were openly raised.

In 2007, in the UK, a weakening real estate market was coupled with the predictable conservatism of valuers reluctant to mark prices down without clear evidence and yet strong external evidence in the derivatives and REIT markets of much lower real estate prices. The September quarter-end valuation of most open-ended funds was too high. Professional investors, primarily fund of funds managers, wished to exploit this anomaly by selling over-valued units in open-ended funds. Several open-ended fund managers deferred redemptions and reduced valuations retrospectively, thereby preventing investors from exiting at valuation. The consequent damage caused to the open-ended fund industry proved to be short-lived, as in retrospect this action protected investors from 'fire sales' of assets.

7.6.2 Valuation lag

As the secondary market trading of funds has begun to grow, pricing of these units has begun to take place at discounts and premiums to net asset value. This challenges market convention, as, unlike REITs, which trade in the stock market at market-determined prices in real time, unlisted funds are priced by reference to market valuations. For higher risk opportunity funds, valuations may be irregular and unimportant, as investors expect to see a return of capital within three to seven years and interim valuations may not be helpful where development or other value-adding activity is the key focus of the fund. For low-risk core funds with longer or indefinite lives, regular valuation is a more accurate and necessary indicator of the manager's progress, and monthly valuations are not uncommon, so secondary market premiums and discounts can appear to challenge the published valuation.

In late 2007, the UK real estate investment market had entered a period of relative crisis. Prices had been falling, liquidity had disappeared and open-ended funds had closed their doors to those trying to exit. Why the loss of liquidity? Why had investors suddenly become trapped within an asset class – and an apparently liquid structure – that had been performing so well but suddenly froze? The answer lies in the unique nature of real estate as a 'big ticket' asset class, but also in the defects inherent within the practice of real estate valuation.

Figure 7.8 shows real estate yields and index-linked gilt yields for the period 1995 to 2014. It shows a remarkable correlation. The market appears to treat these asset types similarly, as excellent inflation hedges.

Figure 7.8: Real estate yields and index-linked gilt yields, 1995–2014

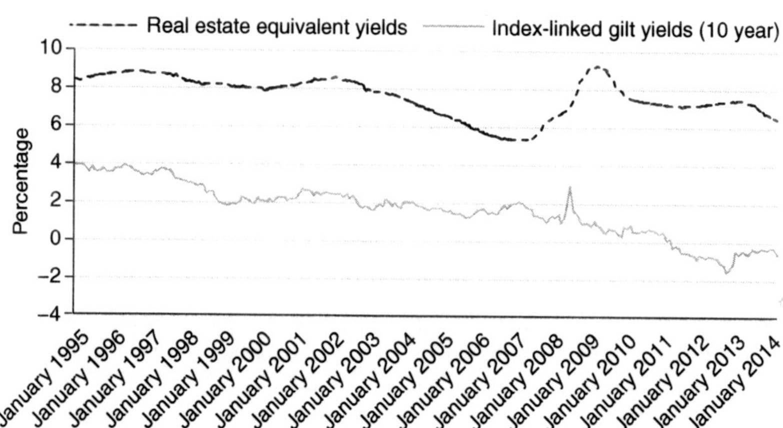

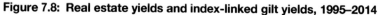

Source: IPD, FT, Property Funds Research

Real estate was looking expensive at the beginning of 2007. By this point, average premiums to NAV on unlisted funds had begun to fall, followed quickly by falls in REIT premiums and derivative margins. However, it was not until the summer of 2007 that returns on the IPD monthly index – the best indicator of prices in the direct UK market – began to turn down.

By late 2006 the gap had closed, making real estate relatively expensive. This is illustrated more clearly in Figure 7.9.

Figure 7.9: Real estate yields less index-linked gilt yields, 1995–2014

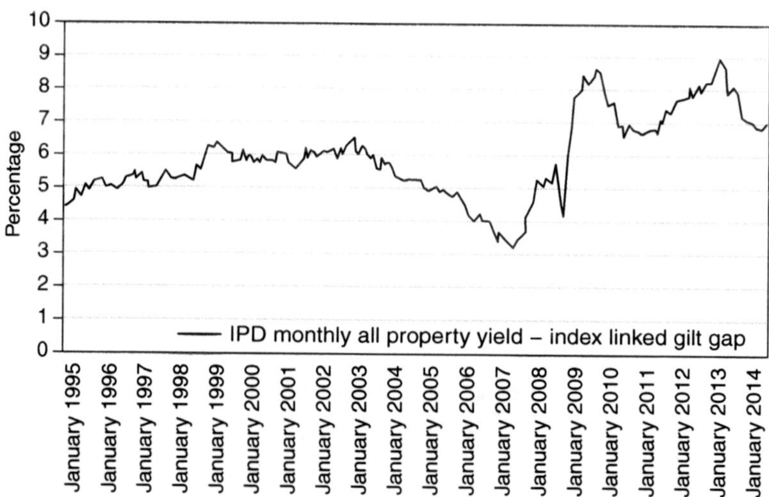

Source: IPD, FT, Property Funds Research

Figure 7.10 shows average three (calendar) year real estate swap margins over LIBOR from August 2006 to September 2007, turning from 0.4 per cent over LIBOR to 9 per cent under LIBOR (Merrill Lynch estimates). Unlisted fund premiums over NAV fell (according to Jones Lang LaSalle estimates) from 4 per cent on average to –9 per cent in September. REIT prices collapsed from premiums to NAV at the start of 2007 to big discounts by summer 2007.

Figure 7.10: REIT and unlisted fund discounts to NAV, real estate swap margins over LIBOR, IPD monthly returns, August 2007 to September 2008

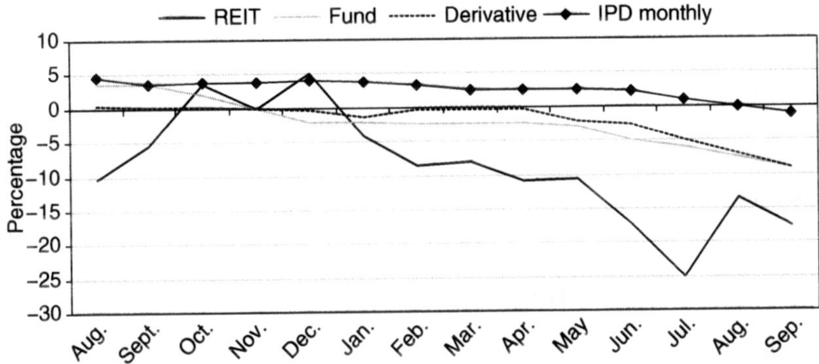

Source: IPD, JLL, CBRE, Merrill Lynch, Property Funds Research

Meanwhile, the IPD monthly index (unlike the other indicators, including income) produced its first negative return (–0.1 per cent) in September 2007. This – at the very least – suggests some lagging in the IPD monthly index.

Why has the IPD monthly index lagged other real estate indicators? The answer lies in the nature of the asset class and the conservatism built into UK real estate valuation practice.

7.6.3 Real estate volatility

Real estate is just one of a set of conventional and alternative assets for investment funds and must compete directly with them. In the UK and US over the long term, equities have performed best, real estate second best and bonds worst. But in the UK the volatility of real estate, as measured by the standard deviation of those returns, is much lower than the other two.

However, there are problems with this argument. The capital values of real estate used in the performance calculations are produced by valuations and are not transaction-based. It is commonly argued that the way in which valuations are produced means they tend to lag market movements, producing a lagging effect in the performance figures which tend to smooth the peaks and troughs of movements in prices (see Chapter 1).

Valuation issues, along with considerations of liquidity and the depreciation of real estate, have been cited as issues which have been used to disadvantage real estate in the asset allocation process. Yet when these differences are exposed they provide an opportunity for professional investors to make money through the identification of pricing anomalies, which hedge funds (for example) increasingly try to do. In the UK, the introduction of a UK REIT and the development of derivative products are both illustrations of the driving together of real estate and the capital markets, the opportunity for arbitrage and the impossibility of real estate appraisal methods standing apart from these markets. This is a good thing for markets, investment managers and investors.

7.6.4 The valuation process

However, real estate is different from liquid assets because market valuations are required for performance measurement purposes. The established doctrine underpinning the identification of market value requires best evidence of trading prices of other similar assets. This doctrine is underpinned by the courts and by the perceived best practice of other competent practitioners.

'Other similar assets' is invariably interpreted as other similar *real estate* assets; and the use of transactions in similar properties means that a lag is built into real estate valuations. Over the period 1996 to 2006, a period of rising prices, IPD estimates that sale prices were around 3 per cent higher than valuations. This suggests some lagging of valuations. As a result, few analysts accept that appraisal-based indices reflect the true underlying performance of the real estate market. Such indices fail to capture the extent of market volatility and lag underlying performance.

Real estate valuation is founded primarily on the use of comparable sales evidence. Similarity in real estate characteristics is paramount and good recent comparables may be rare. Hence (as suggested in Chapter 1) the evidence used to value a property as at 31 December 2014 may be collected over the period July to December. In a rising or falling market, this will again result in a lower variance of prices. As a result, valuations will be based upon the previous valuation plus or minus a perception of change, and the perceived changes, unless the subject of very reliable transaction evidence, will be conservative.

There may also be client influence. The way property fund managers are typically rewarded, with an annual fee and a performance fee based on delivered returns with no reference to risk, may mean they will benefit greatly from a particular performance outcome which will earn a bonus or carried interest, or support a track record to win or retain fee-earning business.

Given that valuations tend to lag price increases and falls, valuations in a bear market will not follow price reductions down as quickly as they occurred. If this bear market continued for a long term, which was the case in Germany, valuations could become higher than prices. It is not surprising therefore that investors would be nervous of this cocktail of moral hazards, with plenty of incentives for the funds to influence valuers, and that some investors lost confidence in the valuation levels being reported.

In the UK, there is thankfully no evidence of client influence maintaining artificially high price levels (Baum *et al.*, 2003). However, there is a secondary market for units in unlisted funds. There is also a growing real estate derivatives market, and a REIT market, not to mention a securitization (CMBS) market. All offer pricing indicators to valuers of direct real estate. Yet while there was patent over-pricing in a falling market in the second half of 2007, valuers claimed a lack of comparable evidence, with few transactions.

Evidence is all around in the capital markets and unlisted real estate vehicles, and valuers are beginning to be influenced by the evidence provided in increasingly integrated markets for direct real estate and real estate funds. Their professional integrity, and a clear absence of client influence, is paramount to the working of the unlisted real estate fund market.

7.7 The case for and against unlisted real estate funds

7.7.1 The case for unlisted real estate funds

Unlisted real estate funds can diversify real estate specific risk

A lot of money is needed to build a diversified real estate portfolio. The capital investment required to mimic the performance of a real estate index depends both on the efficiency of diversification within the segment and upon the average lot size within each segment. Investors with higher levels of risk aversion require more capital investment in real estate segments in order to reduce the specific risk component of the portfolio to the desired level.

For example, Baum and Struempell (2006) found that over £1 billion is needed to build a diversified portfolio of London offices with a 2 per cent tracking error. This presents a very strong case for using an unlisted fund focused on London offices. Assuming that such a fund is financed by 50 per cent debt and 50 per cent equity, 20 investors committing £25 million each will produce enough capital to capitalise the diversified fund. Yet the investor's £25 million is enough to buy only one or two London offices of average lot size.

Unlisted funds are priced by reference to NAV

The above argument could also be used to justify investments in listed property securities. However, (as we saw in Chapter 6) the pricing of listed REITs and property companies will vary from real estate prices and in the short to medium term (zero to five years) equity market factors distort the performance of the securities relative to the underlying real estate market. Since 1990 US REITs have traded at discounts and premiums varying from –35 per cent (in 1991) to +30 per cent (in 1997). On the other hand, core open-ended unlisted funds appear to track real estate NAVs. Figure 7.11 shows how core (lower risk, often open-ended) UK funds have tracked the UK IPD index of direct real estate returns.

Figure 7.11 could be highly misleading. It shows how appraisal-based returns on core funds track appraisal-based returns on the index, but it does not purport to show how

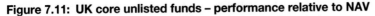

Figure 7.11: UK core unlisted funds – performance relative to NAV

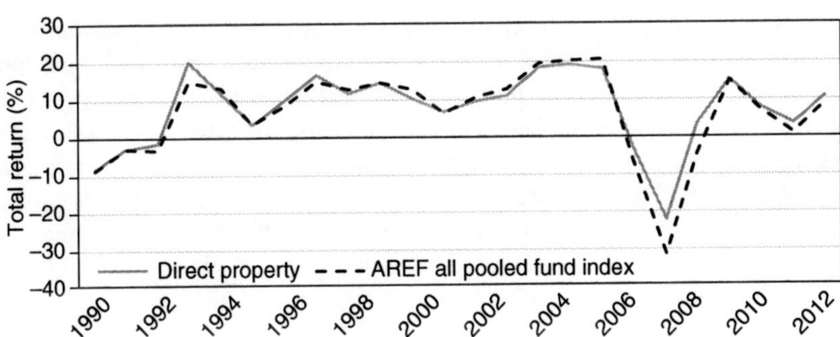

Source: Property Funds Research, AREF

trading prices track the index. This became a problematic issue in 2007–8, as Section 7.6.2 describes.

Unlisted funds provide access to specialist managers

It is likely to be the case that specialist managers, meaning experts in a market sector or a specific geography, will produce better performance than a manager or investor located in a single market yet attempting to buy assets globally. PFR global data shows that the majority of closed-ended unlisted funds are typically focused on a geography (India, London) and sector (shopping centres, London offices). Good fund and manager selection can lead to the holy grail of lower-risk and higher returns.

7.7.2 The case against unlisted real estate funds

Investing in unlisted funds suffers from five key challenges. First, cash may not be taken or returned immediately by the discretionary manager, fund of funds or selected fund(s). This produces liquidity and a slow expected cash drawdown profile. Second, gearing will colour returns. Third, the initial performance will be damaged by the costs involved in the manager buying the initial portfolio, producing what is known as J-curve effect. Fourth, manager fees can challenge thoughtful investors. Finally, trading prices may not track NAV, even for open-ended funds.

The drawdown profile

Managers will not wish to draw cash immediately for a variety of reasons, the key issue being their desire to deliver real estate returns not coloured by cash returns. Hence cash is drawn from investors as and when it is needed to complete the purchase of assets. The result is a delay in attaining full exposure.

Gearing

The typical closed-ended fund is likely to be geared. Adjustments may therefore need to be applied to the direct real estate risk, return and correlation data which encouraged the investor's interest in investing in real estate. Returns may be higher, risk will be higher and correlations may be affected.

A financial structure of 50 per cent equity and 50 per cent debt means that half of the required investment only is needed to attain the same exposure. This increases the appeal and efficiency of unlisted vehicles even more. Unfortunately, this factor carries with it financial risk, which to some extent will offset the reduction in specific risk. It is known that gearing increases risk and volatility (Chapters 1 and 2). It also makes performance more responsive to interest rates and the bond market, depending on whether the interest rate is fixed or floating. Debt can alter the cash flow, and will typically decrease the investor's income return.

In summary, the risk of a geared fund is likely to be higher than the risk of an ungeared fund, as shown by Figure 7.12, in which the shaded area shows the likely spread of returns, increasing as gearing increases.

Hence the price of specific risk reduction achieved by unlisted vehicles may be higher volatility introduced by gearing – albeit balanced by higher prospective returns. This was evidenced in the most extreme way by the GFC period.

Figure 7.12: The impact of gearing on return

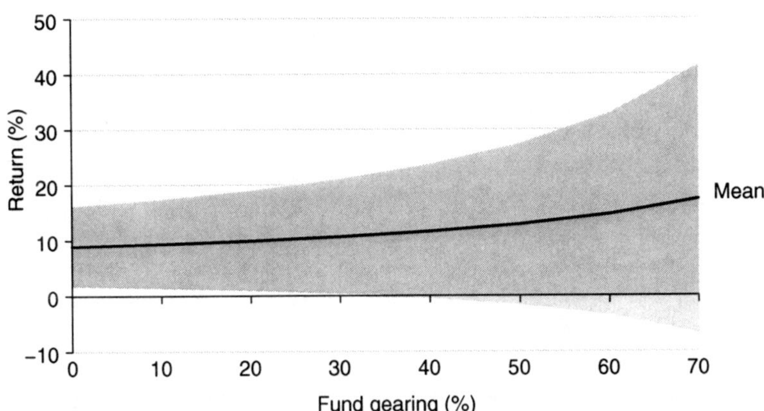

Source: Baum and Struempell, 2006

The 2012 ULI/PFR Report (Have Property Funds Performed?) found disappointing performance across unlisted property funds of all types over the 2001–11 period. The damage was being done primarily by leverage (see also Alcock *et al.* (2013). This is illustrated by Figure 7.13, which shows how powerful are the effects of (i) the market and (ii) leverage upon higher risk funds delivering so-called absolute returns (see Section 7.8).

Figure 7.13: Opportunity fund returns relative to ungeared benchmark, 2001–11

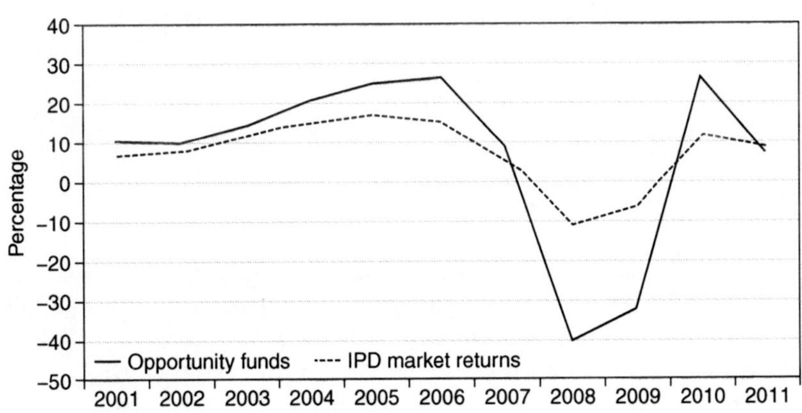

Source: PFR, ULI

The J-curve effect

The performance of an allocation to unlisted funds will also be damaged in the short term by the costs involved in the manager buying the initial portfolio. The result can be poor short-term performance. In the early years, newly launched funds' performance can be negative relative to the direct real estate index – but after fund costs are amortized, and the gearing in the unlisted fund takes effect, the unlisted funds can out-perform the direct market.

The INREV Index, which began in 2001, measures annual net asset value (NAV) based performance for non-listed real estate funds investing in Europe. Performance from 2001 to 2006 averaged 13.67 per cent compared to 9.35 per cent for the ungeared direct property market measured by the Investment Property Databank (IPD) pan-European index. The IPD index for this period and INREV data released in 2006 (see Figure 7.14) describe a classic J-curve relative to the market, showing how fund set-up and acquisition costs damaged early year returns as funds are being established. Figure 7.14 also shows funds out-performing the direct index by an average of over 4 per cent per annum over the 2005–6 period.

Figure 7.14: The J-curve effect

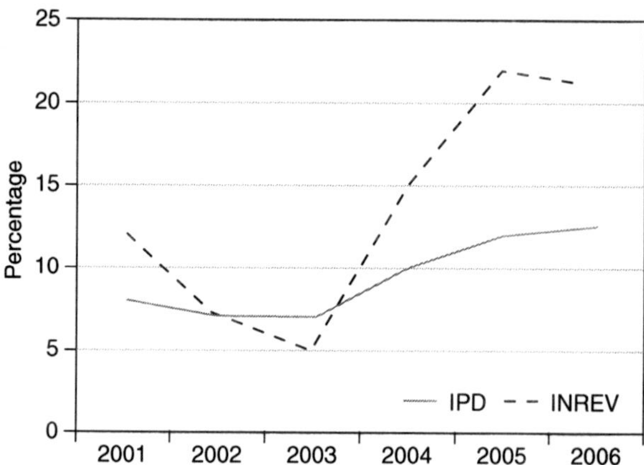

Source: INREV, IPD, Property Funds Research

Fees

Fees charged by the manager of a real estate fund (or a fund of funds) will usually be charged on an annual *ad valorem* basis, typically between 50 bps and 100 bps every year on a growing gross asset value, despite the fact that much of the manager's activity is front-loaded. In addition, performance fees may be charged and related to absolute returns or returns relative to an index. Often, the use of high gearing will mean that the manager has increased the risk profile of real estate investing but, to the extent that this delivers extra returns, will be paid for the risks taken with client's capital. These issues are challenging for managers to justify.

In addition, double fees charged in funds of funds may be hard for clients to bear. Managers need to be able to justify the additional fee layer by proven added diversification and risk reduction, or alternatively by the provision of expert access to out-performing managers at a reduced cost. (For more on the impact of performance fees, see Section 7.8.)

Do trading prices track NAV?

A large component of the case for unlisted real estate funds, as argued above, is that unlisted funds are priced by reference to NAV and can therefore be expected to deliver property-style performance, whereas REITs and listed property companies exhibit volatility and correlation with equities. But the events of 2007–8 call this into question.

Take the case of a UK open-ended fund in mid-2007. The fund is valued monthly by a well-known chartered surveying practice/property services provider. The valuation instruction is to estimate the asset value of the properties in the fund; any adjustments needed to estimate the fund net asset value are usually undertaken internally as an accounting function, dealing primarily with the addition of cash holdings and the deduction of debt.

From January 2007 to June 2007, the IPD monthly index had been showing positive capital growth of between 0.27 and 0.46 per cent for each of the six months of the first half of the year (see Figure 7.14). The fund also showed positive NAV growth.

In the summer of 2007, there was a change in market sentiment. This was evidenced by some circulars from fund managers to their clients warning of poor returns to come. It was reflected to some extent in the IPD monthly index, which produced its last positive total return of the cycle in July, disguising a tiny fall in capital value of 0.22 per cent, followed by a negative capital return in August of 0.4 per cent, marking a turning point in retrospective but hardly indicative of a crash. The fund's values were flat over this period, as they were through the end of September. However, the IPD monthly index for September had taken a more significant downward turn of over 1.5 per cent, a figure which was

Figure 7.15: IPD UK monthly index, monthly total returns, 2007–8

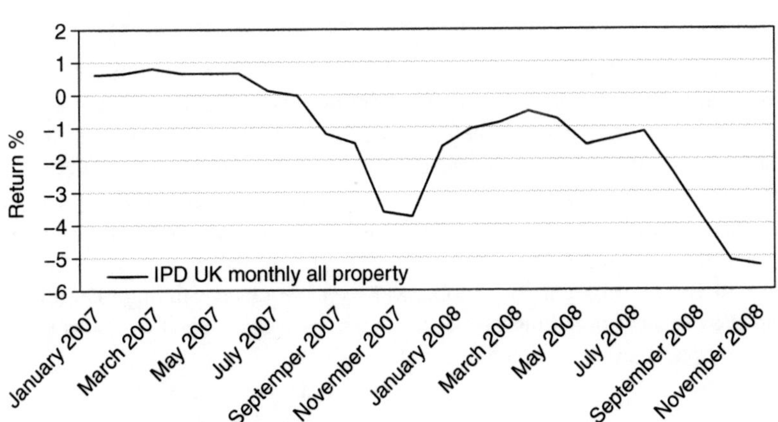

Source: IPD

not available to the valuer of the fund's properties at the time the September valuation was produced. The effect of this was that the fund's values stayed flat over the summer quarter, while the IPD monthly index fell by over 2 per cent for the quarter.

In mid-October 2007, the fund's manager found itself in 'challenging' position. Market sentiment had clearly changed. The UK REIT market had moved to huge discounts to NAV, moving downwards from a small premium in March 2007 to a discount touching 20 per cent in September 2007 (see Figure 7.16).

Figure 7.16: Secondary trading premiums (discounts) in UK closed-end funds and UK REITs, August 2006 to June 2014

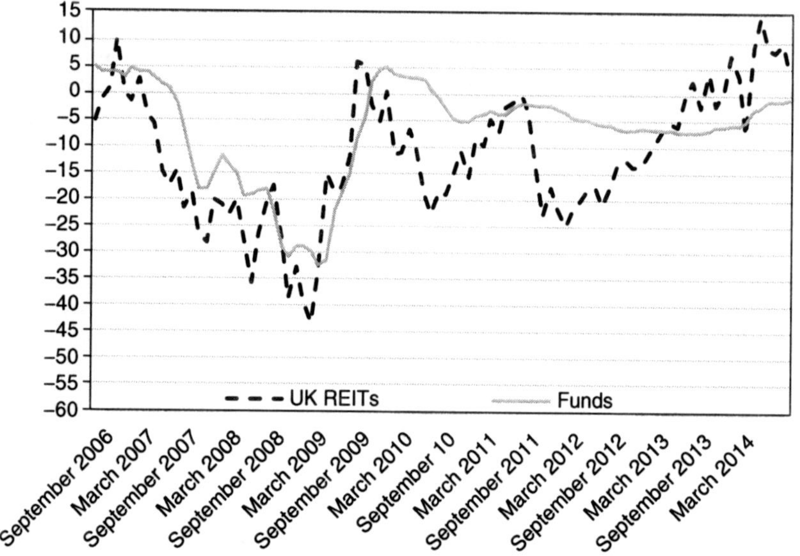

Source: EPRA, JLL

Meanwhile, the fund's NAV had stayed flat over the summer and unlisted funds in general were in a strange position. Secondary trading had dried up as the market sought a new price level, as Jones Lang LaSalle's estimates of closed-ended fund premiums and discounts show (see Figure 7.10). Only by November had the re-pricing become evident.

Professional investors could see a clear arbitrage opportunity, and were prompted to exploit it. They served redemption notices effective at the end of September, expecting to be paid out at the NAV-based bid price. This was broadly the same as it had been in June, at the peak of the market, but by October values were clearly falling. The manager was faced with the prospect of selling properties in a very weak market at prices which would clearly not be as high as the September NAV.

This might be a fair game as far as the exiting professional investor would view it, but it might not be fair from the perspective of an existing unit-holder who wishes to stay in the fund. If a large number of properties are sold considerably below NAV but existing unit-holders are paid out at NAV, the remaining unit-holders suffer the loss. If this is the case, then all unit-holders will be tempted to exit at the same time, challenging the continued existence of the open-ended fund, which had been a perfectly acceptable and stable investment for many small pension funds for over 15 years since the last market crisis of 1991.

The trust deed allowed the manager to defer redemptions, and also to make adjustments to the NAV in exceptional market circumstances. It was judged that these circumstances were indeed exceptional, and a large discount was applied to the NAV in October, and a further discount was applied in January; redemptions were deferred, but sales took place and exiting investors (who had been able to withdraw their redemption notices given the downward price revision) were paid out on time, albeit at the lower bid price, by now revised down to around 80 per cent of the NAV.

So, while unlisted fund NAVs may continue to track the IPD index (see Figure 7.11) and demonstrate high correlation, there is reason to suppose that trading prices of funds on the secondary market, or the prices received by investors exiting open-ended funds, will not always track NAV. This issue is explored in detail by Schneider (2014).

Box 7.1 Pricing an open-ended fund

Open-ended fund units can be redeemed on demand, and new investors will normally be allowed and encouraged to buy new units on demand. The manager will issue units at NAV plus an allowance for the costs of buying new properties with the new cash (the offer price), and will undertake to return capital to the investor at the latest NAV estimate less a deduction for trading costs (the bid price). (Technically, the NAV is adjusted to offer price by adding real estate acquisition costs and offer is reduced to bid by deducting the round trip costs of buying and selling real estate.)

Open-ended funds in the UK typically have quarterly redemptions. The quarter-end NAV is important, as it sets the bid and offer price.

The relevant data for the NCM open-ended fund is as follows.

The fund's properties are valued at £562.15 million. There is cash in the bank of £11.12 million. The fund has debt of £24.96 million. The number of units in issue is 630,201.

GAV is given by (property values plus cash)
NAV is given by (GAV – debt)

The NAV per share is given by (NAV/number of units)

The offer price – the price paid by an investor on entry – is set at NAV plus 5.25 per cent

The bid price – the price received by an investor on exit – is set at offer price less 7 per cent

The bid–offer spread = (offer – bid)/offer

Mid price = (bid + offer)/2

What is offer price, bid price, mid price and the bid–offer spread for the NCM fund?

7.8 Performance measurement and return attribution for property funds

7.8.1 The asymmetry of performance fees

As explained in Section 7.2, performance fees may be charged by managers of unlisted funds, especially those at the riskier end of the spectrum, and will be related to absolute or relative returns.

The use of high gearing increases the risk of the client's capital and should generate extra returns. This can be called beta investing, whereby the manager increases the exposure of the client's capital to the market (see Chapter 5). It is different from alpha investing, whereby the manager uses skill to out-perform the market competition at the relevant risk level. It can be expected that more focus is placed on defining and distinguishing alpha and beta investing in real estate funds, if only because performance fees charged purely for beta are commonplace, yet (all other fees equal) plainly unfair.

This issue, among others, will add to the debate about transparency which is necessary to bring self-regulation to a growing and globalizing market for real estate funds. Aided by the participation of world-class global managers and investors, real estate funds are likely to be the engine which drives best practice in a truly international real estate market.

Since the mid-1990s, in a generally strongly performing property market, fund managers have been able to raise significant capital for unlisted funds which reward them with performance fees, without the manager necessarily being able to provide clear evidence of historic out-performance against market benchmarks or targets.

Table 7.4 shows the delivered and expected returns on a series of high return funds with typical performance fees or carried interests. The average difference between the gross of fees IRRs earned by the fund and the net IRRs delivered to investors is just over

Table 7.4: Total returns, fund series – fee impacts (rounded)

Fund	Gross IRR	Net IRR	Fee impact	Fee impact %
1	29.0%	25.0%	4.0%	13.8%
2	17.0%	13.0%	4.0%	23.5%
3	33.0%	25.0%	8.0%	24.2%
4	35.0%	30.0%	5.0%	14.3%
5	27.0%	21.0%	6.0%	22.2%
6	46.0%	37.0%	9.0%	19.6%
7	21.0%	16.0%	5.0%	23.8%
8	34.0%	27.0%	7.0%	20.6%
9	16.0%	13.0%	3.0%	18.8%
10	20.0%	15.0%	5.0%	25.0%
11	18.0%	14.0%	4.0%	22.2%
12	20.0%	16.0%	4.0%	20.0%
13	14.0%	12.0%	2.0%	14.3%
14	20.0%	15.0%	5.0%	25.0%
Mean	25.0%	19.9%	5.1%	20.5%

Source: Baum and Farrelly, 2008

5 per cent, or just over 20 per cent or one-fifth of the gross IRR. This i
tional fee load for the investor and should therefore be justified in a rela

Property Funds Research data suggests that typical annual fun
excluding performance fees average around 0.8 per cent of gross asset
less than 1 per cent return every year. Hence the fee impact shown in T
and is explained by 'carried interest' or performance fees. High fees n
manager has earned the fee through the exercise of skill. But, as we
risk portfolio should out-perform a lower-risk portfolio on a risk-unadjust
means that the manager could earn a high fee by taking risk with the client's capital. Performance fees should reward alpha, but they may reward pure beta.

In addition, performance fees may represent a form of free option (asymmetrical, as options tend to be) for the manager. High returns may lead to high fees (there is an 85 per cent correlation between the gross IRR and the fee impact in Table 7.4) and limit the investor's upside without limiting the manager's upside; while the opposite situation may describe the downside, as the investor will directly suffer, but the manager will not.

Hence there is a large incentive for managers to create high returns, which is good; but and whether alpha or beta delivers those returns may be immaterial, and that is not good.

7.8.2 An attribution system for funds

To enable performance fees and track records to be judged, risk and return attribution systems need to be developed for property funds and property fund managers. As an example, Baum (2007) focuses on the additional return and risk contribution of fund structure – gearing, for example – to the traditional structure and stock factors. Under this proposed approach, it is necessary to take away vehicle return effects in order to expose the property effect, and then to deduct the structure contribution to reveal the stock contribution.

Fund structure is a factor specific to property held in a vehicle or wrapper. This factor will have an impact on the returns from listed REITs and property companies and from unlisted funds alike. There are two main drivers of the fund structure impact: fund expenses and management fees, and leverage.

Figure 7.17: Time-weighted return attribution for a property fund

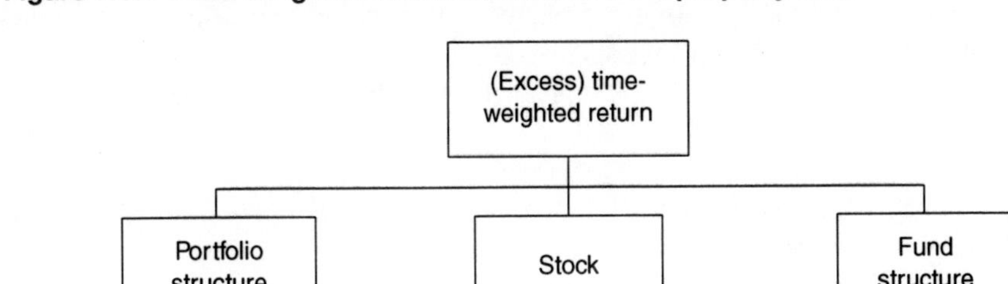

Source: Property Funds Research

Baum (2007) uses empirical evidence derived from the IPD UK Pooled Property Fund ...dex, measuring the fund structure effect by taking the fund returns, the funds' quarterly gearing levels, interest rates and annual fee structures, and 'de-gearing' the gross of fee returns. Deducting this vehicle impact leaves the property contribution. Deducting the structure contribution to the property return from the derived property level return series produces the stock contribution to return (see Chapter 5).

Using the sets of data described above, the tracking errors of 18 funds against the IPD UK Pooled Property Fund Index were computed. In addition, depending on the funds' reporting and data availability, the earliest available period for each fund in which all necessary data were available was used to predict the tracking error given the above approach. The actual fund tracking errors (over the time periods corresponding to each fund's data availability) were then compared to the predicted fund tracking errors. The fit between actual and predicted fund tracking errors was better than the fit between actual and observed property tracking errors, validating the inclusion of gearing and fee factors in a fund risk measure.

Bostwick and Tyrell (2006) show how leverage can change the relationship of return and risk non-proportionately. Nonetheless, as illustrated in Baum (2007) and CBRE (2008) it is clear that the greater the use of debt finance the greater the risk of a property fund. Hence, while there may be some skill in financial structuring, pure leverage is largely a beta generating activity. Expenses and fees simply limit the impact of that beta contribution. Hence fund structure adds beta.

As discussed above, if all portfolio segments are of similar risk, then positive excess returns generated by the portfolio structure relative to a benchmark will produce alpha. If they result from taking overweight positions in high-risk markets, then they generate beta. In the context of unlisted funds, which are largely owned by diversified investors or by fund of fund managers, much of this risk is diversified away. Hence, unless we can observe a strong bias to emerging markets in the portfolio structure, we can suggest that structure contributes alpha.

The same argument can be broadly applied to stock. Property selection can deliver higher initial returns through skill or through taking risk, but unless we can observe a strong bias to risky property types through, for example, pure development exposure or high vacancy rates, then the stock impact can be assumed to deliver pure alpha. This taxonomy is illustrated by Figure 7.18.

Finally, the unlisted fund draws capital from investors over a period of time which could be as much as four years. The timing of the drawdown is within the manager's control, meaning that an IRR approach is appropriate for return measurement. The benchmark, however, will report a time-weighted return, so that the difference can be attributed to investment timing and fund drawdowns.

We arrive at a four-stage first tier of alpha/beta IRR attribution, illustrated by Figure 7.19. This is as follows.

- Fund structure, which is largely the leverage impact, will contribute primarily to beta. Fees will limit the return, however created, and performance fees create a non-symmetric return delivery which is problematic for investors and can, for ease, be assigned to beta.
- Portfolio structure needs to be judged as either an overweight position to more risky markets, or less risky markets, which will produce a beta impact, or as a set of positions

Figure 7.18: Time-weighted alpha and beta attribution for a property fund

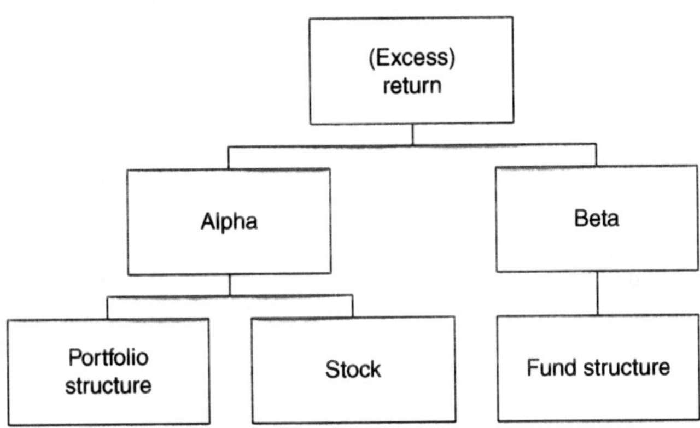

Source: Baum and Farrelly, 2008

with no greater or lesser market risk, in which case any extra return created through portfolio structure is wholly alpha. For most core and core-plus funds this is most likely to be an alpha-generating activity.

- Stock selection also needs to be judged as favouring more or less risky assets, which will produce a beta impact, or as a set of investments with no greater or lesser market risk, in which case any extra return created through stock selection is wholly alpha. For most core and core-plus funds, this is most likely to be an alpha-generating activity.

Figure 7.19: Money-weighted return attribution for a property fund

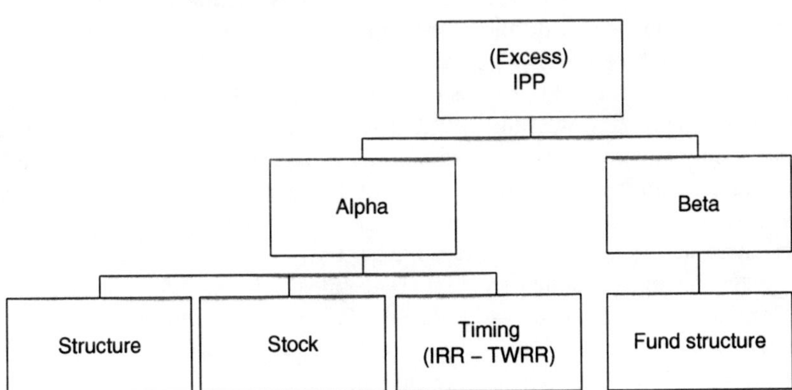

Source: Baum and Farrelly, 2008

- The return impact of timing is attributed to the movement of capital into and out of the fund. The manager's skill in investment timing, which is an alpha activity, would be reflected in this effect. This will be of greater importance in value-added and opportunistic funds, which have shorter investment horizons and look to distribute capital back to investors more quickly.

None of the above is intended to suggest that isolating and measuring alpha or beta will be easy or non-controversial. The choice and/or availability of benchmarks, in particular, are limiting factors.

Judging whether greater risk is being taken at the structure or stock level will be a matter of opinion and is therefore a pragmatic question, best illustrated by an example.

7.8.3 Alpha and beta in property funds: a case study

We use a case study to illustrate the property fund attribution framework set out above.

The case study examines a closed-ended value-added UK-focused unlisted fund, which commenced its acquisition programme in Q4 2001 and was effectively liquidated by Q4 2006. Quarterly performance data was made available for this entire period, although we only had sufficient data to conduct full attribution analysis from Q1 2002. The fund delivered a stunning TWRR of 31 per cent, having purchased 22 assets with an average book cost of £4.5 million and a total portfolio book cost of £99 million. Equity contributions totalled £26 million and leverage ranged from 65–70 per cent throughout the fund's life.

The average holding period of the assets was two-and-a-half years. The manager was looking to exploit deal-making and transaction skills. This level of turnover is not unusual for value-added and opportunistic funds, but it is relatively high. As a result capital was distributed back to investors soon after the investment period had been completed, as illustrated by the overall cashflows of the fund shown in Figure 7.20. Thus the timing effect was expected to be significant.

For property fund attribution analysis, both the fund and property level time-weighted returns were available, but only cash flow data at the fund level fund was available. The property-level time-weighted returns were calculated by IPD and the time-weighted fund returns and cash flow data for the fund were provided by the manager. (We excluded the first quarter's performance for detailed attribution analysis as time-weighted property level returns were not available.)

The fund had a mandate to invest across the UK, so we chose to perform the property fund attribution analysis against the UK IPD universe. The fund was very concentrated from a portfolio structure perspective, with holdings in only four of the 12 UK PAS segments and 55 per cent in one of these. Under Baum and Key's (2000) style definitions we would label this fund manager as specialist, where the manager is holding high weights in segments where selection skills are believed to be strong.

The results of the attribution analysis are detailed in Table 7.5. Addressing property level performance first, the fund has produced relative out-performance of 1 per cent per annum over the five-year measurement period. The manager has under-performed due to portfolio structure by almost 2 per cent per annum.

Performance attribution suggests that the manager has out-performed due to stock selection. With such a relatively high stock score and relatively concentrated segment exposures, we can say that the manager has out-performed by concentrating in preferred

Figure 7.20: Cash flow profile, case study fund

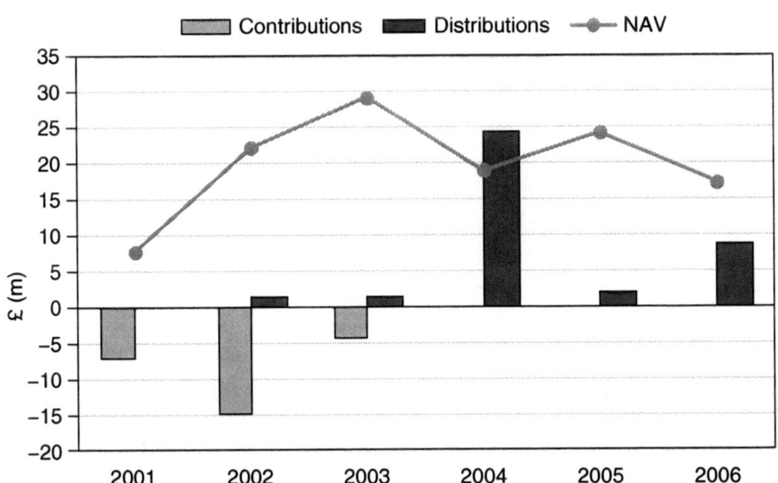

Source: Baum and Farrelly, 2008

Table 7.5: Property fund return attribution

	2002	2003	2004	2005	2006	*5 year*
Property level						
Property TWR	12.6%	10.5%	23.7%	25.5%	8.8%	*16.0%*
Benchmark TWR	9.2%	10.5%	17.4%	19.1%	18.5%	*14.9%*
Relative	3.1%	0.0%	5.4%	5.4%	–8.2%	*1.0%*
Structure score	–2.8%	–3.4%	–2.3%	0.6%	–0.2%	*–1.6%*
Selection score (two component)	5.7%	3.4%	6.9%	4.7%	–8.0%	*2.4%*
Fund level						
Gross TWR	15.7%	20.1%	73.1%	52.3%	5.1%	*31.0%*
Gross fund structure score	2.8%	8.7%	40.0%	21.4%	–3.4%	*12.9%*
Net TWR	11.8%	16.7%	57.6%	40.1%	8.7%	*25.6%*
IM fee reduction	–3.4%	–2.9%	–8.9%	–8.0%	3.4%	*–4.1%*
IM fee reduction %	25.0%	17.1%	21.1%	23.3%	-70.1%	*17.2%*
Net fund structure score	–0.7%	5.6%	27.5%	11.6%	–0.1%	*8.3%*
Net MWR	–	–	–	–	–	*29.9%*
Timing score	–	–	–	–	–	*4.3%*

Source: Baum and Farrelly, 2008

segments. However, at this stage we cannot be sure whether this out-performance has been driven by any alpha, or is simply the result of higher relative risk in the portfolio.

The fund structure effect is presented on a gross and net basis. The gross total returns encompass leverage and all expenses associated with the fund bar investment manager fees, inclusive of performance fees.

The gross structure added 12.9 per cent to the property level return. Fees to the fund manager reduced the gross structure effect by 4.1 per cent (or 17.2 per cent in relative terms), and this impacts on beta. Out-performance peaked in years three and four of the fund, when investments were being realized and value-added initiatives completed.

Finally, over the measurement period the timing of property cash flows added 4.3 per cent to the time-weighted total return, to give investors an IRR of 29.9 per cent. We were unable to conclude how much of this was attributable to alpha, although we suspected that the manager had delivered out-performance given the relatively short hold period of assets in the portfolio.

The fund's annualized total time-weighted return over the measurement period was 25.6 per cent versus its benchmark return of 14.9 per cent. However, the fund's annualized standard deviation was 23.0 per cent compared to the benchmark equivalent of 5.3 per cent. We therefore proceeded to employ the CAPM model to assess the risk-adjusted performance of the fund over the performance measurement period to complement the above attribution analysis. The result is an alpha of zero but a positive and significant beta.

Unfortunately the CAPM regression is not particularly robust statistically, with the alpha coefficient being insignificant. However, the beta coefficient is significant and the equation provides some insight into performance, suggesting that much of the delivered out-performance was a result of a high beta.

The high beta reflects the level of gearing at the fund level, and the asset level and portfolio structure risk. The beta coefficient is also much higher than previous UK property fund beta estimates which have focused on the pooled managed fund universe, and typically have low levels of gearing and are well-diversified.

Figure 7.21: Quarterly time-weighted returns – fund v. IPD index

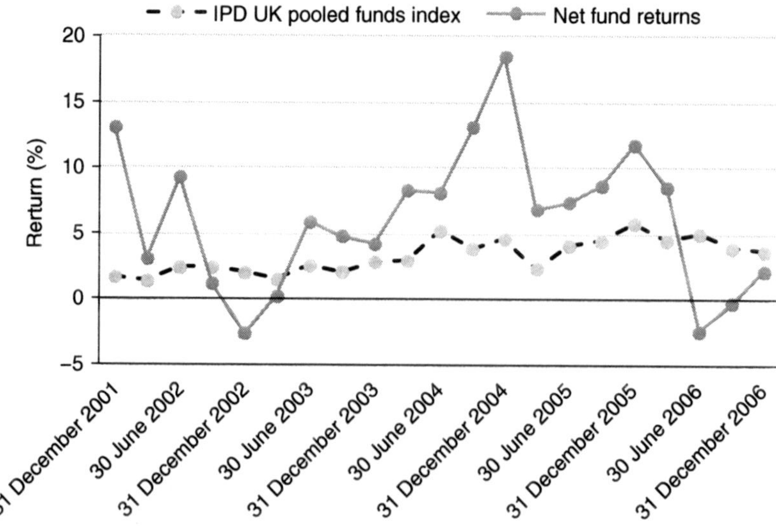

Source: Baum and Farrelly, 2008

Table 7.6: Case study alpha and beta estimates for case study net total returns

	Alpha	Beta
Coefficient	0.00	1.73
t-statistic	–0.04	1.98
R-squared	0.18	–
Observations	20	–

Source: Baum and Farrelly, 2008

The performance data suggests little evidence of alpha. A CAPM equation did point to positive alpha, although this was insignificant. The combination of structure and stock appears to add 1 per cent to return.

This is a small fund, and statistical significance may be elusive. Nonetheless, it appears that a regression-based CAPM approach confirms that (despite the very attractive headline return) there is no evidence of alpha in these performance results. Beta, on the other hand, is significant.

7.8.4 Have property funds performed?

The 2012 Urban Land Institute/PFR Report (Have Property Funds Performed?) found disappointing performance across global unlisted property funds of all types over the 2001–11 period characterized by negative alpha and excessively high betas. The damage was being done primarily by leverage. Alcock *et al.* (2013) explore the same dataset and examine the impact of timing, concluding that managers have not shown timing skills with regard to increasing or reducing leverage.

The impact of leverage – especially in the 2008–9 period – was so punitive that the return delivered by any good work being done by managers was likely to have been obliterated. This affected opportunity funds in particular, despite some evidence of highly positive alphas being achieved by a group of opportunity fund managers and (with the leverage impact corrected for) across the value-added sample.

Results for the core funds sample produced a market beta of close to one, indicating that the property risk is similar to that of the benchmark, and a lower tracking error of around 1.5 to 2 per cent. However, core funds on average under-performed the market by –0.72 per cent p.a. (negative alpha), which can be partly explained by the impact of leverage.

Value-added and opportunity funds were found to have delivered higher returns during a rising market (2001–6) but significantly under-performed core funds during the period of poor market returns (2007–11). Over the whole analysis period (2001–11), value-added funds delivered the highest returns. On a risk-adjusted basis, opportunity funds ranked last in all three time periods, with core and value-added funds delivering similar risk-adjusted returns.

The analysis showed that (as expected) value-added funds took on higher property risk than core funds with a market beta of 1.30, while opportunity funds had the highest property risk exposure with a market beta of 2.05. A single beta model which combines the impact of property risk and leverage identified significant under-performance in all three fund styles. However, when leverage is included as a separate variable in a two factor model, the level of under/over-performance becomes statistically insignificant in the core and opportunity fund sample, suggesting that on average fund managers neither added nor destroyed value and that it is the use of debt that has driven the significant levels of under-performance. In the value-added sample there is evidence that on average fund managers have added value, but again leverage has had a negative impact on returns.

7.9 Unlisted fund performance: conclusions

The growth seen in the unlisted market has helped facilitate growing cross-border property investment in Europe and across the world. Unlisted funds are now the preferred conduit for investors who are looking to invest in direct property outside their own domestic markets. There is therefore a requirement for greater resources and methods to analyse these vehicles and critically examine whether managers can demonstrate reasons for their historical track record and provide evidence of out-performance to justify performance fees.

We used a case study of a single value-added unlisted fund to compare traditional attribution results with an examination of CAPM-style alpha and beta return attribution. Fund structure, which is largely the leverage impact, contributes primarily to beta. In the case study, we found this effect to be very large.

Portfolio structure needs to be judged either as an overweight position to more risky markets, or less risky markets, which will produce a beta impact, or as a set of positions with no greater or lesser market risk, in which case any extra return created through portfolio structure is wholly alpha. For most core and core-plus funds this is most likely to be an alpha-generating activity.

Stock selection also needs to be judged as favouring more or less risky assets, which will produce a beta impact, or as a set of investments with no greater or lesser market risk, in which case any extra return created through stock selection is wholly alpha. For most core and core-plus funds this is most likely to be an alpha-generating activity.

The return impact of the timing of drawdowns can potentially be attributed to the manager's skill in timing. This is an alpha activity, although this is difficult to measure in practice.

Finally, it has been possible to analyse the performance of a large sample of unlisted funds, which suggests that the impact of leverage has been enough to obliterate any evidence of manager skill during the GFC period. The lessons for the market are that leverage needs to be carefully controlled, and that evidence of manager skill needs to be examined rather than taken for granted. Unlisted funds are essential in a world of cross-border investing, and increasing analysis and professionalism in this area of endeavour will benefit investors and managers alike.

8 Property derivatives

8.1 The search for the perfect vehicle

The fundamental problem confronting property investors and property investment managers in the UK and many other European countries is this: to achieve a diversified, liquid property portfolio which delivers pure property-style returns, replicating the return on a property index without specific risk and thereby offering diversification against stocks and bonds. Could this be achieved by investing in a single real estate index derivative vehicle?

A derivative is a financial instrument whose value is 'derived' from the value of another asset or index; thus real estate derivatives would derive their value from real estate indices representing the underlying real estate markets. In its simplest form, a derivative represents a contract between two parties where one party wishes to increase his exposure to a certain asset and the other party wants to reduce his exposure to the same asset. Real estate derivatives could allow investors to increase and decrease real estate exposure without buying or selling properties.

Derivative transactions take place with minimal legal fees and transaction costs, so derivatives could offer less expensive access to real estate exposure than investing directly or in some other indirect vehicles. Derivatives offer well-diversified market exposure, allowing smaller-scale investors to achieve their desired exposure. This potentially overcomes many of the negatives of investing in direct real estate, for example specific risk, illiquidity and high transaction costs, and deals directly with the traditional inability of investors to hedge market risk.

In the last decade many innovative property vehicles have been offered as solutions to this challenge, as industry groups in the UK and elsewhere lobbied regulators to produce changes in tax and listing rules which would enable property derivatives to be efficiently traded. We have seen that listed real estate equity securities are imperfect due to their return characteristics. We have also suggested that unlisted vehicles have their own particular challenges. Derivatives, or synthetics, on the other hand, could potentially overcome many of those problems.

Derivatives have been widely used for some time in the securities markets, but their use in the property market remained limited until 2004. Since then the UK property derivative market experienced significant growth with annual notional volumes increasing from £850 million in 2005 to £7.2 billion in 2007 and £7.1 billion in 2008. Despite a severe slowdown in activity during the GFC, the UK market remains the largest and most liquid property derivative market with over £7 billion or trades being executed between 2009 to 2013 and total cumulative trades of £19.3 billion since the beginning of 2005 (IPD, 2014). We have also seen ground-breaking real estate derivative development in the US, Australia, Hong Kong and elsewhere.

Could this market provide the perfect property vehicle?

8.2 A short history of the UK real estate derivatives market

8.2.1 Introduction

Commercial real estate was, until recently, the only major asset class without a well-developed derivatives market. Early attempts to establish such a market were unable to achieve critical mass or trading volume.

This brief history, taken from Baum *et al.* (2006), highlights the main developments that have led to the current market for total return swaps, structured notes and traded futures. As the leading example, the UK property industry has long sought to develop a derivatives product that would facilitate strategic and tactical portfolio management and enable investors to alter their exposure to real estate without incurring high transaction costs or being exposed to public market price volatility. However, attempts were initially hamstrung by complications concerning regulatory requirements and tax treatment and by the nature of the underlying indices.

8.2.2 FOX, PICs and REIM

The first formal attempt to establish a commercial property derivatives market was led by the London Futures and Options Exchange (FOX). In May 1991 FOX launched a number of simple index derivatives based on the IPD Annual Index. This was a time of severe market illiquidity, and the market failed to develop sufficient depth or volume of trading activity. It was suspended in October 1991 amid allegations of trading irregularities and phantom cross-trading by market makers. The failure of FOX was damaging for the development of a market for property derivatives, blighting attitudes of investors and regulators alike.

In 1994 BZW launched Property Index Certificates (PICs). PICs (a form of structured note – see Section 8.6) are structured as Eurobonds with coupon payments linked to IPD index income returns each year, and a capital redemption value linked to the IPD All Property capital gain over the life of the certificate. If acquired at par, this instrument effectively replicates IPD returns (less any dealing fees and spreads) for the bond holder, although any exit before maturity may result in a price out of line with the index and a consequent tracking error. They provide a low cost means of investing in commercial real estate but are somewhat inflexible as a hedging tool.

PICs and Property Index Forwards (a simple contract for difference product linked to the IPD All Property Index) were issued in 1994, 1995, 1996 and 1999, and again in 2005 and 2009, these last issues being made by Protego Real Estate Investors (now Cornerstone

Real Estate Advisers) and Barclays Capital (who support a secondary market). The issues are listed on the London Stock Exchange. Around £800 million of PICs were issued in the 1990s, and the new issues totalled £464 million. Typical maturities are short: one to four years is typical, and the 2009 issues matured in 2012 and 2013, delivering very strong returns.

Other investors sought to create markets for total return swaps (for example the proposed real estate investment market, or REIM) but development was hampered by regulatory constraints (particularly limitations on life funds holding property derivatives) and by taxation and accounting uncertainties. The UK property industry lobbied for clarifications with considerable success.

In 2002 the FSA confirmed that life insurance companies could use property derivatives for efficient portfolio management. The taxation issue was largely resolved in December 2003, when an Inland Revenue consultation paper confirmed that property derivatives would fall into the 'standard' derivatives regime, with most net cashflows subject to income tax rather than capital gains tax. This was confirmed in the 2004 Finance Act.

Finally, the Financial Services Authority, now the Financial Conduct Authority, allowed authorized retail and non-retail funds to hold property derivatives, subject to various prudential limitations. The constraints that existed in the regulatory environment had largely been removed by late 2004, setting the scene for a successful market launch.

8.2.3 The UK swap and structured note market, 2005–8

By 2005 most of the regulatory restrictions on the development of a property derivatives market had been lifted, and commercial real estate index total return swaps and, later, structured notes were traded from the beginning of that year, marking 2005–8 as the first phase of the new market. During this period, a degree of standardization of commercial terms occurred, and the standard form of total return swap commonly traded in the inter-bank market property became the property derivative structure of choice.

During this period financial intermediaries (derivatives brokers, in particular) and leading banks (acting as market makers and prepared to take positions, warehouse deals and carry inventory costs) were both critical in the development of a more liquid market. Partnerships between real estate service providers and derivatives brokers became common and provided more impetus for the new market.

Banks such as Goldman Sachs began to offer structured notes backed by their own credit, somewhat similar to Barclays PICs.

8.2.4 After the global financial crisis

Following the GFC, the most popular type of UK property derivative contract based on commercial property indices became the IPD index future traded on the Eurex Exchange.

The changing regulatory environment created a number of new protocols and procedures for investors and banks involved with financial markets. As a result, trading in property derivatives declined as banks that had previously traded the market using total return swaps retreated from the market. New regulatory regimes (such as Basel III) required a high on-balance sheet capital requirement for open positions, and the Volcker Rule prevented banks using customer deposits for proprietary trading. These changes forced banks out of the market.

Further to this, derivative transactions now need to go through a central counterparty clearing house, which keeps a record of all transactions in order to remove counterparty risk and reduce systemic risk in markets.

As a result of these changes in regulation, and in response to growing demand from property end-users, in 2009 Eurex (part of Deutsche Bourse) developed a traded future contract based on the IPD Index All Property, followed by IPD index sector contracts on All Retail, All Office and All Industrial in 2011. This was followed by the addition of IPD index segment contracts in 2013 on City Offices, West End Offices, Shopping Centres, Retail Warehouses and South-East Industrial.

8.3 Property derivative products: a review

The three types of derivative structure that have been actively utilized in the global real estate market are:

a total return swaps;
b real estate index notes, or structured notes; and
c traded index futures.

The main difference between these instruments is that swaps and IPD index futures do not require any principal to be exchanged – in other words, there is no up-front price paid, although collateral may be lodged for security – while structured notes are more recognizable forms of investment, with cash invested in return for a flow of income and a capital repayment.

8.3.1 Total return swaps

The structure of a standard total return swap is as follows. At the beginning of the contract, the purchaser of property exposure agrees to pay a fixed price each year for the duration of the contract, based on a notional contract size. In return the buyer receives the annual total return of the relevant index on which the contract is based from the counterparty.

Only the net cash flows which depend on the relative performance of the property index versus the fixed price and on the notional size of the contract, are exchanged.

Figure 8.1 shows how a standard total return swap works between principals on a matched bargain basis.

Figure 8.1: A total return swap – matched bargain

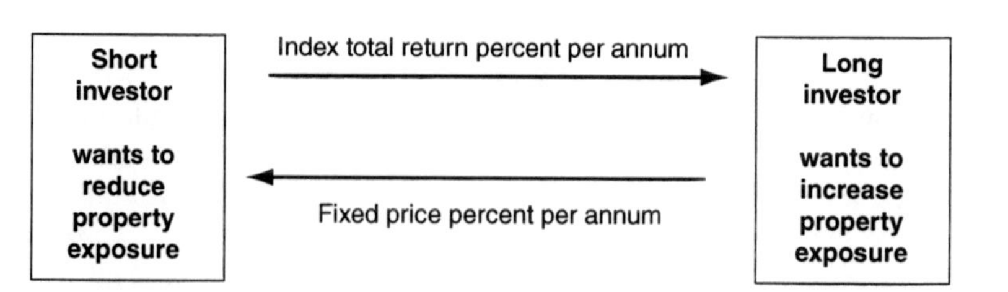

As an example, let us assume a notional contract for £100 million and a duration of one year. The agreed fixed price is 5 per cent. The long investor will be liable to pay £5 million to the short investor. The short investor will pay the notional multiplied by the IPD total return. If this turns out to be 8 per cent, the short investor is liable to pay £8 million to the long investor. However, the only payment made is the £3 million difference, paid in this case by short to long.

These swaps are traded over the counter (OTC) rather than on any formal exchange. Investors entering into a swap need to use an International Swaps and Derivatives Agreement (ISDA) to regulate the terms of the trade. Because the total 'notional' is not usually handed over at the start of the contract, total return swaps have less counterparty risk than a structured note.

Investors are required to post a margin, determined by the investors' credit, generally 5–20 per cent of the notional, to provide 'insurance' for their position. This margin is in effect similar to the equity component invested in the acquisition of a direct property; the remaining 80–95 per cent exposure is synthetically leveraged. Investors can alternatively provide a 100 per cent margin to facilitate an unleveraged investment.

The agreed fixed price might appear to provide an estimate of the expected annual return of the index over the life of the contract. For example, a price of 10 per cent per annum indicates that the expected return on the index is an average of 10 per cent per annum over the life of the contract. The investor buying exposure will pay 10 per cent per annum in exchange for the IPD total return, and this provides investors purchasing exposure with a net expected return of IPD –10 per cent.

If market prices are negative, a price of (say) –10 per cent per annum indicates that the expected return on the index is an average of –10 per cent per annum over the life of the contract. This provides investors purchasing exposure with an expected return of IPD +10 per cent.

It appears that the investor is taking a view on the expected index return compared to the price paid. If investors believe the index return will be higher than as is indicated by the price, they take a buying position. If investors believe the index return will be lower than as is indicated by the price, they take a selling position. However, this is an over-simple view of pricing, which is discussed in more detail in Section 8.6.

8.3.2 Structured real estate index notes

Real estate structured notes are bonds that pay a coupon linked to the performance of a real estate index. These structures involve the payment of a capital sum to the note issuer (investment bank) at the start of the contract and replicate investing in a spectrum of direct real estate. Unlike swaps, structured notes are funded products, meaning that cash is exchanged at the beginning of the trade.

(In a total return swap no principal is exchanged, but the same effect can be engineered by placing cash on deposit to earn the cash interest rate which is paid out in return for the IPD return.)

The structure of the notes can be flexible and determined by the preference of individual investors. There is no need for ISDA documentation and they are relatively simple and straightforward to execute. However, because cash is handed over at the beginning of the contract, structured notes have greater counterparty risk (issuer credit risk) than a total return swap.

Figure 8.2 shows how a standard structured note works. The investor receives the IPD total return plus/minus a premium throughout the life of the contract and the capital sum is

Figure 8.2: A real estate structured note

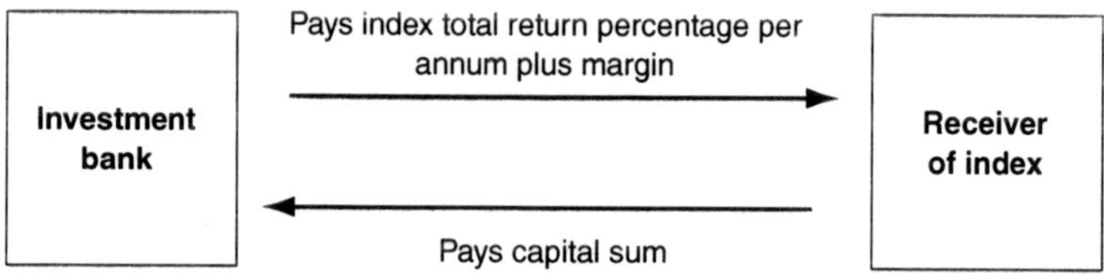

returned to the investor at contract termination. Cash flows can be structured in any custom manner but investors traditionally receive the IPD income payment on a quarterly basis with the capital growth plus the margin premium at the year end.

Pricing is determined by the total return swaps market. When expected returns on the property index are low, these notes can guarantee out-performance of the index by offering a cash-based return, and can be highly attractive to a relative return investor. This is because the investment bank can accept IPD returns from a counterparty by giving away LIBOR, and then hedge (remove) its risk by giving away IPD in return for LIBOR – plus a profit or margin, of course. Figure 8.4 (below) illustrates.

As an example, the implied expected returns on the IPD index as at December 2007 appeared to be as shown in Table 8.1. Given fixed interest rates of around 4 per cent, a bank would be able to take IPD total return risk for calendar year 2009 by giving away LIBOR minus 19 per cent – in other words, being paid 15 per cent to take it on, gaining 19 per cent plus IPD and giving away LIBOR. It can then give away (say, to a relative return investor) IPD returns plus up to 19 per cent – say 17 per cent – in return for taking LIBOR. Then the bank makes 2 per cent, and the relative return investor out-performs the index by 17 per cent. This is a wonderful – unrepeatable? – opportunity for a fund manager charged with delivering relative returns!

Table 8.1 also illustrates the potential for derivatives to provide signals about expected future market returns. Clearly, expectations in December 2007 were very pessimistic.

Table 8.1: Pricing analysis, structured note

Maturity December 2007 to	Note pays IPD +	Expected return	Income return	Capital return
1 December 2008	24.54%	–20.25%	5.50%	–25.75%
1 December 2009	22.96%	–18.95%	7.00%	–25.95%
1 December 2010	17.83%	–4.10%	9.00%	–13.10%
1 December 2011	11.83%	11.55%	10.00%	1.55%
1 December 2012	8.77%	11.75%	10.40%	1.35%

Source: CBRE/GFI, 11 December 2008

8.3.3 IPD index futures

In the beginning there was barley, and then along came farmers and (later) breweries. Breweries want certainty regarding the price of the barley they will have to buy to brew beer, and farmers want certainty regarding the price of the barley they will sell. A deal is there to be done, and it takes the form of a forward contract, whereby the price of the barley is agreed in advance and a contract signed.

Forward contracts lead to traded futures. What happens to a forward contact if the farmer wants to retire before delivering the barley? Can he sell his obligation? If the price of barley has fallen to well below the agreed forward price, then the contract would appear to have value. The mechanism used to capture the gain is likely to be a traded future.

A traded futures contract is a standardized contract, traded on a futures exchange, to buy or sell a standardized quantity of a specified commodity of standardized quality at a certain date in the future, at a price (the futures price) determined by supply and demand among competing buy and sell orders on the exchange at the time of the purchase or sale of the contract. The futures contract has the great advantage over a forward contract of avoiding the need for an equal and opposite, simultaneous coincidence of desires, providing both divisibility and liquidity. It also establishes the basis for the huge traded options market.

A futures contract gives the holder the obligation to make or take delivery under the terms of the contract, whereas an option grants the buyer the right, but not the obligation, to establish a position previously held by the seller of the option. In other words, the owner of an options contract may exercise the contract, but both parties of a futures contract must fulfil the contract on the settlement date.

The seller delivers the underlying asset to the buyer, or, if it is a cash-settled futures contract, then cash is transferred from the futures trader who sustained a loss to the one who made a profit. To exit the commitment prior to the settlement date, the holder of a futures position has to offset his/her position by either selling a long position or buying back (covering) a short position, effectively closing out the futures position and its contract obligations.

Futures contracts are exchange-traded derivatives. The exchange's clearinghouse acts as counterparty on all contracts, sets margin requirements and crucially also provides a mechanism for settlement.

Real estate, formerly recognized as the world's largest asset class without an internationally developed derivatives market, was in 2008 the world's largest asset class without an internationally traded futures market. However, in December 2008 Frankfurt-based Eurex, one of the world's largest derivatives exchanges and the leading clearinghouse in Europe, announced an exclusive ten-year contract with IPD to use its proprietary data on commercial property values (initially in the UK but then throughout Europe and globally) and to launch the first exchange-traded property futures and options in February 2009.

These exchange-traded products provide many new possibilities for investing/hedging/underwriting in the property market by financial institutions, pension funds and insurance companies, property and other corporates, hedge funds and many other interested parties.

The superiority of exchange-listed derivative contracts over OTC contracts such as IPD total return swaps, which rely entirely on banks having credit lines with each other, is clear. Exchange-traded contracts ensure that all parties have the required collateral lodged with the exchange on a real time basis to ensure that losing positions can be covered. The exchange is also AAA-rated and there is therefore minimal counterparty risk.

The potential for growth in this market is significant as IPD index futures contracts traded on the Eurex Exchange allow risk to be managed, with low margins (deposits) and reduced barriers to entry for market participants.

The Eurex Exchange meets all current regulatory requirements and lists nine IPD index futures contracts split into five defined calendar years starting from the current 'front' contract year. Each contract is standardized and based on published contract specifications. The contracts are daily priced, require standard 6.8 per cent margins and are available in equally standard £50,000 lots so that, for example, 200 lots equates to £10 million notional value.

The structure of an IPD index total return future is as follows. The buyer and seller agree a mutually acceptable 'trade price' on the 'trade date'. This is a fixed percentage for a single calendar year (such as 2014 or 2015). When the contract expires, the final cash settlement is the difference between the agreed trade price and the final settlement price multiplied by the notional value. The final settlement price is the IPD index total return outcome for that specific index in that year, so that:

$$\text{Cash settlement} = [\text{final settlement price} - \text{trade price}] * \text{notional value}$$

So, if the notional is £5 million (100 standard contracts) and the calendar year is 2014, and the market return turns out to be (say) 15 per cent, an agreed trade price of 5 per cent would provide a profit to the long investor. The payment would be as follows:

$$\text{Cash settlement} = [\text{final settlement price (15\%)} - \text{trade price (5\%)}\,] * \text{notional value (£5m)} = £500{,}000$$

Figure 8.3 shows how an IPD index futures contract trade works between two counterparties.

Figure 8.3: IPD index future mechanics

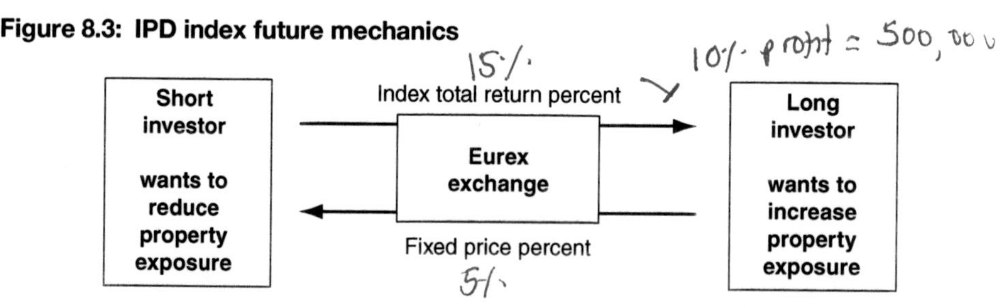

Investors are required to post an initial margin to the Eurex Exchange via their clearing bank. This margin, determined by the Eurex Exchange, is currently 6.8 per cent of the notional value of the contracts traded, or £340,000 in the above example. When this is less than the expected or potential payout, this can create a form of leverage. This margin may need to be topped up with a variation margin if the position goes against one counterparty in a longer-dated contract. To avoid regular variation margin calls, investors can place more margin with their clearing bank. Investors can alternatively provide a 100 per cent margin to create an unleveraged investment.

8.3.4 The mechanics of property swaps and futures

Prior to entering into a contract, investors need to have a clear understanding of the risks and benefits of utilizing derivatives, and the often unique mechanics of this particular derivatives market. A key challenge is the fact that property is an asset class which is alien to derivatives experts and derivatives are difficult for traditional property professionals to understand.

Investors need to be comfortable with property index construction methodology and have a view of expected index returns over the life of the contract. They will need approval to use property derivatives from clients or trustees, and mandates will be required which state allowable contract durations and the maximum allowable derivative exposure.

The UK swap is an over-the-counter contract for difference where parties swap an annual Investment Property Databank (IPD) property index total return for an agreed interest rate. These swap contracts are normally based on a number of calendar years, and trading in the 2014 contract will take place until publication of the IPD return for 2014 in early 2015. Once this is published, attention will focus on the 2015 contract, and as time goes on the publication of the IPD monthly index will change expectations of the calendar year result.

While swap contracts can cover a number of years, IPD index futures contracts are based only on one specific calendar year. For example, if in September 2014 an investor wants to go long until December 2016 he/she would need to trade each individual year 2014, 2015 and 2016, whereas using a swap would necessitate a single (December 2016) swap contract.

Figure 8.4 shows how a bank or exchange can cover its own positions by buying and selling contracts, so that it can focus on the fees and margins (slight differences in prices) it will earn by providing such liquidity. This is clearly a significant advance on a forward contract for barley.

Figure 8.4: A total return trade – bank or exchange as intermediary

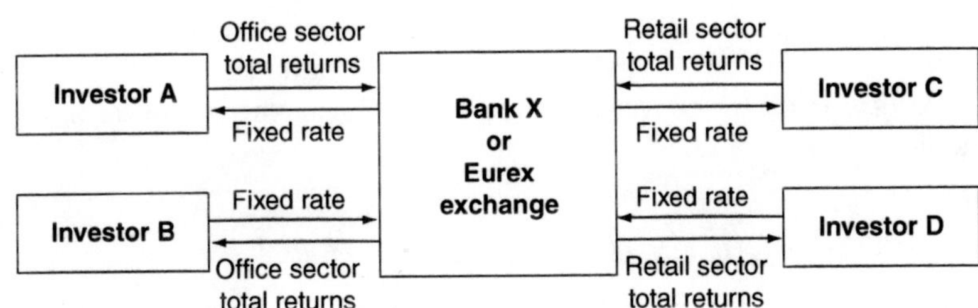

8.4 International developments

Developments in the UK form part of a wider global move towards the creation of property derivatives. While the UK is in most respects ahead of the global market, it now joins the US in having a property futures market.

8.4.1 The US

In the US market, the development of derivative products in the real estate market is also quite recent, although the first real estate-linked swap was launched in 1991. CMBS swaps have existed for some time, based on the Lehman or Bank of America CMBS indices. In 2006, the S&P CME housing futures and options contracts were launched in Chicago, based on the Shiller-Weiss indices.

A total return swap based on the NPI was announced and offered by Credit Suisse First Boston (CSFB) in the US in 2005, and in 2006 Real Capital Analytics and MIT announced a set of indices tracking US commercial property prices which were designed to be the basis for derivative trading.

The US real estate derivatives market has been much slower to develop than the UK market, total notional traded values reaching $0.6 billion at the end of the first quarter of 2008. Once the impact of the GFC fades, this is likely to grow, as the IRS recently ruled that no cross-border tax will be imposed on international investors acquiring US real estate exposure via derivatives, putting the derivative market at an advantage over other forms of cross-border real estate investment into the US, which is notoriously tax inefficient for foreign investors.

The US has offered three commercial real estate indices for derivative trading and two residential real estate indices. Like IPD, the NCREIF NPI is appraisal based, but (uniquely in commercial property as at early 2009) there are also transaction-based indices. The traded indices in the US are shown in Table 8.2.

Table 8.2: US real estate indices for derivative trading

NCREIF NPI	Appraisal based
Moody's/REAL commercial property index (CPI)	Transaction based
S&P GRA commercial property index	Transaction based
Radar Logic's RPX	Transaction based
S&P/Case-Shiller Home Price Indices	Transaction based

The case for a derivative product based on a transactions-based index is strong, to be examined later, but since the GFC there has been no active trading of commercial property derivatives in the US market. If and when market trading re-starts, the NPI is likely to remain the leading index for derivative trading in the US commercial sector in the short to medium term.

8.4.3 A global property derivatives market?

Outside the UK and US, there is an active Listed Property Trust futures contract traded on the Australian Stock Exchange and there are exchange traded products based on the European EPRA indices. Historically, residential property derivatives have been traded in Hong Kong and Switzerland, and commercial real estate total return swaps based on IPD indices have been traded in Australia, Canada, France, Spain, Germany and Japan.

8.5 Using derivatives in portfolio management

Swaps and futures allow for quick re-allocation between asset classes within mixed asset portfolios. For example, let us assume that an investor has a mixed asset portfolio composed of equity, fixed income and real estate and wishes to increase his exposure to real estate quickly. This can be accomplished by selling liquid equities and bonds and buying a 'long' position on the IPD index through a swap or futures contract.

Derivatives can provide immediate access to real estate exposure, without the lead time required to invest in direct real estate. Provided an acceptable index is available, this will allow investors to obtain instant exposure to market returns without the required expertise of locating and underwriting suitable direct investment opportunities. Investors can acquire synthetic exposure and then take their time in locating specific direct investments. The immediate synthetic access creates opportunities to bridge the gap between the decision to invest and the implementation of the investment through traditional direct real estate.

As we saw in Chapter 5, there are two commonly recognized components of risk and return. These are sector structure and stock selection. Sector structure bets can produce out-performance of an index through tactical asset allocation in return for an increase in tracking error relative to a benchmark; while successful stock selection activity produces a reward for successfully taking on specific risk. This is closely related to alpha. Swaps and futures allow investors sensing a real estate downturn to sell market exposure for a pre-determined time using a derivative, while retaining the ownership of preferred assets. This position effectively hedges market exposure and allows investors to retain any excess stock performance generated by the management of the physical assets ('alpha').

In a similar manner derivatives can be employed to more efficiently manage cyclical risk in the property market. Selling 'sector' exposure allows investors to hedge their sub-sector market risk for short to medium timeframes without selling physical assets.

In Chapter 5, Table 5.8, we described an unsuccessful fund that was overweight in Scottish retail largely as a result of holding one very large shopping centre. The managers were removed. The obvious action taken by the succeeding manager was to sell the shopping centre to reduce tracking error despite a very strong forecast for the sector and the asset. He did so, and missed out on rapid and considerable capital growth from an asset with which the fund was highly familiar. A derivative instrument would provide the opportunity for the new manager to retain the alpha of the shopping centre (its out-performance relative to Scottish retails) while reducing tracking error by retaining the shopping centre but swapping out of Scottish retail index performance. This is one of several potential uses of an active property derivatives market, four of which we now discuss.

8.5.1 Single (specific) property swaps

Assume Property Company B, a City office specialist, wishes to access shopping centre performance and exit City offices. It might swap returns on its investment in Widegate, an office complex, for returns on Poolside, a shopping centre.

This (known as a specific property swap) would achieve a property deal with low fees; no actual property exchange would take place. The specific risk of Widegate would be transferred for the specific risk of Poolside. This may, however, create a potential conflict of interest for each owner, because each owner is giving away the returns on the asset he manages.

8.5.2 Property sector (segment) switches

Alternatively, to engineer no loss of long-term control, alpha or specific risk, a sector index switch might be agreed. Company B would switch the City office index for the shopping centre index to achieve portfolio re-balance or tactical asset allocation, while retaining the short-term alpha/specific risk of Widegate, the asset it owns and manages. On the other side of the bargain, the shopping centre owner would achieve a similar result. There would be no conflict of interest. The pricing of this may include a premium or discount payable for one sector or segment versus the other.

This type of trade is also of benefit for developers who wish to hedge market risk (see Section 8.8.3).

8.5.3 Multi-asset level derivatives

Assume Fund A wishes to assemble a synthetic property portfolio, with no management responsibility (and no tracking error or specific risk). It might trade the all property total returns for other asset classes: say equities, using the FTSE index, or cash, using LIBOR (the London inter-bank borrowing rate). On the other side of the bargain would be property investors wishing to reduce their exposure.

8.5.4 International index derivatives

International property investment is difficult partly because of market unfamiliarity and the specific risk which the foreign investor is forced to take on (see Chapter 9). International index swaps would allow this to be avoided.

Assume Fund C wishes to gain continental European exposure, and to do so swaps returns on the UK index for the returns on an overseas index. It does not take on the specific risk of overseas assets, and has no need for specialist local knowledge.

It reduces its UK exposure without selling buildings or increasing its tracking error, and thereby retains alpha/specific risk in the market it knows best, while gaining an indexed exposure to a market it wishes to enter.

8.6 Pricing property derivatives

Understanding the prices paid for property derivatives requires a knowledge of the motivations of the parties involved, which will include speculators buying risk, hedgers selling risk and intermediaries. It also requires a knowledge of the inefficiencies of property markets and property indexes, as well as theories of derivative pricing.

Figure 8.5 shows LIBOR margins for IPD UK all property swap contracts over the period February 2006 to July 2007. It shows how the margin on the three-year 2006–8 contract fell from 200 basis points over LIBOR in early 2006 to negative margins in mid-2007, neatly anticipating the downturn in the IPD monthly index. It also shows how the pricing of the single year 2006 contract booms towards the year end as there was more certainty regarding the final reported value of that year's index, clearly under-stated right up to November.

Academic and practitioner analyses of property derivative prices have been somewhat at variance. Baum *et al.* (2006) introduced a key challenge in analysing derivative prices, specifically that a theoretically sound approach to property derivative pricing appeared to have produced different results from practitioners' typical analyses in the early stages of the market.

We now examine a simple approach to the pricing of a swap and an index future.

Figure 8.5: Indicative LIBOR margins, IPD UK all property swap contracts, February 2006 to July 2007 (basis points)

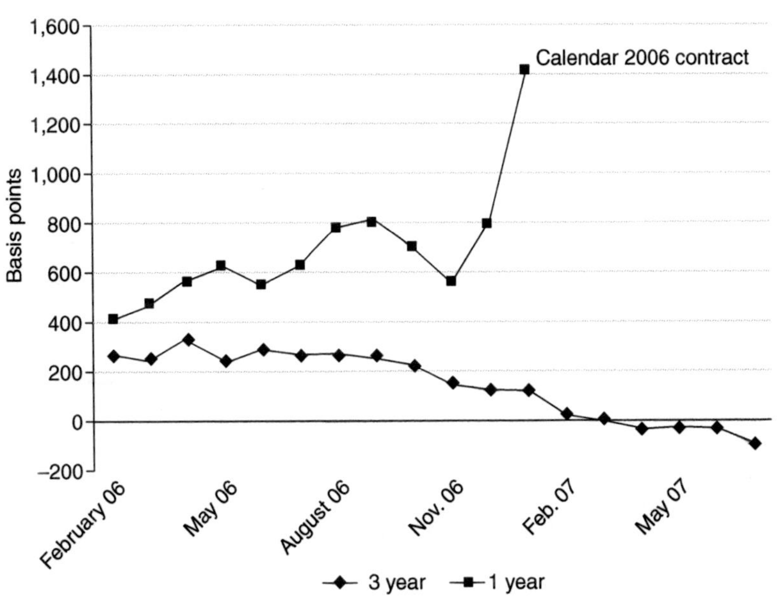

Source: brokers' estimates

8.6.1 Pricing a swap

At first sight, the swap margin would appear to reflect the anticipated difference in performance between the two legs of the swap.

Let us use a simple example. At the end of 2005, the UK Investment Property Forum published a survey of consensus forecasts for the total return on the IPD index for 2006, 2007 and 2008. The mean expected return was 7.8 per cent. At that time, a standard swap would have been with variable rate LIBOR plus a margin. At the time, the expected average LIBOR rate over three years was 4.8 per cent.

Assuming that a three-year swap is to be negotiated, it appears that in very simple terms the buyer of IPD/seller of LIBOR should pay a margin of 3 per cent per annum to receive the IPD return.

If expectations were correct, then no cash would change hands, as the two legs of the swap would equate. If the returns were the same each year, and the notional were £100 million, then the seller of IPD would have to give away 7.8 per cent of £100 million, or £7.8 million, at the end of each year, while the seller of LIBOR/buyer of IPD would have to give away (4.8%+3%)=7.8% on £100 million, or £7.8 million at the end of each year. The two amounts of £7.8 million would net to a payment of zero each year.

In simple terms, this appears to be the way it has to be: if each side has the same expectations, the expected value of the trade must be zero. Of course, expectations usually turn out to be wrong, so one side will likely do better. If IPD does better than 7.8 per cent, say 8.8 per cent, the buyer of IPD/seller of LIBOR will be paid, at the rate of £1 million at the end of each year. If IPD does worse than 7.8 per cent, say 5.8 per cent, the seller of IPD/buyer of LIBOR will be paid, at the rate of £2 million at the end of each year.

This analysis can be made more realistic and complex in a variety of ways. For example, we can take account of time-variant returns. For example, if the IPF consensus forecasts for 2006–8 are 8.6, 6.9 and 7.5 per cent respectively, and LIBOR is expected to deliver 4.5, 4.75, 5 per cent respectively, we can estimate the expected cash flows and discount them.

Table 8.3: A total return swap – cash flows, no margin

Year	IPD	LIBOR	Difference	Value	PV
1	8.60%	4.50%	4.10%	£4,100,000	£3,831,776
2	6.90%	4.75%	2.15%	£2,150,000	£1,877,893
3	7.50%	5.00%	2.50%	£2,500,000	£2,040,745
				Total	£7,750,414

In Table 8.3 we use a discount rate of 7 per cent, a required return for property based on a ten-year gilt yield or risk free rate of 4.5 per cent and a risk premium of 2.5 per cent (see Chapter 4). The cash flows are based on £100 million notional contract value.

If no margin above LIBOR were paid for this swap, the buyer of IPD has an expected gain with a present value of £7.75 million. However, simplifying, the present value of the expected cash flow should be zero. What margin over LIBOR will create a present value of zero?

This is given by the following:

£7,750,414/PV £1 p.a. for 3 years at 7%/£100m
=£7,750,414/2.6243/£100m
=£2,953,308/£100m
=2.95%

Applying this margin to the LIBOR leg, we achieve the present value shown in Table 8.4.

Table 8.4: A total return swap – cash flows, with margin

Year	IPD	LIBOR+2.95%	Difference	Value	PV
1	8.60%	7.45%	1.15%	£1,146,692	£1,071,675
2	6.90%	7.70%	–0.80%	–£803,308	–£701,640
3	7.50%	7.95%	–0.45%	–£453,308	–£370,034
				Total	£0

We can now add a consideration of risk. Which of the two parties' cash flows are most uncertain? From 1987 to 2004, the annual standard deviation of LIBOR was 3.2 per cent, but the standard deviation of the total return on the IPD annual index was 9.6 per cent, so the IPD leg appears to be three times riskier. What is a fair price for that uncertainty? Our analysis uses a risk premium of 2.5 per cent; a 1 per cent increase in this premium would create a 4 bps movement in the margin. This may or may not be a fair value for the risk premium (see below), but its impact appears limited.

This again is simplified. What is the probability of different payouts? The ranges of possible returns for IPD and LIBOR are shown in Figure 8.6.

Figure 8.6: A total return swap – probability of loss

LIBOR
IPD
4.8%
7.8%

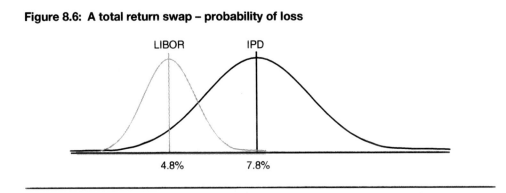

The probability of IPD delivering less than LIBOR is affected by the expected values and standard deviations of the two curves (assumed to be normal), but also by the correlation of the two series. If they are positively correlated, IPD is likely to stay ahead of LIBOR, but if they are negatively correlated, then IPD could fall behind LIBOR. Given that, empirically, the series have been slightly negatively correlated, then this increases the risk of buying (going long) the IPD leg and may add to the risk premium and margin.

There are other considerations: for example, is 2.5 per cent (derived in Chapter 4 as the risk premium for a typical real estate portfolio) a fair risk premium for a property portfolio which has no specific risk? And how can we take account of the trading costs which are avoided by the buyer of an IPD swap when the alternative is buying a portfolio of property with round trip trading costs of around 7.5 per cent?

Figure 8.7 illustrates pricing in the early stages of the UK property swap market. In 2005, in a bullish market for real estate with strong short-term return expectations, short

Figure 8.7: Total return swap margins v. tenor, IPD UK all property

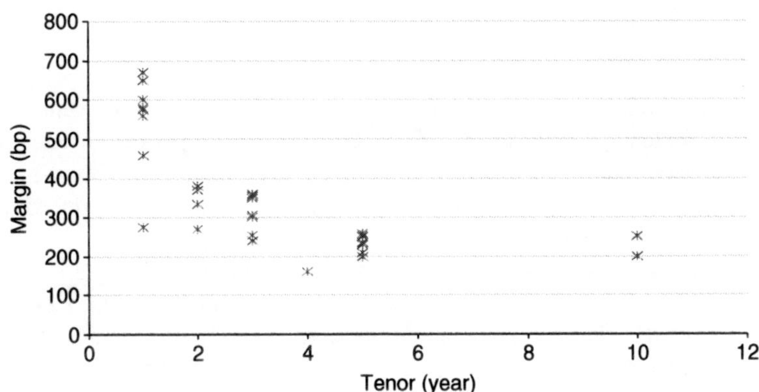

Source: Baum et al., 2006

tenor swaps were earning margins above LIBOR of as much as 7 per cent. At the longer end, by which time long-term return expectations were likely to revert to the mean required return of around 7 per cent (see Chapter 4), the margin had fallen to 2 per cent. This appears to suggest that the margin is affected by the amount by which the market expects that IPD will out-perform LIBOR in the short-term.

8.6.2 Backing out the implied market return

Assuming that the margin reflects an implied market return, how can this implied return be calculated?

In Table 8.5 we showed a margin of 2.95 per cent for a three-year swap. Expected LIBOR rates were 4.5, 4.75 and 5 per cent respectively. We used a discount rate of 7 per cent, a required return for property based on a ten-year gilt yield or risk free rate of 4.5 per cent and a risk premium of 2.5 per cent. The cash flows were based on £100 million notional contract value. Table 8.5 shows how we would estimate the present value of the long LIBOR leg.

Table 8.5: A total return swap – cash flows, with margin

Year	LIBOR	LIBOR + 2.95%	Cash (£m)	PV @ 7%
1	4.50%	7.45%	7.45	6.96262
2	4.75%	7.70%	7.70	6.72548
3	5.00%	7.95%	7.95	6.48957
			Present value	£20.18m

The LIBOR leg throws up a cash flow whose present value must equate with the present value of the expected IPD leg (effectively discounting the net cash flows at the property risk adjusted rate). This value is £20.18 million, which must now be de-capitalized at 7 per cent.

£20.18m/PV £1 p.a. for 3 years at 7%
= £20.18m/2.6243
= £7.69m

This suggests an average expected return on the IPD index of 7.69 per cent, close to the mean of the expected calendar year returns of 8.6, 6.9 and 7.5 per cent used in Table 8.2. Note that the backed-out return is dependent on the risk premium used, but the result is not very sensitive to this input. A 5 per cent risk premium, for example, produced an average return of slightly less (7.68 per cent).

Expected returns for individual years can be backed out by using single year swap data. The results can appear arresting. For example, a typical practitioner analysis of market pricing using a variant of the above logic led to a circular suggesting in January 2009 that the IPD swaps curve was pricing in a peak-to-trough decline in capital value of 59 per cent from July 2007 to December 2010, which was not far from the delivered result.

Box 8.1 Derivatives as leading indicators of the market

Table 8.6, produced in November 2008, shows one house's view of the implied IPD annual index returns per annum based on the derivative market from December 2007. This is compared to the house return forecasts of returns over the same period (and the out-turn). The differences indicate potential trading strategies. Figure 8.8 shows this information broken down to individual year forecasts.

Table 8.6: Derivative-implied cumulative return forecasts

	Implied forecast (%) p.a.	House forecast (%) p.a.	Out-turn
December 2007 to December 2008	−18.90	−17.00	−22.1
December 2007 to December 2009	−18.50	−15.60	−18.6
December 2007 to December 2010	−13.50	−10.20	−3.5
December 2007 to December 2011	−8.00	−6.00	4.3
December 2007 to December 2012	−4.70	0.30	7.8

Figure 8.8: Derivative-implied calendar return forecasts

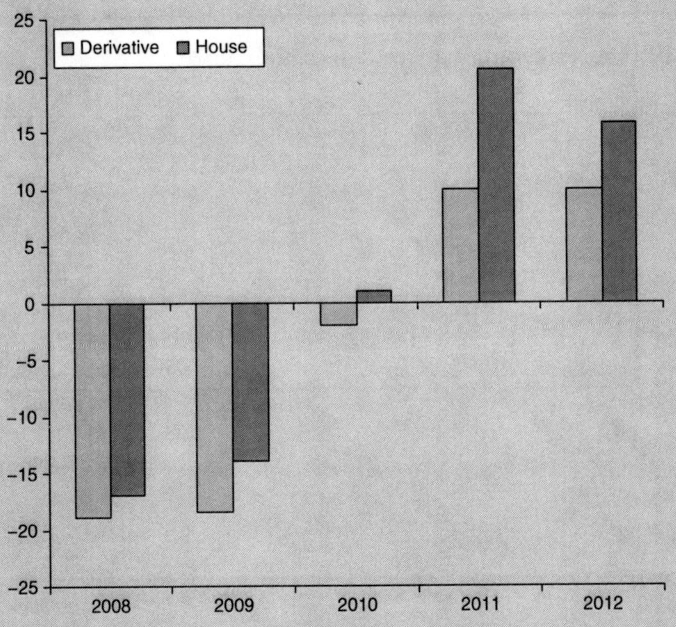

Source: UK property house, November 2008

Note

'The derivative market is pricing in a peak-to-trough fall in UK property values of over 50%, with no recovery until 2011. Thereafter the derivatives market is predicting a total return of 10% per annum, which would be primarily derived from income – since the forecast fall in values would mean that income was in excess of 9%. In other words, the derivative market is pricing in very little recovery in capital values through 2012.'

8.6.3 Pricing an IPD index future

Using IPD index futures, investors trade the calendar year contracts they wish to buy or sell. If in February 2014 an investor wanted to buy exposure until the end of 2015 he/she would buy the 2014 and 2015 contracts, putting down the required initial and variation margins for each. At this time the market prices for the 2014 and 2015 contracts were 6.75 and 5 per cent respectively (indicating expected capital returns only). At February 2014 the IPF consensus forecasts for 2014–15 were 12.1 and 9.2 per cent respectively for total (income plus capital) returns. Assuming income returns of around 4.75 per cent, the buyer was paying a premium of around 0.75 per cent to receive the IPD capital return in 2014 and was buying the IPD capital return at a 1 per cent discount for 2015. The buyer and seller would each need to lodge the required 6.8 per cent margin with the exchange.

At September 2014, the 2014 contract was trading at 18 per cent and the 2015 contract at 7.5 per cent. The year to date return on the IPD monthly index was 12.4 per cent to August 2014. Each counterparty could now decide to trade out of each contract.

In this example, the buyer (especially if he is a speculator) may appear to be more happy with the trade, but the seller might also be happy. If they are long assets, they have essentially hedged or locked in market performance of 6.75 and 5 per cent respectively for each year while retaining the specific asset risk (alpha) of their assets, and they have managed downside market risk (beta) without incurring direct property transaction costs.

Figure 8.9: UK futures contract prices, September 2014

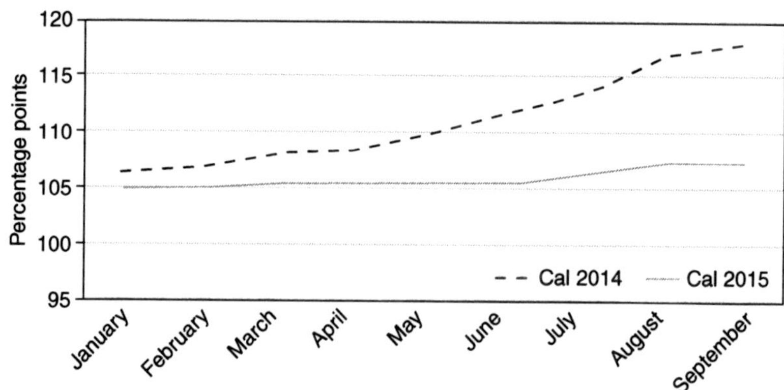

Source: Arca PRM

8.6.4 Theoretical approaches to derivative pricing

The UK experience of derivative market pricing suggests a close relationship between derivative prices and expected market returns. However, this idea is not in harmony with theories of derivative pricing.

A principle common to derivative pricing of all assets is that a riskless, self-financing portfolio can, in practice, be created by an investor. In all cases, a perfectly matched long/short position can be acquired with reasonably low transaction costs. As a result,

Box 8.2 Using derivatives to out-perform the index

It is summer 2007. The client has a relative return mandate with an objective to out-perform the IPD Annual Index by 50 bps per annum over a rolling three-year period, and has cash to invest. Property Index Notes were available, offering IPD returns plus a premium.

Research was complete by October and at this point the offering house priced the note at IPD returns+6 per cent per annum until December 2009. This offered less expensive access to real estate exposure than investing in direct property, and also offered a significant premium return over the benchmark index.

The cost of trading the note was 10–15 bps plus legal fees to review the term sheet.

The client purchased £13 million of IPD exposure through a Property Index Note from October 2007 to March 2010.

However, market sentiment had begun to turn by October 2007. This note was valued at cost (100 per cent) in October 2007, but soon lost value. The monthly mark-to-market values were as follows: November, 96.35 per cent; December, 85.26 per cent; January, 83.12 per cent; and February, 86.26 per cent.

The monthly mark-to-market values result in accounting volatility. However, the intention was to hold the position until maturity. If the client had done this, he would have received IPD+6 per cent throughout the contract. This may be a very poor return in absolute terms, but clearly achieves the relative return objective to out-perform the IPD Annual Index by 50 bps per annum over a rolling three-year period.

differences in risk between the hedge assets become irrelevant. The only reason for a spread, then, relates to the costs involved in creating the position.

The principle of the riskless portfolio forms the basis of the theoretical models of real estate derivative pricing introduced by Titman and Torous (1989), Buttimer *et al.* (1997) and Bjork and Clapham (2002). Such models produce low to zero spreads over the matching interest rate return. However, other authors have noted that extrapolating general principles from interest rate and equity index swap pricing is problematic. Park and Switzer (1996) note problems of basis risk (when the assembled portfolio does not track the market index); and Okata and Kawaguchi (2003) note problems of swap pricing in incomplete markets where the underlying asset is indivisible, has high transaction costs, limited liquidity and unobservable fundamental prices.

Geltner and Fisher (2007) examined pricing issues for swap contracts based on real estate indices. They argue that real estate indices differ from conventional financial market indices since they are based on appraisals and because investors cannot hold the underlying portfolio.

Baum *et al.* (2006) had made very similar arguments, concluding that the spread from property index total return swaps should, in principle, be close to zero but that underlying asset market efficiencies make trading at non-zero spreads rational. While the margins should not reflect return differentials between LIBOR and expected real estate returns once risk is accounted for, there are rational reasons why margins should exist. Constraints facing any investor seeking to create a self-financing arbitrage portfolio include the existence of high transaction costs in the underlying real asset market (see Figure 8.7, which illustrates the premium paid for a long swap contract, probably reflecting saved transaction costs). Other constraints include the time taken to execute transactions and the problem of large lot sizes. This makes it very hard to diversify the investor's exposure to real estate at low cost via the direct acquisition of land and buildings (and certainly not at the same notional cost of most swap and index future contracts). In turn, given high levels of specific risk in commercial real estate markets, this makes it unlikely that any portfolio will effectively track the IPD index (or equivalent), creating basis risk.

The implication of these imperfections in the underlying markets is that it may be rational at certain points in the market for a party buying an index future to pay more than the expected market return for the year. This issue is considered in more detail by Lizieri *et al.* (2009).

8.7 Property derivatives: pros and cons

In Section 8.1, we asked: could this market provide the perfect property vehicle? In this section we provide an answer.

The development of the property derivatives market now adds another method of accessing real estate exposure for investors. It provides portfolio managers with an increased number of options through which to manage real estate exposure and risk. However, over-the-counter derivatives have different advantages and disadvantages from other forms of investment in property. We outline these below.

8.7.1 Property derivatives: advantages

Low transaction costs

Property derivatives have low transaction costs compared to direct property/funds where round trip costs equate to 7.0 to 7.5 per cent.

No management costs

Investment in direct property and funds will incur portfolio management fees whereas exposure through derivatives does not.

Speed of trade

A derivative provides immediate access to property returns without the long lead time associated with investing in direct real estate.

Diversification

Exposure to the property index provides a fully diversified exposure to property returns.

Leverage

For investors using total return swaps or index futures, a margin of up to 20 per cent of the notional size of the contract is usually paid up front rather than the full value of the contract, achieving synthetic leverage without needing debt.

Ability to short the market

Property derivatives for the first time allow investors to take short positions on the direct market, thereby opening up hedging and other strategies.

Tax efficiency

The use of derivatives in international investment could offer advantages regarding withholding tax as they allow investors to enter new markets without the tax implications associated with cross-border investments through direct investment or indirect funds. Under current legislation, derivatives are not subject to withholding tax.

8.7.2 Property derivatives: disadvantages and risks

Illiquidity

Volumes increased over the period 2004–7, but the market remains highly immature and secondary market liquidity is very limited.

Leverage

We know that significant losses can result from highly levered, speculative derivative positions, as the Leeson/Barings and Kerviel/Societe Generale disasters illustrated, well before the many illustrations thrown up by the 2007–8 crisis, AIG being a high-profile example. Investors can acquire positions that attain more leverage than a bank would directly provide for direct investments, and highly leveraged speculative buying and selling positions could result in losses far exceeding margin values on any trade.

Investors taking highly leveraged, speculative short hedging positions could suffer losses if the market turns positive. When taking a short position investors may be expecting lower market returns than the implied price; thus, if the market return increases, short investors have to pay out more than was anticipated at the start of a contract and payments may exceed any collateral or margin available. In order to mitigate this risk, investors may be advised not to take a short position for which they do not manage a matching or closely correlated portfolio of real estate assets.

Counterparty risk

Cash flows from property swaps and structured notes are subject to the counterparty's credit risk. Counterparty risk is the risk that the counterparty will default on their quarterly payments and, in the case of notes, the redemption of principal at the end of the contract. The counterparty has commonly been one of the major investment banks, which was not an issue of concern prior to 2008, but the collapse of Lehman Brothers, a leading player in the UK market with a strong credit rating, changed perceptions somewhat.

IPD index futures have minimal credit risk as risk is managed by the Eurex Exchange and its clearing bank members.

Basis risk

When hedging the market risk of an owned portfolio, there is basis risk between the performance of the portfolio and the underlying index. Basis risk is especially important in a position where an investor sells exposure. The investor is selling (paying) the real estate index return and earning the return on his portfolio. It is important that the portfolio being hedged has a high or known correlation with the index used for the hedge, but this is very challenging, as suggested in Chapter 1.

In-house management risk

The inherent risk of rogue traders and mis-managing derivative positions in-house is a new challenge for property investors and fund managers. As in all positions of fiscal responsibility, appropriate policies and controls need to be in place before derivative positions are taken.

Accounting volatility

The performance of derivatives will be driven by daily pricing, which in turn will be driven by market expectation of returns. As a result, mark-to-market valuations can be volatile and will be different from the performance of the underlying index prior to maturity.

Derivative positions result in significant accounting volatility as the contracts are marked-to-market on a monthly basis. This exposes the investor to the volatility of market pricing as the new price could be very different from the price paid when entering into the contract. Investors could then make or lose money depending on the difference between the original contract price and the new market price.

Re-investment risk

At the end of a swap or futures contract, or as a note matures, the investor is left with a reversed position. There is thus a re-investment risk for an investor looking to achieve a long-term exposure.

To conclude, property derivatives can offer investors an intriguing and attractive addition to the set of tools they can use in assembling a real estate portfolio. However, we cannot conclude that they provide the perfect property vehicle.

8.8 Property derivatives: spin-offs

An active market in property derivatives might not provide the perfect property vehicle, but it will enormously improve the efficiency of the market and attract new capital into the sector. Dealing in put and call options and traded futures will become possible, and the Eurex exchange-traded property futures market launched in 2009 will help this.

Futures in particular will bring access to all segments of the market for all investors and allow quick, cheap and easy-to-achieve tactical asset allocation. This would encourage managers to specialize in property types to retain alpha without being penalized for the tracking error that inevitably accompanies specialization.

The risks of property development will become more manageable, and homeowners (or those seeking to buy) will be able to hedge their exposure (or lack of it).

8.8.1 Hedge funds

A hedge fund is an investment vehicle that can 'go short' – that is, it can sell a liability to pay out future cash based on the performance of a security or index. It is also described as an investment vehicle aiming to be market neutral, meaning that it can deliver a good return even if the market performs badly. By being market neutral it can aim to deliver an absolute return rather than aim to perform well relative to a benchmark. Before the establishment of an active derivatives market, a property hedge fund can only be a fiction; after 2005, several were created.

An example of a hedge fund strategy is as follows. US REITs trade at discounts and premiums to their net asset value, apparently reverting to a mean premium of around 5 per cent. Buying a basket of REITs at a 30 per cent discount to NAV is clearly interesting and possibly attractive: but the risk involved is that the NAV falls by enough to negate the prospective profit even if pricing moves to a NAV premium. Using a swap to short the direct property index will have the effect – albeit imperfect, due to basis risk and other technical imperfections – of neutralizing the NAV movement and capturing the removal of the NAV discount. This was one of the potential strategies used in the Iceberg Fund, described by its manager (Reech AIM) as a relative value, market neutral fund.

Since the launch of Iceberg in May 2007, broadly coinciding with the downturn in UK property market sentiment, the fund delivered +24.51 per cent (net of fees and expenses) in 2008 despite the challenging real estate investment market conditions, whilst outperforming the EPRA UK index of listed property companies by 61 per cent (EPRA UK: –36.8 per cent) and the IPD index by over 40 per cent.

More real estate hedge funds can be expected, and strategies designed to exploit anomalies in the relative pricing of REITs, unlisted funds and other forms of real estate exposure will no doubt be developed in time.

8.8.2 Derivatives funds

In a new market such as the UK property derivatives market, pricing anomalies are likely to exist, especially where trading is thin. Derivatives experts may be able to spot such anomalies and recommend trading strategies to clients, or, alternatively, to take on discretionary mandates to execute those strategies. As an example, the inProp UK Commercial Property Fund claimed to offer:

> a ground-breaking approach to commercial real estate investment. It delivers a diversified, efficient and liquid exposure to commercial real estate by employing a synthetic property investment strategy. Using derivatives means that this approach overcomes many of the problems that face traditional property investment methods.

8.8.3 Managing development risk

Property development is a high-risk activity. Planning risk is an issue, construction costs are difficult to manage and there are many other risks to be controlled. However, the risk that developers have been hitherto powerless to manage is the market.

It is often suggested that land values and development profits are highly geared, and market volatility is the key reason for this. Assume, for example, a development of 1,000 sq m; rental values of $100 p sq m; capitalisation rates on the sale of the property of

5 per cent; building costs of $800psqm; and a land price of $1 million. What is the developer's profit as a percentage of total costs?

Gross development value = cost of land + cost of building + profit

Gross development value = 1,000 * $100/.05 = $2m

Cost of building: 1,000 * $800 = $800,000

Land price: $1m

Profit = $2m − $800,000 − $1m = $200,000, or 25% of costs.

Now assume resale yields rise from 5 to 8 per cent. In the new case, what is the profit?

Gross development value = 1,000 * $100/.08 = $1.25m

Costs: 1,000 * $800 = $800,000

Land price: $1m

Profit: $1.25m − £800,000 − £1m = −$550,000

Hence, for a small change in rental values (a 20 per cent fall) and a rise in yields from 5 to 8 per cent, the impact on profit is to destroy it – and the developer, too. A fall in property values of 37.5 per cent has produced a fall in profit values of 350 per cent. This is the gearing effect – land value and developers' profits are both geared residuals.

Derivatives can help to manage this risk, as suggested in Baum *et al.* (1999a), and as illustrated by the case study shown in Box 8.3.

Box 8.3 Using derivatives to manage development risk

It is late in 2014. Melton Capital, a property development company, is developing a project with total estimated costs of £150 million. The project involves the construction of a 100,000 sq ft office building in the City of London.

On completion, the developer will sell the development at market value. Completion and sale is planned for late 2016.

The initial development appraisal envisaged an average letting value of £90 per sq ft and a resale capitalization rate of 5 per cent. On this basis, the scheme had an anticipated development value of £180 million (100,000 * £90/5%) and was set to deliver a projected profit of £30 million, a profit on cost of 20 per cent.

The average letting value at late 2014 had already reached £100 per sq ft. The market was strong, and the estimated capitalization rate for the scheme at that point had fallen to 4.75 per cent. The development value at the point was £210 million (100,000 * £100/4.75%). However, due to commodity price inflation estimated costs had risen to £175 million.

Nonetheless, the strong market meant that at that point the scheme profit (£35 million) remained as 20 per cent on cost.

At the end of 2014, despite the currently strong market, the development company's advisory board felt that a downturn was a strong probability. Table 8.7 shows the company's views of expected market returns and their associated probabilities.

Table 8.7: Case study return scenarios

Market scenario	2015	2016	Probability
Strong	20%	15%	30.0%
Base case	10%	7.5%	40.0%
Weak	0%	0%	30.0%

The trade prices of calendar (Cal) 2015 and Cal 2016 IPD City Office total return index futures at December 2014 were Cal 2015 at 15 per cent and Cal 2016 at 10 per cent. How could Melton Capital use traded futures to hedge its risk?

Assume the developer, which is less optimistic than the market appears to be, 'sells' IPD City Office exposure at this price as a hedge. Its exposure to date is £175 million, so it could go short or sell £175 million of exposure for the remainder of the development period, best achieved by selling contracts for the 2015 and 2016 calendar years.

1 Assume the market 2015 outcome is strong, a 20 per cent total return. On settlement of the Cal 2015 contract in February 2016, Melton Capital will receive 20 per cent (the futures trade price) on £175m = £35m in payment for the trade. It will pay out the IPD City Office Index total return for 2015 of 20 per cent on £175 million, or £35 million. The total gain/loss for 2015 is zero.

   The 2016 strong outcome is a 15 per cent total return on the IPD West End Office Index. On settlement of the Cal 2016 contract in February 2017, Melton Capital receives 10 per cent of £175 million or £17.5 million for the futures trade, and pays the IPD West End Office Index total return of 15 per cent on £175m = £26.25m, producing a net loss of £8.75 million.

   Melton Capital is also holding the specific risk of the development scheme. There are further cost over-runs in 2015 and 2016. By the completion date, the total cost has risen to £185 million. The completion value of the scheme in a strong market is high at £217 million, with capitalization rates down to 4.5 per cent and rents stronger at £100 (100,000*£110/4.5% = £244.4 million).

   Melton Capital's net position is a profit on the project of £59.44 million, plus a futures loss of £8.75 million. This creates a profit of £50.69 million, compared to a do-nothing (no futures) profit of £59.44 million.

2 Assume the 2015 market outcome is in line with the base case at 10 per cent. On settlement of the Cal 2015 contract in February 2016, Melton Capital will receive 20 per cent (the futures trade price) on £175m = £35m and will pay out the IPD City Office total

return for 2015 of 10 per cent on £175m=£17.5m. The total gain for 2015 is £17.5 million.

The 2016 out-turn is a 7.5 per cent total return on the IPD City Office Index. On settlement of the Cal 2016 contract in February 2017, Melton Capital receives 10 per cent (the futures trade price) on £175m=£17.5m and pays the IPD City Office Index total return of 7.5 per cent on £175m=£13.125m, producing a net profit for 2016 of £4.375 million.

The total project cost is £180 million. Capitalization rates have stayed at 5 per cent and the rent is flat at £100 per sq ft. The completion value of the scheme is around £200 million (100,000*£100/5%).

Melton Capital's net position is a gain on the project of £20 million, plus a futures gain of £21.875 million: this is a net gain of £41.875 million (compared to a do-nothing gain of £20 million).

3 Assume the market 2015 out-turn is weak at a total return of 0 per cent, implying a fall in capital values of around 5 per cent. On settlement of the Cal 2015 contract in February 2016, Melton Capital will receive 20 per cent (the futures trade price) on £175m=£35m and will pay out the IPD City Office Index total return for 2015 of 0 per cent on £175m=zero. The total profit for 2015 is £35 million.

The 2016 outcome is another zero return on the IPD City Office Index. On settlement of the Cal 2016 contract in February 2017, Melton Capital receives £17.5 million for the futures trade and pays the IPD City Office Index total return of 0 per cent on £175m=0, producing a net profit for 2016 of £17.5 million.

The total project cost is £175 million, as competition for labour and materials has eased. Capitalization rates have rebounded back to 5.5 per cent and the rent is weaker at £90 per sq ft. The completion value of the scheme is around £64 million (100,000*£90/5.5%).

The combined position is a loss on the scheme of £11.4 million plus a futures gain of £52.5 million: a net gain of £31 million (which compares to a do-nothing loss of £11 million).

These scenarios are summarized in Table 8.8. The futures trade has a very positive effect on both the average and probability-weighted out-turns, each of which are increased by around £22m. A profit is made in all three out-turns, which is not true if no futures trade is put in place. The range of returns is much tighter. Melton Capital has successfully hedged its position, albeit with some basis risk, by selling market risk at a fixed price.

Table 8.8: Case study out-turn scenarios

	Do nothing (£m)	Futures trade (£m)	Total (£m)	Probability
Strong	59.4	–8.75	23.25	30%
Base case	20	21.875	50.7	40%
Weak	11	52.5	41.9	30%
Range	70.1	–	9.6	–
Mean	22.7	–	44.6	–
Weighted mean	22.4	–	44.3	–

8.8.4 Strips and exotic swaps

Cash flows from property in the form of rentals lend themselves readily to swap analysis using derivative pricing techniques that are now being applied to real estate internationally. However, the UK lease structure offers a particular opportunity to explore this means of analysis because of the complex option-like characteristics of the typical institutional lease.

Property cash flows can be readily 'partitioned' using derivatives pricing techniques with risk-neutral valuation techniques and Monte Carlo simulation (see Baum and Crosby, 2008). The resultant cash flow 'slices' can be swapped or sold both to enable portfolio diversification between funds and to provide funding for developers and corporate owners of property. In effect, a surrogate partial property sale can be synthetically structured for low cost with the reversion belonging to the seller of the swap. For property developers or corporations seeking funding, parties can enter into future or forward contracts to sell the cash flows.

In Baum *et al.* (1999a) we examine pricing and market infrastructure issues surrounding the establishment of markets in both rental swaps and strips or sales. The paper shows how these concepts might be applied to standard UK leases. We show how such structures might be applied to swapping property rentals using an example of a 25-year lease with (a) upward only rent reviews and (b) open market rent reviews. Finally, we offer some indicative pricing parameters based on the above model when swapping a five-year upward only lease on one property for a five-year freely floating lease on another property with the same drift (growth) and the same volatility.

8.9 Conclusions

Looking into the future, the implications of an active property derivatives market are substantial. The availability of property derivatives may increase the aggregate demand for commercial property as efficient risk management becomes possible. A successful traded futures market means that counterparty risk will disappear and more efficient price discovery will reduce barriers to entry. As the global commercial real estate derivatives market continues to grow, property derivatives will offer increasing benefits to real estate investors, including risk management, more efficient portfolio rebalancing and the potential for immediate exposure to new markets.

Since 2009 the property derivatives market has gone through an evolution from being a bank-driven swaps market to being a property end-user exchange-traded futures market with added granularity. Volumes have not increased annually, but the range of end-users has grown to include many UK pension funds and insurance companies. There has been a dramatic decrease in the trading of swaps following regulatory changes in the financial markets and this has led to increased trading of IPD index futures on the Eurex Exchange. We are once again at the start of a new era in the development of this nascent market.

Investors can now manage market risk exposure to different areas of the market in real time using an efficient mechanism. As a result they can focus on generating alpha from the specific risk of their assets whilst managing the market risk beta.

Once established, derivatives markets tend to display impressive growth in traded volumes. Good examples of this include credit derivatives and freight derivatives, both of which have shown exponential growth over prolonged periods. In these cases the market started with a steady but not too spectacular growth rate during which time participants were being introduced to the product and standardization of documentation and commercial terms was occurring.

Within a few years, property derivatives are likely to become part of the core activities of players in the underlying market. Once this occurs volumes can rapidly grow to exceed the underlying market size, and efficient cross-border investment will become increasingly possible as global real estate indexes improve.

International investment is the subject of the final part of this book.

Part 4

International real estate investment

9 International real estate investment: issues

9.1 Introduction

An increased investor appetite for global investment in equities and bonds, and later property, generated a structural market shift in the 1990s. The main impact on the real estate market was a gradual change in strategy away from domestic investing towards international portfolios. Following behind (and closely associated) was a new focus on indirect property investment (investing through securities and funds) which has now become commonplace.

The globalization of business activity was, prior to 2007–8, a continuing process, driven both by the conversion of ownership of successful companies from domestic to multi-national concerns and by the increasing opportunities offered to corporations and institutional investors and banks to own overseas assets through globally traded stock markets. The result has been a surge in foreign direct investment, with Asia-Pacific a particular beneficiary. In this region real estate investment (the construction of manufacturing facilities, for example) accounted for around 40 per cent of all foreign direct investment in the two decades to 2014. Both occupier demand and the ownership of corporate real estate facilities have become increasingly driven by the needs of the multi-national enterprise.

European and global cross-border investment has also been increasing in popularity throughout the 1990s. In the City of London, for example, foreign ownership rose from around 10 per cent in the mid-1980s to over 50 per cent at 2011 (Lizieri *et al.*, 2011).

Diversification by institutional investors is a powerful driver of this activity, while other investor groups seek higher returns by playing the global property cycle. If returns going forward in the US property market are perceived to be disappointing, US money will look abroad. The rise of international benchmarks and improvements in data provision, coupled with globalization in general and the growth of the international investment houses in particular, have added to the appeal of international investment. Sheer weight of money drives some funds such as the Abu Dhabi Investment Authority (estimated assets: around $1 trillion) to place its investments abroad.

The world's top investors have gone global. According to Property Funds Research data (see Chapter 2), of the top ten global investors all now have global real estate portfolios or have announced plans to invest in global real estate. It is now very unusual for a large investor not to have a global property strategy.

Currency hedging is, however, expensive and difficult to achieve efficiently (Lizieri *et al.*, 1998) and vehicles are rarely fully hedged. This problem leaves investors at the mercy of currency movements. The use of debt in the local currency (see Chapter 2 and below) appears to serve a partial hedging function. However, this introduces leverage, and the experience of over-leveraged investors in the GFC should serve to warn of the dangers of investing in a geared vehicle in an overheating economy, quite apart from the added risk of investing equity in a foreign currency.

Other perceived difficulties, including the dangers of operating from a distance with no local representation, increases the attraction of investing internationally through liquid securitized vehicles (Chapter 6) and unlisted funds (Chapter 7).

9.2 The rise of cross-border capital

In 1972, over 94 per cent of the floorspace in a large database of City of London office properties (see Baum and Lizieri, 1999) was owned by UK firms, just less than 3 per cent of space was owned by Middle Eastern interests and around 2 per cent was European owned. Research found no properties owned by German, Japanese or US firms at that time.

By 1997, 21.9 per cent of the buildings covered in the survey were in overseas ownership: 7 per cent of the properties were in Japanese hands, 5 per cent were German owned, 4 per cent were owned by US firms and just under 3 per cent were, as in 1972, in Middle Eastern ownership.

By 2006, 45 per cent of the office space in the City was owned by non-UK firms (Lizieri and Kutsch, 2006). Japanese ownership had been in decline, while the US and German presence had been on the increase, but the most interesting change had been the emergence of international vehicles with indeterminate ultimate ownership – Luxembourg, Cayman and Channel Islands funds, for example.

By 2011, foreign ownership exceeded 50 per cent (Lizieri *et al.*, 2011). This growth was, in part, the child of mid-1980s financial de-regulation. In 1975 the New York Stock Exchange abolished minimum commission rates: 35 broking firms went out of business but stock market turnover exploded. In 1979, UK exchange controls were abolished, allowing capital to move freely around international markets, a move paralleled in other developed economies. By 1986 the implementation of financial deregulation ('Big Bang') meant that merchant banks, jobbers and brokers could combine to become full capacity investment banks, and overseas players could join the London Stock Exchange. Financial business had become global, and London became one of the global financial capitals.

Over the period 1991–6, market globalization intensified, so that the overseas ownership of UK equities increased from 12 per cent to nearly 17 per cent over the five years to the end of 1996. The overseas acquisition of UK finance houses, culminating in 1994–7 in the purchases of Warburgs, Morgan Grenfell, Barings, Kleinworts, Smith New Court, BZW and Mercury by Swiss, Dutch, German, French and American banks, is explained largely by the need of the City economy to access wider markets.

At the same time, savings-based liquidity in Japan, the relaxing of Swedish and German cross-border investment restrictions and changes in German tax policy pushed funds out from these savings-oriented countries, and much of the money flowed into UK property. In addition, international capital flowed into major listed property companies and REITs.

European Monetary Union is another process of radical change which has been gathering momentum since the Maastricht Treaty (and the planned development of the Single European Market it prescribed) made 1992 a landmark date in European history. The 1999 introduction of the euro as a common currency for 11 countries and its subsequent expansion to 18 countries, with more expected to join, is the latest major development in that process.

To a significant extent, currency risk has disappeared for Euroland investors and international investing has been much simplified for non-Europeans entering Europe. Regulation and taxation rules have very slowly begun to converge. Investment benchmarks are slowly becoming global. This will create a significant change in investor behaviour: from a position where any exposure to overseas assets is a risk against a domestic benchmark, growing recognition of wider non-domestic benchmarks would lead to a need to invest overseas to *reduce* risk relative to these benchmarks.

The credit crunch of 2007–8 threatens a return to protectionism and trade barriers, and will likely slow down the globalization process. The strategic trend to international real estate investing nonetheless appears irreversible.

Increasing geopolitical turmoil since the GFC has added to the stimulus for many investors to 'park' capital in the London property market (Badarinza and Ramadorai, 2014). Nonetheless, two dominant styles of international real estate investment vehicle have emerged since the 1990s, driving much of the recent international activity. These are distinguished by the objective being pursued. The key drivers for investing outside the domestic property market and buying global property are the increased opportunities for either or both of (i) diversification and (ii) enhanced return. These potential benefits come at a cost of increased complexity of execution.

9.3 The case for international real estate investment: diversification

It is common to find simplistic assertions that international real estate investment will provide effective diversification for pension plans. This model, which assumes an investor objective defined in terms of expected return and the standard deviation of expected return, is highly flawed, both because it fails to recognize the diversity of real investor objectives and because there are many costs of international diversification which are unrecognized in the measure.

Table 9.1 shows the correlations between various overseas markets and the main asset classes in the UK. The mature property markets appear to have been effective diversifiers

Table 9.1: Correlations between UK assets and global property markets, 2002–13

	UK property	UK equities	UK gilts
France	0.5	0.2	–0.1
Germany	–0.3	–0.3	0.1
Portugal	0.3	–0.1	0.0
Spain	0.6	0.1	0.0
Sweden	0.5	0.4	–0.1
Switzerland	–0.4	–0.3	0.4
Nordic	0.5	0.3	–0.1
North America	0.6	0.2	0.0
Australia	0.6	0.2	–0.1
Japan	0.4	0.1	0.3
South Africa	0.3	0.3	–0.2

Source: IPD, CBRE Global Investors

Table 9.2: Total returns, local currency, global markets, 2002–13

	2002	2003	2004	2005	2006	2007	2008	2009	2010	2011	2012	2013	3 yr	5 yr
UK	9.6	10.9	18.3	19.1	18.1	–3.4	–22.1	3.5	15.1	7.8	3.4	10.7	7.3	8.0
France	8.6	8.0	10.1	15.2	21.7	17.8	–0.9	–1.4	10.0	8.4	6.3	5.1	6.6	5.6
Germany	3.9	2.9	1.1	0.5	1.3	4.5	2.8	2.0	4.2	5.3	4.2	5.2	4.9	4.2
Netherlands	8.8	7.1	7.8	10.2	12.5	11.3	3.3	–0.2	4.6	3.8	1.2	0.5	1.8	2.0
Portugal	13.8	9.8	10.5	10.1	12.1	12.2	2.7	0.2	4.3	0.5	0.8	1.3	0.9	1.4
Spain	8.7	8.2	10.8	16.9	16.9	12.4	–3.7	–9.3	4.8	2.7	–2.2	0.3	0.3	–0.8
Nordic	4.8	4.1	6.4	12.5	14.9	13.5	–0.2	2.7	8.4	7.9	5.6	5.6	6.4	6.0
Canada	8.8	8.3	12.9	18.7	18.3	15.9	3.7	–0.3	11.2	15.4	14.2	10.7	13.4	10.1
United States	6.3	10.1	14.8	19.0	15.1	14.4	–7.4	–17.4	14.8	14.5	10.8	11.4	12.2	6.0
Australia	9.9	11.9	13.8	16.3	19.7	18.4	0.1	–2.4	9.4	10.3	9.5	9.6	9.8	7.2
Japan	na	4.1	6.4	12.2	13.4	11.3	–0.9	–6.1	0.6	3.2	3.6	6.0	4.3	1.4

Source: IPD

against all domestic assets, especially gilts and equities, but more efficient diversification has, surprisingly, been available from certain European property markets.

In addition, both the mature core and emerging markets appear to have acted as good diversifiers against a UK property portfolio over a short period (see Table 9.2). However, these correlations are based on returns in local currencies, and they are based on a short time series. They should be adjusted for future expectations when used to model a potential portfolio.

This data is compiled from IPD global market indices, which are comparable and consistent, but have not been available for very long in several of the markets shown, and are not available at all in other markets. Hence there is a compromise to be made between the length of the data runs and the number of countries to be examined and compared. The result is, unfortunately, a dataset which is so limited as to be non-significant. It also suffers from the following rather large deficiencies, all of which severely limit the ability of investors to replicate these returns in practice.

9.3.1 Index replication

The problem of specific risk, introduced in Chapter 1 and amplified in Chapter 6, means that investors find it very difficult to replicate the return delivered by a national index without suffering a significant tracking error. This sampling error, amplified by the non-substitutability of real estate assets across portfolios, adds a layer of risk which is not represented in the index data shown in Table 9.2.

9.3.2 Currency

The returns shown in Table 9.2 are in local currency. In order that an international investor can achieve local currency returns, there must either be no movements in exchange rates, or the investor must be able to perfectly and fully hedge his currency risk. This is not really possible – see Section 9.6.

The IPD Global Index was published for the first time in June 2008. It reports the market weighted returns for the 22 most mature markets measured by IPD (Austria, Australia, Belgium, Canada, Denmark, France, Germany, Ireland, Italy, Japan, Netherlands, New Zealand, Norway, Portugal, South Africa, South Korea, Spain, Sweden, Switzerland and UK) plus KTI Finland and NCREIF in the US, together worth an estimated $1,296 billion as at the end of 2013.

Table 9.3: IPD global index returns, 2002–13

Currency	2002	2003	2004	2005	2006	2007	2008	2009	2010	2011	2012	2013
Euro	-3.3	-2.1	7.3	22.3	7.2	5.2	-3.8	-6.8	17.8	12.1	4.7	1.4
GBP	3.0	5.8	7.8	18.7	5.1	14.7	26.7	-14.4	13.6	9.3	1.6	4.0
USD	13.9	17.7	15.6	6.1	19.8	16.6	-8.5	-3.8	10.1	8.5	6.3	6.0
JPY	3.2	6.2	10.6	22.0	21.0	9.3	-25.7	-1.3	-4.1	3.0	19.5	28.8
Local	6.4	7.9	10.7	14.2	14.0	11.2	-4.5	-6.7	9.3	9.3	7.1	8.3

Source: IPD

In 2008 the all property total returns across global real estate markets in local currencies were lower than those in 2006, falling from 11.5 to –4.5 per cent. But a UK investor made 26.7 per cent while a Japanese investor made –25.7 per cent, as the pound weakened and the yen appreciated. Currency is clearly a serious issue.

9.3.3 Taxes and fees

Returns achieved by investors will be damaged by taxes and fees. Pension funds which are tax exempt in their own domicile may suffer some taxation when investing internationally. To limit the impact of taxes may involve complex structuring of the investment (see Section 9.9 and Box 9.1) and the payment of legal and consulting fees and investment management fees for international mandates and products will often be higher than domestic fees.

9.3.4 Leverage

Leverage will often be used when investing internationally. There are several reasons for this. First, pension funds will often choose to invest internationally through a special purpose vehicle or unlisted fund. If the investment is through a fund, the fund manager will normally have a selfish preference for using leverage to boost assets under management, and perhaps fees, as well as a mutually beneficial aspiration to boost return on equity (and, less mutually beneficially, risk). If a special purpose vehicle is used by the investor, he may choose to use leverage to boost return, but is more likely to be driven to do so for the following reasons: (i) it is tax efficient to do so; (ii) it permits greater diversification of specific risk; and (iii) it is believed that it can partially hedge currency risk.

We deal with the methods used to hedge currency risk later (Section 9.6); for now, we can state simply that borrowings in foreign currency perfectly hedge the currency risk of the debt component of the investment made.

The tax efficiency of a non-domestic property acquisition by an investor which is tax exempt in its own market can be boosted by using leverage. This is because the tax penalty most likely to be suffered is a withholding tax, applied to income. If net taxable income can be reduced by offsetting loan interest payments against the rent, then income returns are effectively transformed into capital gains on equity, which are less likely to be taxed (see Chapter 2).

Greater diversification is clearly attractive in an international context when the amount of capital needed to buy a globally diversified portfolio is so great (see Chapter 6). Hence the use of (say) 50 per cent leverage is attractive, simply because it allows twice as many assets to be acquired. (Because leverage has so many advantages both for the fund manager and the investor, it went hand in hand with international investing in the 1998–2007 period, and the withdrawal of debt facilities in 2008–9 held a very negative implication for the immediate future of international real estate investing. But by 2014 leverage, and cross-border capital flows, were back in full swing.)

To summarize, the data shown in Table 9.2 appears to offer some promise to investors seeking diversification. But it is not statistically significant, and it does not represent the net of tax and fees, domestic currency, leveraged and specific risk-laden returns available to investors. Data such as this should only be presented with reservations and should only be received with healthy scepticism. Nonetheless, the nature of the economics driving local rental markets coupled with the clear difference between the developed markets of North

America and Northern and Western Europe and the emerging markets in Asia and elsewhere suggests that, theoretically at least, diversification benefits should be available.

The extension of the euro suggests that the diversification benefits offered within the mature Eurozone markets may be a little weaker in future, and the expansion of mature Europe suggests fewer diversification benefits for a commitment to emerging central and Eastern Europe (but see Lizieri *et al.*, 2003; McAllister and Lizieri, 2006). However, it is clear that for a European investor the risk and return characteristics of a domestic portfolio combined with a diversified European exposure to both the core and emerging markets should be significantly better than the domestic portfolio alone, at least before the complications listed above are accounted for. Adding a global exposure to continental European investments introduces the opportunity to include the US (a highly mature market which on its own is as big as the European market) and the Asian and emerging markets.

However, the US has not offered an irresistible market for an investor with an existing UK property portfolio. There is dominant local capital, which limits the opportunities for outstanding performance, including a deep and efficient REIT market with a low cost of capital. The US under-performed the UK over a long period although the US has out-performed the UK over the last 12 years, and was highly correlated with the UK market, very highly indeed until the crash of 2007–8 (see Table 9.4). The correlation of returns for 2002–8 was 88 per cent; for 2002–13 it was around 60 per cent. (Many commentators suspected that a technical index lag rather than fundamentals was the cause of the minor de-coupling.) In addition, US taxes levied on foreign investors is onerous, and difficult – if not impossible – to avoid.

Table 9.4: Total returns, UK and US, 2002–13

	2002	2003	2004	2005	2006	2007	2008	2009	2010	2011	2012	2013	Average
UK	9.6	10.9	18.3	19.1	18.1	–3.4	–22.1	3.5	15.1	7.8	3.4	10.7	7.6
US	6.3	10.1	14.8	19.0	15.1	14.4	–7.4	–17.5	14.8	14.5	10.8	11.4	8.9

Source: IPD

(The high UK/US correlation is in local currency. As Table 9.3 shows, the unhedged domestic currency returns have been very different. A dollar investor would have had far worse returns than a mere –22 per cent in the UK in 2008 thanks to the pound weakening against the dollar. The average number of dollars bought by a pound in January was 0.5; in December it was 0.67. If –22 per cent were a simple capital return in sterling, in dollars it would have been –42 per cent.)

Asia includes several interesting mature markets (Japan, Korea, Singapore, Hong Kong) and also holds many of the large emerging markets (China, India, Pakistan, Middle East, Indonesia, Vietnam and others). The mature markets have been highly volatile, offering tactical opportunities, while the emerging markets should offer the highest long-term returns. In both cases, performance will be underpinned by the fastest expected global rates of economic growth, which drives real estate demand. In addition, it appears that an Asian exposure can be expected to act as an effective diversifier against UK property, which would compensate for higher volatility.

However, we do not yet have sufficiently good data to be confident that long-term diversification benefits have been available, and a view formed from a combination of economics, property research and institutional (property market) experience is required.

9.4 The case for international real estate investment: enhanced return

Europe alone combines large and relatively mature, liquid and lower risk markets with risky emerging markets, with the result that investments are available across the risk spectrum in what are known as core, core-plus, value-added and opportunity categories. (See Chapter 2 and Figure 7.5, which summarizes the risk/return characteristics of typical property funds in these categories.) Enhanced returns are likely to be available in the riskier markets and funds.

International investment can provide access to higher potential returns than are available domestically. Figure 9.1 demonstrates the returns that would have been achieved in different markets in one year, 2013. UK returns were strong at 10.7 per cent, but well behind those achieved in South Africa (15.3 per cent). Meanwhile, Spain suffered capital value falls and struggled to deliver a positive return (0.3 per cent).

The range of these (local currency) returns means that a global unconstrained mandate is usually likely to offer the potential for higher returns than a domestic-only strategy.

Figure 9.1: Direct property total returns, 2013

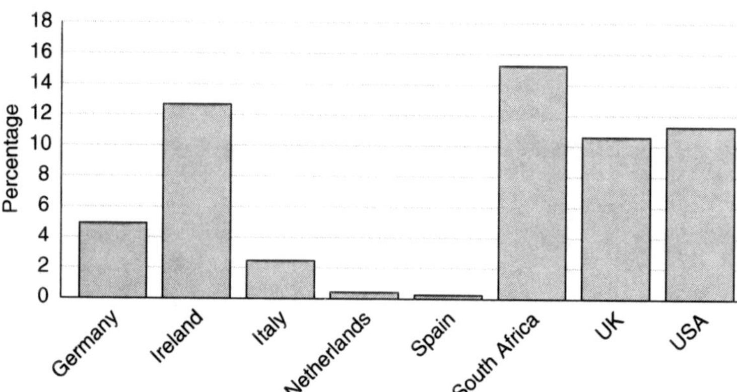

Source: IPD composite indices

9.5 Other drivers

9.5.1 Liability matching

Insurance companies build books of liabilities to pay out insurance claims and protect savings in international markets. As an example, the UK insurance conglomerate Norwich Union changed its trading brand to Aviva in 2002 as a sign that its business was international. The insurance fund has to match liabilities with assets in order to remain in business, so it is natural to build investment portfolios in different markets and currencies, including real estate assets.

9.5.2 Lack of local product

There are stark examples of very wealthy investors based in one domicile which contains a very small real estate market in global terms. These investors are forced to invest internationally. Examples include sovereign funds in the Middle East (Qatar, Abu Dhabi) and others. The argument has also been used by pension funds in larger markets, such as the Netherlands and Australia.

In addition, the Government of Singapore Investment Corporation (GIC) and other sovereign wealth funds are prevented by their mandates from investing in their domestic (real estate) markets. This is related to the size of the domestic market and is designed to prevent (i) over-heating of the market through weight of capital, (ii) poor return prospects and (iii) poor diversification.

9.5.3 Fee generation

Part of the wave of international real estate investing has been encouraged by investment managers making a stronger case for diversification than the data permits, perhaps because higher fees can be earned for international property investing. Because higher fees can be earned does not mean there is more profit to be made, but there is little doubt that fund management businesses with a mission to build a global franchise have been very keen to sell international products and take capital across national boundaries.

9.5.4 Fashion

It has also been evident that international real estate investing happens in waves, affecting both the capital source and the target destination of the capital. This can be grounded in market pricing and institutional economics, but it can also be influenced by fashion – peer group pressure – and by the opinions of firms of investment consultants with influence over client groups. Hence many Dutch pension funds went international in the 1990s, using a mixture of REITs and unlisted funds, while UK pension funds made the move roughly ten years later, using unlisted funds, funds of funds and (rarely) REITs.

A more positive effect of this fashion is to introduce education to otherwise domestically focused professionals and analysts who gain transferable skills and knowledge. Marketing is another side effect. For example, it may be an unpriced benefit of real estate development to use a multi-storey tower to advertise the brand of an international bank in red neon.

However, neither training nor marketing per se are good arguments for international real estate investing which, to return to the beginning of this section, should be driven either by diversification or by the search for high returns. But what are the costs?

There are significant challenges involved in executing a global property investment strategy. Research and expertise is needed. Property comes in large lot sizes, so it is very difficult to buy enough assets to build a diversified portfolio. There may be political risks in certain countries, for example a risk of taxation of foreign investors, title risk or even forced land nationalization.

There will be a currency risk that may be impossible to perfectly hedge. International investment may result in less liquidity, and gearing the portfolio may be unavoidable. We now deal with these issues.

9.6 Currency risk

9.6.1 Introduction

As we saw in Section 9.3.2, movements in currency exchange rates have a large impact on delivered returns to investors, and greatly complicate a global strategy. Currency fluctuations can be significant and, if left unhedged, currency exposure would significantly increase the overall riskiness of the investment.

Given that, as we have seen, as much as two-thirds of the returns from an international property portfolio can be explained by currency movements and one-third by property returns, it can be more important to develop a currency strategy than a property investment strategy. At the same time, given that property investors and property fund managers are not currency experts, and that forecasting currencies is notoriously difficult, our focus needs to be on the risk component of currency and not its return potential.

There are other side-effects of currency movements which can be damaging to investors and fund managers. The quick and steep devaluation of sterling in 2008, for example (see Figure 9.2), had an unforeseen impact on investors who had committed to non-sterling investments. We saw in Chapter 7 how the drawdown period for an unlisted fund might extend to three years. Investors make forward commitments, say in euros, while their domestic currency may be sterling. There may be an initial drawing (say 10 per cent of the commitment) but if 90 per cent remains undrawn and sterling depreciates by 20 per cent the capital required is now 118 per cent of the original sterling commitment.

Generally, investors and managers will focus on neutralizing currency risk as much as they can. Here are three main approaches.

Figure 9.2: The sterling/euro exchange rate, 1999–2014

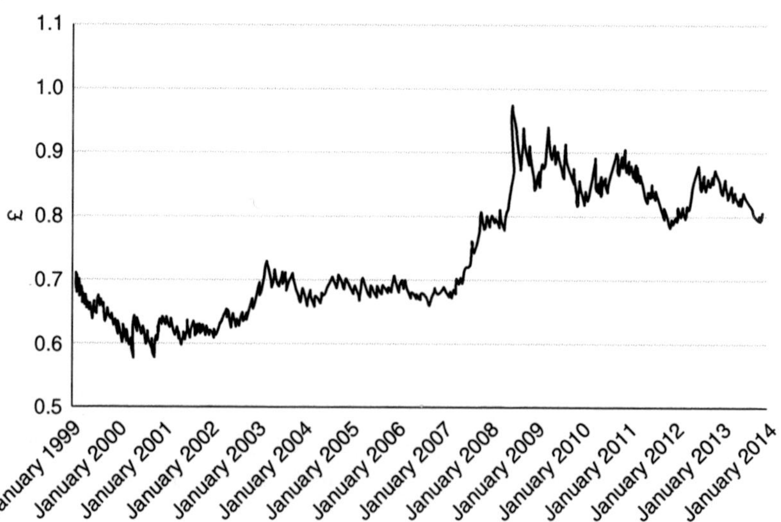

Source: European Central Bank

9.6.2 A currency overlay

Large multi-asset investors and managers may have the luxury of an in-house team of currency experts whose job it is to maximize the risk-return profile of the house's net global currency exposure. This exposure will be attained through all asset types, including private equity, hedge funds, real estate, stock and bonds as well as cash, held either for liquidity or specifically to access an attractive currency.

The currency team will have an optimal currency exposure policy, perhaps influenced by liabilities. It will measure the undesired currency exposure and manage it. It can use a variety of instruments to manage currency exposure, but the most common instrument used will be the currency swap, which hedges (neutralizes) an undesired exposure. If a currency team operates in this way for the house, then a 'currency overlay' avoids any need for the property investment team to manage currency exposure. The price of this may be a directive to avoid or limit investment in certain property markets because the undesired currency exposure is too unattractive or too expensive to manage.

9.6.3 Using leverage

When and where debt finance is available, property funds investing in non-domestic property typically employ local currency leverage, in the range 50–70 per cent. The leverage has more than one benefit. It enhances the income return if property yields exceed debt rates, so that dividend yields for continental European property funds were generally higher in nominal terms than for UK property funds when (as in 2000–7) the UK interest rate exceeded the euro interest rate.

Leverage enhances the prospective total return/IRR as long as the prospective IRR exceeds the cost of debt (see Chapter 2). Leverage also provides a partial hedge against the effect of currency movements on capital values. For example, if the leverage ratio is 50 per cent, 50 per cent of the property capital value will be hedged by equal and opposite changes in value of the local currency debt.

Let us assume that a UK property is acquired in 2003 for £100 million by a US investor. The sterling–dollar exchange rate at the time of purchase is £0.5:$1. The investor exchanges $100 million for £50 million and borrows £50 million from a UK bank.

He holds the investment for five years, sells the building in 2008 for the price he paid, and achieves a 5 per cent total return on the project, all through income. At the time of the sale the sterling–dollar exchange rate has weakened to £0.7: $1.

His capital gain in dollars is negative. He owes the bank £50 million, which he can pay back out of the sale proceeds of £100 million, leaving his equity of £50 million, now worth $71 million. He has lost $29 million.

If he had financed the building through 100 per cent equity, he would have lost $58 million, so he has been approximately (because we have not dealt with income) 50 per cent hedged. If he had used 75 per cent leverage, he would have lost only $14.5 million. His upside gain would have been similarly limited by increasing levels of gearing.

However, this is only half the story, as it ignores property risk. The above example assumes that the investor receives a 5 per cent return on the investment. But what would happen if he borrowed at 5 per cent and earned –10 per cent? The greater the leverage he takes on, even in local currency, the worse his financial position would become (see Chapter 2). So leverage provides a partial hedge against the effect of currency movements on capital values, but it exaggerates the property risk taken on by the remaining equity component of the investment.

9.6.4 Hedging

The value of the equity investment in a non-domestic property investment or fund can be hedged in the money market. Taking as an example a UK fund investing in the Eurobloc, the euro equity exposure can be hedged by using currency swaps.

We saw in Chapter 4 that Fisher's equation explaining interest rates has three explanatory variables: these are the real risk free rate, or a reward for liquidity preference, the expected rate of inflation and a risk premium.

$$R = l + i + RP$$

Hence, there is a unity relationship between the rate of interest (*R*) and the expected inflation rate (*i*). There is also a theoretical unity relationship between the expected inflation rate and the currency exchange rate, suggested by the theory of purchasing power parity. Imagine that goods are made in Japan and the UK, and that the UK suffers an inflation rate of 5 per cent while prices in Japan are stable. The prices of goods in the UK rise by 5 per cent every year, while prices in Japan stay the same. After ten years, prices in the UK are 63 per cent higher than in Japan. UK manufacturers would be tempted to source parts in Japan. To buy them, they would have to sell sterling and buy yen. This would be a profitable arbitrage until the yen appreciated against sterling by 63 per cent. As long as it remained profitable, it would continue to happen, resulting in net sales of sterling and net purchases of yen, driving the yen upwards against sterling until parity is reached. In an efficient market, the adjustment would be daily.

There is also a direct unity relationship between interest rates and expected movements in currency exchange rates, posited by the concept of interest rate parity. This idea suggests that the interest rate differential is a predictor of currency exchange movements, and the banking system holds and uses this information on a real time basis as it makes a market for currency swaps.

Let us refer back to our example of the US investor buying a UK property. He may use 50 per cent leverage but wishes to hedge the equity component. What he would like to do is guarantee that he can exchange £50 million for $100 million in five years' time, or five years forward. There is an active currency swaps market, so he can offer this deal to a bank or 'inter-dealer broker'.

The bank is being asked to swap $100 million of its own cash for the investor's £50 million in five years' time. Is this an attractive proposition? This depends on expectations of the future exchange rate. If the pound is expected to weaken against the dollar, it is not attractive; if the dollar is expected to weaken against the pound, it is attractive. As we showed above, the market consensus expectation of future currency exchange rates is given by the interest rate differential.

The cost of a currency hedge is therefore related to the interest rate differential between sterling and the dollar over the relevant time horizon. If US interest rates are 2 per cent when UK interest rates are 4 per cent, sterling will be expected to depreciate by 2 per cent each year against the dollar. The bank will then charge 2 per cent of the hedged amount every year in order to guarantee to swap £50 million for $100 million in five years' time (although in practice a series of shorter period swaps is more common).

Using another example, assume that the expected return on a Eurobloc property is 8 per cent (6 per cent through income). The expected return on a UK property over the same period is also 8 per cent (6 per cent through income). The euro base rate is 4.25 per cent, while the UK interest rate is 5.25 per cent.

A UK investor is looking at each alternative for a five-year hold. The property value of each property is the same – £6 million and €10 million, with an exchange rate of £0.6: €1.

Assume that the expected value of the Eurobloc property in five years is, as expected, €10m * $(1.02)^5$=€11.04m. What is the value in sterling? This is £6.62 at the current exchange rate, but the exchange rate is expected to change. What is the expected value of €11.04 million in sterling? The 1 per cent interest rate differential suggests a decline in the value of sterling of 1 per cent each year against the euro (€11.04 * $(1.01)^5$ * 0.6=£6.96). The UK investor could let the currency bet ride and get a capital return of £6.96/£6=1.16=3% p.a., 1 per cent better than the UK alternative. But this is risky!

If the investor arranges a forward swap of euros for sterling by a euro bank, the bank will be happy. It is beneficial to be promised euros in exchange for sterling in five years' time, because the euro is expected to appreciate. The UK investor is happy to get sterling in exchange for euros in five years' time. The markets expect euros to appreciate by 1 per cent per annum, so the swap margin is 1 per cent.

Assume the investor swaps €1 one year forward for £0.60. The bank expects to pay a margin of 1 per cent, so the property investor will get €1.01 for £0.60. In five years he will get €1.01^5=€1.051. So he sells the property for €11.04, swaps into £ at €1.051, gets £11.04 * 1.051 * 0.6=£6.96. The capital return is again 3 per cent, but this time there is no currency risk.

In 2014, the UK/euro interest rate yield curve is the reverse of the case in our example. The interest rate differential is a little over 1 per cent (the euro is higher) for most maturities, strengthening the UK property market relative to continental Europe and going some way to explaining low cap rates and high prices in London.

In practice, hedging is implemented through the money markets, either using forward foreign exchange (FX) contracts or options. Nonetheless, it is difficult if not impossible to achieve a perfect hedge. The practical issues arising include the following.

Figure 9.3: UK and euro interest rate yield curves

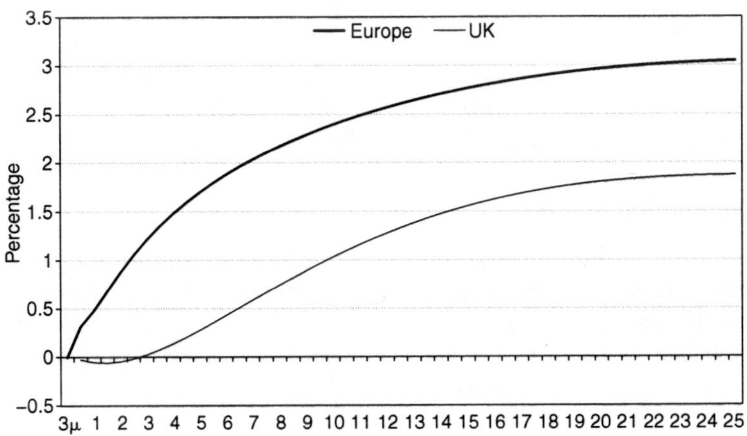

Source: Bank of England, European Central Bank

ı/loss on the investment is unrealized, while the gain/loss on the hedge is the event of a loss on the hedge, this gives rise to a funding requirement in tched by cash flow from the asset.

n value are not immediately hedged. The investment will be hedged at cost. ue of the investment changes, the change in value is unhedged. This can be n by using shorter duration hedges and renewing the hedge based on the new n at each quarter end.

- Regulators may not allow a 100 per cent hedge, as this may result in an over-hedged position when values fall. For example, in Ireland the regulatory maximum is a 97 per cent hedge.
- The dividend yield on the investment remains unhedged using the approach described.
- The hedging transaction will involve transaction costs, so the net benefit will be less than the full interest rate differential. Transaction costs (spreads), typically very low in the three-month euro/GBP and other major markets, are higher for minor currencies.
- Forward commitments are difficult to hedge. Once an investor has made a commitment to a project or fund, it may not be possible to know how much will be drawn, and it is very unlikely to be known at what time.

Nonetheless, something approaching the elusive 'free lunch' (in this case a higher return for a lower risk) may hover into view. In the 2004–7 period, for example, nominal returns in euros were enhanced by the interest rate differential flowing from the hedge, resulting in attractive returns in GBP, while neutralizing the majority of the currency exposure.

9.7 Political and title risk

Poor or stressed government action will often express itself in the form of inflation, currency devaluation, high taxation, low economic growth and other impacts which are not conducive to successful property investment.

A purer form of political risk can encompass a range of hazards, from punitive taxation of foreign investors, exchange controls, new limits on non-domestic ownership of real estate assets, and even land and property nationalization.

Political risk can also be extended to cover the risk of defective legal title, a potential problem in the former communist countries of Central and Eastern Europe. This issue can be exaggerated by international investors who are ignorant of a country's history and institutions. At its most extreme, however, grounded or ungrounded perceptions of political risk can make a country uninvestable: see Chapter 10.

9.8 Specific risk

Specific risk has a technical meaning in the context of modern portfolio theory: see Chapter 1. It also has a popular meaning in the context of international real estate investing. Both concepts are relevant here.

The technical meaning was explored in this context in Chapter 6 (Section 6.2). A large amount of capital is needed to purchase a portfolio of directly owned real estate assets. If this is concentrated in the domestic market, and the benchmark is domestic, then specific risk will be a challenge for all investors except the very largest. If the benchmark is global and the same amount of investment capital is, alternatively, spread around the world then the specific risk – and tracking error – will be greater.

The popular meaning concerns the perception that foreign assets are, dollar for dollar or pound for pound, more risky than domestic assets through 'information asymmetry', or the belief that local players know more about the asset, the legal and tax environment and the market than a foreigner. This may be the case, and explains why international investors will often choose to invest through a joint venture with a local partner.

To some extent, and on occasion, this may be balanced by the perspective advantage an external buyer might have when looking into a market where local players have lost confidence (Baum and Crosby (2008, Ch. 9), describes a case where German buyers did very well in these circumstances in London in 1993).

9.9 Other problems

9.9.1 Fees and costs

The structures set up to invest internationally can be very expensive to create and to manage, as will be clear from the remainder of this chapter. Consulting fees, legal costs, directors' fees, accounting and audit fees, fees charged on the provision of debt and the costs of annual reporting combine to produce a hefty initial and annual expense which means that the tax savings created are not wholly for the benefit of the investor.

Fund management fees have tended to be higher for international funds and mandates than for domestic investment allocations. A domestic fund may cost an additional 25 bp (around one-third of the typical fee) in total annual management charges excluding performance fees.

9.9.2 Global cycles, converging markets

It has been suggested that the impact of globalization in its broadest sense has been to increase correlations between markets and thereby reduce the benefits of international diversification. It is not possible to test this hypothesis by producing convincing evidence of changes in the diversifying benefits of an international real estate programme, due to deficiencies in the available data (see Section 9.3). However, Lizieri *et al.* (2003) and McAllister and Lizieri (2006) examine the changing diversification benefits available to cross-border investors using listed property securities in the newly converging Eurobloc and find evidence of continuing benefits.

9.9.3 Loss of focus and specialization

For a REIT or investment manager which has a strong track record and long experience of a particular market, especially when specialized in a single sector, there is much to be said against diversification. It is commonly held that diversification is better achieved by the investor, and that REITs and funds should 'stick to the knitting'.

9.10 Taxation issues

9.10.1 Introduction

Pension funds are usually tax exempt in their own domicile, but may suffer withholding taxes – and other taxes specific to the foreign environment – when investing abroad. Withholding tax is a tax on income, so called because the income is withheld from the foreign investor at source. Using leverage to reduce net income, if permitted, is a natural way to mitigate this.

In addition, there may be tax shocks. Examples of specific tax shocks include a French tax on non-domestic owners of immovable property, which can be 3 per cent of the market value of such properties, charged annually. All legal entities in the ownership structure are jointly and severally liable for the payment of this tax, which can often be avoided, but at a cost.

Sometimes, properties will be held within single asset companies to allow shares rather than the building to be sold or other taxes to be minimized. This may be tax advantageous, but introduces another taxable layer: as a result we will now have potentially taxable properties, companies, fund entities and investors.

Taxes may be applied to investors in the domicile of the fund (for example, withholding tax, and taxes on capital gains). Taxes may be applied to the investor in its home domicile (income tax, taxes on capital gains). Taxes may be applied to the investor in the domicile of the property (for example, the French 3 per cent tax). Taxes may be applied to the holding entity in the domicile of the property (local taxes); or the domicile of the fund (corporate taxes, withholding tax). Taxes may be applied to the entity in the domicile of the entity (corporate taxes). Taxes can be applied to the property in the domicile of the property (VAT, stamp duty and other transfer taxes).

There are many other tax risks facing the global investor, and the complexity of the problem is perhaps best illustrated by case studies and examples. Suffice it to say, expert tax advice is unhesitatingly used by professional investors and fund managers when contemplating non-domestic investment and new international property funds, and the resulting structures can be mesmerizing. Established offshore, corporate vehicles can be highly tax efficient and hence attract international investors. Companies set up in the Channel Islands, for example, can sell property free of all UK capital gains tax. For this reason and others, the UK is seen to some extent as a tax haven for international investors.

Much international property investment utilizes this type of vehicle. It raises some interesting questions. A UK life fund may typically consider this type of vehicle in allocating cash to international property investment. Its decision may be based on the returns available after tax on equity, compared to the gross returns available in their domestic market. Its domestic investments are unlikely to be geared, and the false comparison of similar returns on low risk domestic investment and high risk, highly geared or levered international investment may be tempted.

We use two examples to illustrate these issues. A relatively simple example is presented in Section 9.10.2, and a more complex illustration in Box 9.1. Both concern investment into French assets by non-French investors.

9.10.2 Tax case 1 – a French property fund, late 1990s

A UK investment manager with a captive (in-house) insurance fund has determined in 1998 that performance prospects for French property, especially Paris offices, are attractive. There is also known to be demand from a Dutch pension fund as a likely co-investor. Attractive fees can be earned from an unlisted fund set up to access this market, and the in-house insurance fund will benefit from higher return prospects than are available in the UK.

However, there is a tax penalty for overseas investors in France (see above). There was also (at the time) a transfer tax of 18.5 per cent on the purchase of buildings.

There is a 1.75 per cent tax on the transfer of companies. In addition, a company with limited liability is helpful in making sure there is a layer of protection between the fund's operations and the fund itself.

There is a tax treaty between France and the Netherlands, and a tax treaty between the UK and the Netherlands, but no tax treaty between France and the UK. (Tax treaties are set up to avoid double taxation of legal persons who are resident or domiciled or otherwise have interests in two locations. The tax treaty also means that pension funds which do not pay tax at home may be shielded from tax when investing internationally.)

There is income tax relief on loan interest in France, and lower taxation of loan interest than equity dividends in the Netherlands.

The structure used is shown in Figure 9.4.

The way the fund works (in simplified terms) is as follows. The fund is a Dutch limited liability company, which must be controlled by a majority of Dutch nationals based in the Netherlands, where board meetings will be held. The Netherlands–UK tax treaty means that no tax is paid in the Netherlands by a tax exempt UK life fund.

The fund owns a single limited liability holding company (BV) to allow a sale of the entire portfolio without collapsing the fund, and to insert a layer of limited liability. This in turn owns a series of special purpose Dutch BVs which in turn each own a single French property company. This structure widens the net of possible tax-efficient buyers.

The tax treaty between the Netherlands and France means that no tax is paid by Dutch tax free entities on French income. The French companies own the French buildings in order to avoid the transfer tax of 18.5 per cent on acquisitions and to put in its place a 1.75 per cent company transfer tax. The French property companies use debt to reduce taxable income and to reduce French income tax on dividends paid.

Figure 9.4: French property fund, 1998

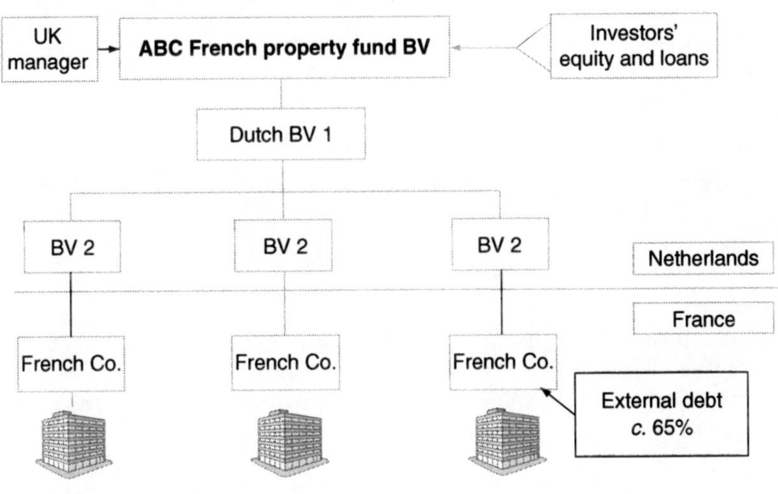

Source: Manager

At the fund level, the investors provide loans to reduce the tax on income received, but 'thin capitalization' rules limit the extent to which loans can be used in place of equity. The loans pass down through the structure subject to the tax efficiency of the structure at each stage.

Each company will have its own cash and its own revenue statement. If the structure works well, the loans and equity pass down through the various companies, and are used to provide the equity for the property acquisitions. The companies will receive rents, and pay operating expenses and two sets of loan interest (one to the local bank, and one back up to investors), and make a small profit which is available for distributions up through the structure, with enough cash to fund them, but not so much cash so that it becomes trapped in the subsidiaries.

9.11 Conclusion

International property investment is not straightforward. Tax and currency issues are considerable, and the data required to fully support a case in the face of these obstacles is not yet available. But at the peak of the market in 2007 the investment management teams were in place and the vehicles were available. A period of reflection and retrenchment was inevitable following the 2007–9 crash, but a continued recovery in the appetite for and supply of global real estate investment solutions was well established by 2013.

The data available to support a decision to invest internationally is illustrative of possibilities and of limited value: it describes investments in direct property, and also describes the performance of diversified market indexes, which cannot be perfectly captured. The argument needs to be set in the context of the execution model, by which we mean the use of unlisted property funds and listed REITs.

How can a global investor capture the desirable performance characteristics described in this section? This is dealt with in Chapter 10.

Box 9.1 A detailed tax case

This fund structure was set up in 2007 for the purposes of establishing a fund for multi-domicile investors investing in a variety of European markets. This was a pan-European fund holding French property through a Luxembourg structure. The case refers to tax rules in place at the time, which may have since been changed.

The manager had identified the following key requirements. The fund structure had to be:

a tax efficient, putting investors, as far as possible, in as good a position (as regards income, capital gains, transfer and other taxes) as if they had bought property directly;
b capable of benefiting from an exemption from the French 3 per cent tax;
c subject to regulation which is not unduly limiting given the fund's investment strategy;
d capable of accommodating VAG investors (investors subject to the provisions of the German Insurance Supervision Act), using their equity quota;
e flexible enough to accommodate a wide range of European investee jurisdictions and a wide range of international institutional and high net worth investors; and
f in a recognizable and market-familiar fund structure that investors will generally be comfortable with.

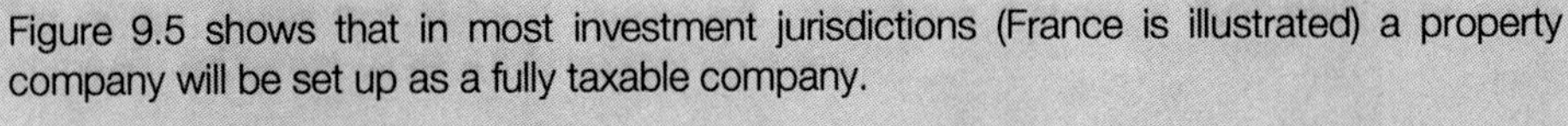

Figure 9.5 shows that in most investment jurisdictions (France is illustrated) a property company will be set up as a fully taxable company.

Figure 9.5: The investment structure – France

Fund
Debt
LuxCo 1
Debt
LuxCo 2
Debt
(Used if acquisition is of shares in a French property company)
French HoldCo
Debt
French PropCo
Debt
Bank

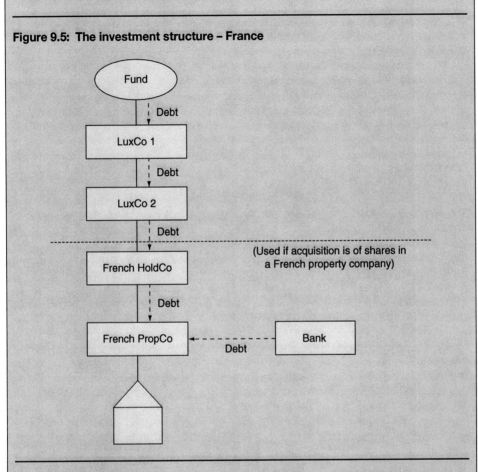

The holding of investments via PropCos provides maximum flexibility in structuring disposals via a sale of the underlying investment out of a PropCo, or via a sale of the shares in the PropCo (or intermediate holding company).

The fund, an English limited partnership, will finance LuxCo 1 up to 99 per cent by debt and up to 1 per cent by equity. LuxCo 1 will then finance LuxCo 2 up to 99 per cent by debt, which mirrors the loan from the fund to LuxCo 1, and 1 per cent by equity. This allows the effective rate of withholding tax on income paid from LuxCo 2 to LuxCo 1 and then from LuxCo 1 to the fund to be reduced to as little as 0.42 per cent.

This structure enables the fund to minimize tax on dividends and capital gains derived from the PropCos (via intermediate holding companies where applicable) and on the disposal of the PropCos (or intermediate holding companies). Subject to the observance of local borrowing limits, interest payments made by each PropCo to LuxCo 2 will not be subject to withholding tax in the jurisdiction of residence of PropCo, and will be subject to reduced taxation in Luxembourg due to the ability of the investor to shelter interest income in LuxCo 2.

Debt from XBank and other senior lenders would normally be provided to the PropCo, so that:

- a ring fencing on a property-specific or at least country-specific basis can be achieved (institutional investors would expect this);
- b effective security can be given locally; and
- c interest payable under the loans can be deducted against the income of the PropCo for corporate income tax purposes.

In both Germany and the Netherlands, rules restricting the deductibility of interest paid on connected party loans will restrict gearing to 60:40 in the case of Germany and 75:25 in the case of the Netherlands and, subject to certain exceptions, 60:40 in the case of France. Unless external lending is utilized, the denial of the deductibility of interest to the extent that the gearing exceeds the prescribed limits will result in tax leakage in the relevant jurisdictions.

The French 3 per cent tax provides that legal persons that own immovable properties in France must pay an annual tax of 3 per cent on the market value of such properties. All legal entities in the ownership structure are jointly and severally liable for the payment of this tax. The general partner (GP, a UK company fully taxable in its own jurisdiction) will benefit from an exemption provided that the GP complies with certain filing requirements. The GP's direct or indirect shareholders would have to be able to claim the exemptions themselves with respect to the French 3 per cent tax. The tax does not apply to the fund since, as an English limited partnership, it does not have a separate legal personality.

LuxCo 1, LuxCo 2, French HoldCo and French PropCo (all being Luxembourg companies fully taxable in Luxembourg or French companies) will also all benefit from an exemption provided that they comply with certain annual filing requirements.

The investors, insofar as they are non-natural persons, need to identify where they have their corporate seat, so that the French 3 per cent tax position applicable to them can be determined. The same applies to their direct or indirect shareholders.

Why Luxembourg?

Luxembourg is often chosen as an intermediate jurisdiction for the incorporation of holding companies acting as special purpose vehicles because of its flexible company law, its large treaty network and the favourable domestic participation exemption, whereby dividend and capital gains from substantial participations may under certain conditions be tax exempt (under, for example, the 'Soparfi' regime).

The Luxembourg Soparfi regime covers three different aspects of tax exemption:

- a exemption from corporate tax on dividend income received at the level of LuxCo 1 and LuxCo 2;
- b exemption of capital gains on the alienation of shares realized by LuxCo 1 and LuxCo 2; and
- c exemption of withholding tax on dividend distributions made to the shareholders of LuxCo 1 and LuxCo 2.

Corporate tax

LuxCo 1 and LuxCo 2 are fully taxable Luxembourg companies. As such, they are in principle subject to corporate income tax at a rate of 22 per cent (*impôtsur le revenu des collectivités*), municipal business tax at a rate of 6.75 per cent in Luxembourg-City (*impôt commercial communal*; the rate varying from one municipality to another, although most municipalities apply a tax rate of 7.5 per cent) and a contribution to the unemployment fund of 4 per cent on the corporate income tax. The overall tax burden (at 2006) thus stood at 29.63 per cent in Luxembourg City.

LuxCo 1 and LuxCo 2 are assessed on the basis of their worldwide profits, including interest income from loans and bank deposits, trading income, real estate rental income or foreign exchange gains, after the deduction of allowable expenses and charges, determined in accordance with Luxembourg general accounting standards.

In addition, LuxCo 1 and LuxCo 2 will be subject to wealth tax (*impôtsur la fortune*) at a rate of 0.5 per cent, assessed on the estimated realization value of its assets on the wealth tax assessment date. Retained earnings and portfolio investments held each year on the wealth tax assessment day will be subject to wealth tax.

Article 166 of the Luxembourg income tax law (LIR) provides for the corporate income tax exemption of dividend income through a set of conditions, which pertain to the tax status of the parent and of the subsidiary, as well as to the participation threshold and the holding period. The participation exemption is available to Luxembourg fully taxable companies having capital divided into shares, to certain public entities and to permanent establishments of foreign companies. Luxembourg companies which have their capital divided into shares are public limited companies (*sociétés anonymes*), private limited companies (*sociétés à responsabilité limitée*) and partnerships limited by shares (*sociétés en commandite par actions*). LuxCo 1, being a fully taxable company having a capital divided into shares, will thus qualify as a parent company.

A direct participation of the parent (LuxCo 2) in its subsidiary (PropCo or an intermediate holding company) is required, and the owner (LuxCo 2) must have full ownership of the relevant shares. The participation held by the parent company must also be substantial. A participation of at least 10 per cent in the share capital of the subsidiary or with an acquisition price that amounts to €1,200,000 is deemed qualifying.

The above qualifying participation in PropCo (or HoldCo) has to be held by LuxCo 2 for at least 12 months. Each foreign subsidiary has to be fully taxable in its jurisdiction. Under Luxembourg tax administration practice, a company is deemed fully liable to corporation tax in its jurisdiction of residence if:

a the nominal foreign corporation tax rate is at least 11 per cent; and
b the tax basis is determined by the application of rules similar to those existing in Luxembourg; or
c the company is listed in the EU Parent/Subsidiary Directive 90/435, as amended by Council directive 2003/123 dated 22 December 2003 (the Parent/Subsidiary Directive).

Capital gains

The structure will benefit from Luxembourg's tax treaties on capital gains made on the disposal of shares in a company whose assets principally comprise immovable property. However, the treaty with Spain expressly provides that such gains are taxable in the state where the immovable property is situated, so that a Dutch fully taxable holding company needs to be interposed between LuxCo 2 and the Spanish PropCo, as the double tax treaty between the Netherlands and Spain does not provide for taxation in Spain on the sale by a Dutch company of shares in a Spanish company whose assets consist mainly of Spanish real estate.

In the treaties with Italy, the UK, the Netherlands and Poland such gains fall within a 'catch-all' provision for all gains not expressly mentioned, and are taxed in the state of residence of the company making the gain (Luxembourg). The treaty with Germany also provides for such gains to be taxed in the state of residence of the company making the gain, under provisions stating that any income not specifically mentioned in the treaty is to be taxed in the state where the beneficiary (LuxCo 2) is resident.

A Luxembourg parent company (LuxCo 2) may benefit from an exemption from capital gains realized on the transfer of shares (in PropCo or HoldCo) forming part of a substantial participation. The exemption may be claimed on a sale, but also on other changes of ownership, such as a contribution to the share capital of a company. To be eligible for this exemption, similar rules to those used for the exemption of dividend income apply.

The Luxembourg parent (LuxCo 2) which realizes a capital gain may be a public or a private limited company or a partnership limited by shares. The subsidiary whose shares are sold (PropCo or HoldCo) must be fully taxable in its jurisdiction.

The availability of the participation exemption is conditional on a holding period requirement. The parent company must have held a participation of 10 per cent in the subsidiary's share capital or, alternatively, the acquisition cost of the participation must have been at least €6,000,000. The qualifying participation must have been held for at least 12 months at the beginning of the financial year in which alienation occurs.

Withholding tax

Under Luxembourg domestic law, dividend distributions and other (deemed) profit distributions, as well as interest payments on certain profit sharing bonds made by Luxembourg resident companies, are, in principle, subject to 20 per cent Luxembourg withholding tax (WHT). To the extent that distributions by a Luxembourg company are subject to dividend WHT, the applicable dividend WHT rate may be reduced by treaty claims from eligible shareholders.

In the fund structure, a limited partnership is interposed between the investors and any Luxembourg company. However, Luxembourg doctrine considers that the setting-up of a transparent entity should not prevent members of this transparent entity, who are residents of another contracting state, being granted treaty benefits for income derived through that transparent entity from the other contracting state.

An exemption may be secured on the basis of an applicable double tax treaty or on the basis of the Parent/Subsidiary Directive. This exemption applies to dividends allocated by a

Luxembourg company having a capital divided into shares (which will be the case fo[r] LuxCo 1 and LuxCo 2) to, in particular:

- a another Luxembourg resident company having capital divided into shares;
- b a company benefiting from the Parent/Subsidiary Directive;
- c a permanent establishment of an EU company; or
- d a permanent establishment of a company having capital divided into shares, enjoying treaty protection.

In relation to payments by LuxCo 1, the benefit of the withholding tax exemption may also be secured if, as here, a tax transparent partnership is interposed between LuxCo 1 and the investors. In the case of investors who do not benefit from either the Parent/Subsidiary Directive or an applicable double tax treaty, the effective rate of withholding tax may be brought down to 0.42–0.45 per cent.

The participation threshold and the holding condition are the same as those for the dividend exemption, namely a 10 per cent participation in the subsidiary's capital or a participation having an acquisition value of €1.2 million which must be held for at least 12 months.

The liquidation proceeds distributed upon the liquidation of LuxCo 1 and LuxCo 2 are not subject to Luxembourg dividend WHT under current law, regardless of the residence of the investors.

Debt financing and thin capitalization issues

Each Luxembourg company (LuxCo 1 and LuxCo 2) will be financed through a mix of debt and equity. Unlike dividend payments, payments in relation to indebtedness (interest and reimbursement of principal) are *a priori* not subject to withholding tax and interest payments are in addition tax deductible for corporate income tax purposes, subject to compliance with Luxembourg thin capitalization requirements.

LuxCo 1 and LuxCo 2 are financed up to 99 per cent by debt, which exceeds the 85 per cent limit pursuant to the Luxembourg thin capitalization rules. Interest payments on the excessive portion of the debt may therefore be deemed by the tax administration to be a hidden profit distribution, subject to dividend withholding tax (currently 20 per cent) and no deduction will be available to LuxCo 1 and LuxCo 2 in respect of this excessive interest.

However, even if LuxCo 2 is over-indebted, no withholding tax is due in Luxembourg by virtue of the EU parent–subsidiary regime as LuxCo 1, which is the beneficiary of the dividend payments, is a Luxembourg fully taxable limited company, provided LuxCo 1, at the time of the distribution, has held or commits itself to hold for an uninterrupted period of 12 months at least 10 per cent of the share capital of LuxCo 2.

At the level of LuxCo 1, 15 per cent of the loan to LuxCo 2 will be considered a hidden participation. Consequently, 15 per cent of LuxCo 1's debt corresponding to this hidden participation will in turn be excessive indebtedness generating hidden dividends subject to withholding tax at a rate of 20 per cent. This implies an overall effective rate of withholding tax of 0.42–0.45 per cent depending on the precise level of equity.

realized by investors

holdings in the fund, investors may realize a capital gain on such ...ed as a disposal of shares in LuxCo 1). Under current applicable ...estor, having no permanent establishment in Luxembourg to which ...ocated, is in principle not taxable in Luxembourg on the capital gains ...osal of the shares held in LuxCo 1, provided:

... not held (via its holding in the fund) more than 10 per cent of the ... LuxCo 1; or

b ...as held (via its holding in the fund) more than 10 per cent of the share capital of LuxCo 1, such investor has not alienated its shares within six months of their acquisition.

If all the shares held by a non-Luxembourg resident shareholder, not holding their shares through a Luxembourg permanent establishment, are redeemed, and this shareholder thus completely exits the company, the redemption is not taxable in Luxembourg as it is considered a partial liquidation.

Issues specific to French holdings

According to the France–Luxembourg tax treaty dated 1 April 1958 (as amended), rental income generated by French property is currently not taxable in France provided that such rental income is not derived through a French permanent establishment of a Luxembourg company. The same applies in respect of capital gains made by a Luxembourg resident company on the disposal of a French property. Since such income or gains are also exempt in Luxembourg, French property investments are usually structured in a way such that the French property assets are directly held by a Luxembourg company.

For this reason, real estate investments in France would be owned by a French PropCo, incorporated and resident for tax purposes in France. The French PropCo would itself either be a wholly owned subsidiary of another French incorporated and tax resident company (French HoldCo) or it would be wholly owned by LuxCo 2. French PropCo and, as the case may be, French HoldCo would be financed by a combination of debt and equity from their respective members and possibly with third party (bank) debt.

Taxation of French PropCo and French HoldCo

Rental income arising from the French property would constitute taxable income for the French PropCo. Such income will be taxable at the standard corporate tax rate (up to 34.43 per cent) after the deduction of allowable charges such as general expenses, interest (subject to certain restrictions concerning interest on intra-group loans) and capital allowances. Capital gains made upon the disposal by a French PropCo of the underlying property would be subject to corporate tax at the standard corporate tax rate.

French Holdco will only receive periodical dividend income and, as the case may be, interest paid by the French PropCo. Dividends received should be exempt from French corporate tax under the participation exemption. To qualify for the participation exemption, dividends must be paid on shares that represent at least 5 per cent of the share capital of the distributing company, and the shareholder must hold such shares for a period of at least two years. Interest received would be subject to corporate tax, to the extent that it exceeded allowable expenses. Improvements (as opposed to land) and the various components of the building (fittings, lifts) can be depreciated over their individual useful life.

Capital gains made upon the disposal by French HoldCo of its shares in French PropCo would be subject to corporate tax at the standard corporate tax rate if the shares have been held for less than two years. If shares have been held for two years or more, capital gains will be subject to tax at a rate of up to 15.49 per cent.

Thin capitalization rules mean that intra-group loans made to French HoldCo from related parties would need to be granted on market terms and would be subject to the following restrictions:

a the amount lent must not exceed 150 per cent of the borrower's net equity;
b interest paid on such loans must not exceed the amount of interest received from a related company; and
c interest paid on such loans must not exceed 25 per cent of the company's adjusted EBITDA.

These restrictions would not apply to interest on loans granted by a non-related entity (for example, a bank as senior lender).

Disposal by LuxCo 2 of its investment in French HoldCo (or in French PropCo)

Capital gains made by LuxCo 2 upon the disposal of shares in French HoldCo (or in French PropCo) should not be taxable in France because of the relevant tax treaty. Disposal of the French investments should therefore be more tax efficient if made by LuxCo 2 selling the shares in its French subsidiary than if made by way of having French HoldCo selling its investment in French PropCo or French PropCo selling its real estate investment.

Profit extraction

Profits made in French PropCo may be paid upstream by way of dividends. If dividends are paid to French HoldCo, no taxation would arise at this stage by way of withholding tax. French HoldCo should be subject to tax on this dividend income, but it should be able to benefit from the participation exemption in respect thereof, resulting in no effective tax being payable in France.

Dividends paid to LuxCo 2, whether by French PropCo or by French HoldCo, should be exempt from withholding tax in France on the basis of the Parent/Subsidiary Directive, as implemented under French domestic law.

In broad terms, the Parent/Subsidiary Directive will apply if:

a the dividend paid by French PropCo or by French HoldCo is paid to a company that is a resident of Luxembourg where it is subject to corporate tax; and
b this Luxembourg company is the beneficial owner of the dividend and holds at least 10 per cent of the capital of the distributing company.

In addition, the French tax authorities require that the Luxembourg company provides evidence that it is not ultimately controlled by entities that are not resident in an EU Member State.

Profits may also be extracted by way of interest payments. Such payments, if made to LuxCo 2, should in practice be exempt from any withholding tax in France. Dividends received by LuxCo 2 from its French affiliates will be received free of Luxembourg corporation tax by virtue of the Luxembourg participation exemption.

French tax should not be chargeable on profits distributed or on interest payments made by French PropCo to French HoldCo. French HoldCo may distribute its profits to LuxCo 2 free of Luxembourg corporation tax by virtue of the Luxembourg participation exemption.

VAT

In some cases, VAT rather than registration duties may be payable upon acquisition of a French property (for example, for properties which are disposed of for the first time within a period of five years following completion). This VAT, charged at 19.6 per cent, is, however, recoverable if the property is let to a tenant and the rent is subject to VAT.

The letting of French commercial property may be subject to VAT upon election of the lessor. Such an election could be tax efficient if the acquisition of the French property has been subject to VAT or if the lessor incurred some VAT (for example, on refurbishment costs), as it enables the lessor to recoup the VAT incurred.

Local tax

A local tax (*taxe foncière sur les propriétés bâties*) is assessed annually on companies that own French property. This tax is charged at rates decided by the local governmental authorities and is assessed on the administrative rental value of the property (which in practice is much lower than market value).

The tax is assessed by the tax administration in the name of the owner. Other taxes may also be due in certain circumstances, but they are usually charged back to the lessee.

French 3 per cent tax

Under article 990 D et seq. of the French Tax Code, legal entities which, directly or indirectly through affiliate(s), hold French property may be subject to an annual 3 per cent tax charged on the fair value of the underlying property.

For these purposes a legal entity means any legal person (as opposed to a natural person), notwithstanding the form of the entity concerned, that has, under the laws of the jurisdiction in which its statutory seat is located, a legal personality which is distinct from that of its members. The 3 per cent tax is charged without taking into account any indebtedness (i.e. on gross, not net, asset value), and is charged in proportion to the total interest owned (directly or indirectly) by the taxpayer in such property.

However, a large number of exemptions may apply to companies resident in a country that has signed an appropriate tax treaty with France, subject, however, to (generally burdensome) compliance obligations. In practice, therefore, this tax is mainly applicable when a French property is ultimately (directly or indirectly) owned by a legal entity based in a jurisdiction that has not entered into an appropriate tax treaty with France. The investors should also ensure that they can individually benefit from an exemption from the 3 per cent annual tax.

Filing requirements are not only imposed on the investor, but on every entity with a direct or indirect interest in that investor and on every entity holding French property in which that investor has an interest.

Transfer tax

Acquisitions of French real estate by French PropCo will be subject to registration duties at an effective rate of 5.19 per cent (including a 0.1 per cent land registry fee). Where French real estate acquired by French PropCo is subject to VAT, registration duties are charged at an effective rate of 0.815 per cent (including a 0.1 per cent land registry fee). Notary fees are payable in addition to registration duties.

Further, the sale of shares in a company whose assets mainly consist of French-based properties will be subject to registration duties at a rate of 5 per cent (assessed on the fair value of the shares transferred), even if the company is not a French company.

Registration duty is usually payable by the purchaser unless otherwise agreed by the parties.

10 Building the global portfolio

10.1 Introduction

As we saw in Chapter 9, international property investment is not straightforward. Tax and currency issues are considerable, and the data required to fully support a case in the face of these obstacles is not yet available. But investors and managers are creating solutions, albeit with varying degrees of efficiency, with an intended net effect which is advantageous to the investor seeking higher returns and/or diversification of real estate exposure. In this chapter we describe a recommended approach for a large institutional investor with say €500 million to invest.

While direct investment is popular with individuals and wealthy family offices, unlisted funds are the natural route to gaining global property exposure for most institutional investors of this scale. This is because their performance characteristics are most in line with the direct market over the short to medium term, so that efficient diversification is possible against financial market assets. Building exposure to a portfolio of unlisted funds also provides a means of accessing property-style returns with diversification at the property level, meaning that specific risk is reduced.

Sufficient unlisted funds with the right risk and return characteristics exist in most developed markets, with some exceptions where listed REITs are the dominant routes to market. REITs may be a useful addition, providing useful liquidity, a different tax treatment and on occasion very attractive pricing. While the overall exposure to REITs should be limited by the sector's short- to medium-term performance characteristics, the limitations on unlisted fund investment in certain geographies, coupled with the occasional pricing advantages of the listed sector, mean that the addition of a selection of REITs brings several benefits at the property portfolio level.

Table 10.1 illustrates a view of the relative strengths of the unlisted fund and listed security routes to overseas investment.

Table 10.1: Unlisted fund and REIT characteristics

	Unlisted funds	Listed REITs
Pure property exposure	* * *	*
Diversification against other assets	* * *	* *
Management quality	* * *	* * *
Investment size	* *	* * *
Diversification of specific risk	* *	* * *
Liquidity	*	* * *

Source: CBRE Global Investors

10.2 The global real estate market

10.2.1 Core, developing, emerging

Many US investors and most UK investors going international looked first at investing in continental Europe driven by familiarity and perceptions of risk. However, US opportunity funds opened up the new emerging markets of Central and Eastern Europe in the early 1990s and entered Latin American and Asian markets in force in the following decade.

Table 10.2 shows a split of the main countries of Europe into core, developing and emerging markets as defined in the first edition of this book. Low-risk investors would be more likely to go to core markets; high return investors such as opportunity funds might seek out emerging markets.

The allocation of countries to core, developing and emerging property investment markets is somewhat arbitrary and changes over time. (Several of the developing markets shown in Table 10.2 are now core markets, and some emerging markets are better described as developing.) Nevertheless, broadly speaking, core markets have a benchmark (for the relevance of this, see Chapter 3), are politically stable, have a stable currency, offer professional services necessary for institutional investment and are liquid and transparent.

Table 10.2: Market definitions

Core	Developing	Emerging	Opaque
UK	Portugal	Czech Republic	Belarus
Germany	Spain	Hungary	Moldova
France	Italy	Poland	
Ireland	Denmark	Slovakia	
Sweden	Austria	Baltic States	
Netherlands	Norway	Turkey	
Switzerland	Finland	Greece	
Belgium	Luxembourg	Slovenia	

Source: CBRE, 2002

Developing markets generally have no benchmark, are smaller, have less liquid markets (but liquidity is either growing or is expected to grow) and are politically stable with a stable currency. Emerging markets have low liquidity, less political or currency stability, fewer professional services and no benchmark.

10.2.2 Transparency

Baum *et al.* (2014) investigate the factors that determine the volume of cross-border capital flows into direct real estate markets. In particular, they set out to establish how existing institutional, regulatory and real estate specific barriers affect cross-border real estate inflows and outflows in a sample of 24 developed and emerging countries. They show that economies with more liquid real estate markets attract more real estate capital flows.

Transparency is important, and Jones Lang LaSalle's Real Estate Transparency Index (TI) is a great help in understanding transparency differences across markets. The TI, first published in 1999, with the latest (eighth) version published in 2014, defines the 102 markets covered as high transparency, transparent, semi-transparent, low transparency and opaque. This survey-based measure uses judgements about the following:

a the availability of investment performance indexes;
b market fundamentals data;
c listed vehicle financial disclosure and governance;
d regulatory and legal factors; and
e the transaction process.

This information is used to arrive at a single index measure, with the best transparency scores awarded to the UK and (next) the US. The most opaque markets included Libya, Myanmar and Senegal.

The Middle East and North Africa had the lowest average transparency scores when compared to other regions, with Sub-Saharan Africa performing slightly better. While Europe as a region performs best in the JLL Index, there are significant variations between sub-regions within the continent, with countries outside Western Europe performing less well. Asia Pacific is next best, containing high transparency markets such as Australia,

Table 10.3: JLL Transparency Index 2014: extract (top nine, each category)

High	Transparent	Semi	Low	Opaque
UK	Switzerland	Taiwan	Slovenia	Ghana
US	Sweden	Romania	Zambia	Kazakhstan
Australia	Germany	Israel	Colombia	Jamaica
New Zealand	Singapore	Slovakia	Serbia	Nigeria
France	Hong Kong	Greece	Bulgaria	Venezuela
Canada	Belgium	Turkey	Saudi Arabia	Mozambique
Netherlands	Denmark	China – tier 1	Vietnam	Guatemala
Ireland	Poland	Thailand	Jordan	Algeria
Finland	Spain	Russia – tier 1	Russia – tier 3	Dominican Republic

Note
Tier 1, 2 and 3 identifies cities of reducing size.

New Zealand, Hong Kong and Singapore, with the Americas ranked in the middle, split between transparent Northern America and the less transparent rest.

10.2.3 The limits to globalization

Baum (2008b) sets out to describe the role played by unlisted property funds in facilitating cross-border investing. In particular, our research focused on the development of unlisted funds as intermediary structures carrying institutional capital from developed to developing markets.

The research relates the number of funds targeting particular countries to population and GDP per capita. It finds that there is a very strong relationship between the popularity of a country for investment through this vehicle format and these independent variables. More interesting, perhaps, is the identification of outlier countries where the amount of investment is significantly less – or greater – than that predicted by population and GDP per capita.

In the research, we define the emerging markets as the regions outside Europe, Australasia and North America, and focus on the largest 55 countries in these regions by population. This produces a country cut-off of a minimum of roughly 20 million population and includes Asia, Latin America, Africa and the Middle East.

GDP per capita and population were used as independent variables to explain the number of funds targeting an emerging country. Both appear to be correlated with our measure of investment. GDP per capita is a reasonably good explanatory variable but population is better. This equation explains 84 per cent of the variation in the number of funds targeting any country. The two independent variables are highly significant.

The predicted number of funds targeting the country can be compared with the observed number. The countries receiving significantly more investment than that predicted by the equation are Brazil, Malaysia, Mexico, Argentina and Vietnam. Three of these are located close to the US, the main supplier of capital in the survey.

More interesting, perhaps, are the countries receiving significantly less investment than that predicted by the equation. These are Taiwan, Saudi Arabia, Venezuela, Indonesia, Iran, Pakistan, Columbia, Nigeria, Bangladesh, Algeria, Thailand and Peru.

We find that the JLL Transparency Index results fit well with countries receiving significantly less investment than as predicted, while the countries receiving significantly more investment than that predicted by the equation are generally semi-transparent or improving.

10.2.4 Risk and return

In Europe, the core markets are defined broadly in terms of all or most of the following criteria: membership of the EC; membership of the Euro; political stability; generally having a benchmark (the exceptions are Belgium and Switzerland); size; quality of professional services; liquidity. The developing markets are less liquid (although they are likely to have growing liquidity) and have no benchmarks, but are politically stable, either within the European Community or the Eurozone.

In 2000, using CBRE data describing returns notionally available on new buildings, this core/developing classification proved to be surprisingly meaningful. In both retail and office markets, the group of core markets showed both lower returns and lower volatility of returns over the period 1985–97, confirming the different market maturities of these two groups. This is shown in Table 10.4.

Table 10.4: Core and developing countries, return and risk, 1985–97

Market group	Return (%)	Risk (SD, %)
Core retail	12.01	17.56
Developing retail	16.44	25.88
Core office	11.56	17.65
Developing office	13.43	25.76

Source: Henderson Global Investors, CBRE

By 2000, several funds had already assembled capital to attack these developing markets, typically short of capital to fund the property development programmes that were needed to support their economies as they emerged from communist influence. Hence high returns were obtained by pioneer investors, who limited their risk by the payment of rents in US dollars (Poland) or euros (Hungary), and by achieving going-in yields as high as 15 per cent.

By 2009, many of these markets were no more attractively priced than the UK and had completed a transition from emerging to developing markets. At this point, huge changes in the risk and return relationships around the world suggested a temporary retrenchment to the core markets, with the possible exceptions of the powerhouse economies of China and India. By 2014, global investment programmes had re-started and markets such as Brazil were attracting large capital flows.

The global geography of real estate market attractiveness is constantly changing, and forms the first key challenge in developing an investment strategy.

10.3 Building a strategy

How can this information be used together with capital market, currency, economic and property pricing data to assemble a global portfolio?

We suggest a top-down approach, which assumes that tax and structuring issues are generally soluble without prohibitive cost. The following issues need to be considered.

i pricing;
ii the regional allocation;
iii the property type allocation;
iv the fund risk style allocation;
v leverage.

As a start, we need to identify investable and attractive markets. We have already considered which markets may be investable. Tax advice will be needed to further refine this checklist. Otherwise, market attractiveness is a function of pricing. We consider pricing in Section 10.4 and portfolio construction in Section 10.5.

10.4 Pricing

10.4.1 Pricing models and currency

In Chapter 4 we built a property appraisal model which combined Fisher and Gordon equations to produce the following:

$$K = RFR_N + RP - (G_N - D)$$

Using assumed data, we may have the following information:

$$K = 4.5\% + 3\% - (3\% - 2\%) = 6.5\%$$

The correct yield appears to be 6.5 per cent. If the current yield is 5 per cent, offices are over-priced. Can we use this approach when looking at international markets? Unfortunately, we cannot, without adjustment. This is because currency movements are excluded from the analysis, and perfect hedging is both unavailable and may reduce or enhance returns. Without knowing anything else, a high yield makes a market look attractive, but might simply imply high bond yields, high inflation and a depreciating currency.

Remember that the Fisher equation considers the components of total return on an investment. It states that:

$$R = l + i + RP$$

where:
R is the total required return;
l is a reward for liquidity preference (deferred consumption);
i is expected inflation; and
RP is the risk premium.

From this we can see that the bond yield may be high only because expected inflation is high, in which case the currency can be expected to depreciate, damaging returns in the home currency. In Chapter 9 we also saw that the cost of a hedge will be equal to the interest rate differential, so the high bond yield again suggests that return prospects will be reduced, this time by the cost of the hedge.

10.4.2 A total return model

Figure 10.1 takes a modified approach to the yield as an indicator of value, neutralizing the effect of the expected inflation rate and currency movement by deducting the bond yield from the property yield in each country.

The data shows that in 2006 Poland had the highest positive difference between its property market yield and its bond market yield, and the UK the smallest. At first sight, this makes Poland more attractive than the UK. But this does not provide the full picture. The data identifies the size of a positive yield gap between property and gilt yields by using the following re-arrangement of the formula we have seen already:

$$K - RFR_N = RP - (G_N - D)$$

Figure 10.1: All property yields v. local ten-year government bond yields, 2006

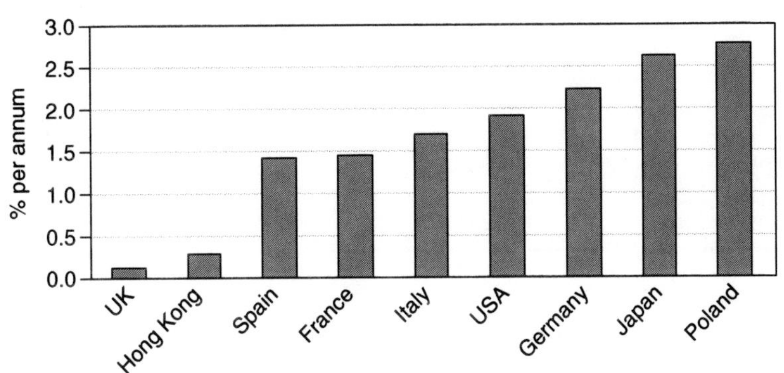

Source: CBRE Global Investors

It is clear from this that a positive yield gap between property and bonds could indicate a high risk, or low net rental growth, or both. If these variables were the same across the markets examined, then the analysis suggests an attractive market where the left hand side has a lower value than the right hand side.

So we need a more comprehensive pricing model which deals with the following: how risky is the market? What is the required risk premium? How much net growth will the market deliver? Given answers to these questions, we can then estimate the expected IRR on the market and the 'excess' return (IRR versus required return).

Assume we have a market where the following data has been estimated:

$$\text{the required return} = RFR_N + RP = 4.5\% + 3\% = 7.5\%$$

$$\text{the expected return} = K + G_N - D = 5\% + 3\% - 2\% = 6\%$$

The property market is expensive; negative excess returns are on offer.

Assume we have a market where the following data has been estimated:

$$\text{the required return} = RFR_N + RP = 4.5\% + 3\% = 7.5\%$$

$$\text{the expected return} = K + G_N - D = 5\% + 6\% - 1\% = 10\%$$

Here the property market is cheap; positive excess returns are on offer.

In Chapter 4 we presented an analysis of required and expected returns, which is repeated in an international context in Table 10.5. How does this analysis work across international markets?

Difficulties of analysis arise because *RP* and *G* are both affected by currency. *RP* may be influenced by other variables relevant to differences between the international markets, but what risk does currency introduce?

More challenging, perhaps, is the following question. What growth in income is to be expected? Let us assume that expected rental growth in all property markets is 2 per cent.

Table 10.5: Hypothetical required and expected returns, international markets

	RFR_R	+i	+RP	Buy?	K	$+G_N$	−D
UK bonds	1.5	2.0	0.5	=	4.0	0	0
UK property	1.5	2.0	4.0	=	6.5	2.0	1.0
Japanese bonds	1.5	2.0	?	?	1.0	3.5	0
Japan property	1.5	2.0	?	?	4.5	?	?
France property	1.5	2.0	?	?	5.5	?	?
South Africa property	1.5	2.0	?	?	12.5	?	?

But if the return is in the domestic currency of the investor, it not only comprises market growth but also currency appreciation.

The total required return comprises three parts:

$$R = l + i + RP$$

where:
l is a reward for liquidity preference;
i is expected inflation; and
RP is the risk premium.

As we saw in Chapter 9, interest rates and expected inflation rates are directly related.

Purchasing power or interest rate parity also directly relates interest rates and exchange rates. The identity is theoretical: there is evidence to support as well as to refute the concept. Interest rate parity says that the spot price and the forward or futures price of a currency incorporate any interest rate differentials between the two currencies. So interest rate differentials and expected currency exchange rate movements are directly related.

In theory, interest rates and expected inflation rates are directly related, interest rate differentials and expected currency exchange rate movements are directly related, and therefore expected inflation rates and expected currency exchange rate movements are directly related. A higher inflation currency will depreciate relative to a lower inflation currency – and will have higher interest rates (absent government policy distortions). Hence, if we know that UK government bonds earn yields of 3 per cent more than Japanese bonds, then we can expect 3 per cent higher inflation in the UK and a 3 per cent appreciation in the yen against sterling.

(In practice, interest rates, expected inflation rates and currency exchange rate movements may not be related in the short term. In what is known as the carry trade investors might borrow in low interest rate currencies and lend/invest in high-yielding markets. This is effective in periods of global financial and exchange rate stability, but it is risky.)

So, to recap, we might be initially attracted to high nominal returns in the local currency, but this is subject to currency risk and promotes high risk markets. We might therefore aim for high nominal returns in our domestic currency, but this requires a forecast of the currency exchange rate, and again promotes markets which are risky. Instead we should be looking for high excess returns over local bonds, which will often point capital towards low interest rate environments.

10.4.3 The positive effect of leverage

Low interest rate markets are attractive because the currency risk can be managed more easily, and (if hedged) can even deliver return while reducing risk. They have other advantages, as less equity is needed and greater diversification is possible. In addition, positive leverage is more likely to be achieved in a low interest rate environment, and, as we saw in Chapter 2, this can add to return (and risk).

Cash-on-cash yields (income return on equity) can also be enhanced. If we buy an asset for \$100 million, with a \$10 million income, we achieve a 10 per cent income yield. If we use 50 per cent leverage and an interest-only loan at a rate of 5 per cent, we lose \$2.5 million in interest but now receive a cash-on-cash return of \$7.5 million, which as a percentage of equity is \$7.5 million/\$500 million = 15 per cent.

Box 10.1 includes an illustration of the positive effect of leverage.

10.4.4 Using local excess returns

For reasons we develop in this section, we recommend looking for high nominal excess returns in the local currency. This takes account of market risk, takes out the inflation – and currency – effect and requires no currency forecasting skill.

Note that where k is an initial yield, R is the required return, D is depreciation and and G_N (nominal) = G_R (real) + i (inflation):

$$RFR_R + i + RP = K + G_R + i - D$$

High nominal *excess* returns are delivered where the expected return (the right hand side) is higher than the required return (left hand side). Because i appears on both sides of the equation, this rule holds in theory in high and low inflation markets. A high nominal return is not attractive per se. Investors should therefore aim for high excess returns on property relative to returns on local bonds plus a risk premium (high excess returns). This rule is not affected by high inflation, because this boosts both expected and required returns, but not excess returns. But this measure there is no expected return from currency movement. How can we deal with this?

As an example, let us re-visit the example used in Chapter 4 (Tables 4.7–4.10) and take four government bond markets: UK, Japan, France and South Africa, with ten-year issues yielding 4, 2, 3 and 10 per cent respectively. UK indexed bonds yield 1.5 per cent.

A pricing analysis is shown in Table 10.6. The analysis is from the perspective of the local investor. All fixed interest bond issues carry a small inflation risk premium of 0.5 per cent: there is no currency risk. The real risk free rate is given by the UK indexed bond yield of 1.5 per cent. All markets, being efficient for local investors, are in equilibrium.

Table 10.6: Bond pricing analysis

	RFR_R	+i	+RP	=	K	$+G_N$	-D
UK indexed bonds	1.5	2.0	0.0	=	1.5	2.0	0.0
UK bonds	1.5	2.0	0.5	=	4.0	0.0	0.0
Japanese bonds	1.5	0.0	0.5	=	2.0	0.0	0.0
France bonds	1.5	1.0	0.5	=	3.0	0.0	0.0
South Africa bonds	1.5	8.0	0.5	=	10.0	0.0	0.0

The differences in expected inflation rates signify expected movements in currency exchange rates against the pound. The yen is expected to appreciate by (4%–2%=)2%, the euro is expected to appreciate by (4%–3%=) 1% and the rand is expected to depreciate by (10%–4%=) 6%.

From the perspective of a UK investor, all fixed interest bonds are expected to deliver the same return in sterling, as shown in Table 10.7, which adds *Gc*, growth from currency movements, to the analysis.

Table 10.7: Bond returns – UK perspective

	Return	=	K	+G	+Gc	-D
UK indexed bonds	3.5	=	1.5	2.0	0.0	0.0
UK bonds	4.0	=	4.0	0.0	0.0	0.0
Japanese bonds	4.0	=	2.0	0.0	2.0	0.0
France bonds	4.0	=	3.0	0.0	1.0	0.0
South Africa bonds	4.0	=	10.0	0.0	–6.0	0.0

We can now extend the analysis to property. Let us assume that property yields in the UK, Japan, France and South Africa are 6.5, 4.5, 5.5 and 12.5 per cent respectively.

Table 10.8 is an equilibrium pricing analysis from a local perspective. Returns on offer to local players in the UK, Japan, France and South Africa are 7.5, 5.5, 6.5 and 13.5 per cent respectively. These are all excess returns over bonds of 3.5 per cent, the additional risk premium for property over fixed interest bonds.

Table 10.8: Property returns – local perspective

	RFR_R	+i	+RP	=	K	$+G_N$	-D
UK property	1.5	2.0	4.0	=	6.5	2.0	1.0
Japanese property	1.5	0.0	4.0	=	4.5	2.0	1.0
France property	1.5	1.0	4.0	=	5.5	2.0	1.0
South Africa property	1.5	8.0	4.0	=	12.5	2.0	1.0

From a UK perspective, growth in income from the expected currency movement – or hedge – must be added. The UK analysis is shown in Table 10.9.

Table 10.9: Property returns – UK perspective

	RFR_R	+i	+RP	=	K	$+G_N$	+Gc	-D
UK property	1.5	2.0	4.0	=	6.5	2.0	0.0	1.0
Japanese property	1.5	0.0	4.0	=	4.5	2.0	2.0	1.0
France property	1.5	1.0	4.0	=	5.5	2.0	1.0	1.0
South Africa property	1.5	8.0	4.0	=	12.5	2.0	–6.0	1.0

All four property markets are offering the UK investor a return of 7.5 per cent in sterling. However, this assumes that the investor estimates the same risk premium, the same rental growth potential and the same depreciation for each market.

In practice these estimates will differ greatly. Given that rental growth is partly inflation-driven, we can expect more rental growth in South Africa and less in Japan. The economies may be offering different real growth prospects. Market leasing practice and construction standards may drive differing depreciation. The risk premium in non-domestic markets is likely to be higher, largely to deal with the risk of currency movements but also to cover the costs and risks systematically incurred by international buyers.

Table 10.10 is a possible (hypothetical) analysis from a UK perspective. (On the required return side of the equation, remember that the UK investor needs to beat UK inflation.)

Table 10.10: Property returns – UK perspective, non-equilibrium

	RFR_R	+i	+RP	Req	K	$+G_N$	+Gc	–D	Exp
UK property	1.5	2.0	4.0	7.5	6.5	2.0	0.0	1.0	7.5
Japanese property	1.5	2.0	5.0	8.5	4.5	1.0	2.0	0.5	7.0
France property	1.5	2.0	4.5	8.0	5.5	3.0	1.0	0.5	9.0
South Africa property	1.5	2.0	8.0	11.5	12.5	5.0	–6.0	2.0	9.5

On the basis of this analysis, the UK market is a hold, Japan a sell, France a buy and South Africa a sell: see Table 10.11.

Table 10.11: Property excess returns – UK perspective

	Expected	Required	Excess	Decision
UK property	7.5	7.5	0.0	Hold
Japanese property	7.0	8.5	–1.5	Sell
France property	9.0	8.0	1.0	Buy
South Africa property	9.5	11.5	–2.0	Sell

Note that UK property is expected to deliver the UK bond yield plus the additional UK property risk premium over bonds. Japan property delivers the UK bond yield (4 per cent) plus the additional Japan property risk premium (4.5 per cent), less the excess (–1.5 per cent)=7 per cent. France property delivers the UK bond yield (4 per cent) plus the additional France property risk premium (4 per cent), plus the excess (1 per cent)=9 per cent. South Africa property delivers the UK bond yield (4 per cent) plus the additional South Africa property risk premium (7.5 per cent), less the excess (–2 per cent)=9.5 per cent.

Our recommended simple rule, therefore, is to look for high nominal excess returns in the local currency. This takes account of market risk, takes out the inflation – and currency – effect and requires no currency forecasting skill. A full analysis of our summary is shown in Table 10.12.

Table 10.12: Property excess returns – recommended approach

	Bond	+RP	Req	K	$+G_N$	−D	Exp	Excess	Decision
UK property	4.0	3.5	**7.5**	6.5	2.0	1.0	**7.5**	0.0	Hold
Japanese property	2.0	4.5	**6.5**	4.5	1.0	0.5	**5.0**	−1.5	Sell
France property	3.0	4.0	**7.0**	5.5	3.0	0.5	**8.0**	1.0	Buy
South Africa property	10.0	7.5	**17.5**	12.5	5.0	2.0	**15.5**	-2.0	Sell

The expected sterling returns remain as shown in Table 10.10. South Africa is not attractive, despite having the highest initial yield and the highest expected return in local currency; France is attractive, despite having a lower initial yield than the UK.

(Note again that the risk premium in this table is the additional risk premium above the bond risk premium of 0.5 per cent. This ensures that the local required return is correctly estimated.)

Seeking high nominal excess returns (expected returns less required returns) in the local currency will therefore put in place a process which is designed to deliver a minimum of the *domestic* risk free rate plus the *local* risk premium, and to select markets on the basis of their excess returns without the complications of currency forecasts.

10.4.5 Leverage, tax and fees

How can currency risk be managed? As we saw in Chapter 9, investors can use local debt to reduce the capital at risk. The equity can be hedged, and the cost of hedging will be determined by interest rate and inflation differentials. This will add to return if the target market has low interest rates.

If a UK investor hedges an international investment, this will damage return if the target market has higher interest rates. It will enhance return if the target market has lower interest rates. In addition, leverage will have a more positive effect on returns if there is a positive carry (property yields are higher than borrowing costs).

Using funds means that returns will be geared or leveraged. Returns will be net of tax, and also net of fees. In a pricing analysis, we need to use excess returns which are leveraged and net of fees and taxes. If using a hedge is attractive because the target market has low interest rates then this is easily taken into account, as shown in Box 10.1. (The analysis would be the same, albeit with more risk, if no hedge were used but we instead relied upon currency appreciation.)

Box 10.1 A cross-border comparison

A UK investor has a choice of buying a UK shopping centre for £100 million or one based in France, a euro currency area, for €100 million. He plans to use 50 per cent gearing. The UK shopping centre has a yield of 5 per cent, and throws off a rental income of £5 million. The French shopping centre has a yield of 5.5 per cent, and throws off a rental income of €5.5 million.

Management fees of 6 per cent (£300,000) in the UK are higher *pro rata* in France where there is less competition to provide such services, and where the structure used to shelter

Table 10.13: Shopping centre comparison, Eurobloc and UK

£100m shopping centre with 50% leverage			€100m shopping centre with 50% leverage		
	£m	**Return on equity**		**€m**	**Return on equity**
Net rental income	5.0	–	Net rental income	5.5	–
Management fees	–0.3	–	Management fees	–0.5	–
Interest	–3.1	–	Interest	–2.6	–
Net income	1.6	3.2%	Net income	2.4	4.8%
Capital growth	2.0	–	Capital growth	2.5	–
Tax leakage	0.0	–	Tax leakage	–0.3	–
Total return	3.6	**7.2%**	Total return	4.6	9.2%
			Hedging return	–	1.0%
			Total return incl. hedge		**10.2%**

tax involves some administrative expenses, totalling in this case €500,000 or 9 per cent. Interest is charged at 6.2 per cent in the UK and 5.2 per cent in the lower interest rate euro area, a cost of £3.1 million (6.2 per cent of a £50 million loan) in the UK and €2.6 million (5.2 per cent of a €50 million loan) in France. The net income on equity is £1.6 million and the cash-on-cash yield is 3.2 per cent in the UK, and the net income on equity is €2.4 million and the cash-on-cash yield is 4.8 per cent in France.

It is reckoned that rental and capital growth in the UK will slightly under-perform rental and capital growth in France, running at 2 and 2.5 per cent respectively, and adding £2 million and €2.5 million respectively to the investor's equity and total return each year.

The French centre will be held in a tax efficient structure, but there will still be some leakage, estimated at €300,000 each year. The UK property shows a net annual total return of £3.6 million, 7.2 per cent on equity, while the French centre shows a net annual total return of €4.6 million, 9.2 per cent on equity.

Finally, the interest rate differential of 1 per cent will add 1 per cent to the sterling return each year, either though currency appreciation or through the hedge. The result is a return in sterling of 7.2 per cent in the UK and 10.2 per cent in France, the out-performance coming from a combination of property, leverage and currency factors.

10.5 Portfolio construction

10.5.1 The top-down process

Given a view of target markets, how can we think about the top-down portfolio construction process?

We begin with a recap. For real estate as an asset class, we expect long-term returns superior to bonds but inferior to equities. Volatility (by reference to appraised valuations) is low, but smoothed. Real estate is a good diversifier against bonds and equities, with a high Sharpe ratio (see Chapter 1). An optimizer can be used to model the ideal property weight, and the ideal geographical portfolio distribution. Given the rule we developed in Section 10.4, we would optimize excess returns in local currency.

Direct portfolios carry high property specific risk, because property is not homogeneous and individual lot sizes may be large. Listed and unlisted funds can diversify specific risk; unlisted property is illiquid, but listed property companies and REITs provide limited diversification against stocks and bonds.

Using funds means that returns will be geared or leveraged, and significant specific risk will remain relative to a global index or benchmark. Returns will be net of tax, and also net of fees. So what returns should be optimized? Given the pricing analysis, we need to optimize excess returns which are leveraged, and net of fees and taxes.

We conclude this chapter, and the book, by describing the approach we propose, as adopted by a US endowment fund.

Box 10.2 The global portfolio

We manage a US state university endowment fund with a new $500 million real estate investment allocation. We have only dollar-denominated liabilities. The fund has no current exposure to real estate, has a long-term horizon, a moderate risk appetite and a skeleton in-house team.

The issues to be confronted are as follows:

- What allocations should be made to direct and indirect forms of property, including derivatives? What allocations should be made to domestic and international property respectively?
- How much of an indirect allocation should be listed and how much unlisted? How much should be allocated to funds with core, value-added or opportunity styles?
- What regional and geographic split of the allocation is advisable? What sector split is to be recommended? Should we use optimization, or an equilibrium (market value weighted) approach?
- What execution model is appropriate? Should the fund hire in-house personnel and choose funds? If so, where should they be located? If not, what mandate can be designed and how many advisers or managers are required? Should funds of funds or a multi-manager approach be used?

The board has determined the following. There will be no direct property – this is regarded as too lumpy for a global $500 million allocation. There will no use of derivatives, as the appropriate risk controls are not in place. As a US investor, the fund will be overweight US assets because liabilities are dollar-denominated and the tax treatment of domestic assets is favourable. The long-term investment horizon and limited requirement for liquidity encourages an exposure to unlisted funds at the expense of listed securities, but there is a preference for the risk profile of REITs over REOCs and other listed property securities.

The fund's risk appetite allows an exposure to some opportunity funds and also to currency risk. The minimum/maximum investment to each fund is $25/50 million (say 20 unlisted funds maximum). A single advisory manager is to be used to guide fund selection and ongoing review, with the fund board retaining discretion over investment decisions. Funds of funds will not be selected in order that we can avoid paying double fees.

After a working session between fund and adviser, using a neutral or equilibrium approach adjusted by an optimization of excess net returns, the recommended regional and sector allocations and fund style choices have been made. The regional and sector allocations are shown in Tables 10.14 and 10.15. The recommended weights are summarized in Table 10.16. They can be broken down further as shown in Table 10.17.

The adviser has reminded the fund that gearing – typically 33 per cent for unlisted core, 50 per cent for listed and 65 per cent for opportunity funds – will alter the equity required to attain the desired geographical and sector exposure. The impact of this is shown in Table 10.18.

Table 10.14: Regional allocations

	Neutral	Position	Bet
US	41%	50%	9%
Asia	15%	10%	–5%
Europe	36%	25%	–11%
Emerging	8%	15%	7%
	100%	100%	0%

Table 10.15: Sector allocations

	Neutral	Position	Bet
Office	40%	25%	–15%
Retail	25%	35%	10%
Industrial	10%	20%	10%
Residential	15%	5%	–10%
Other	10%	15%	5%
	100%	100%	0%

Table 10.16: Property style allocations

	Neutral	Position	Bet
Direct	0%	0%	0%
Listed	44%	30%	–14%
Unlisted core	49%	55%	6%
Opportunity	7%	15%	8%
	100%	100%	0%

Table 10.17: Fund style and regional allocations

	US	Asia	Europe	Emerging	Total
Listed	15.0%	5.0%	5.0%	5.0%	30.0%
Unlisted core	35.0%	0.0%	20.0%	0%	55.0%
Opportunity	0.0%	5.0%	0.0%	10.0%	15.0%
	50.0%	10.0%	25.0%	15.0%	100.0%

Table 10.18: Equity allocations

	Position	Gearing	Equity (m)
Direct	0%	0%	$0
Listed	30%	50%	$132
Unlisted	55%	33%	$321
Opportunity	15%	65%	$46
	100%	–	$500

Afterword

Property is a factor of production, a place to work and the main input into the production of food. It provides shelter and leisure facilities. It is the essential source of work, rest and play.

For a corporation, property is of key importance as a factor of production. For a bank, it provides ultimate security for the majority of all loans. For an investment manager, it represents a significant source of fees. For a country, it is the basis of a large proportion of the nation's savings, investments and future pensions. While its performance in the past 25 years has not matched that of equities, it has sufficient advantages in terms of liability matching to continue to be a popular investment class in future.

Forces of change will continue to challenge our perceptions of the place and importance of property. Globalization means that domestic markets cannot remain insular. Securitization is a response to global investors placing more emphasis on the liquidity and divisibility of investments, and in tandem with this more unquoted pooled vehicles will be provided to enable global investors to diversify more effectively.

A growing and more affluent population is leading to congestion and a re-emphasis on town centres for sustainability and lifestyle. Careful planning and sensitive land management and development are ever more important. Property investment managers will be required to look beyond the demands of fees and returns, and to play their part in the efficient and sensitive management of this global asset.

Bibliography

References

Ackrill, A., Barkham, R. and Baum, A. (1992): Property Company Performance: A Report for Boots Properties plc, University of Reading, Reading.

Alcock, J., Baum, A., Colley, C. and Steiner, E. (2013): The Role of Financial Leverage in the Performance of Core, Value-add and Opportunistic Private Equity Real Estate Funds, *Journal of Portfolio Management*, 39(5), 99–110.

Alcock, J., Lizieri, C. and Steiner, E. (2011): Real Estate Returns and Financial Assets in Extreme Markets: Empirical Evidence for Asymmetric Dependence in the Returns from Listed and Unlisted UK Real Estate Returns, Investment Property Forum Working Paper 4, November.

Anson, M. (2002): *Handbook of Alternative Assets*, Hoboken, NJ: Wiley Finance.

Antwi, A. and Henneberry, J. (1995): Developers, Non-linearity and Asymmetry in the Development Cycle, *Journal of Property Research*, 12, 217–39.

Association of British Insurers (2012): UK Insurance Key Facts, September.

Badarinza, C. and Ramadorai, T. (2014): Preferred Habitats and Safe-Haven Effects: Evidence from the London Housing Market, Oxford-Man Institute of Quantitative Finance and Centre for Economic Policy Research (CEPR), Oxford.

Barkham, R. and Geltner, D. (1995): Price Discovery in American and British Property Markets, *Real Estate Economics*, 23, 21–44.

Barkham, R. and Ward, C. (1999): Investor Sentiment and Noise Traders: Discount to Net Asset Value in Listed Property Companies in the UK, *Journal of Real Estate Research*, 18(2), 291–312.

Barras, R. (1994): Property and the Economic Cycle: Building Cycles Revisited, *Journal of Property Research*, 11, 183–97.

Barras, R. (2009): *Building Cycles: Growth and Instability*, Oxford: Wiley-Blackwell.

Barras, R. and Clark, P. (1996): Obsolescence and Performance in the Central London Office Market, *Journal of Property Valuation and Investment*, 14(4), 63–78.

Baum, A. (1991): *Property Investment Depreciation and Obsolescence*, London: Routledge (see www.andrewbaum.com).

Baum, A. (1997): *Trophy or Tombstone? A Decade of Depreciation in the Central London Office Market*, London: Lambert Smith Hampton and HRES (see www.andrewbaum.com).

Baum, A. (2005): Pricing the Options Inherent in Leased Commercial Property: A UK Case Study, Paper delivered at the European Real Estate Society Conference, Dublin, June.

Baum, A. (2006): Real Estate Investment through Indirect Vehicles: An Initial View of Risk and Return Characteristics, in Bone Winkel, S., Thomas, M., Schafers, W., Leopoldsberger, G., Tilmes, R., Sotelo, R. and Rottke, N. (eds) *Stand und Entwicklungs: tendenzen der Immobilienokonomire*, Cologne: Rudolf Muller.

Baum, A. (2007): Managing Specific Risk in Property Portfolios, *Property Research Quarterly* (NL), 6(2), 14–23.

Baum, A. (2008a): The Emergence of Real Estate Funds, in Peterson, A (ed.) *Real Estate Finance: Law, Regulation and Practice*, London: LexisNexis.

Baum, A. (2008b): Unlisted Property Funds: Supplying Capital to Developing Property Markets? International Real Estate Research Symposium, Kuala Lumpur, April.

Baum, A. and Brown, F. (2006): Pricing the Options Inherent in Leased Commercial Property: the Impact of Rental Growth Volatility, Working Paper, University of Reading.

Baum, A. and Crosby, N. (2008): *Property Investment Appraisal* (3rd edn), Oxford: Blackwell.

Baum, A. and Devaney, S. (2008): Depreciation, Income Distribution and the UK REIT, *Journal of Property Investment and Finance*, 26(3), 195–209.

Baum, A. and Farrelly, K. (2008): Sources of Alpha and Beta in Property Funds, Paper delivered at the European Real Estate Society Conference, Cracow, June.

Baum, A. and Hartzell, D. (2012): *Global Property Investment: Strategies, Structures, Decisions*, Oxford: Wiley Blackwell.

Baum, A. and Key, T. (2000): Attribution of Real Estate Portfolio Returns and Manager Style: Some Empirical Results, European Real Estate Society Conference, Bordeaux, June.

Baum, A. and Lizieri, C. (1999): Who Owns the City of London? *Real Estate Finance*, Spring, 87–100.

Baum, A. and Moss, A. (2012): Are Listed Real Estate Stocks Managed as Part of the Real Estate Allocation? EPRA, Brussels, March.

Baum, A. and Moss, A. (2013): The Use of Listed Real Estate Securities in Asset Management: A Literature Review and Summary of Current Practical Applications, EPRA, Brussels, October.

Baum, A. and Sams, G. (2007): *Statutory Valuations* (4th edn), London: Elsevier.

Baum, A. and Struempell, P. (2006): Managing Specific Risk in Property Portfolios, Pacific Rim Real Estate Society Conference, Auckland, January (see www.andrewbaum.com).

Baum, A. and Turner, N. (2004): Retention Rates, Reinvestment and Depreciation in European Office Markets, *Journal of Property Investment and Finance*, 22(3), 214–35.

Baum, A., Beardsley, C. and Ward, C. (1999a): Using Swaps to Manage Portfolio Risk and to Fund Property Development, Paper presented at the RICS Cutting Edge conference, Cambridge, September.

Baum, A., Beardsley, C. and Ward, C. (1999b): Derivatives Pricing Approaches to Valuation Models: Sensitivity Analysis of Underlying Factors, Paper presented to the European Real Estate Society, Sixth European Conference, Athens, June.

Baum, A., Crosby, N., McAllister, P., Gallimore, P. and Gray, A. (2003): Appraiser Behaviour and Appraisal Smoothing: Some Qualitative and Quantitative Evidence, *Journal of Property Research*, 20(3), 261–80.

Baum, A., Fuerst, F. and Milcheva, S. (2014): Cross-Border Capital Flows into Real Estate, *Real Estate Finance*, 31(3), 103–22.

Baum, A., Key, T., Matysiak, G. and Franson, J. (1999): Attribution Analysis of Property Portfolios, ERES conference, Athens, June.

Baum, A., Lizieri, C. and Marcato, G. (2006): Pricing Property Derivatives, Investment Property Forum, August.

Bjork, T. and Clapham, E. (2002): A Note on the Pricing of Real Estate Index Linked Swaps, SSE/EFI Working Paper Series in Economics and Finance, No. 492.

Bjorklund, K. and Soderburg, B. (1997): Property Cycles, Speculative Bubbles and the Gross Income Multiplier, Working Paper No. 24, Royal Institute of Technology, Stockholm.

Blake, N., Goodwin, A., McIntosh, A. and Simmons, C. (2011): Property and Inflation, Investment Property Forum, April.

Bond, S. and Glascock, J. (2006): Performance and Diversification Benefits of European Real Estate Securities, European Public Real Estate Association, Strasbourg, www.epra.org.

Bond, S. and Lizieri, C. (2004): Defining Liquidity in Property, Working Paper One in Bond, S., Crosby, N., Hwang, S., Key, T., Lizieri, C., Matysiak, G., McAllister, P. and Ward, C. (eds), Liquidity in Commercial Property Markets: Research Findings, Investment Property Forum, April, pp. 8–21.

Bostwick, J. and Tyrell, N. (2006): Leverage in Real Estate Investments: An Optimisation Approach, European Real Estate Society Conference, Milan, June.

Bradley, M., Capozza, D.R. and Seguin, P.J. (1998): Dividend Policy and Cash-flow Uncertainty, *Real Estate Economics*, 26(4), 555–80.

Brinson, G., Hood, L. and Beebower, G. (1986): Determinants of Portfolio Performance, *Financial Analysts Journal*, 42(4), 39–44.

Brooks, C. and Tsolacos, S. (2010): *Real Estate Modelling and Forecasting*, Cambridge: Cambridge University Press.

Brown, G. and Matysiak, G. (2000a): *Real Estate Investment: A Capital Market Approach*, Upper Saddle Rive, NJ: Prentice Hall.

Brown, G. and Matysiak, G. (2000b): Sticky Valuations, Aggregation Effects, and Property Indices, *Journal of Real Estate Finance and Economics*, 20(1), 49–66.

Brown, G.R. (1988): Reducing the Dispersion of Returns in UK Real Estate, *Journal of Valuation*, 6(2), 127–47.

Burnie, S., Knowles, J. and Teder, T. (1998): Arithmetic and Geometric Attribution, *Journal of Performance Measurement*, Fall, 59–68.

Buttimer, R., Kau, J. and Slawson, V. (1997): A Model for Pricing Securities Dependent upon a Real Estate Index, *Journal of Housing Economics*, 6, 16–30.

Cacciapaglia, J. (2011): Core, Core Plus, Value Add, and Opportunistic: Four Commercial Real Estate Strategies, www.activerain.com.

Callender, M., Devaney, S., Sheahan, A. and Key, T. (2007): Risk Reduction and Diversification in UK Commercial Property Portfolios, *Journal of Property Research*, 24(4), 355–75.

CALUS (1986): *Depreciation of Commercial Property*, Reading: College of Estate Management.

CBRE Investors (2008): *The Case for a Global Unconstrained Property Strategy*, CBRE Investors, London.

Chandrashekaran, V. (1999): Time-Series Properties and Diversification Benefits of REIT Returns, *Journal of Real Estate Research*, 17, 91–112.

Chin, H., Topintzi, E., Hobbs, P., Keng, T.Y., Billingsley, A. and Naylor, S. (2007): Global Real Estate Insights, RREEF, October.

Chin, W., Dent, P. and Roberts, C. (2006): An Explanatory Analysis of Barriers to Investment and Market Maturity in Southeast Asian Cities, *Journal of Real Estate Portfolio Management*, 12(1), 49–57.

Chong, J., Miffre, J. and Stevenson, S. (2009): Conditional Correlations and Real Estate Investment Trusts, *Journal of Real Estate Portfolio Management*, 15(2), 173–84.

Clapham, E., Englund, P., Quigley, J. and Redfearn, C. (2006): Revisiting the Past and Settling the Score: Index Revision for House Price Derivatives, *Real Estate Economics*, 34(2), 275–302.

Clayton, J. and MacKinnon, G. (2000): Explaining the Discount to NAV in REIT Pricing: Noise or Information? University of Cincinnatti, OH.

Clayton, J. and Mackinnon, G. (2003): The Relative Importance of Stock, Bond, and Real Estate Factors in Explaining REIT Returns, *Journal of Real Estate Finance and Economics*, 27, 39–60.

College of Estate Management (1999): *The Dynamics and Measurement of Commercial Property Depreciation in the UK*, Reading: College of Estate Management.

Consilia Capital (2012): Growing the European Listed Real Estate Market, September.

Corgel, J., McIntosh, W. and Ott, S. (1995): Real Estate Investment Trusts: A Review of the Financial Economics Literature, *Journal of Real Estate Literature*, 3(1), 13–43.

County NatWest (1992): Solving the Risk Premium Puzzle, Equity Briefing Paper 26, London, 29 July.

Crosby, N. and Hughes, C. (2011): The Basis of Valuations for Secured Commercial Property Lending in the UK. *Journal of European Real Estate Research*, 4(3), 225–42.

Crosby, N. (2007): German Open Ended Funds: Was There a Valuation Problem? Working Papers in Real Estate & Planning, no. 05/07, University of Reading, p. 15.

Crosby, N. and McAllister, P. (2004): Deconstructing the Transaction Process, Working Paper Two in Bond, S., Crosby, N., Hwang, S., Key, T., Lizieri, C., Matysiak, G., McAllister, P. and Ward, C. (eds), Liquidity in Commercial Property Markets: Research Findings, Investment Property Forum, April, pp. 23–39.

Crosby, N., Hughes, C. and Murdoch, S. (2005): Monitoring the 2002 Code of Practice for Commercial Leases, Office of the Deputy Prime Minister, London.

Crosby, N., Lizieri, C. and McAllister, P. (2010): Means, Motive and Opportunity? Disentangling Client Influence on Performance Measurement Appraisals: *Journal of Property Research*, 27(2), 181–201.

Damodoran, A. (2013): Musings on Markets, 19 May, http://aswathdamodaran.blogspot.co.uk/2013/05/equity-risk-premiums-erp-and-stocks.html.

Daude, C. and Stein, E. (2007): The Quality of Institutions and Foreign Direct Investment, *Economics and Politics*, 19(3), 317–44.

Devaney, S. and Scofield, D. (2014): Time to Transact: Measurement and Drivers, Investment Property Forum, September.

DTZ (2008): *Money into Property*, London: DTZ.

Elton, E. and Gruber, M. (1977): Risk Reduction and Portfolio Size: An Analytical Solution, *Journal of Business*, 50(4), 415–37.

Evans, J. and Archer, S. (1968): Diversification and the Reduction of Dispersion, *Journal of Finance*, 23(4), 761–7.

Farrelly, K. (2012): Measuring the Risk of Unlisted Property Funds: A Forwards- Looking Approach, Paper presented at the European Real Estate Society conference, Edinburgh.

Feldman, B.E (2003): Investment Policy for Securitized and Direct Real Estate, *Journal of Portfolio Management*, Special Real Estate Issue, 112–21.

Fisher, I. (1930, reprinted 1977): *The Theory of Interest*, Philadelphia, PA: Porcupine Press.

Fuerst, F. and Matysiak, G. (2013): Analysing the Performance of Non-listed Real Estate Funds: A Panel Data Analysis, *Applied Economics*, 45(14), 1777–88.

Geltner, D. (1991): Smoothing in Appraisal Based Returns, *Journal of Real Estate Finance and Economics*, 4(3), 327–45.

Geltner, D. (2003): IRR-based Property-level Performance Attribution, *Journal of Portfolio Management*, Special Issue, 138–51.

Geltner, D. and Fisher, J. (2007): Pricing and Index Considerations in Commercial Real Estate Derivatives, *Journal of Portfolio Management*, Special Real Estate Issue.

Giliberto, S.M. (1990) Equity Real Estate Investment Trusts and Real Estate Returns, *Journal of Real Estate Research*, 5(2), 259–63.

Glascock, J., Lu, C. and So, R. (2000): Further Evidence on the Integration of REIT, Bond and Stock Returns, *Journal of Real Estate Finance Economics*, 20, 177–94.

Gordon, J. (1994): The Real Estate Capital Markets Matrix: A Paradigm Approach, *Real Estate Finance*, 11(3), 7–15.

Gordon, M.J. (1962): *The Investment, Financing and Valuation of the Corporation*, New York: Irwin, reported in Brigham, E. (1982) *Financial Management: Theory and Practice* (4th edn), Chicago, IL: Dryden Press.

Goshawk/IPD (2014): The Asset Management Report, London, June.

Grenadier, S. (1995): Valuing Lease Contracts: A Real-options Approach, *Journal of Financial Economics*, 38, 297–331.

Gyourko, J. and Keim, D. (1992): What does the Stock Market Tell Us about Real Estate Returns? *Real Estate Economics*, 20, 457–85.

Hamilton, S. and Heinkel, R. (1995): Sources of Value-added in Canadian Real Estate Investment Management, *Real Estate Finance*, Summer, 57–70.

Hoesli, M. and Macgregor, B. (2000): *Property Investment: Principles and Practice of Portfolio Management*, London: Longman.

Hoesli, M. and Oikarinen, E. (2012): Are REITs Real Estate? Evidence from International Sector Level Data, Swiss Finance Institute Research Paper Series, Nos 12–15, Zurich.

Houston, J., Lin, C. and Ma, Y. (2012): Regulatory Arbitrage and International Bank Flows, *Journal of Finance*, 67(5), 1845–95.

Hudson-Wilson, S. and Guenther, P. (1995): The Four Quadrants: Diversification Benefits for Investors in Real Estate: A Second Look, *Real Estate Finance*, 12(2), 82–99.

Ibbotson Associates (2006): Commercial Real Estate: The Role of Global Listed Real Estate Equities in a Strategic Asset Allocation, Washington, DC, November.

Investment Property Forum (2005): *Depreciation in Commercial Property Markets*, Investment Property Forum/IPF Educational Trust, July.

Investment Property Forum (2011): *Depreciation of Commercial Investment Property in the UK*, Investment Property Forum/IPF Educational Trust, November.

IPD (2014): www.ipd.com/real-estate-indexes/other-market-data/property_derivatives.

JLL Transparency Index (2014): www.jll.com/GRETI.

Jones Lang LaSalle (2008): *Real Estate Transparency Index*, London: Jones Lang LaSalle.

Jones Lang Wootton (1987): *Obsolescence: The Financial Impact of Property Performance*, London: Jones Lang Wootton.

Keeris, W. and Langbroek, R.A.R. (2005): An Improved Specification of Performance: The Interaction Effect in Attribution Analysis, European Real Estate Society Conference, Dublin, June.

Kennedy, P. and Baum, A. (2012): Aligning Asset Allocation and Real Estate Investment: Some Lessons from the Last Cycle, Working Paper, Henley Business School, Henley-on-Thames.

Key, T. and Law, V. (2005): The Size and Structure of the UK Property Market, Investment Property Forum, July.

Knight, J., Lizieri, C. and Satchell, S. (2005): Diversification when It Hurts? The Joint Distributions of Real Estate and Equity Markets, *Journal of Property Research*, 22, 309–23.

Kuhle, J. (1987): Portfolio Diversification and Return Benefits: Common Stocks vs. Real Estate Investment Trusts (REITs), *Journal of Real Estate Research*, 2, 1–9.

Law, V. (2004): The Definition and Measurement of Rental Depreciation in Investment Property, Unpublished PhD dissertation, University of Reading, Reading.

Lee, M.L. and Chiang, K. (2010): Long-run Price Behaviour of Equity REITs: Become More like Common Stocks after the Early 1990s? *Journal of Property Investment and Finance*, 28(6), 454–65.

Lee, M.L., Lee, M.T. and Chiang, K. (2008): Real Estate Risk Exposure of Equity Real Estate Investment Trusts, *Journal of Real Estate Finance and Economics*, 36(2), 165–81.

Lee, S. (2003): The Persistence of Real Estate Fund Performance, American Real Estate Society Meeting, Monterey, FL.

Lee, S. and Stevenson, S. (2002): A Meta Analysis of Real Estate Fund Performance, American Real Estate Society Meeting, Naples, FL.

Lee, S. and Stevenson, S. (2005): The Case of REITs in the Mixed-asset Portfolio in the Short and Long Run, *Journal of Real Estate Portfolio Management*, 11(1), 55–80.

Lee, S., Lizieri, C. and Ward, C. (2000): The Time Series Performance of UK Real Estate Indices, www.reading.ac.uk/rep/indices.pdf.

Lee, S.L. (2010): The Changing Benefit of REITs to the Mixed-asset Portfolio, *Journal of Real Estate Portfolio Management*, 16(3), 201–15.

Li, J., Mooradian, R.M. and Yang, S.X. (2009): The Information Ccontent of the NCREIF Index, *Journal of Real Estate Research*, 31, 93–116.

Liang, Y. and McIntosh, W. (1998): REIT Style and Performance, *Journal of Real Estate Portfolio Management*, 4(1), 69–78.

Liang, Y., Hess, R., Bradford, D. and McIntosh, W. (1999): Return Attribution for Commercial Real Estate Investment Management, *Journal of Real Estate Portfolio Management*, 5, 23–30.

Lieser, K. and Groh, A.P. (2014): The Determinants of International Commercial Real Estate Investment, *Journal of Real Estate Finance and Economics*, 48, 611–59.

Ling, D. and Naranjo, A. (2012): Returns, Volatility, and Information Transmission Dynamics in Public and Private Real Estate Markets, Bergstrom Centre for Real Estate Studies Working Paper, Gainsville, FL, August.

Ling, D. and Naranjo, A. (2014): Returns and Information Transmission Dynamics in Public and Private Real Estate Markets, *Real Estate Economics*, forthcoming.

Litterman, R. (2003): *Modern Investment Management: An Equilibrium Approach*, Hoboken, NJ: Wiley Finance.

Litterman, R. (2008): Beyond Active Alpha, *CFA Institute Conference Proceedings Quarterly*, March, 14–21.

Liu, C.H. and Mei, J. (1992): The Predictability of Returns on Equity REITs and their Co-movement with Other Assets, *Journal of Real Estate Finance and Economics*, 5, 401–18.

Lizieri, C. and Kutsch, N. (2006): *Who Owns the City 2006: Office Ownership in the City of London*, Reading: University of Reading and Development Securities plc.

Lizieri, C. and Pain, K. (2013): International Office Investment in Global Cities: The Production of Financial Space and Systemic Risk, *Regional Studies*, Special Issue, 48(3).

Lizieri, C., Alcock, J., Steiner, E., Satchell, S. and Wongwachara, W. (2013): Real Estate's Role in the Mixed Asset Portfolio: A Re-Examination, Investment Property Forum/University of Cambridge Department of Land Economy, Cambridge, March.

Lizieri, C., McAllister, P. and Ward, C. (2003): Continental Shift? An Analysis of Convergence Trends in European Real Estate Equities, *Journal of Real Estate Research*, 23(1), 1–23.

Lizieri, C., Marcato, G., Ogden, P. and Baum, A. (2009): Pricing Inefficiencies in Private Real Estate Markets: Using Total Return Swaps, Working Paper presented at the AUEREA conference, January.

Lizieri, C., Marcato, G., Ogden, P. and Baum, A. (2012): Pricing Inefficiencies in Private Real Estate Markets: Using Total Return Swaps, *Journal of Real Estate Finance and Economics*, 45(3), 774–803.

Lizieri, C., Oughton, M. and Baum, A. (2001): *Who Owns the City, 2001*, Reading: University of Reading and Development Securities plc.

Lizieri, C., Reinert, J. and Baum, A. (2011): *Who Owns the City 2011: Change and Global Ownership of City of London Offices*, University of Cambridge Department of Land Economy/Development Securities, Cambridge, March.

Lizieri, C., Worzala, E. and Johnson, R. (1998): *To Hedge or not to Hedge?* London: RICS.

McAllister, P. and Lizieri, C. (2006): Monetary Integration and Real Estate Markets: The Impact of the Euro on European Real Estate Equities, *Journal of Property Research*, 23(4), 289–303.

MacGregor, B. (1994): Property and the Economy, RICS Commercial Property Conference, Cardiff, June.

Mackinnon, G.H. and Zaman, A.A. (2009): Real Estate for the Long Term: The Effect of Return Predictability on Long-horizon Allocations, *Real Estate Economics*, 37(1), 117–53.

Markowitz, H.M. (1952): Portfolio Selection, *Journal of Finance*, 12(March), 77–91.

Maxted, W. (2013): The UK Commercial Property Lending Report Lending Survey, De Montfort University, Leicester.

Mitchell, P. (2013): The Size and Structure of the UK Property Market 2013: A Decade of Change, Investment Property Forum, March.

Mitchell, P. and Bond, S. (2008): Alpha and Persistence in UK Property Fund Management, Investment Property Forum, April.

Modigliani, F. and Miller, M. (1958): The Cost of Capital, Corporation Finance and the Theory of Investment, *American Economic Review*, 48(3), 261–97.

Modigliani, F. and Miller, M. (1963): Corporate Income Taxes and the Cost of Capital: A Correction, *American Economic Review*, 53(3), 433–43.

Morrell, G.D. (1993): Value-weighting and the Variability of Real Estate Returns: Implications for Portfolio Construction and Performance Evaluation, *Journal of Property Research*, 10, 167–83.

Mueller, A.G. and Mueller, G.R. (2003): Public and Private Real Estate in the Mixed-asset Portfolio, *Journal of Real Estate Portfolio Management*, 9, 193–203.

Mueller, G.R., Pauley, K. and Morrill, W.A. (1994): Should REITs be Included in a Mixed-asset Portfolio? *Real Estate Finance*, 11(1), 23–8.

Myer, F.C.N and Webb, J.R. (1993): Return Properties of Equity REITs, Common Stocks, Retail REITs, and Retail Real Estate, *Journal of Real Estate Research*, 9, 65–84.

NAPF (2013): Trends in Defined Benefit Asset Allocation: The Changing Shape of UK Pension Investment, NAPF, July.

Niskanen, J. and Falkenbach, H. (2010): REITs and Correlations with Other Asset Classes: A European Perspective, *Journal of Real Estate Portfolio Management*, 16(3), 227–39.

Oikarinen, E., Hoesli, M. and Serrano, C. (2011): The Long-run Dynamics between Direct and Securitized Real Estate, *Journal of Real Estate Research*, 33(1), 73–103.

Otaka, M. and Kawaguchi, Y. (2003): Hedging and Pricing of Real Estate Securities under Market Incompleteness, Meikai University Working Paper Series, Japan.

Pagliari, J.L., Scherer, K.A. and Monopoli, R.T. (2005): Public versus Private Real Estate Equities: A More Refined, Long-term Comparison, *Real Estate Economics*, 33, 147–87.

Park, T. and Switzer, L. (1996): Mean Reversion of Interest Rate Term Premiums and Profits from Trading Strategies with Treasury Futures Spreads, *Journal of Futures Markets*, 16, 331–52.

Phalippou, L. and Baum, A. (2014): Hilton Hotels: Real Estate Private Equity, Saïd Business School, University of Oxford.

PREA (2013): Why Real Estate? Hartford, CT.

PREA/various (2007): *Global Commercial Real Estate: A Strategic Asset Allocation Study*, PREA-sponsored special real estate issue of the *Journal of Portfolio Management*.

Prudential Real Estate Investors (2012): A Bird's Eye View of Global Real Estate Markets: 2012 Update, February.

Real Estate Strategies (2014): Original Data, Innovative Thinking, Better Decisions, Effective Strategies, London, June.

Rees, D., Wood, M. and Wright, K. (2006): The Four Quadrant Investment Model, Mirvac/Quadrant Real Estate Advisors, Sydney.

Robinson, B.L. (2012): Risk of Income Shortfall in Portfolios of Short-lease Industrial Assets, Paper presented at the ERES conference, Edinburgh, June.

Royal Institution of Chartered Surveyors (2002): Property Valuation: The Carsberg Report, January.

Schneider, P. (2014): Price Discovery in UK Unlisted Real Estate Funds, University of Cambridge, Department of Land Economy, Cambridge, March.

Schuck, E.J. and Brown, G.R. (1997): Value Weighting and Real Estate Risk, *Journal of Property Research*, 14(3), 169–88.

Scott, P. (1996): *The Property Masters: A History of the British Commercial Property Sector*, London: Taylor & Francis.

Sharpe, W. (1988): Determining a Fund's Effective Asset Mix, *Investment Management Review*, November/December, 59–69.

Sharpe, W.F. (1964): Capital Asset Prices: A Theory of Market Equilibrium under Conditions of Risk, *Journal of Finance*, 19(3), 425–42.

Simon, S. and Wing, L. (2009): The Effect of the Real Estate Downturn on the Link between REITs and the Stock Market, *Journal of Real Estate Portfolio Management*, 15(3), 211–19.

Stevenson, S. (2001): The Long-term Advantages of Incorporating Indirect Securities in Direct Real Estate Portfolios, *Journal of Real Estate Portfolio Management*, 7(1), 5–16.

Titman, S. and Torous, W. (1989): Valuing Commercial Mortgages: An Empirical Investigation of the Contingent-Claims Approach to Pricing Risky Debt, *Journal of Finance*, 44(2), 345–73.

Tyrell, N. and Bostwick, J. (2005): Leverage in Real Estate Investments: An Optimization Approach, *Briefings in Real Estate Finance*, 5(3–4), 143–54.

ULI/PFR (2012): Have Property Funds Performed? Urban Land Institute.

University of Aberdeen and IPD (1994): *Economic Cycles and Property Cycles*, London: RICS Books.

Urban Land Institute (2012): Have Property Funds Performed? ULI Europe Policy and Practice Committee Report, October.

Wang, K., Erickson, J. and Gau, G. (1993): Dividend Policies and Dividend Announcement Effects, *Journal of the American Real Estate and Urban Economics Association*, 21(2), 185–201.

Westerheid, P. (2006): Cointegration of Real Estate Stocks and REITs with Common Stocks, Bonds and Consumer Price Inflation: And International Comparison, Discussion Paper No. 06-057, Centre for European Economic Research, Mannheim.

Wheaton, W. (1999): Real Estate 'Cycles': Some Fundamentals, *Real Estate Economics*, 27(2), 209–30.

World Bank (2013): World Development Indicators, Washington, DC.

World Economic Forum (2012): The Global Competitiveness Report 2012–2013, Geneva.

World Heritage Foundation (2013): The Index of Economic Freedom, www.heritage.org/index/book/methodology.

Worzala, E. and Sirmans, C.F. (2003): Investing in International Real Estate Stocks: A Review of the Literature, *Urban Studies*, 40(5–6), 1115–49.

Yungmann, G. and Taube, D. (2001): FFO: Earnings or Cash Flow? Real Estate Portfolio, NAREIT, May/June.

Yunus, N., Hansz, A. and Kennedy, P.J. (2012): Dynamic Interactions Between Private and Public Real Estate Markets: Some International Evidence, *Journal of Real Estate Finance and Economics*, 45(4), 1021–40.

General reading

Ball, M., Lizieri, C. and MacGregor, B. (1998): *The Economics of Commercial Property Markets*, London: Routledge.

Barkham, R. and Geltner, D. (1994): Unsmoothing British Valuation-based Returns Without Assuming an Efficient Market, *Journal of Property Research*, 11, 81–95.

Barkham, R. and Geltner, D. (1995): Price Discovery in American and British Property Markets, *Real Estate Economics*, 23, 21–44.

Barkham, R. and Ward, C. (1996): The Inflation-hedging Characteristics of UK Property, *Journal of Property Finance*, 7, 62–76.

Baum, A. (1991): Property Futures, *Journal of Property Investment and Valuation*, I(3), 235–40.

Baum, A. (1993): Quality, Depreciation and Property Performance, *Journal of Real Estate Research* (USA), 8(4), 541–66.

Baum, A. (1995): Can Foreign Real Estate Investment be Successful? *Real Estate Finance*, 12(1), 81–9.

Baum, A. (1999): Changing Styles in International Real Estate Investment, *Australian Land Economics Review*, 5(2), 3–12.

Baum, A. (ed.) (2000): *Freeman's Guide to the Property Industry*, London: Freeman Publishing.

Baum, A. and MacGregor, B. (1992): The Initial Yield Revealed: Explicit Valuations and the Future of Property Investment, *Journal of Property Valuation and Investment*, X(4), 709–26.

Baum, A. and Schofield, A. (1991): *Property as a Global Asset*, in Venmore-Rowland, P., Brandon, P. and Mole, T. (eds), *Investment, Procurement and Performance in Construction*, London: E & FN Spon.

Baum, A. and Wurtzebach, C. (1992): *International Property Investment*, in Hudson-Wilson, S. and Wurtzebach, C. (eds) *Managing Real Estate Portfolios*, New York: Irwin.

Byrne, P. and Lee, S. (1998): Diversification by Sector, Region or Function? A Mean Absolute Deviation Optimisation, *Journal of Property Valuation and Investment*, 16(1), 38–56.

Byrne, P. and Lee, S. (2000): Risk Reduction in the United Kingdom Property Market, *Journal of Property Research*, 17(1), 23–46.

Byrne, P. and Lee, S. (2001): Risk Reduction and Real Estate Portfolio Size, *Managerial and Decision Economics*, 22, 369–79.

Byrne, P. and Lee, S. (2003): An Exploration of the Relationship between Size, Diversification and Risk in UK Real Estate Portfolios: 1989–1999, *Journal of Property Research*, 20(2), 191–206.

Crosby, N., Lavers, A. and Murdoch, J. (1998): Property Valuation Variation and the Margin of Error in the UK, *Journal of Property Research*, 15(4), 305–30.

Economist Intelligence Unit (1997): *Global Direct Investment and the Importance of Real Estate*, London: RICS.

Eichholtz, P. and Lie, R. (1999): Property Capital Flows: Moving the Frontiers, ING Bank/ING Real Estate, The Hague.

HM Treasury (2005): UK Real Estate Investment Trusts: A Discussion Paper, HM Treasury and Inland Revenue, London.

Hoesli, M. and MacGregor, B. (2000): *Property Investment: The Principles and Practice of Portfolio Management*, London: Pearson Education (Addison Wesley Longman).

Investment Property Databank (1999): *The UK Property Cycle: A History from 1921 to 1997*, London: RICS.

Investment Property Forum (1996): *Readiness for Sale: The Code of Practice for Streamlining Commercial Property Transactions*, London: Investment Property Forum.

Investment Property Forum (2005): *Understanding Commercial Property Investment: A Guide for Financial Advisers*, London: Investment Property Forum.

Kinnard, W., Lenk, M. and Worzala, E. (1997): Client Pressure in the Commercial Appraisal Industry: How Prevalent is It? *Journal of Property Valuation and Investment*, 15(3), 233–44.

Lai, T. and Wang, K. (1998): Appraisal Smoothing: The Other Side of the Story, *Real Estate Economics*, 26, 511–35.

Laposa, S.P. (2007): The Foreign Direct Investment Property Model: Explaining Foreign Property Demand and Foreign Property Capital Flows in Transitional Economies, PhD thesis, University of Reading.

Lee, S. (2001): The Relative Importance of Property Type and Regional Factors in Real Estate Returns, *Journal of Real Estate Portfolio Management*, 7(2), 159–68.

Lee, S. (2003): The Persistence of Real Estate Fund Performance, American Real Estate Society Meeting, Monterey, CA.

Matysiak, G. and Wang, P. (1995): Commercial Property Prices and Valuations: Analysing the Correspondence, *Journal of Property Research*, 12, 181–202.

Mitchell, P. and Bond, S. (2008): *Alpha and Persistence in UK Property Fund Management*, London: Investment Property Forum.

Quan, D.C. and Quigley, J.M. (1991): Price Formation and the Appraisal Function in Real Estate Markets, *Journal of Real Estate Finance and Economics*, 4, 127–46.

Renaud, B. (1998): Property Cycles and Banking Crises, IPD conference paper, November.

RES (2014): www.realestatestrategies.com.

Roche, J. (1995): *Property Futures and Securitisation: The Way Ahead*, Cambridge: Woodhead Publishing.

Royal Institution of Chartered Surveyors (2002): *Property Valuation: The Carsberg Report*, London: Royal Institution of Chartered Surveyors.

Schofield, J.A. (1996): Inflation Hedging and UK Commercial Property, *Journal of Property Finance*, 7, 99–117.

Scott, P. and Judge, G. (1999): Cycles and Steps in British Commercial Property Values, mimeo, Department of Economics, University of Portsmouth.

Tsolacos, S., Keogh, G. and McGough, T. (1998): Modelling Use, Investment and Development in the British Office Market, *Environment and Planning A*, 30, 1409–27.

University of Reading and Oxford Property Consultants (2001): Liquidity and Private Property Vehicles: Where Next? www.propertyfundsresearch.com/publications.

Wolverton, M. and Gallimore, P. (1999): Client Feedback and the Role of the Appraiser, *Journal of Real Estate Research*, 18(3), 415–32.

Websites

Association of Investors in Non-Listed Real Estate Vehicles, www.inrev.org
Association of Real Estate Funds, www.aref.org.uk
European Public Real Estate Association, www.epra.com

Investment Property Databank, www.ipd.com
National Association of Real Estate Investment Trusts, www.reit.com
National Council of Real Estate Investment Fiduciaries, www.ncreif.com
Pension Real Estate Association, www.prea.org
Property Funds Research, www.propertyfundsresearch.com
Royal Institution of Chartered Surveyors, www.rics.org.uk/research
Urban Land Institute, www.uli.org

Index

Page numbers in *italics* denote tables, those in **bold** denote figures.